Kindness and the Good Society

**SUNY series
in the
Philosophy of the Social Sciences**

Lenore Langsdorf, Editor

Kindness and the Good Society

Connections of the Heart

William S. Hamrick

State University of New York Press

Published by
State University of New York Press, Albany

© 2002 State University of New York

For information, address State University of New York Press,
90 State Street, Suite 700, Albany, NY 12207

Production by Michael Haggett
Marketing by Michael Campochiaro

Library of Congress Cataloging-in-Publication Data

Hamrick, William S.
  Kindness and the good society : connections of the heart / William S. Hamrick.
    p. cm. — (SUNY series in the philosophy of the social sciences)
  Includes bibliographical references and index.
  0-7914-5265-4 (alk. paper) — ISBN 0-7914-5266-2 (pbk. : alk. paper)
  1. Kindness   I. Title.   II. Series.

BJ1533.K5 H35 2002
177'.7—dc21   2001049516

10 9 8 7 6 5 4 3 2 1

*For my parents, and for
Eldora Spiegelberg,
the kindest living person I know,
who understands intuitively the sense of the question,*

*"[W]hat is the use of studying philosophy if all that it does for you
is to enable you to talk with some plausibility about some
abstruse questions of logic, etc., & if it does not improve
your thinking about the important questions of everyday life?"*
—Ludwig Wittgenstein

Contents

Acknowledgments

It would be the unkindest cut of all not to express my gratitude to several people and organizations that have helped me in various ways to complete this book. Sincere thanks are due, first, to Professor Wolfe Mays, Editor of the *Journal of the British Society for Phenomenology*, for permission to quote short passages from some of my articles published therein. They are listed in the Bibliography. I am also grateful to the Graduate School of Southern Illinois University Edwardsville for a summer research fellowship that provided the time to finally complete the book, and to the National Endowment for the Humanities for awarding me a place in Thomas Pavel's 1996 summer seminar, "After Poststructuralism: The Individual in Contemporary French Thought," at Princeton University. The influences of that seminar are present throughout the following pages. I am deeply indebted to Professor Pavel and my fellow seminar participants.

I am likewise grateful to Eldora Spiegelberg, who has always been a fresh, instructive example of the fact that the life of kindness can mean a life worth living. To her, and to my parents, who both died during the writing of this book, this work is affectionately dedicated. I thank John Compton for his stimulating discussions of Philip Hallie's reflections on cruelty and much else. I also am grateful to Ms. Dixie Golden for her expert proofreading. Additionally, I owe a great debt to my family, colleagues, and other friends, especially Michael Barber, Frank Flinn, James Marsh, and Thomas D. Paxson, Jr. They did not let me give up, even when I came close to death myself. They have taught me much about the importance of a community of good people for living a life of kindness, and I hope that they will find their lessons here well learned.

While this book was in press, William Desmond's *Ethics and the Between* (Albany: State University of New York Press, 2001) appeared. The present book offers a phenomenology of kindness which is, in several ways, consistent with the ontology of goodness which Desmond's work provides. I regret that it was impossible to refer here to that book because the careful reader will note in both texts, albeit for different purposes, overlapping and complementary descriptions of human actions and values as well as similar concerns for ambiguity, perplexity, goodness, evil, and hermeneutical interrogation.

Finally, the sad and horrible terrorism of September 11, 2001, which also took place while this book was in production, dramatically showed both the obstacles to, and the array of possibilities of, kindness and compassion in a world in violent struggle. In the extreme circumstances of destruction, shock, pain, and the disorienting awareness of unsuspected vulnerability, countless kind acts of strangers created and reinforced community not only in New York and Washington, but across the country as well. The achievement of goodness is indeed fragile, as Martha Nussbaum points out, but the tough resolve to reassert it gives one reasons for hope after all. I gratefully and humbly acknowledge that indomitable spirit.

Introduction

I never forget to speak of humans as acting and suffering.
—Paul Ricoeur, *Oneself as Another*

Theoretical and Social Context

Up until about twenty-five years ago, deontological and utilitarian moral theories dominated Anglo-American ethics. These theories took various forms, of course, and still greatly influence the contents of textbooks used in university ethics courses, the deliberations of hospital ethics committees, the writings of professionals in diverse fields of "applied" ethics and—in the case of Kant—the critical theory of Jürgen Habermas. But over the last two decades, several philosophers (and others) have raised critical questions about these two main theories of normative ethics, a questioning that has led them to seek an alternative in virtue ethics characteristic of ancient Greek philosophy.[1] These thinkers have reconsidered ancient theories of the good life, *eudaimonia*, or "human flourishing." The work proposed here attempts to extend and deepen that reconsideration.[2]

Anyone who wishes to think seriously about kindness today is in a rather curious position. On the one hand, praise of kindness is a staple of ordinary discourse, community interest news stories, fairy tales and other genres of children's stories, poetry, and even bumper stickers. These references usually share Wordsworth's opinion (in *Tintern Abbey*) of

> *. . . that best portion of a good man's life;*
> *His little, nameless, unremembered acts*
> *Of kindness and love. . . .*

However, most of these references are superficial in the extreme and often rest on demonstrably false presuppositions about their subject. As a result, to use Heideggerean language, they end by concealing the phenomenon rather than genuinely disclosing it.

On the other hand, philosophers have only seldom shown any interest in pursuing a more reflective understanding of kindness, and so what Wordsworth thought the best part of the moral life has only rarely attracted the attention of ethicists. It is not likely that they are ignorant of this particular human quality, or that they value it less than do the rest of humankind. More probably, they have not thought kindness worth discussing. Why this has been so is in part fairly clear and in part a matter of speculation, but both are philosophically important.

First, deontological and utilitarian ethical theories provide internal reasons for their neglect of kindness. On the one hand, Kantians and other deontologists might argue that kindness is (1) a function of character, and thus cannot be the object of the good will's moral legislation; and/or (2) a result of physical actions, and so irrelevant to the state of the good will itself. Or they might construe kindness very differently by identifying it with benevolence or beneficence, or at least they might believe that all references to these phenomena logically include kindness as well. Kant himself takes this line in describing "kindness done from duty" as "*practical*, and not *pathological*, love" (1964a, 67; emphasis in original), and H. J. Paton adopts the same interpretation (1965, 152). They are not alone in these beliefs, since the synonymy is found in most dictionaries. On the other hand, utilitarians, and consequentialists in general, misled by the same identification of beneficence and kindness, focus solely on questions of social utility and restrict themselves to calculating the moral score of any given action, rule, social policy, law, and the like. Thus they tend to lose sight of—what is of only secondary interest for them anyway—the character of moral agents themselves. Individual feelings, closely bound up with the experience of kindness or doing acts of kindness, become suspect to the degree that they can interfere with the rational calculation of consequences. And, as we shall see, the lack of any sort of calculus of actual or possible results frequently characterizes certain types of acts of kindness.

There are three exceptions, of varying degrees of importance, to the utilitarian disregard of kindness, and to the neglect of kindness in ethics generally. David Hume, in a minor sort of way, discusses kindness as a type of benevolence. He wants to explain "that merit, that is commonly ascrib'd to *generosity, humanity, compassion, gratitude, friendship, fidelity, zeal, disinterestedness, liberality*, and all those other qualities that form the character of good and benevolent" (1967, 603; emphasis in original). Further, he approvingly cites Juvenal's remark that the "principal advantage" of a "more extensive" benevolence is that it "gives us larger opportunities of spreading our kindly influence than what are indulged to the inferior creation" (Hume 1957, 10). Also, Henry Sidgwick (1913) discusses duties of kindness under the general heading of "Benevolence" in Chapter IV of *The Methods of Ethics*. Finally, and much more substantively, Moritz Schlick (1939) dedicates his entire major work on moral philosophy to laying the foundations of an ethics of kindness to replace a Kantian ethics of duty. But Schlick himself does not adequately address the question of what kindness is, and his analysis is limited by his utilitarianism.[3]

A third reason for the neglect of kindness is that, reflecting a world continuously in (often violent) struggle, philosophers have confined most of their moral attention to questions of justice. In light of these legitimate and urgent concerns, kindness and its cognate phenomena have almost certainly appeared with a considerably diminished importance, or as an unaffordable luxury. It seems to be something "soft" as distinct from the "hard" real world of power and injustice. One English graduate student, swayed perhaps by such considerations or by Hume's view that benevolence is one of the "softer affections" (1957, 9), even called the idea of a phenomenology of kindness "wet." This response is revealing, and perhaps even a common misunderstanding. Why it is a misunderstanding will be clear at several junctures in this book, and especially in the final chapter. The student did concede, however, that Moritz Schlick's writings were the last place she would look for something "wet."

A fourth reason for the traditional inattention to kindness lies outside of ethical theory. It is that philosophies tend to develop in a dialectical interchange with the growth of the language in which they are situated, and it is worth noting that the use of the word "kind," as indicating something morally praiseworthy, emerged since the Renaissance, at least in English. Its anterior usages referred to natural kinds and natural abilities. For example, Hamlet remarks to his mother (Act III, sc. 4) that:

> *I must be cruel, only to be kind;*
> *Thus bad begins, and worse remains behind.*[4] (Shakespeare 1939, 142)

Here "kind" refers to Hamlet's natural duties as a son in avenging the murder of his father. The relationships between kindness as a morally praiseworthy object and as natural kinds are still on the social agenda. They appeared explicitly in the reflections of sociobiologists and subsequently in those of evolutionary psychologists. These relationships are also implicitly present in such diverse social phenomena as the bitter racial divisions laid bare by the Rodney King beatings, the O. J. Simpson trial, and racial harassment in the workplace. They are equally embedded in trends toward voluntarily and involuntarily segregated schools, concerted attacks on affirmative action policies, virulent racial confrontations on once-liberal college campuses (of all places), and in the rise of racist hate groups here and abroad. As an example of the latter, the Ku Klux Klan has trained its admirers in Germany (hands across the sea) and perhaps still does so, with the inevitable and familiar rise of (neo?) Nazi violence to immigrants. And the racial hatreds that consumed Rwanda, Bosnia, and then Kosovo have produced unspeakable dimensions of torture, rape, and murder. Meanwhile, here at home, the white hate group called the World Church of the Creator now solicits children with a slick Web page of bright colors, a white supremacist coloring book, and crossword puzzles containing racist clues.[5]

These racial divisions are only one class of a great number of contemporary social phenomena that provides an impetus for this book outside of ethical theory. Most of these phenomena reflect an accumulating disintegration of social life and community and unprecedented assaults on civility and basic human decency.[6] One example is the way that the 1980s became a decade of greed—which Ronald Reagan made acceptable in America (again)—that spawned, among other things, yuppies, corporate raiders, the junk bond scandal, and the savings-and-loan fiasco.[7] For too many people in this country, where there was once a conscience, there remains now only a vacuum in the wastes of crass self-interest. From 1977 to 1989, the richest 1 percent of American families collected 60 percent of after-tax income and 75 percent of pre-tax income. Indeed, at the end of the decade, the highest 1 percent was worth more than all of the remaining 90 percent (the *bottom* 90 percent?) put together.

Looking back at the 1980s, such numbing facts both uncover the true meaning of the "trickle-down" theory of economics and provide an infallible vector to the all-too-well-known economic realities underlying such a disproportionate accumulation of wealth. These familiar markers on the social landscape included widespread failures of small farmers and other small business owners, corporate downsizings to make American companies "lean and mean" to fight world competition,[8] an ever-widening gap between a living and working wage, homelessness, along with its police repression,[9] and a general closure of hearts (and wallets) to those without shelter. Moreover, by the end of the 1990s, despite the booming economy and the lowest unemployment rates in living memory, the gap between rich and poor in this country, far from narrowing, became even wider.[10]

In terms of homelessness, many of those without permanent shelter have full-time jobs, but at the low end of the wage scale. They are the working poor for whom affordable housing no longer exists. In fact, for many Americans, "affordable housing" has become one of the most familiar oxymorons of urban life. Despite skyrocketing Dow Jones averages and the federal government's continued claims of economic prosperity, following the Welfare Reform Bill of 1996, as Peter Edelman pointed out, there were "millions of people who don't earn enough to support their families. . . . [T]wo million people work full time all year and can't get their families out of poverty. More than 70 percent of poor children live in families where somebody has income from work."[11]

Also in the wake of the Welfare Reform Bill of 1996, more and more people were dropped from state welfare rolls. Those who lost jobs had trouble getting welfare payments, and available positions were often not steady or well paying. Correlatively, recent national surveys of hunger in America show that more and more people in bread lines are the working poor and those from double-income, formerly middle-class families. One study found that Second Harvest, the largest organization for charitable hunger relief in the country, had alone fed 21 million people in 1997—more than the population of the entire state of Texas.[12]

We have also seen, hardly coincidentally, increases in aggressive and senseless violence, although violent crime decreased significantly by the end of the 1990s. Even so, as former Surgeon General Joycelyn Elders told Congress on November 1, 1993—and things did not seem to improve by the end of the decade—for many young people it is simpler to find a gun than a friend. Shootings and mass murders within and outside of schools themselves provide a grim realization of Elders' fears, though she could hardly have foreseen recent examples of parents brawling (and, in one case, killing) over the calls of officials at their youngsters' sports matches.

Poverty, unemployment, violence, and drugs are certainly the kinds of social phenomena that keep moral philosophers locked on to issues of justice, and these are not the only ones that make for a most unkind society. Two other highly visible examples of this sort were attempts by House Republicans to finance tax cuts for the wealthy and balance the federal budget at the expense of Medicare/Medicaid and school lunch programs—a simultaneous attack on what were, or what were perceived to be, the politically weakest members of society. These attacks were only symptomatic of a much wider social trend of demonizing the poor for political benefit. (In Newt Gingrich's famous parlance, "Are there no prisons? Are there no workhouses?") They are also politically victimized, in that corporate influence on legislation makes elderly people without health insurance pay 15 percent more for medicines than those who are insured. They are also consistently and legally the targets of predatory lending practices for such things as furniture, automobiles, home mortgages, and "payday loans"—practices that even Alan Greenspan condemned in a speech in March 2000.[13]

Kindness is certainly implicated in such pressing and momentous justice issues, but it is also central to other, less justice-related examples of cultural disintegration and incivility that coarsen and disfigure contemporary social life. For instance, there is the way that nastiness came into its own on television in the late 1980s in the form of confrontational entertainment (Morton Downey, Geraldo Rivera) and attack comedy (Andrew Dice Clay). In addition, there are several well-known daytime television programs that take advantage of their guests by getting them to reveal either outright lust or other embarrassing details of their most private lives. These shows exploit and humiliate their contestants—one of whom was actually provoked to a now well-known murder—and then abandon them immediately after the telecast and do not help find therapy for those who so obviously need it.

Such programs also succeed in turning their studio and home audiences into voyeurs—as did the O. J. Simpson trial for much of the country. Indeed, the camera as voyeur, or rather ourselves turned into voyeurs through the unblinking lens, has become a regular feature of televised spectacles. There is even a recognized genre of "exploitative reality TV specials." Perhaps the most spectacular was the Fox network's *Who Wants to Marry a Multimillionaire?* that reduced matrimony to entertainment. At least Fox's ratings were spectacular— until the subsequent PR fiasco occasioned by the allegedly violent past of the groom. But although Fox vowed to bow out, other networks dug in, most notably with CBS' *Survivor* and *Big Brother.* However, Fox's resolution did not last long. At the beginning of 2001, it launched *Temptation Island,* which featured "four real-life 'committed couples' being tempted toward infidelity by a bevy of models and other hyper-attractive singles"[14] Since Fox admitted that it paid these hyper-sexed tempters for their services, it is not easy to see how the show differed from straightforward prostitution—except that prostitutes normally do not perform for millions of voyeurs.

Voyeurism also extends to scenes of (previously) intimate pain and suffering. Cameras zoom in on broken bodies and pain-wracked faces of injured athletes, on victims of natural disasters, and on sobbing relatives and friends at funerals, for example, those killed in the Oklahoma City bombing. Increasingly feeding and feeding on the pathological desires of its viewers, television has lost the ability *not to look,* and perhaps the worst case of all is that of Elián Gonzalez.[15] Similarly, the only two consistently profitable sectors of e-commerce are pornography and stock trading.[16]

Nastiness also spilled over the borders of televisionland to help define the culture of the 1990s. It was not only Justice Clarence Thomas who worried about the decline of civility. Trash talk, rudeness, and aggressive behavior were and are ubiquitous. One such case was the way "gangsta rap" flourished within a widespread debate on its relationship to violence. In this context, its most successful producer, Death Row Records, is deeply symbolic. Then again, there was the epoch in which, in both form and lyrics, pop music—particularly at the intersection of hard metal, hip-hop, and grunge—celebrated pain, a joyless, destructive sexuality, aggressive misogyny, and other types of abuse. Hard-edged anger, conjugated with an iconoclastic despair, shredded anything like warm, nurturing love.

Indecency, in a variety of senses, is also now a staple of the radio waves during well-known talk shows, and off the air it defines the contours of many urban dwellers' daily lives. It manifests itself in angry exchanges with panhandlers to whom they have become involuntarily and ambiguously habituated, at least in those cities in which the police have not driven them out of town or put them in jail. In the corporate world, meanwhile, according to a recent survey by the University of North Carolina School of Business, incivility is increasing. It shows up not only in the overt actions of racial and sexual harassment but also in omissions to act, such as not returning phone calls or forwarding messages. The lack of civility is similarly embodied in the fact that, in several Midwestern states, the Salvation Army can no longer keep open deposit bins, because they are being used as dumpsters. Likewise, the NFL "(throat) slash" or the "in-your-face" style of basketball, typical of the NBA, has become the metaphor of choice for how many exist. One NBA player settled a beef with his coach by trying to strangle him—twice yet—while other sports figures have bitten off ears and spit on umpires.

Further, there is the contemporary vogue of celebrating dumbness, a particularly depressing unkindness to oneself, which has generated unkindnesses to others in the form of bumper stickers such as, "My kid just beat up your honors student." And finally, if there is a "finally" in this sordid litany, there was the dismal fact that, after the Oklahoma City bombing, certain critics verbally attacked President Clinton for merely urging people to stop spewing out hate on the airwaves. He neither argued for censorship nor even named names. All he did to earn such opprobrium was to urge self-restraint.[17]

A 1993 article in *The New York Times* tried to explain a great deal of such incivility as a honest recognition by the working class of, and the means to assert power against, the cold-blooded cruelty of those who have power and money. As captured in television shows such as *The Simpsons, Married with Children,* and *Roseanne,* this "blue-collar rudeness stands for honesty, simplicity, and sincerity, as opposed to the sneaky, passive-aggressive style that goes under the name of politeness." Further, the story claimed, when we consider the class under the working class, rejection replaces skepticism about the possibility of civility.[18] Doubtless, this clarifies at least partly why some people are provoked to strike out at others, but it does not explain the fate of those Salvation Army deposit bins and countless gratuitous offenses against civility that are irrelevant to economic injustice.

"Things fall apart; the centre cannot hold," wrote Yeats (1976, 184). But disintegration is not merely a falling into disorder. It is also, and more deeply, a lack of wholeness and integrity, words that are also derived from the Latin *integer,* and it is precisely this lack, individually and collectively, that runs through all of the above instances of social disintegration. Within philosophy, we are especially indebted to Gabriel Marcel for his penetrating social diagnoses of a disintegrating "broken world" as well as a philosophy of hope as its antidote—what Paul Ricoeur once referred to as a "sociology of shadows" and "a metaphysics of light" (1973, 253). The latter clearly depends on the (re-)establishment of community, for which kindness in a multiplicity of social forms is a necessary condition. Part of the aim of this book is to describe phenomenologically the manifold ways that kindness occurs in order to show how community is possible and how it can fail to be possible. Thus while the facts referred to above update the diagnosis of a "sociology of shadows," there is also counterbalancing evidence to maintain some hope in human beings despite all.

Consider, for example, the recent push toward volunteerism, which reveals both aspects of Marcel's vision. The great social needs underscored by such efforts disclose both what has to be remedied as well as an enduring capacity to develop those qualities that Marcel and other philosophers, such as Hume, thought our highest possibilities.

Phenomenological Method

Throughout the following pages, I want to use phenomenology as a method to reach a concrete understanding of kindness in individual and social life. The knowledge desired here is neither a purely conceptual understanding of an essence nor an empirical inventory of all the ways we can be kind or unkind. It is a philosophical understanding, but one distilled from reflections actively engaged with our times. It is a *theoria* bound dialectically to *praxis* in order to fulfill Hegel's observation that, "Whatever happens, every individual is a child of his time; so philosophy too is its own time apprehended in thoughts" (1967, 11). This book incorporates practical examples from a variety of cultures, old as well as current, but it is neither culture bound in a philosophically defeating way nor dedicated to an exclusive preoccupation with multicultural diversity per se. It is not history alone or solely a sketch of kindness and unkindness in contemporary American life. The focus here is, then, not a "history of the present" so much as it is an "ontology of the present," to use Vincent Descombes' distinction (1993, 21). That is, the central theme of this book is what it means to be kind and unkind in our own time. The answer will appeal both to reason and the evidence on which it is based because, finally, truth lies in the details. As Philip Hallie remarks correctly, "[G]ood and evil and help and harm dwell in detail, or they dwell nowhere" (1997, 7).

It follows that the notion of evidential rationality to be defended here is not that which underpins modernism's commitment to universal, timeless truths stripped of their references to particularity. Reason is embedded, and always functions, in specific historical contexts conditioned by multiple layers of what Maurice Merleau-Ponty referred to as "sedimented" meanings (1964b, 89). It is a question, therefore, of bringing reason "down to earth" (Merleau-Ponty 1964a, 13). Neither reason nor evidence is to be repudiated. Rather, reason has the capacity to be self-critical as well as critical of its own evidence. It is not so weakened that it is inherently deceptive or empty.

This is not to say, however, that well-known postmodern (and other) challenges to reason are not serious or deserving of a response. They are, but this brief introduction is not the place for it. Rather, the entire text is intended to constitute a performative answer, and in a manner distinguishable from Dr. Johnson's memorable stone kicking. That is, the book itself will attempt to do phenomenology in such a way that our understanding of the phenomenon of kindness will be enhanced by a successful appeal to evidence and the relevant philosophical problems in making that appeal will be resolved. In other words, I adopt as a working hypothesis the twin premises that there is such a thing as evidence and that it is given to us in phenomenologically distinctive ways as the point of departure for our philosophical investigations. If the attempt to describe these evidences and make sense of them is successful, it will allow us to see phenomenology as a *recovery* of experience and of itself as a way to understand it.

The phenomenology developed in the following pages will consist of three distinct but interrelated levels of development. Part One will stay as close as possible to the descriptive level, while Part Two will focus on the interpretive and, in the last chapter, the critical. This does not mean that Part One will contain no references to the ethical, or even try to avoid such references. But it does imply that all such references will themselves attempt to describe kindness and related phenomena instead of taking normative positions.

We must begin with the descriptive for two reasons. First, interpretation and critique themselves are intentional—always of something—that is, some types of evidence. Just as a science is naive and dishonest by forgetting the experiential origins necessary for its own foundations (Merleau-Ponty 1962, ix), so also interpretation and critique must remember their own evidential origins. Rather than springing full-blown into being as Athena from the head of Zeus, interpretation and critique have identifiable, meaningful roots in our experience that phenomenology must illuminate.

The second reason is that interpretation has a double intentionality. Its point of departure is not only whatever is described but also the descriptions of it. That is, we shall see that description has an internal momentum that pushes it beyond itself into interpretation. These are passages from what can be experienced consciously to what is experienced unconsciously. Here phenomenology must embrace a hermeneutics of suspicion—following Ricoeur's reference to Nietzsche, Freud, and Marx as the three great "masters of the school of suspicion" (1970, 80–86)—in order to deepen the analysis of the nature of kindness and question its value. It is part of this questioning to scrutinize both the evidence and the way it is described, and especially the ways in which such descriptions play a role in people's actions, social practices, customs, and the like. In a similar way, as we shall see at the end of Part Two, interpretation will open into critique to seek a synthesis of the descriptive and skeptical questioning. Here kindness will pass from being an object of suspicion to a vehicle of critique of the social world. This will be the third level of development.

To begin with the descriptive level, phenomenology here has the sense of Merleau-Ponty's conception of a method for describing what appears to us as it appears—the world as we live it, as opposed to the ways that scientific or

historical explanations derivatively represent it. These descriptions of the phenomenological evidences do not exist for their own sakes, however, but rather
for a certain coinage. The aim is to understand their essential meanings, or
essences, as Edmund Husserl proposed, and these essences are supposed to
bring with them "all the living relationships of experience, just as the [fisher-
man's] net pulls up fish and pulsating algae from the depths of the sea"
(Merleau-Ponty 1962, xv).

To look for the essences of phenomena is to search for what actually presents itself to us before any explicitly reflective thematization of it. Pre-
thematically, the essence of a phenomenon is the "unique manner of existing
which gets expressed in the properties of the pebble, the glass or the bit of
wax, in all the facts of a revolution, in all the thoughts of a philosopher" (Merleau-Ponty 1962, xviii). This "unique manner of existing" is the concrete unity
of "matter" and "form," sensibility and intelligibility, particular and universal.
It is, in short, the "Idea in the Hegelian sense" (Merleau-Ponty 1962, xviii)—
the *Inhalt* or Content—or, in the language of Merleau-Ponty's last writings,
its "style" (1968, 188).

Thus, for example, there is no such thing as pure color. Rather, it is always
qualified by its material surface. As Jean-Paul Sartre showed in analyzing the
red of a carpet in one of Matisse's paintings—referenced by Merleau-Ponty
(1962, 5) without explaining Sartre's example—the artist "has chosen precisely
a carpet to redouble the sensual value of this red . . . it is a *woolly* red because
the carpet is of such a woolly matter" (Sartre 1963, 276). The red is part of a visual field where it gets its value as a part internally related to other internally related parts of the whole Gestalt. We shall see in what follows that much the
same thing happens to gestures of kindness as they emerge in different types of
social situations.

This concrete unity of particular and universal, matter and form, implies
that, as against Husserl, fact and essence cannot be sharply distinguished. In
the language of *The Visible and the Invisible*, "As the vein bears the leaf from
within, from the depths of its flesh, the ideas are the texture of experience, its
style, first mute, then uttered . . . [and] could not be detached from it" (Merleau-Ponty 1968, 119; translation altered). Each individual thus has a particular way of being, "in the active sense, a certain *Wesen*, in the sense that, says
Heidegger, this word has when it is used as a verb" (Merleau-Ponty 1968,
115).[19] In virtue of this concrete way of being, every essence, as Merleau-Ponty
indicates, is situated historically and geographically in a domain that includes
both our life and thought.

A second important implication of the concrete unity of particular and universal consists of a rejection of eidetic intuition as belonging to a pure spectator, the "attitude *above* the subject-object correlation that belongs to the world
and thus the attitude of focus upon the *transcendental subject-object correlation*"

(Husserl 1970, 181). In rejecting this "pensée de survol," or high-altitude think-ing, Merleau-Ponty quite rightly notes that it would deprive us "of that very cohesion in depth (*en épaisseur*) of the world and of Being without which the essence is subjective folly and arrogance" (1968, 112).

There is a third anti-Husserlian implication of the concrete unity of partic-ular and universal that is equally important for understanding kindness. It is that essences are open rather than closed. Since essences present themselves to us within our perceptual fields that are open, figure-ground structures with horizons of meaningfulness always to be filled in, and since, "There is no other meaning than carnal, figure and ground" (Merleau-Ponty 1968, 265), essences are characterized by the same open horizonality. This is true of simple exam-ples such as the "woolly red" of the carpet, but it equally holds for more com-plex universals in sociopolitical and moral life.[20]

Given this unavoidable openness of horizonality, essences are, just as are all perceptual data, contextual and ambiguous. Reciprocally, our way of under-standing of them is very different from a constitution of meaning in the im-manence of consciousness or holding them arrayed before us in the clarity of a complete eidetic intuition. Rather, we apprehend them "laterally, *by the style*" in which they manifest themselves (Merleau-Ponty 1968, 188). Especially in complex sociopolitical and moral contexts, instead of the rationalist's confident, secure possession, the sense of universals emerges uncertainly, indirectly, and approximately. As Václav Havel has argued, intellectuals should follow Sir Karl Popper's rejection of the siren call of holistic social engineering, but at the same time search for concrete ways to improve the world. They must do this, he tells us, although their success may always be limited in specific contexts, despite the fact that they will not know in advance if the changes they sought were the cor-rect ones, and "though they must always be prepared to rectify whatever life has shown to be wrong."[21]

However uncertainly grasped, essences are, to vary a bit Merleau-Ponty's metaphor of the fisherman's net, rather like the knots of the net. They are nodal points, intersections of connecting threads. They are themselves only cer-tain ways that these threads are woven together. Hence, their being is deter-mined by the way that the threads come to be bound up with each other. Furthermore, in conceptual nets, no less than in those in the world of the fish-erman, the knots have no sense apart from the threads that make them up, and are themselves only the ways that those strands of thought intersect. Thus it is only by appreciating how kindness is manifested concretely in the affairs of daily life, as well as how it fails to get manifested, that we can approach the nodal point of its essence.

Despite this non-Husserlian conception of essences, Husserl was right that a necessary first step for phenomenologists consists of breaking with the naïveté of the "natural attitude," and that to break with this uncritical acceptance, we have to impose an "epoché" or "bracketing" of as many of our presuppositions as possible about the particular phenomenon being studied. Imposing the epoché marks a basic move from mere thinking to reflection, from an interested to a disinterested consciousness, and hence Richard Schmitt correctly notes that, "It is here, in reflection, that the distinction between true belief and knowledge is first drawn" (1959, 243).

For Husserl, and phenomenologists generally, the epoché has had both an exclusive and a revelatory function. Husserl's own beliefs notwithstanding, there is nothing very novel about its exclusive function. That we must set aside as many as possible of our prejudices, biases, and other types of presuppositions to see the phenomena objectively and impartially has been a shop-worn nostrum for philosophers at least since Plato. But the revelatory function of the epoché was novel. Its aim was to break with the natural attitude and to prepare for a philosophy constructed on the basis of a new attitude toward the world—what Eugen Fink called an "astonishment" in the face of the world (Merleau-Ponty 1962, xiii).

In the present book, the epoché will have similarly exclusive and revelatory functions. The exclusive function poses less of a problem here than with certain other phenomena because, in the absence of philosophers' (and others') general lack of serious interest in kindness, there is no fully developed theory, still less a set of theories, to bracket. On the other hand, there are value assumptions and judgments embedded in the natural attitude that we would do well to place in parentheses—for example, that kindness is identical to benevolence or beneficence, that it is or is not a moral duty, and that it is always good.

The revelatory function of the epoché will be visible in this book in two different but interrelated contexts. The first of these parallels its appearance in Merleau-Ponty's *Phénoménologie de la perception*. There the author was able to illuminate our normal bodily powers of inhabiting the world by studying pathological behavior—chiefly Gelb's and Goldstein's famous patient, Schneider—in which those powers were severely atrophied.[22] This adaptation of the epoché turned out to be a very fruitful strategy. The lived-body appeared as a system of motor-intentional powers of inhabiting a world spatially and temporally, as involved in perceptual and cultural relationships with other people and physical objects, and as situated in a history in which one takes up existing "sedimented" meanings and freely creates others through multiple powers of expression. It is, in the nice expression of Kym Maclaren, an "improvisatory body."[23] In the first part of this book I shall adopt a similar tactic, though on a more limited scale, in terms of the sick and injured body.

Since my task initially will be to describe the manifold ways in which kindness appears to us and to disengage from these phenomenological evidences as much as can be said about the meaning of kindness, the chapters making up Part One will therefore be divided according to the relevant phenomena—what things appear to us as kind. In sequence, these will be acts and omissions to act (Chapter 1), persons (Chapters 2 and 3), indeterminate social atmospheres and technological uses of nature (Chapter 4), and social institutions and communities (Chapter 5).

There are three sources of these phenomenological evidences. The first two are personal and collective social experiences, as well as insightful writings of phenomenologists such as Merleau-Ponty, Marcel, Ricoeur, Emmanuel Levinas, Werner Marx, and Mikel Dufrenne. These thinkers reflect in diverse ways on the philosophical importance of the body, and almost all of our immediate and clearest experiences of kindness and unkindness affect the welfare and "illfare" of the body. The third source consists of literature—that "incomparable storehouse of knowledge" (Barthes 1985, 246–47)—and other works of art.

Literature is an important and even a crucial source of evidence, because novels can reveal in a unique way who we are and, along with it, the significance of kindness in human existence. This is so partly because of the notion of narrative identity that Ricoeur first explored in volume 3 of *Time and Narrative* and later much more thoroughly in *Oneself as Another*. In relevant part, for Ricoeur, through the act of reading, a dialectic emerges to enable the reader to belong at the same time to the imaginative world of the work and to her own concrete existence. Reading becomes the context in which "the transfer between the world of the narrative . . . and the world of the reader takes place"; as such, reading "constitutes a privileged place and bond for the affection of the reading subject" (1992, 329). In this "transfer," or, using Merleau-Ponty's language, "chiasm between history and fiction" (Ricoeur 1992, 114, n. 1), the reader can come to understand her own life as narrative. As Mark S. Muldoon expresses it succinctly, "As Ricoeur likes to quote from Gadamer, through a 'fusion of horizons,' the reader belongs to both the experiential horizon of the work imaginatively, and the horizon of his or her action concretely [citing Ricoeur 1984, 77]" (Muldoon 1997, 41). Thus the interpretation of stories that we recount about people make their lives "more readable," and the stories themselves achieve greater lucidity to the degree that we can interpret them in terms of "the narrative models of plots—borrowed from history or from fiction (drama or novel)" (Ricoeur 1992, 114, n. 1).

This is also an additional way that the epoché will find a place in this book because novels (and other genres of art) can function as such by "depragmatizing" the Lifeworld of the reader (Ricoeur 1988, 169). As Martha Nussbaum argues in the course of her extensive commentary on Henry James' *The Golden Bowl*, "A novel, just because it is not our life, places us in a moral position that is favorable for perception and it shows us what it would be like to take up that position in life. . . . [I]t does not seem far-fetched to claim that most of us can read James better than we can read ourselves" (1990, 162).[24] Or, as Emmanuel Bury states it in a very different context, "[I]n the end, literature offers us a moral picture of the human condition. Far from purely speculative philosophy, it wants to demonstrate the truth of certain values in action: it is fundamentally Socratic" (1996, 240).

Ricoeur is also correct to note that literary narrative not only provides us with past self-understanding, but also opens us up through imaginative variations on our corporeal existence that the story provides and invites us to rethink the sense of our lives. To the degree that characters in novels or on the stage closely resemble us thinking, speaking, and acting subjects, they invite us to see the lived-body as "a dimension of oneself [and], the imaginative variations *around* the corporeal condition are variations on the self and its selfhood" (Ricoeur 1992, 150). These imaginative variations in turn provoke us to reflections on "the ethical aim of life" (discussed in Chapter 3).

Exactly the same theme appears in Nussbaum's *Poetic Justice*. When we read novels—she takes Charles Dickens' *Hard Times* and Richard Wright's *Native Son* as cases in point—there is a dialectic between the story and our reflections on people in our own society. These and other novels make us think about the conditions of their characters' flourishing, or lack thereof, and the sense of contingency in their and our social arrangements. This dialectic stimulates us to wonder what, as concerned citizens, we could do to improve things. As a result, for Nussbaum, "the novel constructs a paradigm of a style of ethical reasoning that is context-specific without being relativistic, in which we get potentially universalizable concrete prescriptions by bringing a general idea of human flourishing to bear on a concrete situation, that we are invited to enter through the imagination" (1995a, 10).

Thomas Hardy once remarked, "[A] novel is an impression, not an argument" (1978, 38). This is both true and false. Novels are not philosophy, and one cannot argue with good literature the way one can with philosophy. But novels, and other works of art as well, are not collections of discrete, Humean-like impressions either. As Friedrich Nietzsche pointed out, well before the advent of Gestalt psychology, "It cannot be doubted that *all sense perceptions are permeated with value judgments* (useful and harmful—consequently, pleasant or unpleasant)" (1968a, no. 505, 275; emphasis in original).[25] We might also add that literary impressions can be insightful, personally illuminative, and philosophically exciting. Great literature—for instance, the story of *Job*, Tolstoy's *War and Peace,* Shakespeare's *King Lear,* George Eliot's *Middlemarch,* or Toni Morrison's *Beloved*—does this not only by developing characters within their contexts and informing us about the historical milieu they reflect, but also by telling us something philosophically important about ourselves.

Furthermore, a crucial dimension of this revelation is, as Ricoeur and Nussbaum maintain, ethical. As Ricoeur indicates, "Literature is a vast laboratory in which we experiment with estimations, evaluations, and judgments of approval and condemnation" (1992, 115). These experiments illuminate, among other things, moral responsibility, gaps between our intentions and the results of our actions, and the complexity and moral ambiguities involved in making choices. They also show us unsuspected problems associated with the unintended consequences of our actions and the reversal of our usual value schemes in assessing the nature of the good life. In addition, novels sensitize us to suffering by confronting us with struggles between powerful people and those who must submit to them, as well as the experiences of suffering that these conflicts entail.

Novels will provide the most important stock of non-philosophical examples of kindness and unkindness represented here, but there are other sources. We shall find relevant evidence in poems, short stories, plays, and non-literary art as well, such as paintings, drawings, and sculptures. These also have a compelling power to present us with imaginative, morally complex experiences, and hence to sketch more graphically problems for philosophers to untangle.

In general, then, the view defended here is that literature (as well as other artistic media) has a cognitive function. Art can disclose truth for the reasons that Aristotle gave for poetry: "[T]he function is to describe, not the thing that has happened, but a kind of thing that might happen, i.e. what is possible as being probable or necessary. . . . Hence poetry is something more philosophic and of graver import than history, since its statements are of the nature rather of universals, whereas those of history are singulars" (1941, 1451a:37–1451b:11, 1463–64). Novels, as well as other artworks, can be illuminating sources of evidence for doing philosophy, and they can reveal truths to us in ways that standard works of philosophy cannot.[26] This is why, for instance, Merleau-Ponty often refers to authors such as Stendhal, Balzac, and Proust for inspiration, and why Gabriel Marcel found so many reference points for his philosophy in music and the theatre. So also, to take examples almost at random, R. S. Thomas' poem, *Children's Song*, has a startling power to show us certain relationships between the child and the adult that illustrate our lateral participation in the complex of essences involved in childhood and how they are inscribed in Being (Thomas 1985, 21).[27] George Eliot's sublime prose can shed an equal amount of light on Heidegger's memories of his high school and his reflections on Being as verbal,[28] and Henry James' *The Golden Bowl* provides an instructive example of Merleau-Ponty's notion of the "chiasm."[29]

In short, philosophy and literature, as well as other artistic media, are parallel and supplementary. Their relationship is not one of generality to particularity, but rather of a rational logos to an immanent intelligibility. To once again recur to Merleau-Ponty's metaphor, good novels and insightful examples from other artistic media are like the knots of the fisherman's net—expressions of a certain localizable time and place, but without having their meaning restricted to that spatio-temporal anchorage. They provide philosophy with a richer, unique source of evidence for its reflections. Philosophy does not turn into literature to fulfill itself. Rather, as Dufrenne puts it, "[P]hilosophy [should take] art as an object of reflection, but in transposing into its own language and in integrating into its own system what it finds of truth in it" (1973, 323). And within philosophy, I take phenomenology to be best situated to push beyond the usual abstractions of moral and political discourse to fully appreciate what good art shows well, namely, the kinds of human interactions in which even bodily gestures take on the weight of commitment in kind and unkind relationships with others.

Good literature and other works of art will also play an important role in Part Two of this book which, as noted above, will deal with a hermeneutics of suspicion about, and a critical defense of, kindness. Merleau-Ponty was right to argue that, "The greatest lesson of the [phenomenological] reduction is the impossibility of a complete reduction," that "there is no thought that embraces all our thoughts" (1962, xiv).[30] Since experience is inevitably interpretive, it follows that descriptive phenomenology cannot be a complete phenomenology. It must become hermeneutic in order to fulfill itself. Accordingly, this hermeneutic interpretation will attempt to uncover what lies beyond and beneath the appearances, and therefore is not openly presented to us.

This is to say that the problem with appearances is not that they are not real (usually). On the contrary, the world is already there, what we take up as the presupposed foundation of any experience and our point of departure for doing philosophy to begin with. The difficulty is, rather, that appearances are all there and have to be unpacked to get at their full meaning. Here truth becomes *aletheia,* "disclosure" in Heidegger's sense of "taking entities out of their hiddenness and letting them be seen in their unhiddenness (their uncoveredness)" (1962, 262). The historicity of concrete social actors, received moral codes, politics, and so forth reveals hidden frameworks of interpretation themselves that contextualize, often at our ignorance, particular actions, rules, policies, and the like situated within those frameworks. As we shall see in undertaking a hermeneutics of kindness, the phenomena increase in complexity by involving self-perception and deception in addition to the perceptions of others, individually and as whole classes. In addition, a hermeneutic phenomenology of kindness, unconstrained by brackets imposed at the descriptive level, will not maintain a value-free stance. The very nature of the types of questions raised in interpretation will lead quickly to an exploration of exploitation and coercion, as well as to a fresh encounter with Nietzsche on the will to power and the genealogy of morals. To reach that end, however, we must first undertake the difficult labor of attempting to get back to, in Husserl's famous phrase, "the things themselves."

PART I

To betray humanity would be to betray, quite simply, to fall short of virtue—
that is, short of the virtue of fraternity. In that humanity, one should never
betray one's brother. Curse or speak ill of him. Another way of
saying: only the brother can be betrayed. Fratricide is the general form
of temptation, the possibility of radical evil, the evil of evil.
—Jacques Derrida, *Politics of Friendship*

Chapter 1

Acts and Omissions

What do we live for, if it is not to make life less difficult to each other?
—George Eliot, *Middlemarch*

Kindness and the Body: The Epoché

All of us have a "perceptual faith" in the world as we perceive it, and our beliefs about this world "rest on a fundamental basis of mute 'opinions' implied in our life" (Merleau-Ponty 1968, 3). In a similar fashion, we assume kindness as a given in our cultural world. We believe that it exists, at least sometimes, and we also hold "mute" as well as, very occasionally, explicitly formulated opinions about it. Given the exclusive function of the epoché, none of these beliefs will be appealed to here. For the reasons given in the Introduction, we will begin with as few presuppositions as possible in describing the manifold ways in which kindness appears to us—its unique manner of existing—through bodily actions and omissions to act.

Kindness emerges in our relationships with others and their reciprocal relationships with us. Kindness is, therefore, one modality of our primordial situation, I-in-the-world with-others. Just as Sartre demonstrated that no one can be obscene or ashamed all by herself, so also no one can be kind by herself, though she could be kind to herself. Moreover, this "I" is no Husserlian (or Kantian) transcendental ego—and still less a Cartesian *cogito*—any more than it is the other in whose existence I am enmeshed. Rather, it is what Merleau-Ponty described as the "lived-body" (*le corps propre*), "existence, that is to say, being in the world through a body" (1962, 309). (It is also true, though, let us remark in passing, that Merleau-Ponty's notion of the lived-body is greatly indebted to Husserl's distinction in the *Cartesian Meditations* and other texts between *Leib*—"flesh," "my body"—and *Körper*, the body as object.)

I am in the world through a body by existing in a perceptual circuit with things and other people. It is a Hegelian concrete universal, a "thought-in-act,"

3

because it is a system of motor powers for exploring and making sense of the world as it presents itself to us. The lived-body is thus an "I can" as well as an "I think." The mobile body and consciousness are like two sides of the same sheet of paper: they are mutually implicatory, because they comprise "two abstract aspects of one existence" (Merleau-Ponty 1970, 8).

Accordingly, it is within this field of corporeal motility that we find our most evident, directly presented instances of kindness and unkindness, namely, actions and omissions to act. Of course, actions and omissions to act occur between persons in the context of social atmospheres and institutions, and these phenomena, distinguished here only for the sake of analysis, are the subjects of the following chapters. But the fact that actions and omissions are primordial presentations of kindness is why the epoché of the sick and injured body can have such revelatory power. When awareness and motility are disrupted, our relationships with others and the world around us change profoundly. We become more sharply conscious of power relations, dependencies, the reliance of our wills on all of the involuntary aspects of nature and culture that simultaneously support and threaten us, and finally of the capacity of others to help and harm us. The "gift of sorrow," as George Eliot once said, is the "susceptibility to the bare offices of humanity that raises them into a bond of loving friendship" (1985, 269). Even when the consequences do not extend as far as Eliot conceives them, it is still true that, in suffering, there is the danger of self-centeredness and despair that can be conquered only by being liberated from myself. That freedom in turn requires "attachment to the other" (Marcel 1984, 201).

Certainly not all acts of kindness involve sick or injured bodies, but those that do make us more keenly aware of how such acts occur. Hence, sickness and injury can function as an epoché. Throughout our normal perceptual and behavioral life, as phenomenologists such as Merleau-Ponty have shown, the rays of a motor-intentional consciousness stream out pre-reflectively to embrace objects and other people. The body disappears in these projects because, rather than being the focus of a thematic concern, it forms only the anonymous, pre-personal background of all of our acts. There is also a "depth" disappearance in that the inner, or visceral, life of the body likewise remains hidden. Thus it is *"the body's own tendency to self-effacement* that allows for the possibility of its neglect or deprecation" at the hands of philosophers such as Descartes (Leder 1990, 69, emphasis in original).

The body does not come to mind, literally and figuratively, until something happens to make it the explicit object of thematic attention. This is what happens in the pain of injury and sickness, and then the body appears as fallible and untrustworthy. In these cases, the body "dys-appears," that is, in the Greek sense of *dys,* meaning "'bad,' 'hard,' or 'ill,' and [which] is found in English words such as 'dysfunctional'" (Leder 1990, 84). "Dys-appearance" is not, however, identical to "dys-function." Rather, the latter is only one possible case of the former, because the body can become an object of thematic concern outside of the contexts of injury and illness—as, say, the object of reflections on the normal process of aging.

How do these dys-appearances come about? Let us consider pain first and then illness. Not all pains create dys-appearances. Some experiences of pain are congruent with our projects, as Nietzsche pointed out with reference to the sufferings of the artist, but it is also true of athletes, students, writers, and masochists (these classes are non-disjunctive). However, other pains do lead to dys-appearances, because they are involuntary, invasive, and destructive. At a sensory level, these types of pains fix attention on the body in three ways. They create a "sensory intensification," they possess an "episodic structure," because they disrupt the normal "amorphous" state of well-being with novel sensations, and, finally, they compel us to attend to them (Leder 1990, 71, 72, 73).

When pain becomes severe enough, it disrupts our intentional relationships with other people, it constricts our lives spatially and temporally, and it draws our attention unwillingly to the body as an alien and a passive "other." The first of these effects comes about because pain strikes at us individually and isolates us from others among whom we live and with whom we work and play. The tennis player overcome by angina pains announcing an immanent heart attack becomes acutely aware of the way in which pain singles out and isolates its victim from other players on the court. The victim alone can feel the spreading fire of internal toxicity and the crushing weight in the chest, and even the clamminess of skin is experienced as something that would not feel the same to others. The sufferer alone feels it and feels quite alone in the consciousness of being the only one who feels it. The tense, worrying faces of the other players crowding around can only reinforce this aloneness, since they but create a consciousness of being the intentional object at the intersection of anxious gazes. Uncomfortable men tend to talk loudly—with a loudness that, like whistling in the dark, betrays a certain self-conscious futility and awareness of their own vulnerability visible in the victim. Or, as John Updike has expressed it so poignantly, they "challenge silence with laughter," while women, smiling, bestow the kindness of their "eyes of famous mercy."[1] Such kind gestures strike the sufferer isolated by and in pain as well-intentioned superfluities.

This same effect is present in other phenomena that result at least partly from pain—for example, the weakened and atrophied body. On crutches, the previously gentle slope of the sidewalk becomes the coefficient of an arduous task. Things and other people take on a new appearance that reflects diminished capacities to sustain one's usual motor-projects. Entering a restaurant door, for example, means discovering that the door is no longer a tool employed unthinkingly but an impediment compounded by other users. In a crowded room, bodies no longer slide by each other with pre-reflective grace and fluidity but rather collide in awkward bunches around the crutches. (One incredulous individual resolved her uncertainty by trying to go *through* them.)

In the second effect of pain, the spatio-temporal narrowing of my world, that world does not totally collapse, but through motor and perceptual constriction, I tend to reflect more on myself and on my isolation. Pain tears through the normal ec-static structures of consciousness by which I project myself in the world; it tends to fix me in place. Pain also constricts me temporally by pinning me down to the present. It has a "phenomenologically 'centripetal' force, gathering space and time inward to the center" (Leder 1990, 76). Often, too, this centripetal force is balanced by one that is centrifugal, by which we try to escape pain in the present through imagination and fantasy and through memories of a painless past. This desire to escape is a response to the fact that suffering—a phenomenon wider than, but inclusive of, pain—strikes at our sense of self-esteem by decreasing our power of acting—the "I am able to"—of the lived-body (Ricoeur 1992, 320).

Chronic pain presents a special case of these centripetal and centrifugal forces at work in our self-consciousness, because there is much more of the centripetal and much less of the centrifugal. To the degree that those who suffer are no longer able to remember a past without pain, they lose a refuge in memory and a concomitant ability to construct a better future in fantasy. The world eventually runs out of opportunities. In the experience of unwanted pain generally, a fault line opens up between the body and the self, and the body disharmoniously appears as alien. This third effect of pain is exacerbated in chronic sufferers, so that they eventually lose sight of what the wholeness of self-integrity was like. Alienation from the body achieves permanency. In non-chronic pain, in contrast, a future-looking demand opens up in us for both a hermeneutic interpretation of the pain and then for action to reachieve a painless existence. The chronic sufferer eventually tends to lose this hope.[2]

Illness, or "dis-ease," sets in motion many of the same experiential kinds of changes as does pain. Sick people also lose motor possibilities and recognize that the lived-body is temporarily or permanently no longer an "I can." They also experience a rupture of intersubjective relationships as they turn inward in self-absorption with illness. There is likewise a spatio-temporal compression of existence and the sense of the body as an alien presence. Finally, when disability is recognized as permanent, a corresponding lack of hope and self-esteem becomes more likely.[3]

Our bodies, whether or not alienated from our selves, are, as Merleau-Ponty pointed out, always with us, our point of view on the world from which we perceive objects and have something to do. Our bodies are not distinguishable from us, as are tools, coffee cups, or glasses, which we can misplace or lose. It follows, therefore, that our perceptions of our bodies as an "alien presence" in pain and sickness always come into existence within the perspective of the lived-body. However much victims of injury and illness may wish, and however much of a wedge that pain and sickness drive between the body and the self, there is no final cleavage between the two. Thus the patient in the coronary care unit who sees all vital signs recorded and sounded on multiple pieces of monitoring equipment knows that there is some deep connection after all between the self and the mysterious alien presence that the inner body has become.

It is in this field of corporeality—mine and that of others—whether well or sick, fully able or injured, fully capacitated or pained, that acts of kindness and kind omissions to act appear to us. Some of these acts and omissions strike us immediately as kind, and we shall study them next. Other acts and omissions are only recognized as such through the mediation of reflective, conscious acts across temporal intervals of varying duration, and we shall consider these later in this chapter.

Immediately Presented Acts and Omissions

Immediate presentations of kindness strike us spontaneously as kind. No inferences or other reflective, positing acts of consciousness are necessary (or sufficient) to bring about such experiences. We may later change our minds about their meanings, for one reason or another, but our first impression is that someone is doing us a kindness.

Various examples exist of such experiences that are more or less familiar to us all. Strangers who have no special duties of care to victims of tragedies sometimes flood them with monetary and other types of gifts. Someone may call my attention to a letter I have dropped while on the way to the post office. A stranger might put money in my parking meter to prevent me from getting a ticket—in Cincinnati, even at the cost of legal prosecution—or merely listen to me when no one else will. A stranger in a foreign city may alert me that I have to validate my subway ticket in the platform machine. Less familiar, however, are experiences such as those of patients in a coronary care unit. They have lost all sense of the taken-for-granted character of the world of the natural attitude and therefore appreciate the overpowering weight of a compassionate word or gesture, the sheer astonishment that caring others are there to begin with and, correlatively, the sense of not being forgotten.[4] Conversely, we take it as evidence of unkindness, though not always definitively, when people are able but unwilling to help us in these various ways—when they "turn their backs on us"—through either indifference or refusal.

There are likewise diverse examples of kind omissions to act. Past acquaintances may have the power to embarrass us by revealing facts that we would like to keep hidden, and yet refrain from doing so. Friends do not utilize a public forum to refute certain claims that we have made, either out of consideration for our feelings or to not jeopardize our chances of attaining whatever might be the goals of our present projects. Conversely, we would be inclined to view contrary acts as unkind when omitting to act was equally possible.

In general, these are familiar and unremarkable instances of kind acts and omissions. Now let us consider certain cases of each more closely. Suppose that someone opens my office door for me while I am struggling with my briefcase and keys and balancing clumsily on my crutches. My most immediate awareness here is of another person intervening in my (so far unsuccessful) motor-projects because of my body image as an awkward powerlessness. I am simultaneously aware of the other doing for me what I cannot do for myself, and of my own handicap.[5]

How someone performs an act of kindness is equally, if not more, important than *what* has been done. To begin with, the act must have at least two interrelated qualities common to all acts in order to be one of kindness. The action must be intentional, in the sense of being purposeful. Someone who trips, falls against the door, and causes it to open just when I want to enter, would not have acted. The agent must be aware of what is being done and must mean to do it. The action must also be voluntary in some significant sense. It is part of this necessary voluntariness that actions not be performed because of direct physical or psychological compulsion. Nor can they result from indirect compulsion produced by coercion applied to someone else, or by "causes internal to the person, such as reflexes, ignorance, or disease, that decisively contribute, in ways beyond his control, to the occurrence of the behavior" (Gewirth 1978, 31). More positively, an individual's choice is voluntary when under her own control, when "unforced and informed choice is the necessary and sufficient condition of the behavior" (ibid.). Thus someone opening the door for me at gunpoint, under hypnotic or post-hypnotic suggestion, or (even more bizarrely) while sleepwalking, again would not have acted. In the absence of any effective will and self-control, the external motions at best would have imitated a voluntary and an intentional act.[6]

To say that all actions, and therefore those of kindness, are purposeful and voluntary means that they evidence what Merleau-Ponty, Ricoeur, and Alfred Schutz have variously described as a motivated freedom.[7] Inscribed in this freedom is a third quality of kind acts, namely, that they possess a particular type of vector quality: the actions are done *for* a certain person (s), and not simply aimed *at*, or done *to*, them. If the agent meant to do something else instead—say, opening my office door to retrieve some files, paying me no heed on the way in—then the experiential identity of the action would be changed irrevocably. My presence would be acknowledged only as an impediment to entry—not minded as long as it did not interfere with the completion of the project.

The content of this interested vector quality in acts of kindness, which is part of their underlying motivated freedom, is that it embodies a sensitivity to the need of the other and a resolve to attempt to remedy the need. In less transitory relationships, acts of kindness can also transcend the minimal level of remedying needs and, as we shall see in the following chapter, actively seek the other's spiritual flourishing. But at whatever level of commitment, the other takes a more or less momentary and momentous interest in my welfare, and this is why I respond to the action differently than in the case of many others that I witness day in and day out. I am aware that my needs have registered in the eyes of the other, and I resonate the offered help with thanks for her solicitude. Equally importantly, if not more so, I am cognizant of the fact that the interest that the other takes in my welfare is for my sake, and not hers. Neurotic do-gooders, for example, take an active interest in our welfare—early and often—and yet their actions do not manifest kindness. Their interest rides along on, so to speak, and testifies to, their interest in us for their own sakes.

When I register in the eyes of the other to solicit acts of kindness, I cannot determine the gravity of my claim on the other's freedom. I may end up counting with more or less importance. As a result, acts of kindness may be located anywhere along a extensive scale of seriousness—from normally fairly trivial actions, such as opening doors, to, say, important life-saving actions, such as warning someone of her intended sexual partner's exposure to the AIDS virus. There is also a special class of actions located at the high end of the scale that Claude Lanzmann's epic Holocaust documentary, *Shoah*, illustrates poignantly. At a certain point in the Warsaw ghetto uprising, a man was killed and given only a hasty burial (under fire). Later, a woman, at considerable personal risk, disinterred the body and gave it a proper Jewish burial. As Judith Jarvis Thomson has noted, there are several types of Samaritans: those who are (only) minimally decent, those who are good, those who are very good, and those who are splendid (1971, 62-64). The woman in the Warsaw ghetto was splendid, just as were the actions of Magda Trocmé who, along with her pastor husband, André, organized the handful of hungry, straitened villagers of Le Chambon-sur-Lignon to shelter and rescue thousands of Jews during World War II.[8] Such actions teach us that there are not only corresponding degrees of sensitivity to our welfare but also of the resolve to act on those sensitivities. Effectively the Chambonnais used the same weapons as did Gandhi, "*ahimsa* ('non-violence, the refusal to hurt any living thing'), truthfulness, courtesy, and love" (Zaehner 1962, 228).

We can increase our understanding of this sensitivity by examining instances of unkindness in which our need for help goes unheeded. In these cases, we are struck first by the absence of response, a lack that is not nothing. On the contrary, it is pregnant with meaningfulness, because it consists of a failure to respond to an appeal, whether explicit or implicit. I am left without a justification, but one that I consider is owed me. Hence, the lack of response endows the behavior of the other with a normative dimension best described as a deficiency or shortcoming, but one that is expressed by a very different sense of "ought" than that captured by the usual language of rights and duties. In that interpretive framework, unless the other has a special duty of care toward me, I have no right to aid. Nonetheless, in cases of ordinary, rather than heroic, or "splendid" Samaritanism, other things being equal, when the other can heed my appeal and does not, the lack of response carries along with it the sense of having to be justified. Blame attaches to heedlessness, just as it does in the parable of the Good Samaritan to the priest and the Levite, who likewise had no special duty of care to the injured and pained victim, nor he a correlative right to their assistance.

When I try to grasp the reasons behind unkind acts, I tend to construe the lack of response as an expression of either insensitivity and/or awareness. These two factors are non-disjunctive, for either may reinforce and perpetuate the other. Insensitivity takes many forms and can characterize an agent's actions in which there is no lack of purpose and no voluntariness of conduct, and in which there is often full awareness of what is being done and to whom. When acts of unkindness are motivated chiefly by insensitivity, the object of those actions becomes aware of simply not counting, or not counting enough, in the agent's eyes to solicit the response needed. This is a double revelation: that one has been judged and in the judgment has been not only left in need but also found unworthy of being helped.

It was this insensitivity that Moritz Schlick had in mind when he argued that the "peculiar characteristic" of egoism is "inconsiderateness." By this he meant that the egoist is "quite untroubled by the desires and needs of others. When he pursues his ends with such inconsiderateness that he coldly ignores the joys and sorrows of his neighbors. . . . he remains deaf and blind and cold to the happiness and misfortune of his neighbor" (1939, 75–76). Schlick does not point out, but there is no reason to think that he would dispute it either, that there are many degrees of such deafness, blindness, and coldness.

Some are appallingly grotesque, as, for example, the Austrians who for six years lived in full view of the stone quarries in the Mauthausen concentration camp and "saw nothing" of the tortures and killings of Jewish prisoners. Such cases can easily make us believe that the depths of human callousness have no limit. At the other extreme are all of the little unkindnesses that make up daily life, such as rude and dangerous drivers who are not even conscious of the endangered motorists that they leave in their wake, or noise polluters who never give a thought to the possibility that they are disturbing someone else's peace.

Coldly ignoring the welfare and "illfare" of one's neighbors is an important part of inconsiderateness, albeit, as we shall see shortly, not the whole of it. Such insensitivity clearly evidences appraisals of others that find them wanting—as, for example, when one of my students, who is paralyzed from the waist down, once tried to park his specially outfitted van in the only available parking place for the disabled in a certain shopping center. (It was also the only available parking place in the entire lot.) A departing shopper foiled the attempt when, despite her clear recognition of his handicapped license place, she rolled her empty cart in his way. (He had to return home.)

Coldly disregarding the welfare or "illfare" of the other is also responsible for certain examples of unkindness in cases of what Drew Leder calls the "social dys-appearance" of the body and attendant unkindnesses. In this type of dysappearance, for a variety of reasons, a split opens up between self and body as a result of the other's gaze that is "highly distanced, antagonistic, or objectifying"; thus the social dys-appearance of the body amounts to "disrupted cosubjectivity" (1990, 96, 97). When, for example, a woman attempts to internalize the way she is a sex object for others, or the ways that her body fails to please, a split opens up between herself and her body, so that she cannot appear to others, or herself, as herself.[9] Likewise, the same mechanism of unkind alienation is inscribed in the ways that our culture socializes women to believe that social acceptability is predicated on physical appearance.[10]

Specifically thematizing the body is often conjugated with imbalances in power relationships. In inferior-superior relationships—for example, women to men, students to instructors, patients to doctors, or prisoners to jailers—the less powerful often tend to an enhanced self-awareness. The difference in power makes co-subjectivity difficult and impossible when the superior replaces, rather than supplements, the experience of the inferior. Thus the body is, as Foucault showed in *Discipline and Punish* and elsewhere, vulnerable to sociopolitical as well as biological forces.

Coldly ignoring the welfare or "illfare" of the other is not the whole of our inconsiderateness, because a particular type of unawareness can also be a sufficient condition of such attitudes. That is, ignoring something or someone requires reflective, positing acts of consciousness to avoid (re) cognition and to put them out of mind. But there are other forms of inconsiderateness that presuppose no such conscious acts or judgments. Instead, they rest on a lack of awareness that takes the form of thoughtless indifference. Unkind acts that are the products of such a lack of awareness are not acts of ignoring but rather consist of a peculiar failure to register, as in cases such as our scanning the morning paper's stories of the latest atrocities abroad and of crime victims in our own communities. Reading the papers is a comfortable because insulated way of learning about the latest disasters and misfortunes. As such, "the practice always verges on seeming frivolous and in bad faith" (Descombes 1993, 5). It is also a convenient way of not recognizing how few are the times when we really are ready to aid other people. As Hallie notes, our usual response to "the sufferings and deaths of strangers" is one of boredom (1997, 5).

But "not registering" other people's sufferings is itself a very complex phenomenon that occurs in both personal relationships and on a more general social level. At the individual level, it may include, but not necessarily, a lack of visual recognition. My first impression of the unencumbered person who simply walks by when I am struggling with crutches to open a door is not of someone whose perceptual acuity must be urgently deficient. Rather, I am presented with someone in whom my injury fails to resonate, someone in whom there is a basic lack of sensitivity. Similarly, as noted above, our criticisms of the priest and the Levite who simply "passed by" are not that they were perceptually deficient—or, for that matter, that they lacked consciousness, intelligence, or dedication to their tasks. It is, rather, that they could not make room in themselves for the victim. In contrast, the Good Samaritan's response to the victim's pain was such that he was "moved with compassion" (Luke 10:33).[11]

This type of inconsiderateness is, then, not only thought-less, but feeling-less as well. Rather than an outright rejection of the other, it comprises a pre-reflective, affective failure, because one's sensitivities have been anesthetized through indifference. We will study this subject further in Chapter 3 in terms of the peculiar phenomenon of self-absorption, but here suffice it to say, again, that this insensitivity presents itself as having a normative dimension that merely failing to perceive something or someone does not. My lack of awareness of the cardinals building a nest near my window, or the expensive sports car with which a friend is enthralled, is typically due to concentration on other things, and usually no blame attaches to such a lack of awareness. But if I am insensitive to someone's fatigue because I was engrossed in telling a story—it simply "never occurred to me" that they might not be enjoying it—then criticism is usually thought to be the appropriate response. It is a deficiency, because I should have known better. It is a shortcoming, because its foundational ignorance is not innocent. As Levinas argued, the prescriptive appeal of the Other is inscribed in our face-to-face relationships, because the face of that Other puts my freedom in question: "The Face, whose ethical epiphany consists in soliciting a response . . . is not satisfied with a 'good intention' and a benevolence wholly Platonic" (1979, 225).

When the prescriptive appeal of the other is answered, how is that possible through kind *omissions* to act? To take some typical examples, a parent might witness a child struggling to rise to some challenge and feel a great temptation to intervene in order to save time or to spare the child the possible experience of embarrassed failure. Still, the parent resists. I have committed a *faux pas* and come to be aware of it. Witnesses now have the power of public reproof. I look anxiously, if furtively, into their eyes to measure the impact of my gaffe. Perhaps blushing a little, I see no resolve to embarrass me. They may be looking down or a little to one side in a transparent pretense of having not heard or seen my foolishness—a putative "failure" to hear and see that manifests itself as purposively self-contradictory. Or, they may continue to speak and look at me with poker faces, "as if nothing had happened." Their kind omission becomes my reprieve.

Again, I might be telling a joke to a group that includes someone who has already heard it. I can tell that the listener's impatient gestures and anticipative pleasure in a collateral, silent telling of the story reveal a temptation to beat me to the punch line. But she refrains: there is a smile of confederation, a co-conspiratorial look that gives me to understand that not speaking was a way of taking my side. Our projects interweave as my benefactor laughs along with the rest, lets me take credit for the entertainment, and refrains afterward from the mild revenge of announcing prior knowledge of the joke.

In all of these and similar kinds of cases, the object of the kind omission who is aware of what has transpired becomes cognizant of an absence of response, but one radically different from those of unkind acts of indifference described above. Here the lack of response presents itself as purposive, voluntary, and subtended by a vector quality that mobilizes a sensitivity to help. A choice has been made, and the omission to act is therefore another type of action, that of remaining silent. In such cases, Sartre's early theory of freedom has a certain truth: one cannot not choose (1956, 479).[12] There is a silence, but it is not nothing. It is sensuousness pregnant with meaning—here tact or courtesy—that presents itself as "instead of speech." It is not the silence of an unintelligible void represented by a corpse or a coma patient but rather of a free, purposive refusal to act that gives me the impression of complicity with my interests.

This is what George Eliot describes in *Middlemarch* when Will Ladislaw had refused a loan by Bulstrode, the banker. Dr. Lydgate, much to his subsequent regret, had accepted a similar offer. Will discovers this fact and, in the course of a conversation with Lydgate, "had a delicate generosity which warned him into reticence" (1965, 840). He remained silent rather than tell Lydgate that he had rejected Bulstrode's money. Phrased differently, this type of "delicate generosity" amounts to a respectful and tactful concern.[13] As Suzanne Cataldi has pointed out, "All forms of respect suggest the keeping of a deferential *distance—and* an observance of tact" (1993, 9). It is a question of a distance that is thought-full, rather than thought-less.

Similar cases of kind omissions to act are clearly evident in the lives of the sick and injured. The cardiac patient, for example, may be struggling to regain something like a normal purchase on the world, and others may witness her fear, tenuous motility, and diminished energy. When others see but pointedly do not notice or comment, the patient becomes aware of their recognition and also of their kind omissions to call attention to it. Their not speaking or manifesting other gestural recognition is thus distinguishable from the indifference of the egoist. Their non-acts constitute an effort to keep the bonds of intersubjectivity from being disrupted any further than they have been by the patient's pain and illness. They have registered and refused to comment on the patient's weakness. In contrast, the egoist's not commenting constitutes a failure, rather than a refusal, and the failure to comment is parasitic on the deeper one of not registering the patient's suffering at all.

When kindness and unkindness are immediately present in the gesture, speech act, or purposeful omission to act, we know that they are such in and through a bodily knowledge not otherwise possible. This is so for reasons found in Merleau-Ponty's descriptions of the body as an expressive corporeal schema. The chiasm of the flesh, that which makes the body both seeing and seen, touching and touched, feeling and felt, means that, "The schema of the lived-body, because I see myself, can be participated in by all other bodies that I see. It is a lexicon of corporeity in general, a system of equivalences between the inside and the outside which prescribes to one to accomplish itself in the other" (1970, 129).

Since my body is a concrete unity of the "mental" and the "physical," and since others can participate in the lexicon of my corporeity and I in theirs, it follows that, as phenomenologists have long pointed out, emotions or feelings are not inner realities or "psychic facts" of which behavior is only the physical and inherently meaningless sign or re-presentation. On the contrary, emotions and feelings such as love, anger, fear, and so forth exist only in and through gestures and speech; they are but various modalities of our relationships with the other and the world around us that we express through our bodies. Since meaning is "immanent in the sensuous," that meaning "can be read by feeling or elaborated upon by reflection only if it is first received and experienced by the body, that is, if the body is intelligent from the beginning" (Dufrenne 1973, 341). Thus, for instance, in *A Room with a View*, George Emerson and Lucy Honeychurch "were close to their pension. She stopped and leant her elbows against the parapet of the embankment. He did likewise. There is at times a magic in identity of position; it is one of the things that have suggested to us eternal comradeship" (Forster 1986, 52).

The same is true of kindness. Kindness is in the gesture or the speech act just as immediately as is love or joy, with which it often overlaps, or anger and fear. Kindness is also just as primordially a modality of our relationships with others: it is a way that the texts of our lexicons of corporeity interweave and thus can both read and be read. Kindness, just as emotions, is one of a variety of "types of behavior or styles of conduct visible from the outside. They are *on* this face or *in* these gestures and not hidden behind them" (Merleau-Ponty 1964c, 52-53).[14] This is why we can discover in the body of the other "a miraculous prolongation of my own intentions, a familiar way of dealing with the world. Henceforth, as the parts of my body together comprise a system, so my body and the other person's are one whole, two sides of one and the same phenomenon" (Merleau-Ponty 1962, 354).

The upshot here for the experience of kindness is that my most immediate, primordial knowledge of the other is bodily; it is reached through perception, discourse, and behavior. A given action that appears to me immediately as kind or unkind does not do so as a conclusion of one or more reflective acts but as an immediate perceptual and linguistic presence. Arguments from analogy, Cartesian in inspiration, if not origin, presuppose and are based on this real presence.

My body can resonate and respond to the real presence of kindness (and unkindness) because, as part of the text of the lexicon of corporeity, it is embodied in an inherently meaningful sensuous immediacy. In the case of kindness, I can recognize and respond to the non-threatening deployment of the body of the other, the expense of uncalled-for effort, the concerned facial expression that provides an invitational rather than a threatening greeting, and so forth. Here, as in our perception of things, sense is not imposed on the world but instead emerges in our complicity with it.

Answering the question of how I know that a particular action is one of kindness leads to two other important and related questions. First, even in its simple physical presentations, how can kindness be in the gesture or speech act as a simple feeling or emotion can be? Is not kindness different from emotions and feelings at least in part because it has a motive hidden behind the action and to reach which I have to perform inferences of varying complexity? Second, because any theory of perception has to account for the possibility of error, if we can read kindness in the body's lexicon of corporeity, is it not also possible to misread the text? Let us consider these questions in turn.

It is true that kindness has a motive (s), and therefore it differs in certain ways from feelings and emotions. It is also the case that actions are not self-interpreting: nothing can do away entirely with the ambiguity inherent in perceptual life. Inferences to the agent's reasons and purposes are thus sometimes necessary. But neither of these facts entails that when I have a veridical perception of kindness, I have encountered a meaningless gesture, a mechanical, corporeal re-presentation of a Cartesian-like inner psychical reality. For there is no self-contradiction in saying that kindness has a motive, which is hidden, and is also expressed in an observable gesture, any more than there is in saying that a person can both think and act. Motives qua motives are hidden, but nothing prevents them from being expressed. The possibility of deception does not imply that what we perceive, even when we are mistaken, is inherently meaningless and awaits its intelligibility from the imposition of mental acts. Rather, "[T]he mental life of the other becomes an immediate object, a whole pregnant with immanent meaning" (Merleau-Ponty 1962, 58).[15]

This "whole pregnant with immanent meaning"—the immediate presence of kindness in the gesture—is what we see distinctly in the way that *A Room with a View* describes the elder Mr. Emerson: "The kindness that Mr. Beebe and Lucy had always known to exist in him came out suddenly, like sunlight touching a vast landscape—a touch of the morning sun?" (Forster 1986, 177). This real presence is also clear in Toni Morrison's *Beloved,* when Paul D. comes up behind Sethe at the stove: "Behind her, bending down, his body an arc of kindness, he held her breasts in the palms of his hands. He rubbed his cheek on her back and learned that way her sorrow, the roots of it; its wide trunk and intricate branches" (1988, 17).[16] In a very dissimilar setting, the same phenomenon is evident in Josephine Hart's *Damage*, when the protagonist, a former doctor turned politician, ponders the deaths he has experienced: "A competent easer of pain, I was often the last person the dying saw. Were my eyes kind?" (1991, 13).[17] How strange it would have been if he had asked himself, as a consistent Cartesian ought to have done, whether his eyes re-presented an accurate copy of his inner mental disposition. On the contrary, the gesture was a sensuousness pregnant with meaning, and such experiences serve as a touchstone for all of our inferences in cases in which there is uncertainty.

The second critical question posed above about the embodied nature of kindness concerned the possibility of deception. If mistaken perceptions are possible, how can we tell when we are having a veridical perception of kindness? To answer that question, we must turn to the wider perceptual and social context of acts of kindness. All gestures and speech acts, and therefore those of kindness, appear to us as do perceptual objects—in Gestalt structures of focal points against background contexts that affect their experiential identity. An act of kindness or a kind omission is situated in at least three different types of contexts. There is the immediate perceptual scene, both in terms of the totality of the bodily comportment of the agent, the presence or absence of others, the relevant social situation of the agent, and the like; there is also our knowledge, or lack thereof, of the agent's character. (This is the subject of Chapters 2 and 3.) If we already believe the agent to be a kind person, we anticipatively structure our perceptual fields to expect similar future actions. When we cannot do this, the meaning of the gesture is more nearly bound to its immediate presence and surrounding perceptual context and is therefore more open-textured and ambiguous. This is typical of urban life: many of those who do us kindnesses, or whom we observe doing them for third parties, are anonymous others whom we probably will never meet again.

The third type of context that conditions the appearance of acts of kindness, which we will explore in Chapters 4 and 5, is one of broader cultural meanings. This network of meanings usually does not have to be articulated, since it is learned and lived pre-reflectively, in the same way that we breathe in air. But it is real and important nonetheless, and it has important implications for Schlick's discussion of the smiles of kindness. He asserts that, "Man smiles when he is gay, and also when he feels sympathy." Because happiness and kindness are inscribed in the "same facial expression," nature offers the best lessons, " the inner relationships of happiness and a noble disposition" (1939, 194). But Schlick's confidence about the illuminative power of the smile is not a lesson "which nature itself offers," since any human "nature" is also necessarily cultural.[18] Language and behavior are inevitably biological but at the same time always "escape from the simplicity of animal life" (Merleau-Ponty 1962, 189).[19] Thus there are *"many ways for a body to be a body, many ways for a consciousness to be a consciousness"* (Merleau-Ponty 1962, 124; emphasis in original). As a result, the smile is inherently meaningful, although that meaning (s) will differ from one culture to another and will still be intelligible to those who live the culture from the inside, or at least to subcultural groups within it, though perhaps hidden from outsiders.[20]

These three sorts of contexts all provide reasons why we can mis-take a given action for one of kindness, either because of our perceptual failings or because of a successful intent to deceive. The perceptual setting of gestures and speech means that, among other things, kind acts and omissions are situated against a background of indeterminacy and have to be disclosed against these horizons that get filled in through further experiences. It follows, therefore, that even in simple corporeal presentations of kindness, there can be the same ambiguity that Merleau-Ponty held to be the watermark of all perceptual experiences— that is, that the perceived always has more than one possible meaning.

It is also the case that, both with acts of kindness and kind omissions, the resulting ambiguity can vary widely in complexity. A minimal amount of ambiguity comes into play when, say, the person holding open the door of my hotel is the door attendant. The gesture might constitute a kind response to the sight of a guest limping along on crutches, and/or might amount to job performance. On the other hand, there are also highly ambiguous instances—say, in the intricacies of institutional politics—in which what purports to be an act of kindness carries with it a living sense of many other possible motives. There is meaningfulness in the behavior of the other, but in these cases it is much less clear what that meaning is. We must resort to one or another strategy to work out indirectly what the motive was. We might try to remember if we have acted similarly in such situations. If we know the agent, we can consider how the act or the omission to act coheres with other behavior in such circumstances. I can reflect on the general cultural framework of the situation and the likelihood that the other has been conditioned to act in the way that we take her to be acting. We can likewise reflect on future consequences: what can be gained in performing such and such an act?[21]

The upshot here is that we rarely achieve anything like absolute certainty in our reading of the other's actions. Deception, fraud, and seduction are still always part of the social agenda. To construct a minor variation on an actual misfortune of a friend, the stranger who points out the letter that I have dropped on the way to the post office may, when I bend down to retrieve it, take my wallet along with my thanks.[22] As François La Rochefoucauld pointed out, "It is very hard to distinguish between kindness to all, and sundry, and consummate cleverness" (1959, §620, 122). On the other hand, as we shall see shortly, there are cases of veridical perception of kindness that, for all practical purposes, provide us with enough certainty to justify beliefs in kindness.

Accounting for error in the perception of kindness looks, then, to be closely analogous to explaining perceptual error generally. This becomes clearer when the act of kindness, heretofore isolated artificially as a discrete event, is rein-serted into the temporal flux of experience in which each present comes into being with a double pre-reflective intentionality, a retention of its past and a protention of its future. These horizons of pastness and futurity provide the present with a context that, just as that of a perceptual object, conditions its ex-periential identity. In perception, the whole object appears to us from any given perspective, albeit incompletely, and its meaning is filled in through subsequent perspectives as those previously experienced "shade off" (Husserl's *Abschattun-gen*) in the past. These perspectives are filled in through the unity of time-con-sciousness as the meaning of the perceived unfolds before me. Correlatively, it is not the inference that a perceptual object exists that is crucial to constituting the experience, but rather its perception that makes the inference possible.

This is why, for instance, Merleau-Ponty can hold that the perceived world is the foundation of all rationality, and the latter is expressed as a convergence of perspectives: "The phenomenological world is, not pure being, but the meaning that shows through at the intersection of my experiences and at the intersection of my experiences and those of others" (1962, xix–xx). Conversely, perceptual error is explained in terms of a failure to achieve a perspectival con-gruence. I may think I am standing before a house, but when I walk around it, I discover it is only a clever, two-dimensional stage set. Or I may be convinced that I see the cobra that escaped from the zoo, but closer inspection reveals only the coiled garden hose.

Similar considerations obtain in the perception of kindness, as well as in other phenomena in the social world. I take up situations in which I find my-self involved with the other who appears to be doing me a kindness. As noted above, the presentation of that act is conditioned by immediately past experi-ences, those of a longer duration reflecting my knowledge of the agent, if any; my awareness of socially appropriate behavior in such circumstances, and so on. Likewise, in terms of my protentive intentional relations with the future, such experiences leave me set with certain anticipations about the unfolding of sub-sequent events. When my expectations are not fulfilled—when, say, I discover that my wallet is missing—I am faced with a dissonance of disconfirming, in-consistent evidence about the other whom I took to be kind.

There are also other cases in which no convergence or dissonance is possible, because it is a question of anonymous others whom I may never meet again. Here the absence of disconfirming evidence is as important as the fact that the stranger has helped me, and my initial uncertainty about how to classify the ac-tion eventually yields to a belief in the kindness of a good Samaritan.

The process of convergence and divergence of perspectives is present as well in our experience of kind omissions to act. For example, I may take the other's silence about some gaffe I have committed as a kind disinclination to embar-rass me or harm my reputation, but I may discover later that the reticence was due to an expected reward (a mild form of blackmail) or a neurotic desire for gossip mongering. My original perception of the kind omission shades off into my past, but it gets changed when held retentively against the backdrop of intervening experiences.

For both kind acts and omissions, however, there are some significant differences from perceptual experience in the way that the process of confirmation and falsification of perspectives works. A confirming series of perspectives on a perceptual object fills in the content of the given with new information. I see the house now from the side, then from the back, then from the other side, and so on. In the case of acts of kindness and kind omissions—unique events—a confirming series of subsequent perspectives provides no new information. Only disconfirmation through inconsistencies reveals anything new. Second, confirmation and falsification do not happen at the same rate or with the same rhythm as in the perceptual world. Usually I can discover that the "house" is really a stage set in a rapid, straightforward manner that is often impossible in the perception of kind acts and omissions. However, not only will I often have no further interaction with passing strangers, but also, even with people with whom I do, I cannot control the flow of events that will provide me with inconsistent evidence.

In sum, then, we have a matrix of six possibilities in our perception of simple physical acts of kindness and omissions. (1) I believe that kindness is really present in the action or omission, and it is. This is a case of veridical perception. (2) I believe that kindness is really present, but it is not. I am mistaken: I have, say, been duped by "consummate cleverness." (3) I do not believe kindness is present, and it is not—a second possible case of veridical perception. (4) I do not believe that kindness is present, and it is: I am again mistaken, perhaps because I have been "burned too often" and am overly suspicious. I am not certain whether an act is one of kindness, and (5) it is, or (6) it is not. My frame of reference may have been inadequate to appreciate what I experienced, I may not have been paying close enough attention, and so on. But whatever possibility happens to be instantiated in a particular instance, it is still the case that the gesture or speech act remains inherently meaningful behavior that sometimes is and is not correctly perceived. The possibility of error does not entail taking refuge in a Cartesian-like dualism.

Neither is a totalizing and crippling skepticism or cynicism warranted just because deception is always possible. To say that we can be deceived rests on the ability to perceive correctly, and this is as true in the social world as in the life of perception. Total deception, that last Cartesian spectre haunting phenomenology, is incoherent, because the very sense of a mistaken perception derives from veridical perception (Austin 1962, 118–19). Or, in Levinas' idiom, "[D]eceit and veracity already presuppose the absolute authenticity of the face" (1979, 202). Thus in the case of kindness, I cannot know what it means to be deluded without also having the experience of being right with which to contrast it. There are simple acts of kindness that seem so compelling that the possibility of false impressions reduces to the mere logical possibility of clever acting, fraud, and seduction. Such cases are analogous to certain emotional presentations in which one would not even be inclined to raise the hypothesis of doubt—as, say, when confronted with a parent whose child has died and whose grief is so fierce that it is frightening. As Wittgenstein said, "Just try—in a real case—to doubt someone else's fear or pain" (1968, §303). Similarly, the coronary care patient can only logically doubt the presence of kindness in the smiles and encouraging words bestowed by worried relatives.

Beyond such experiences of kindness, however, and in direct proportion to the absence of confirming evidence, a kind of faith takes over so that we credit (in both senses) the other with an act of kindness. In the supermarket checkout lane, for example, if the shopper with the fully laden cart lets me go ahead of her with my hand basket, I thank her for her kindness. I might be wrong in this ascription because, say, I mistook an inattentive, coincidental eye contact for an invitation to help speed me through. But the possibility of being wrong rested on that of being right, or, as William James noted in another context, "Truth lives, in fact, for the most part on the credit system." Our thoughts and beliefs are credited just in case nothing contests them, just as bank notes are, provided that people do not refuse to take them. "But," James continues, "this all points to direct, face-to-face verifications somewhere, without which the fabric of truth collapses like a financial system with no cash-basis whatever" (1910, 207–208). An experience of kindness that provides the foundation for that credit we extend to others, as Merleau-Ponty said in another context, "hollows itself out, loses its opacity, reveals a transparence and itself makes sense forever . . . if one wanted to contest it, one would no longer even know for what one is searching" (1973, 121).

Mediately Presented Acts of Kindness and Kind Omissions

Immediate presentations of simple, physical acts of kindness and kind omissions serve as our original and clearest objects of the experience of kindness. They are perceived directly as kind, and their meaning gets disclosed in their original contexts as well as subsequently through either confirmation of our original impressions or as thrown into doubt by inconsistent evidence. However, kindness is notably more complicated than these simple examples, and all of the considerations sketched above about veridical perception and the possibility of error apply in an even more complex way to these more difficult sorts of cases. Those kindnesses, both of acts and omissions, become apparent only after their occurrence, and sometimes long after. In these cases, kindness appears mediately, and the mediation is usually accomplished by a number of inferences about what was originally undetermined.

When I eventually come to perceive a previously undetermined act or omission as kind, I see the act or omission invested with a motivated freedom, purpose, and sensitivity to my welfare—the qualities described above that I find in immediate presentations of kindness. But I also become aware of the fact that I did not originally get it, and I am then led to focus on the reasons why I misunderstood the situation. Sometimes there is a fairly simple answer: I may have been tired, distracted, wrapped up in my own enjoyment of life, in pain or injured, and consequently my ties with other people were severely disrupted. Or, more interestingly, I can sometimes detect, retrospectively, in the behavior of the agent an originally invisible sense of strategy to distinguish between what really was in my interest and the immediate gratification of my desires.

For example, someone might deny me something I want very much, or do something to me that I find odious, and only after the fact can I detect how the other sought my long-range good at the price of my immediate gratification. I discover that, in addition to doing something to me, she was actually doing something for me as well. In such cases we must distinguish a double gratification of desires, that of the object of the act of kindness and that of the agent herself. Thus, for instance, while it is no kindness to children to spoil them,[23] those inclined to do the spoiling might be less firm than they ought to be and experience a reciprocal pleasure in being so.

Conversely, when we manage to resist the temptation successfully, we can do so in a kind and an unkind way, and the former can always be misinterpreted as the latter. This can happen when, say, heads of organizations need to let personnel go because they are not good enough. However, delivering bad news in kind fashion poses multiple challenges, because disrupting illusions and breaking up "fool's paradises" become notoriously difficult without attacking the dignity of the person (s) involved.

Nevertheless, it is no kindness to give an addict a hit, or a student a "charity D" when such generosity may create a real possibility of greater future pain and suffering—although the addict or the student would certainly press for the chance to run the risk, and the addict's benefactor or the instructor might be sorely tempted to give in. The intensity of such temptations led the Partnership for a Drug-Free Greater New York, along with the New York Business Alliance, to take out a full-page advertisement in The New York Times on August 23, 1993 (p. C8) to urge employers not to ignore addicted employees. The copy that accompanied the picture of a pleading addict said in relevant part, "You could kill an addict with kindness. . . . An addict's only chance is treatment. But kindness won't help somebody who's hooked. . . . It's not pleasant. Confrontations and threats never are. But your toughness may be the addict's only hope." However, this is a seriously mistaken view of kindness. It is no kindness to be an accessory to an addict's self-destruction, no matter how much one's short-term help is begged for. It is, rather, a kindness to seek the addict's longer-term, but initially more painful, good. Therefore, the Jewish Theological Seminary in New York got it right in another full-page advertisement in the *Times* on Wednesday, September 15, 1999 (p. A10). The ad begins with a quotation from Leviticus 19:14: "Do not put a stumbling block before the blind." The copy then continues: "But there's more than one kind of blindness. And this teaching is a wake-up call to all of us who'd never think of ourselves as cruel or dangerous. It says we are answerable if we put the young, the impressionable, or the vulnerable in harm's way." There then follow five different ways that we do that: "Abet an addiction, fill teen magazines with ultra-thin models, make lethal weapons available to children, support entertainments that glamorize violence, [and] push the sale of chances for 'easy money' to people in poverty." We could also add very different types of stumbling blocks, such as creating markets for human organs and seducing people into becoming donors as a way of escaping their grinding poverty.

Mediately presented acts of kindness, as distinct from those that manifest themselves to us immediately, are often marked by conflict, alienation, and sometimes, real pain. Thus their sense is generally not apparent in the gesture or speech act and frequently cannot be communicated otherwise. The true meanings of these actions or omissions must therefore await their explication when subsequent events unfold—if they do at all—possibly when the recipient of the kindness takes the place of the agent at some time hence. For example, it is not unusual for new parents to gain insights into their own childhood experiences and to them change their view of their parents. Or, in a different sort of case, the recipient of a past act of unacknowledged kindness might chance to hear the original events described in a different light, or in a manner providing new information, which changes her view of them.

A different type of credit system and verification thus takes over in such cases. There is no initial credit that has to be paid back with subsequent experiences to which I am sensitive for such purposes. Rather, when the sense of the kindness can be constituted after the fact, I accredit the action and credit the agent at the same time through a juxtaposition of my memories and present experiences. The accrediting and the verification are one and the same thing. In addition, the subsequent experiences that mediate the appearance of the past event might have nothing to do with the agent of the original, unperceived kindness. For that reason, these later experiences might well never lead me to understand and appreciate the original kindness.

Mediately presented acts and omissions teach us also to distinguish kindness from a cluster of cognates with which it is often identified: niceness, courtesy, and gentleness. Kindness may overlap these qualities, but the connection is always contingent. In the types of examples we have been examining, kindness can exist in the absence of these qualities—I can "get tough" with the addict or the able student who is unintelligibly failing, because I fear that any gentleness, niceness, and so on would only offer illusory comfort. Such qualities can also exist when no act of kindness is present, from which it follows that they are not sufficient conditions of kindness either.

Considering first niceness, there are several reasons it is not identical to kindness. I can be nice to an addict by providing another hit, or to an alcoholic by buying a drink, but, for the reasons given above, it would be unkind to do so. Someone can be nice to me as a sort of general posture toward the world, a kind of neutral stance of noninvolvement or noninterference that is not an act even directed toward me, let alone intending my welfare. That is, niceness can be a social strategy of the least involvement and responsibility possible in order to get by with the fewest inconveniences. Niceness can also be, as Virginia Woolf shows us, a technique of insincere social convention. For example, in *To the Lighthouse*, Lily Briscoe turns the dinner conversation favorably in the direction of Charles Tansley. "She had not been sincere. She had done the usual trick—been nice. She would never know him. He would never know her. Human relations were all like that, she thought, and the worst . . . were between men and women" (Woolf 1992, 86).

A close relative of this type of unkind niceness consists of the plastic friendliness that hospital patients often experience. The forced smiles, the overspirited talk that is just a bit too loud, the brisk demeanor, and the avoidance of eye contact and direct answers to questions announce and instantiate a strategy of non-involved managing of a "problem." The patient's sick and/or injured body lies at the core of her existence. Plastic friendliness relegates that suffering to the status of an obstacle to the smooth functioning of the bureaucratic machine, hence the inevitable dissonance in the phrase "managed care."

In a very different sort of context, the work of Lyn Mikel Brown and Carol Gilligan has shown that niceness and kindness are held to be equivalent in American society as a goal of a complex socialization process for girls. But in this process, the latter are expected to undergo the unkindness of suppressing their personalities, silencing themselves, and muting their ambitions to the profit of boys and then men. In this equivalence, as Brown and Gilligan also appear to construe it falsely, kindness is said to function as a tyranny.[24] In Chapter 7 we shall see that this socially constructed niceness is deeply unkind to both boys and girls, as well as to men and women.

Another reason for rejecting the identification of kindness with niceness is that the latter, but not the former, can serve as a cover for repressed hostility. Indeed, Florence King claims that, "Niceness as practiced by Americans is a festival of misanthropy denied" (1992, 9). In her view, random expressions of niceness merely hide anger and animosity. Citizens who do not necessarily hate all of their fellow citizens are still appalled by "compulsory gregariousness, fevered friendliness, we-never-close compassion, goo-goo humanitarianism, sensitivity that never sleeps, and politicians paralyzed by a hunger to be loved" (1992, 8).

Some cases of niceness are therefore not cases of kindness, and vice versa, and the same relationships obtain between courtesy and kindness. Some instances of kindness, especially those associated with "tough love," are not typified by the graceful politeness that we associate with courtesy. Conversely, some examples of courtesy cannot be acts of kindness. Someone can courteously rob us, denigrate us socially, or even kill us. As for the latter, Isabel Allende tells us about the most powerful man in a particular dictatorship. He was the "Chief of Political Police, the Man of the Gardenia." He had "slicked-down hair and manicured fingernails, impeccable white linen suits—always with a flower in the buttonhole—and French cologne. . . . He personally directed the torture of prisoners, elegant and courteous as ever" (1989, 69).

Gentleness has an equally contingent relationship with kindness, though much more subtle and variable than niceness and courtesy. For, in fact, most of the simple corporeal acts of kindness of the types described above are marked by a gentleness of non-domination that leads to their false identification. Think again of Updike's poignant description of women who bestow their "eyes of famous mercy" on those in pain, as well as the constantly conjoined description of some social phenomenon as "kinder and gentler." Nonetheless, kindness is not the same as gentleness because, as Rousseau's criticisms of Montesquieu remind us, gentleness is sometimes a "weakness of the spirit," since "there are cowardly and faint-hearted souls . . . who are gentle only through indifference to good and evil."[25]

We can also see clearly the lack of synonymy between gentleness and kindness in Philip Hallie's comments on William Hogarth's engravings, *The Four Stages of Cruelty*, but this case is more philosophically instructive. In the first of these pictures, a smiling boy is tying a bone to the tail of a dog that is, in turn, licking the boy's forearm. This is a preparation for torture, and for Hallie, "[A] process that ends in horror often begins gently. In fact, the gentleness helps put the victim in the power of his oppressor" (1982, 24). For "oppressor" we can also substitute "seducer," "confidence man," and the like to indicate a number of unkind processes for which gentleness is a necessary condition of success.

Hallie actually uses this example to identify kindness with gentleness. He refers to the boy's action as a "momentary kindness" that "often is a part of the cruel act; cruelty can be going on when there is not yet any dramatic pain" (ibid.). However, a gentle gesture and a smile to an animal as a prelude to torture do not show that tying on the bone was an act of kindness any more than, as McTaggart pointed out in another context, "the refreshments administered in the intervals of tortures proved the humanity of the torturers" (1906, 256).

Even if the agents in both cases wanted their victims to perceive their acts as kind, it would be seriously misleading to describe them as such. Both acts involved a protentive intentional relation to a future objective that gave them their identity. Clearly these horizons of futurity provided no intent to increase the welfare of the victim. On the contrary, as Hallie notes, it was simply to make the victimization easier and, in the instance cited by McTaggart, to make the torture last longer. For, as Foucault points out, "[D]eath-torture is the art of maintaining life in pain, by subdividing it into a 'thousand deaths.'. . . Torture rests on a whole quantitative art of pain" (1977, 33-34).[26]

Hallie's misidentification of gentleness with kindness is also found in literature upon which the U. S. Supreme Court based its famous *Miranda* decision. The Court was concerned about techniques of interrogation in which it was said that kindness was employed as psychological coercion in an atmosphere of privacy—the suspect alone with the interrogator(s). The Court noted the following description of such techniques: "In the preceding paragraphs emphasis has been placed on kindness and stratagems. The investigator will, however, encounter many situations where the sheer weight of his personality will be the deciding factor" (O'Hara 1956, 112), *Miranda v. Arizona*, 384 U. S. 436 (1966), at 451. But then O'Hara proceeds to give the lie to the label of kindness, because he equates "kindness and stratagems" with "emotional appeals and tricks."

There are, unfortunately, actual cases of McTaggart's descriptions of the torturer, and not just in the age of the Spanish Inquisition. Kurt Franz, commander of the Nazi concentration camp at Treblinka, "personally killed 139 prisoners and was convicted by a German court for complicity in the deaths of 300,000 others. He used to pummel Jews to death at a whim, even reviving them with water during the beatings so that their suffering and his unconcealed pleasure could be extended."[27] It would have been stupefying if Franz's victims or Franz himself viewed the proffered water as an act of kindness.

There is at least one more important feature of acts of kindness and kind omissions that only makes sense as such after the fact. This is how we assess their consequences in terms of the important moral and legal distinction between harming and hurting. If someone spreads a scurrilous rumor about me and I never find out about it, I will have been harmed but not hurt. If someone uses me as an experimental subject and I never discover the fact, I will also have been harmed but not hurt. An act of kindness, in contrast, can hurt—if I fail instead of receiving a "charity D, or if I am dropped from a sports team—but it cannot intend to harm the person to whom it is directed.[28] This is the sense of the interaction between Margaret Schlegel and Leonard Bast in E. M. Forster's *Howards End*. Margaret's sister, Helen, has brought Mr. Bast to talk about a job with Margaret's husband, the elder Mr. Wilcox. Margaret must tell Leonard that it will not work, so she says, "I can only advise you to go at once. My sister has put you in a false position, and it is kindest to tell you so" (1985, 178). Margaret realizes that this refusal will hurt, but she wishes to save Mr. Bast from harm and further hurt.

Actions are done, or omitted to be done, by persons, and it is not only the act or omission which can be said to be kind or unkind, but also the agent. Since, as we have seen, our perceptions of agents themselves as kind or unkind are closely related to our perceptions of their actions and inactions, references to some qualities of the kind Other have already surfaced. We shall now consider what it means for persons themselves to be kind. In that way, Chapter 2, like the others that follow in Part One, will deepen and extend the present chapter by filling in the concrete contexts of kind acts and omissions.

Chapter 2

Personal Kindness

For Mercy has a human heart,
Pity a human face;
And Love, the human form divine;
And Peace, the human dress.
  —William Blake, *Songs of Innocence*

Persons and Acts

We saw in the previous chapter that kindness is really present in the gesture, the speech act, or silence—in each case, a sensuousness pregnant with intelligibility. Kindness is not a meaning hovering behind or above the phenomena but rather inscribed in them, credited in the present through a perceptual faith, and awaiting, when available, confirmation in subsequent experiences. In a similar fashion, we also credit persons as such with the quality of kindness. Since, as noted above, the appearance of the agent contextualizes the experience of a kind act or omission, we are led naturally from the perception of the latter to ascribe the same quality to the former. We express this connection in ordinary language by saying, "That is kind of you," or "You are very kind," instead of, "That was a kind act," or (more strangely), "That was a kind refraining to act." We reinforce our belief in the connection by saying "is" instead of "was," because in uttering the former, we effectively refuse to confine the validity of our observation to an isolable past event. Thus perceiving the other and the act or omission as kind are closely related. As Montaigne pointed out, "That is why when we judge a particular action we must consider many circumstances and the whole man who performed it, before we give it a name" (1958, II:11, 311).

On the other hand, before we can consider "the whole man," we are also aware of the inevitably contingent relationship between person and act. The other may strike us neutrally: we do not know how to "read" the lexicon of her

27

corporeity. Then again, we know that a kind act does not necessarily prove the kindness of the agent. As Alexander Pope noted in his (1903) *Moral Essays* (*Epistle* I, line 110):

> *Not always actions show the man, we find*
> *Who does a kindness is not therefore kind;*

This can be so for any number of reasons, as Pope also points out:

> *Perhaps prosperity becalm'd his breast,*
> *Perhaps the wind just shifted from the east: (1903, 158)*

The author's observation is part of the stubborn truth of the old French proverb that one should distrust first impressions because they are always right—or, as Merleau-Ponty would rephrase it, because they are always ambiguous.

Moreover, just as unkind people can sometimes transcend their own egoism, kind people can also do unkind things. Anyone can have bad days (or longer). Hence, we should conclude, "Who does a kindness may be kind," and "Who does an unkindness is not necessarily an unkind person." As a result, we need to understand how we come to believe that a particular individual is a kind person and what that process reveals about the meaning of a person's being kind—that is, what we mean apart from the performance of a kind act. To answer these questions, both this chapter and the next will be concerned with the kindness of persons, or personal kindness. Since consciousness is intentional—that is, consciousness of something—its unity has both objective and subjective aspects. This chapter will describe the objective side of the phenomenon of personal kindness, how the other manifests herself as a kind person to us, and the beneficiaries of her acts. Chapter 3 will then focus on the subjective side of the phenomenon, personal kindness from the agent's own point of view. There we shall attempt to enter into the enactment of personal kindness as it comes into being.

Forming the Judgment: The Constitution of Character

As a matter of first impressions, others, even strangers, can strike us as kind or unkind persons—just as they may strike us as funny, melancholy, or ambitious. These first contacts with strangers constitute another case of perceptual faith, and if we have further contact with them, the impressions that underlie this faith may turn out to be right or wrong. As John Wild observed, "He is far from me and other than myself, a stranger, and I cannot be sure of what this strangeness may conceal. Hence the need to show friendly intent which brought forth the earliest forms of introduction and greeting" (Levinas 1979, "Introduction," 13).[1]

Strangers can strike us as kind people, but with those whom we know better, the evidence for their being kind goes far beyond a "striking." We see them as kind on the basis of judgments informed by our ability to read their bodies' lexicons of corporeity expressed in social acts. We come to make these judgments in a manner parallel to that in which we come to believe that a particular act is one of kindness. Here also there is a convergence of perspectives so that the sense of what sort of people particular individuals are, just as the sense of their actions, can emerge through patterns of evidence. These patterns in turn lead to judgments that may be true or false, sustained by beliefs that are justified or unjustified.

Actions, omissions to act—where observable—and the way that actions are carried out are evidence of the kindness of others in both a weak and a strong sense. The weak sense consists in the fact that a kind act or omission reveals others as *capable of* such acts or omissions. As Dufrenne notes correctly, "In this respect, every action we perform is a means of self-expression. Actions can haunt us, because they define us" (1973, 381). And this is why, for Sartre, the whole of consciousness is disclosed in any given gesture: "[T]here is not a taste, a mannerism, or a human act which is not *revealing*" (1956, 568). Hence, other people manifest themselves to me as I do to myself, as a fundamental unity. Their acts do not, therefore, present themselves as isolable events existing externally to each other.

The strong sense in which acts and omissions are evidence of personal kindness consists of capabilities actualized into patterns of kind actions. The repetition of kind acts and omissions establishes a behavioral constancy over time. In this sense, "kind," just as "trustworthy," "responsible," or "loyal," is a predicate signifying temporal duration. Generally unavailable for most of the strangers with whom we interact daily in urban environments, this behavioral constancy creates in those we know more fully a reference point for future generalization. It permits us to conclude reliably that particular individuals turned out to be what they appeared to be. Patterns of doing kind acts are thus the first essential characteristic of personal kindness.

These patterns instituted in a person's life are an important aspect of character. "Institution" here means what provides our experience "with durable dimensions, by relation to which a whole series of other experiences will have meaning, will form a thinkable continuation or a history" (Merleau-Ponty 1970, 40–41). In virtue of such institutions, the lived-body is not simply a motor-intentional presence in the world but also a habitual body. It is not merely an "I-am-able-to" but also an "I-can-remain-committed-to." Paraphrasing Kant, we may say that the freedom of a motor-intentional body without habits is empty, while habit without freedom is blind. Both are involved in the social relationships with the other that Aristotle had in mind when he described the connection between moral virtue and habit (*ethos*) (1962, II, 1103a, 15–20, p. 33).

The convergence and divergence of perspectives involved in coming to see patterns of behavior is both similar to and different from what is involved in the experience of a single kind act or omission. On the one hand, there is a consistency that underwrites our beliefs, mistakes are possible, one cannot say *a priori* how much evidence is required for falsification, and deceptions do not imply a crippling skepticism. Adapting the Austinian argument from Chapter 1, we may say that we can be deceived about whether a certain person is kind only because of the possibility of a veridical experience of personal kindness.

On the other hand, there are important dissimilarities in the two types of judgment. In the case of a perceptual object, I can determine when the evidence has been presented fully. Austin, for example, pointed out that, if I am skeptical that something really is a telephone, I can take it apart or actually use it, and that it would be unreasonable to require any more evidence (1962, 119). Similarly, if I am mistrustful that something is a stage set or clever *trompe d'oeil* painting rather than a house, other things being equal, I do not have to walk around and through the house more than once to be sure. In contrast, judgments about a person's character can rest on sufficient, though never complete, evidence. That is, we may have all the evidence we need to make a reliable judgment about certain people being kind or unkind—we know them well enough. But people can change in ways that perceptual objects cannot, and they also possess an inherent inexhaustibility that does not usually attach to things. As Merleau-Ponty put it, "Where is the other in this body that I see? He is (like the meaning of a sentence) immanent in this body (one cannot detach him from it to pose him apart) and yet, more than the sum of the signs or the significations conveyed by them" (1968, 209).

A second type of dissimilarity lies in the fact that the meaning of character revealed through the habitual body emerges at a different tempo and with different rhythms than with simple, perceptual meanings. It is a question of a more subtle process based on much more complex evidence. For example, we cannot say *a priori* how much evidence is required to falsify a certain belief about someone, because we have to make allowances for some inconsistencies while still believing in the pattern of behavior. Acting "out of character" is different from the various modalities of non-veridical perception—for example, hallucinations or illusions. Sick and injured people who are frustrated by the necessity of negotiating an indifferent or a hostile world can display the unevenness of alternately kind and unkind behavior for which there is no analogue in the perception of physical objects. So also can those who bear the invisible burden of accommodating unsympathetic or uncomprehending people across a barrier of chronic pain.

Considering kind acts within a habitual pattern thus gives us another perspective on the fact that "unkind" is not necessarily a value predicate. The emphasis on habit allows us to preserve judgments that a given person has developed an *ethos* of kindness while taking into account behavioral inconsistencies considered aberrations or, as described above, acting "out of character." On the other hand, if the number of apparent aberrations began to increase substantially and even outnumbered the instances of identifiable kindnesses someone performed, we might not know what to say about the *ethos* itself. A new *ethos* of unkindness might or might not be emerging. But even if it is not possible to specify *a priori* a maximum number of aberrations consistent with a belief in an *ethos* of kindness, this does not mean that inconsistencies cannot be seen as such and that the pattern of behavior constituting the *ethos* of kindness could not exist. We can understand the non-convergence of rays of light in a single focus—the optical meaning of aberration—only because we can have the experience of convergence with which to compare it. However, given that, as noted above, behavioral habits can change into even contradictory patterns, our knowledge of the other is always in a certain sense conditional and tentative. Even those thoroughly devoted to a life of kindness over many years are not kind in the way that a perceptual object is blue or square.

Such inconsistencies flow from the fact that, among other things, even firmly entrenched behavioral patterns are malleable in the face of a variety of cultural influences. These include education, the presence of evil or extraordinary goodness, persuasion among friends and coercion among others, extraordinary events—as, say, a near-fatal heart attack or Scrooge's nocturnal terrors—and other similar upsurges of non-conscious motivation that make us change our ways. As such cases show us clearly, patterns of behavior can disappear and give way to new and even contradictory patterns. As a result, in understanding a person's character, truth lives on the credit system differently than at the simple level of perception.

There is another important complexity in the context dependence of personal kindness, namely, that such kindness is usually situated in a cluster of values that it inevitably reflects. Kindness is therefore expressed selectively in their light. For example, most of us would not hesitate to swat a fly as the quickest way to dispatch a nuisance. But in Laurence Sterne's *Tristram Shandy*, Uncle Toby carefully catches one and puts it outside. He explains to the fortunate insect, "[W]hy should I hurt thee?—This world surely is wide enough to hold both thee and me" (1987, 91).[2]

A very different sort of example of value selectivity and its impact on kindness appears in Leo Tolstoy's short story, "The Forged Coupon." He describes a certain revolutionary, Katya Turchaninova, who is willing to use any means to destroy the social order. She would cheerfully murder aristocrats, and attempts to do so, but at the same time, she "was also a truly kind-hearted and self-effacing woman who was forever putting herself out for the sake of other people's advantage, enjoyment and well-being, and who was always genuinely glad of an opportunity to do favours, whether for children, old people or animals" (1985, 217).[3] In *Middlemarch*, George Eliot has one of her characters muse, "It is curious what patches of hardness and tenderness lie side by side in men's dispositions" (1965, 753). Such inconsistencies may be "curious" in some people, but Tolstoy does not portray Katya Turchaninova as conflicted in her selective expressions of kindness. Rather, her choices look to be guided by clearly fixed principles.

The intricate contextuality of personal kindness (and unkindness) means that, when we consider, with Montaigne, "the whole man," we have to keep in mind these other value commitments. In practice, they have to be broad and diverse enough, as well as temporally enduring, to justify a belief about personal kindness. If certain people were kind *only* to lobsters, or only sometimes and inconsistently to a wider range of objects, there would not be enough evidence to warrant the belief that they were kind persons.

It is impossible to specify *a priori* just how several and diverse the objects of their kindnesses must be to provide sufficient evidence. As Aristotle said in another context, the decision rests with perception. Even so, this theoretical impossibility does not authorize us to say that there is no difference between being a kind and an unkind person. In practice, there are degrees of personal kindness so that it is possible not to be truly kind without therefore being unkind: "The conscientious Kantian and the caricature of piety who is concerned only to help others as a means to his own salvation illustrate this possibility" (Cullity 1994, 116). At the other end of the scale, there are the Chambonnais "who exclude[d] no one from their love" (Hallie 1997, 53)—neither the Jewish refugees nor the German soldiers whom they wished to protect from more sinful killing.

Disposition

In the previous section we saw that we could reach a reasoned conclusion that given individuals are kind persons by coming to appreciate simultaneously one essential quality of personal kindness itself, that these individuals incarnate a consistent *ethos* of doing kind acts directed toward sufficiently diverse objects. Their behavior allows at least enough predictability to not be surprised at their kind acts. The pattern itself provides a temporally thick duration required for the institution of kindness in their lives, and because we do not consider personal life apart from the habitual body, we say that those are the sort of persons they are.

We have also seen that, whereas some individuals strike us right away as kind, others who are kind do not. For the former, appreciation of patterns of kind acts can confirm our original impressions: these persons turn out to be what they appeared. For those people who are kind but do not immediately manifest themselves as such, an appreciation of an *ethos* of doing kind acts has the function of resolving original doubts, uncertainties, suspensions of belief, and so forth.

Nonetheless, the fact that some people do strike us immediately as kind, and do turn out to be such, shows us that there is more to personal kindness than the habitual performance of kind acts. From all that appears, there are at least three other qualities that are also essential to being a kind person. These are (1) an active disposition to leading a life of kindness, where possible; (2) a warm generosity, and (3) self-mastery. The rest of this chapter will focus on (1) and (2), while Chapter 3 will take up (3). These four qualities may also be sufficient for personal kindness, though that claim is not defended here. Rather, what a phenomenology of personal kindness discloses is that all four qualities are necessary, and that people are kind in various degrees as they manifest one or more of these qualities.

To say that persons have an active disposition to kindness is to say that, analogous to the way that Gestalt psychologists described the anticipative "set" of perceptual consciousness, kind individuals are actively prepared to be of service to others. That is, they are sensitized to the presence of appeals for help, because they are already "on the lookout" for them. They do not regard others with indifference—the "inconsiderateness" of Schlick's egoist—and of course not with malevolence either.

Furthermore, the disposition to kindness means more than that a certain individual actually does kind acts or even behaviorally institutionalizes a rich pattern of them. Some individuals, once sufficiently alerted to an appeal for help, are perfectly willing and able to respond. They are not egoists, in Schlick's sense. However, for whatever reasons, they usually remain unaware of the appeal to begin with. Once they are pointed in the correct direction, so to speak, their response is unproblematic, but they require being turned. They can be kind, but they are not initially compassionate enough to trigger kind acts by themselves. In a sense, they lack the freedom of a moral motility and spontaneity that Gelb's and Goldstein's patient, Schneider, did with his brain-damaged body (if he was not faking). In the case of kindness as in perceptual life, there is also an "intentional arc" uniting us with other people and the world around us that can go "limp" (Merleau-Ponty 1962, 136).[4]

The active disposition to kindness functions at two different but related levels, the first of which consists of a readiness to respond to a perceived need. As such, the disposition consists of an "active receiving" without which the given need "would remain merely the offered which by-passes us" (Spiegelberg 1984, 72). The disposition to respond with kindness implies a prospective surveillance for such needs, an acknowledgment of their existence, once found, as well as a preparedness to provide remedies.

Even at this basic level, such a disposition already transcends Hallie's sense of a "negative" or "minimal morality," as explained in the Introduction. Likewise, the seriousness and effort involved in such actions can be anything but minimal. On the contrary, sick and injured people occasionally confront us with pain and suffering sufficient to consume all of our responsive energies. The truly helpless patient's appeals to us are marked with a desperation that is the obverse of her feelings of vulnerability. In these kinds of cases, what is "minimal" about our response is not the trouble and effort invested in the rescue attempt, but rather that the need to be filled is a basic, minimal ability to live anything like a stable, satisfactory life.

At a higher level, however, the disposition to kindness more fully reflects Hallie's "positive" or "maximal" sense of morality, because it consists of an active commitment to transcend the performance of duties required for retaining "clean hands." As noted in the previous chapter, all kind acts and omissions have a vector quality of being directed "for" rather than merely "at" the Other. "Acting with" displaces merely "acting toward." At the higher level of a disposition to kindness, this structure of "withness" carries us far beyond filling lacks. In Levinasian language, there is also a sense of "Desire" that is a positive rather than a negative attraction, and it seeks its expression in the mutual accomplishment of goodness for the agent and the Other. Desire is "the 'measure' of the Infinite which no term, no satisfaction arrests (Desire opposed to Need)" (Levinas 1979, 304). This is precisely how Tolstoy describes Katya Turchaninova's motivation: apart from aristocrats, anyway, she constantly sought the "advantage, enjoyment, and well-being" of vulnerable others.

Some people's dispositions to kindness strike us as the expression of effortless spontaneity, while others give us the impression that they have had to work to develop it through the performance of kind acts. Either way, the disposition functions primordially at the level of feeling rather than rational inference. The positive Desire incarnated in being-for-the-other, although cognitive instead of a blind, unintelligible, affective irruption, is not fundamentally an intellectual construct. Rather, it rests on a non-representational, non-inferential understanding of the other in which a persisting capacity for feeling attuned to the other's welfare can flourish. Therefore, when we encounter someone who appears to be truly kind, we have the distinct impression that that kindness is not something reached at the end of a ratiocinative process or intellectually manufactured for the occasion. Were this the case, phenomenologically, this state of development could at best reveal someone capable of kindness. Rather, our impression is that there is much stronger evidence that the kindness is more lasting and deeply seated, and that it authentically expresses the agent.

The level of feeling in which this commitment is located is what Heidegger referred to as *Befindlichkeit*, or "disposition"—a word whose meaning includes both how and where we are. *Befindlichkeit* is always particularized in definite

Gestimmtheiten—usually translated as "moods," but better understood as "modes of attunement" to the world, other people, and ourselves. In turn, our attunement is always particularized in some definite mood or other—joy, sorrow, contentment, anger, and the like—that can disclose or conceal. Joy, for instance, has the capacity to open us up and disclose, just as anger can not only close me off from the other but also from myself—I can go "blind with rage."

Philosophers such as Levinas and Werner Marx are correct to criticize Heidegger for privileging the ontological over the personal. Nevertheless, Heidegger did correctly point out that our disposition of feeling, specified in various modes of attunement, is anterior to, and presupposed by, a constituting consciousness, such as Husserl described it. Our disposition to be for-the-other is a crucial dimension of such feeling and presupposes several modes of attunement such as joy or sorrow, lightheartedness or fear, and so forth.

Werner Marx has studied the disposition to kindness, resting on modes of attunement to the other's welfare, in his efforts to establish a phenomenological ethics based on compassion (1987, 1992). His efforts to elucidate the nature of compassion and its ethical consequences have important implications for personal kindness. To liberate one's capacity for compassion, he asserts, an individual needs to be shocked out of herself—thoroughly unsettled (dis-posed)—from her selfish isolation in order to adopt a new attitude toward herself and others.

The key to this unsettling is an awareness of the individual's own mortality that can effect a transformation so that the "*measure for the capacity for compassion* is disclosed as an existential possibility" (Marx 1992, 38; emphasis in original). In such a changed state, a given individual's "naive security" shows itself to be "mere illusion" (1992, 50), and her *ethos* could develop into the virtues of kindness and others referred to above. Further, the object of this transformational awareness is not death in the sense of a terminal event, but rather what the early Heidegger meant as the Being of Dasein, the daily process of living that is inexorably also a passing away, just as the wick of a candle produces its light only by being used up.

This disrupting awareness of our own mortality stems not from an exercise of will or calculative reason but from feelings or emotions. The latter are not destructive and irrational, in contrast to most of the Western philosophical tradition. On the contrary, Heidegger's notions of disposition and its diverse modes of attunement underscore the fact that *Befindlichkeit*, like Aristotle's sense of *nous*, has its own kind of intuitive intelligibility. Hence, emotion is not primordially a blind, affective explosion but the bearer of a pre-predicative, pre-reflective understanding of the world, other people, and ourselves.[5]

For Marx, a sudden change in our emotional attunement can produce a radical transformation of understanding within us, and it is this transforming force that accounts for the way that the awareness of our own mortality can emerge from feeling. Our "horror" at our daily passing away can produce an unsettling, disrupting, or "displacing" anxiety—the play on spatial metaphors is keyed to the spatial meaning of *Befindlichkeit*. Once emotionally disrupted, we can see things differently; as noted above, our "naive security" turns into "mere illusion."

In turn, this emotional displacement can point us outward and generate further transformations that make sociality and the moral life itself possible. These transformations begin when I open myself to the other in a changed relationship in which the capacity for compassion becomes a "healing force" (Marx 1992, 47). When I open myself to the other emotionally, reason functions as an Aristotelian *nous*, because it becomes an "intuitively rational seeing and listening to the other and not a cold, calculating, and planning reason" (ibid., 65). Through it, the other and I can participate sympathetically in each other's fates, because we both recognize ourselves in distress and mutually in need of help. I reach out to the other with an appeal. This appeal is a calling (from the French *appeler*) for responsibility—answering the call—a disposition to kindness as the capacity for compassion.

When we answer this call, for Marx, we become full persons. The force of compassion consolidates itself and develops into social forms of virtue and character. When operative for a certain person, this force "could develop his *ethos* in the virtues of sympathy,[6] acknowledgement, and neighborly love to such an extent that he could participate sympathetically in the fate of others" (1992, 38). For whole societies as well as for particular members of them, a compassionate ethics should provide "a measure of responsible action" (ibid., 43): "[T]he operative force of the capacity for com-passion is the *measure* that determines the individual forms of acknowledgment, sympathy, and neighborly love through and through" (ibid., 55). This type of compassion includes kindness (Marx 1987, 21), and kind persons are those who understand their disposition (*Befindlichkeit*) as open rather than closed off from the other (Marx 1992, 135).

(One should compare here not only Schlick's criticisms of the indifferent egoist, but also Camus' indictment of affectlessness, expressed first in *L'Étranger* and then later in plays and other writings. For both Marx and Camus, moral commitment is anchored primarily in feeling, the absence of which creates horrible loss and evil.[7] Both thinkers could have had an interesting conversation with Kurt Franz and the judges who released him from prison.)

In terms of personal kindness, Marx's ethics shows us that openness and closedness are fundamental categories, and that our active disposition to be of service to the other is located primarily at the level of feeling, with intuitive reasoning woven into it. This does not mean that will and calculative reason can never be involved in an active disposition to kindness. Indeed, in the previous chapter we already examined certain kind acts and omissions that require strategy and calculation to be effective. Even so, will and calculative reason are not the sources of the disposition, and this is why Hume argued correctly that reason cannot by itself motivate (1957, 6).[8] Marx's ethics also shows us that kindness embodies a compassionate response to the other in need, and that this need can become visible when the agent herself is dis-posed from her self-centered, unexamined understanding of her existence.

Since Marx argues in a particular context for specific purposes, there is much about the disposition to kindness that he does not discuss, though there is no reason he could not accept the following supplementary remarks. First, since that disposition is not necessarily all or nothing, there are the differences sketched above between remedying needs and a more positive desire for the welfare of the other. In addition, the gravity of one's commitment does not have to be total or inconsequential but may take on any intermediate degree of weight. Marx could also accept that, conversely, unkind people have no such dispositions, because they are in some measure closed off from me, and that if openness incarnates a bond of human solidarity in diverse forms of acquaintanceship, friendship, and love, then closedness expresses a mutilation of the spirit, some type of alienation.

The characteristic non-openness of an indisposition to kindness can be expressed in many types of demonstrative negativity. There is, for example, hostility in the form of fear, anger, violence, hatred, and the like—in short, much of the depressing litany of daily life described in the Introduction. There is also a sort of "cool" hostility—lower key and less visible, often generated in selfishness and fears of inferiority, and expressed in envy. As George Eliot masterfully described it, "There is a sort of jealousy which needs very little fire; it is hardly a passion, but a blight bred in the cloudy, damp despondency of uneasy egoism" (1965, 243). Even otherwise impeccable actions and motives can trigger such a hostile response. For example, courtesy to someone whom a given individual has already placed at a humiliating disadvantage can easily be perceived as pouring salt in the wound, even when not meant to be such.

Other forms of demonstrative negativity closely linked to hostility consist of various aversions. Four obvious and important contemporary examples of such unkindnesses are those based on pain and suffering, race, the lack of physical attractiveness or other characteristics, and poverty. Chapter 1 argued that pain and suffering provide a privileged access to kindness for the one who is suffering. It is open to question whether, for the sufferer, the sick and injured body is not a better source of motivation to compassion than is the realization of death, in Marx's sense. Our enhanced sense of fragility and vulnerability may well sensitize us to the need for compassion for fellow sufferers far more effectively than would the authentic consciousness of our mortality. It is true that sickness and injury testify to our fragility and vulnerability, and thus they indirectly raise questions of our mortality. However, it does not follow that we must be consciously aware of mortality in order to be moved by sickness and injury, and the latter are much more likely to be what we do think of when we are suffering.

In contrast, when we are faced with pain and suffering that is foreign to our experience, the common response is not compassionate kindness but rather indifference—as when we read the newspaper—or even repulsion. Whereas the sufferer is repelled by and seeks relief from her pain, the other tends to be repelled by and seeks relief from the sufferer.[9] Anton Chekhov shows this clearly in his classic short story, "Heartache," of which Marx could have made significant use. Iona, the hunchback cab driver, tries to share his grief over his son's death with several of his fares, but none will listen. In "anxiety and torment," he seeks in vain someone who will help him carry the burden of his "immense, boundless" grief (1988, 123), so he ends up sharing his anguish with his horse: "The nag chews, listens, and breathes on her master's hands. Iona is carried away and tells her everything" (ibid., 125).[10] Pain and suffering can illuminate the nature of kindness for the sufferer, but far less for the observer.

Racial aversions highlight the second (non-moral) sense of kindness and point to a relationship between the two meanings. Except for the lunatic fringe, few these days make an argument for racial discrimination—and still less for its especially horrifying consequences, such as the skinhead violence in Denver, the dragging death in Texas, and the execution of the African-American student in Littleton or the Filipino mailman in Los Angeles. Racism does not persist as a product of intellectual demonstrations but rather as a visceral phenomenon. For whatever reasons, evolutionary or otherwise, most people seem to identify with the family group, the tribe, and so forth, and to be suspicious of difference. This is surely why the counter-message of the *Star Trek* television programs appears so obviously didactic, and also why, regardless of the greater acceptability of interracial marriages, most people do not appear to view it with equanimity when the possibility arises in *their* families. Analogously, in a society that has our present racial composition, the child of adoptive preference is Caucasian. Since demand far exceeds supply, the results are fierce competition and a lucrative black market. At the same time, the supply of minority group children available for adoption far exceeds the demand.[11]

The subject of repugnance based on physical attractiveness and other characteristics includes well-known feminist protests against making physical attractiveness the standard of social acceptability for women, but there are other types of such repulsion. Consider, for example, gender-neutral aversions to what is perceived as ugliness because of obesity. One striking feature of televised news stories that sample opinions on thinness is how many people positively abhor even looking at those perceived as fat. In one such broadcast recently, interviewees described the overweight as "disgusting," "revolting," and "sickening," but none showed even the slightest awareness of the related topic of causes, especially genetics. Similarly, barriers get erected between the hypercritical and those with physical difficulties—say, with disfiguring handicaps—and between homophobic observers and those who have unacceptable gender preferences. Homosexuality now functions for too many people as the new witchcraft.

Poverty appears to be an equally substantial obstacle to kindness, and this type of aversion is well attested in literature. "We are not concerned with the very poor," pronounces the elder (and wealthy) Mr. Wilcox in E. M. Forster's *Howards End*. "They are unthinkable, and only to be approached by the statistician or the poet (1985, 34). Apparently he is so thoroughly insulated from the poor that he has even lost sight of the feelings by which they tend to repel us. Those feelings derive at least in part from the fact that, as George Eliot observes, "[T]here is a chill air surrounding those who are down in the world, and people are glad to get away from them, as from a cold room: human beings, mere men and women, without furniture, without anything to offer you, who have ceased to count as anybody, present an embarrassing negation of reasons for wishing to see them" (1985, 372). Perhaps this is one reason there is less and less direct contact with the poor—say, delivering baskets of food at Thanksgiving—and that it has proved entirely convenient to have charitable institutions mediate our contact with them. Likewise, the increasing social stratification in this country, reflecting the increasingly widening gap between rich and poor, as described in the Introduction, contributes to this diminished contact. In this context, it is instructive to remember that Dorothy Day founded the Catholic Worker movement not so much to help the poor but to develop the discipline of exposing people to them.[12]

These feelings of hostility are also due to recognition of the fundamental *dependence* of the poor. That is, we tend to recoil at the very possibility of some sort of claim being made on us, and especially in regard to financial resources. In D. H. Lawrence's *Sons and Lovers*, for instance, this is the situation in which Paul and Mrs. Morel find themselves when they go to Jordan's factory to get some type of position for Paul. They "sat quiet and with that peculiar shut-off look of the poor who have to depend on the favour of others" (1982, 95–96).

On the other hand, if we are inhibited from being kind to the poor, the converse does not seem to follow. Jane Eyre "could not see how poor people had the means of being kind" (Brontë 1966, 57). But in fact, from the myth of Philemon and Baucis[13] to the joy of those who live in the Haitian slum of Le Soleil and John Steinbeck's migrant communities, the absence of an economic measure of human dignity appears to open up people for a great range and depth of kindness. Of course, one does not have to be poor in order to refuse this measure of human dignity,[14] even if this rejection is a necessary condition of kindness. In this light, it is interesting how often the parable of the Good Samaritan gets twisted into a moral tale about the obligations of the wealthy to care for the poor. In truth, "[T]he Samaritan is a social outcast, and yet he is the one who shows compassion. It is not about us, the privileged, showing kindness to the downtrodden. It is about them showing kindness to us" (Wuthnow 1991, 184).

The story of the Good Samaritan returns us again to the egoist's indifference. Such indifference can manifest other types of non-openness to the other that are phenomenologically distinguishable from the forms of demonstrative negativity described above. Many of Jane Austen's characters display one form of such non openness. In *Persuasion*, for example, Anne Elliot's cousin, Mr. Elliot, was "rational, discreet, polished—but he was not open. There was never any burst of feeling, any warmth of indignation or delight, at the evil or good of others. This, to Anne, was a decided imperfection" (Austen 1982, 173).[15] What is to be stressed here is how this indifference evidences Camus' sense of affectlessness or, as Marx would say, lack of modes of compassionate attunement in human solidarity.

Another type of non-openness occurs through insulation in social roles—say, those of officials and other institutional representatives. It is not simply that "rules are rules" and "business is business," revealing tautologies though they are. Even when this is the only defense, there are, as noted in the previous chapter, kind and unkind ways of delivering bad news. When, for example, an instructor must explain to a student—on the grounds of merit, consistency, and fairness to other students—a refusal to change a failing course grade to an "incomplete," it is equally possible for the explanation to evidence a concern for the student's welfare or to leave her dignity in shreds.[16] The problem is not that rules or laws are per se antithetical to kindness. Rather, it is a question of a certain wooden attitude that elevates them above the people for whom they were created, and which therefore can create conflicts between the human being and the official, and between officials and those subject to them.

In Tolstoy's "The Forged Coupon," for instance, the Tsar refuses an appeal for the lives of two peasants about to be hanged. He simply shrugs, "The law's the law." Later, after the executions take place, a famous monk preached in the court chapel on the evils of capital punishment and its inconsistency with Christian principles. Because of this impertinence, the church administration sacked the monk and sent him to a distant monastery, but not in time to save the Tsar from nightmares of hanged corpses. Like Scrooge after his own nocturnal terrors, the Tsar began to reflect on his responsibilities, and he remembered all that the monk had said to him. However, unlike Scrooge, he could not yield to the human being within because of all the official demands made on him. Tolstoy tells us that he was not strong enough to admit that the demands of being human outweighed those of his office.

A different form of affectless indifference consists of smug satisfaction, or self-completion, in one's own projects. In this satiation, or saturation, of self, there is no feeling connection to the other, because the bloated sense of self appears to absorb all of one's concerns. We usually refer to this attitude as "thoughtlessness," but the suggested mental emptiness is mistaken. It is more nearly a question of a self-reflexive thought*ful*ness that is parasitic on an underlying affectlessness. Self-absorption and a consequent indifference to the other's welfare or "illfare" are not the products of reasoning. They are, rather, the basis for selfish reasoning.

There is also a type of affectless indifference based on the composition of a person's value structure, which is at least of partly intellectual origin. For, if feelings shape and condition reasoning, the opposite half of the dialectic is also true. Both kindness and unkindness in the form of affectless indifference can be expressed within, and conditioned by, a particular set of values. In Joseph Conrad's *Heart of Darkness*, for instance, the company's chief accountant goes on implacably entering figures in a book, while below him, in a grove of trees, native slave laborers are dying. The narrator tells us that the accountant "bent over his books, was making correct entries of perfectly correct transactions; and fifty feet below the doorstep I could see the still tree-tops of the grove of death" (1985, 47). The accountant's indifference stems from his untroubled conviction that Africans are not human. Thus when they make too much noise outside of his office, he complains, "When one has got to make correct entries, one comes to hate those savages—hate them to the death" (ibid., 47).

An equally depressing, real-life type of affectless indifference, one that appears to be conjoined with sadism, runs as follows. On April 4, 1991, Mary Jo Frug, a well-known feminist legal scholar, was slashed to death on the street in Cambridge, Massachusetts. Exactly one year later, the *Harvard Law Review* threw its annual gala banquet, at which time the new editors of the *Review* are recognized. The organizers of the banquet invited the dead woman's husband, John Frug, who was on the Harvard Law School faculty. Had he attended, he would have discovered on his plate a parody of his wife's final article that, after a heated dispute, had been published posthumously in the *Review*. The satire, written by the *Review's* editors and paid for by the law school, "depicted Ms. Frug as a humorless, sex-starved mediocrity and dubbed her the 'Rigor-Mortis Professor of Law.'"[17]

Professor Alan Dershowitz, also on the Harvard Law School faculty, labeled this grotesque satire "an unintentionally offensive parody,"[18] but there is such a thing as over-explaining the obvious, for this account would assume one of two things. Either the students were ignorant of the fact that a grieving husband (and others) *whom they had invited* would be offended by finding an insult to his dead wife on his and everyone else's dinner plates, or the students' value-structure as expressed in the parody blocked all sensitivity to women and grief-stricken survivors. The first possibility is implausible, because it presupposes the students to be too dense to have been admitted to the law school in the first place. The second possibility implies an unconscious sadism, a moral pathology that no one, including Dershowitz, should defend. The only other possibility is that the satire was intentionally offensive—that is, consciously sadistic. In short, either the students at issue were stupid or evil, unconsciously or consciously. Whatever the true explanation, when William Blake asked,

> *Can I see another's woe,*
> *And not be in sorrow too?*
> *Can I see another's grief,*
> *And not seek for kind relief?*[19]

it is clear, unhappily, that the answer to both questions is "yes."

Marx's ethics of compassion follows in the footsteps of Martin Buber and Gabriel Marcel, and the discussion across the last several pages about obstacles to a disposition to kindness can be seen as detailed elaborations of the negative side of Marcel's reflections on human existence, as explained in the Introduction. On the positive side, Marcel also holds that the disposition to perform kind acts, the second main characteristic of personal kindness, originates not in an intellectually constituting consciousness but in an intuitively reasoned feeling that gets expressed in various modes of attunement to the world. Both the negative and the positive sides of Marcel's views are important for understanding our disposition to kindness, because they will prepare us to grasp the third essential characteristic of personal kindness, warm generosity. They will also set the stage for much of the analysis of society in Chapters 4 and 5.

Taking the negative side first, the key diagnostic word for Marcel is "function." In his view, we have lost our awareness of the sense of being human, because we have been reduced to sets of functions, both vital (the body) and social (roles such as producers, consumers, and so forth). Marcel does not argue that it is wrongheaded to talk of the functioning of, say, the immune system, or that it is inherently degrading to fill social roles. Rather, his point is that we have been led to see ourselves "as a mere assemblage of functions" (1964b, 10),[20] as in the example cited in the previous chapter of hospital patients who are viewed only as sets of functions and problems to solve within a bureaucratic rationality. Being gets degraded into having: I am no longer a body; I have a body. The other, such as my wife, is no longer a Thou. She becomes something I have, like an object on my mantel ("the wife," "the little woman"). The other gets degraded from a Thou to an "it," no longer a person, but a thing, because she has been reduced to a set of objective properties. Thus objectified, the person becomes a convenient instrument of manipulation and control. Hence, when Balzac opined that for a woman to give herself to a man was like placing a violin in the hands of an ape, his intention to praise women misfired, because he failed to see that a violin is also an instrument, passive and compliant, (with) which one plays.[21]

There are many other examples of such functionalization. The Vatican's insistence on reducing human sexuality to the unobstructed functioning of a plumbing system is one such case. Also, soldiers killed in battle and downsized employees—linked together in the headlines of *The New York Times* series on downsizing, referred to in the Introduction—can be viewed by their respective superiors as "simply replaceable"—"Scandalous, and even sacrilegious words" (Marcel 1963, 139). Surgical operations can be seen functionally as successes, even if the patient dies. Death, which was once viewed as part of the spiritual life—Native Americans, for example, traditionally dressed for it—has now largely been reduced objectively and functionally to the failure of the machine and the scrapping of the remains (a revealing description). Hospices apart, death, the final affectlessness, tends to be treated as affectlessly as possible—no doubt partly because, as Heidegger and Marx point out, we maintain our studied avoidance of death so that we can continue to flee from an authentic realization of our ultimate possibility.

For Marcel, this functionalized world generates an overwhelming impression of sadness to both spectators and those caught up in it, and a deep suspicion that something has gone dreadfully wrong. One thinks, for example, of paintings such as Manet's *Plum Brandy* and Degas' *L'absinthe*—as well as the countless real-life bar scenes that faultlessly mimic those works' melancholy atmospheres—and several of Hopper's paintings that take up the same motif, such as *Nighthawks*, *Automat*, and *Sunlight in a Cafeteria*. The world depicted in those works is "empty," as opposed to the "full" world of human being (Marcel 1964b, 12), and has a "feeling of *staleness*" (Marcel 1964a, 153) ("staleness" is in English and italicized in the original text). For Marcel, an empty world centered on function reduces everything to a problem to solve by calculational thought, and hence leaves no room for mystery. Since it dis-integrates persons into functions—Thous into its—its typical results are "despair, betrayal, and suicide" (1964b, 27).

The language of functions and objectification expresses well the types of closedness described above that are implicated in unkindness. The French hotel owner instantly sensed its degradation. In addition, aversions and hostilities based on class, social roles, and poverty reduce the value of their targets to that of objects that do or do not have certain properties and the corresponding ability or inability to perform certain functions. Mr. Wilcox, a descendant of Dickens' immortal characters of Bounderby and Gradgrind in *Hard Times*, consigns even thinking about the poor to the calculating statistician and—what in his view is completely useless anyway—the non-calculating poet. Conrad's accountant explicitly values the clarity and correctness of figures over human flesh, just as George Eliot's descriptions of the chill air surrounding the poor correlate exactly to a value structure based on having. For people like Wilcox, Bounderby, and Gradgrind, the poor are only to be counted, and when the value of the masses is flattened and distorted into their place in the social calculus, they end up failing to count at all.

For Marcel, as for Marx (1992, 38), technology is the principal cause of de-humanizing reduction of persons to functional objectification. Technology, he argues, feeds desire with the specious optimism that everything central to our welfare is a problem that it can solve. When the inevitable disappointment comes, frustrated desire gives way to fear that generates greater efforts toward technological achievement, and that in turn will spawn more fear, and so forth. In truth, in this never-ending spiral, "man is *at the mercy of his technics*. . . . he is increasingly incapable of controlling his technics, or rather of *controlling his own control*" (Marcel 1964b, 31). Philosophy itself, he wrote thirty-five years later, has the job of articulating our own malaise that stems from bureaucratic, technological mutilation of human being (Marcel 1973, 13; see also Marcel 1963, 162–66). We need a "tragic wisdom," because human beings perceive that they have been "betrayed" by "the exaggerated development of a global technology which can only lead to emptiness," an emptiness that Nietzsche was correct to label "nihilism" (Marcel, 1973, xxxiv–xxxv).

In contrast, the positive side of Marcel's thought, a "metaphysics of light" (Ricoeur), celebrates the integrity of human being motivated by hope, creative fidelity, and "presence" (Marcel 1964b, 40). In rejecting my degradation into a mass of functions, I recoil into myself as self-recovery, a self-conscious recol-lection *recueillement*). But this centripetal moment of spiritual discovery is bal-anced by a centrifugal moment through which I affirm myself as a totality of my concrete relationships with others at a meta-problematical level (the level of mystery). By realizing the difference between my life and my being, I am liber-ated from being reduced to an ensemble of functions. The capacity to hope re-turns to "the soul which is at the disposal of others": it is dedicated to others with a freedom that transcends self-interest. Recognizing that it belongs to others "is the starting point of its activity and creativeness" (ibid., 43).[22]

Disponibilité is Marcel's word for the disposition that we have been dis-cussing as the second main characteristic of personal kindness. It is that by which I am "available" to, "at the disposal (disponible) of," the other. It is "pure charity" (ibid., 39) through which I am actively, not passively, at the service of the other—*prêt à servir*—"it implies the state of 'being ready to'" (Marcel 1984, 201). As Marx would appreciate later, this contrast of activity versus passivity, readiness rather than unreadiness to be at the service of the Other, can also be expressed as openness as opposed to closedness, life instead of death (ibid., 1984, 201–202). As Hallie points out, the "iron axiom" of the Chambonnais who rescued thousands of Jews during World War II was a "habitual readiness" to be *prêt-à-servir*" (1997, 38).

This active receptivity to the other funds me with the freshness of hope, a "creative fidelity" (Marcel 1964b, 34) in I-Thou relationships, and this hope is the very opposite of an inert, passive waiting that Marcel takes to be central to Stoicism. Hope is, rather, a dynamic, joyful commitment to the other. It creates a concrete relationship with the other that is a "permeability" in and through which we "participate" in each other's being (Marcel 1964a, 87) as opposed to experiences in which, for all the façade of openness, we remain closed off from each other. As the Dalai Lama points out, "Some smiles are sarcastic. Some smiles are artificial—diplomatic smiles. These smiles do not produce satisfaction, but rather fear or suspicion. But a genuine smile gives us hope, freshness," because it bespeaks "compassion" (1990, 124). Marcel, in fact, more than once uses the distinction between freshness and staleness to designate the corresponding difference between genuine and spurious disponibilité.

Marcel also translates the distinction between genuine and spurious disponibilité as a difference between real presence and mere physical presence. "The most attentive and the most conscientious listener," he indicates correctly, "may give me the impression of not being present; he gives me nothing, he cannot make room for me in himself, whatever the material favours that he is prepared to grant me. The truth is that there is a way of listening which is a way of giving, and another way of listening which is a way of refusing, of refusing *oneself*" (1964b, 40; emphasis in original). Conversely, as we have also seen, "Unavailability is invariably rooted in some measure of alienation" (ibid.)—"in some manner not only occupied but encumbered with oneself" (ibid., 42).[23]

The kindness inscribed in creative fidelity must also be distinguished from faithfulness to a moral principle, a political slogan, or an institution as such. Each of those types of fidelity imply conformism, as Marcel sees it, and the desire to commit oneself to a principle for its own sake. However, "Fidelity to a principle as a principle is idolatry in the etymological sense of the word"; when "life has withdrawn" from a given principle, I have a duty to myself to change my allegiance so as not to betray myself (ibid., 35).

Thomas Hardy's *Tess of the D'Urbervilles* provides us with a graphic illustration of both this sense of idolatry and the alienation of being "encumbered with oneself" in terms of Angel Clare's reaction to Tess' post-wedding confession that she is not a virgin (she was raped). His exclusive reliance on the principle that virginity is a necessary condition of honorable marriage deflects all of her pleas for mercy. She breaks down in tears and turns away from him, but to no avail. "Within the remote depths of his constitution, so gentle and affectionate as he was in general, there lay hidden a hard logical deposit, like a vein of metal in a soft loam, which turned the edge of everything that attempted to traverse it" (1978, 311).

The Chambonnais, in contrast, were not faithful to a principle (of Christian love) just because it was a principle. On the contrary, they were faithful because it was only through their rescues that that principle had any meaning. They demonstrated that kindness is not merely the subject of an ethics of internal moral spiritual order but rather a project in the world. It cannot be conceived of apart from action—it is more nearly *bonitas* than *benignitas*.

For Marcel, the type of thought that *is* appropriate for thinking human being is what imposes a restraint on calculational thought, namely, a Heideggerean *Gelassenheit*: an art "whose principle resides precisely in the heart and is not reducible to a technique, to some kind of textbook know-how. This art implies a gift of self, a reverential attitude designated by the term 'piety.' This attitude is inconsistent with the pretension of mastering something in order to exploit it" (1973, 114). *Gelassenheit,* "which is so contrary to the disposition of the pure technician . . . finds its most perfect expression in the poet" (ibid.).[24]

Marcel's conception of *disponibilité,* along with the closely related notions of freedom and responsibility, is central not only to the Christianity to which he himself was committed but to a number of other belief systems as well. For instance, these notions are embodied in the Confucian virtue of *chun-tzu,* and also in Native American thought. The Dakota notion of responsibility, for example, as George W. Linden points out, held that, "To grow in manliness, in humanness, in holiness, meant to plunge purposively into the relatedness of all things. A Dakota never *assumed* responsibility, because responsibility was had, was there always. . . . It remained for the Dakota to recognize his relatedness, and his responsibility; it was there for him to discover" (Lee 1959, 61; cited at Linden 1977, 31; emphasis in original).

Chun-tzu and the Dakota notion of responsibility both mean not accountability but "something like spiritual availability, or perhaps, reciprocity, for responsibility is responding, re-spondere, speaking-back-to. . . . And it means to be responsive in a web of relationships already objectively existing" (Linden 1977, 31).[25] Moreover, Dakota culture was a shame, rather than a guilt, culture. Kind generosity was the highest virtue, because the responsibility in which it was inscribed meant caring for the others" (ibid.). Personal and family honor turned on such generosity: "Undistinguished and stingy men . . . ['] just live,' said a brave old warrior. It was really the worst one could say about anybody" (Erdoes 1972, 35).[26] Therefore, as Linden also notes, one of the most slanderous labels in the English language is "Indian-giver."[27]

To conclude these reflections on Marcel's work, the chief value of his thought for understanding personal kindness lies, on one side, in its diagnosis of one main cause of unkindness—a reduction to objective functions through which we come to be alienated from the Other in various types of hostilities, aversions, and indifference. On the other side, Marcel's thought stresses positively creative fidelity, dedicated freedom, and human solidarity that are all involved in our *disponibilité* to perform kind acts. It is this *disponibilité* that constitutes the second main quality of personal kindness. From this angle, it is worth remembering that what was really monstrous about Dr. Frankenstein's creation, more chilling even than its appearance, was its complete isolation from humanity. Its disposition to acts of kindness died at the same time as did its hopes for acceptance in the human community. Hence, it is deeply symbolic of its isolation that the creature, contrary to Hollywood, has no name, and that its self-destruction takes place in the Arctic. He suffers from "a cold loneliness 'more frightening than death itself' " (Gilligan 1982, 1993 printing, citing Erikson 1976).

At the same time, there are at least three closely related weaknesses in Marcel's view that are also significant for understanding personal kindness. The first concerns his indictment of calculational thought, and I have already described above and in the previous chapter contexts in which the benign use of calculation is not only consistent with kindness but actually necessary to bring it into being. Marcel's wholesale indictment of calculative thought is closely related to the second weakness, which is his almost totally negative view of technology, as sketched above, and its consequences for human dignity. We shall examine that deficiency, along with calculational thought again, in Chapter 4. The third weakness consists of his almost entirely negative approach to objectification. Since the third weakness is presupposed in the other two, we shall start with it here.

As we have seen, Marcel does not perceive objectification (into functions and properties) as inherently dehumanizing. Rather, dehumanization starts when human beings are considered nothing but assemblages of functions, "Thou" reduced to "its." Put this way, his view mirrors Kant's criticism of treating persons as mere means to ends, albeit not based on the capacity to reason as a criterion of personhood. But this theoretical distinction aside, in practice, virtually all of Marcel's references to objectification are negatively prescriptive, and this is especially so in the context of technology. He very rarely even suggests the possibility of the humanizing use of objectification. Doubtless, he was persuaded to conflate objectification with exploitation, and technology with evil, by the horrifying events of his own times. Perhaps he was also convinced by Nietzsche's conviction of our "human, all too human" tendency to try to gain power over others. Indeed, Marcel ends his "Preface" to *Tragic Wisdom* by agreeing with those who find the meaning of the contemporary human condition better expressed by Nietzsche than by Karl Marx and subsequent Marxists.[28]

Nonetheless, it is possible to objectify and even manipulate people while treating them as "Thous," and hence with kindness. Good parenting and classroom pedagogy are common examples. Calculative thought, inscribed in a sense of strategy, enters into such benign objectification as it does into certain acts of kindness described at the end of Chapter 1. Also, in a complex, urban, industrial society, we use people daily to perform various functions—letter carriers, doctors, teachers, store clerks, and the like—all without the slightest necessity of exploitation. Thus as Harvey Cox argued some years ago against Buber, I-Thou and it-it relationships constitute a false dichotomy. We do not have to choose between them, because our functional, yet humane, relationships with other people most often comprise what Cox calls "I-you relationships" (1966, 42). Correlatively, kindness can be embedded just as much in I-you as I-Thou relationships.

Moreover, kindness is not only consistent with the objectification present in I-you relationships, but as Cox's own examples show, such objectification is actually necessary for kindness to exist in these daily social transactions. He notes correctly that, "Supermarket checkers or gas-meter readers who became enmeshed in the lives of the people they were serving would be a menace. . . . Urban life demands that we treat most of the people we meet as persons—not as things, but not as intimates either" (ibid., 36).[29] Kindness can coexist with objectification in I-you relationships, because they treat the other as a means, but not as a *mere* means, to an end. Thus the Kantian proscription can be observed when, for example, I make use of a surgeon to restore my health, and she makes use of me for both the purposes of healing and practicing a profession. The word "can" is crucial here, because there is always the possibility of slipping over into using the other as a mere means, abusing rather than merely using her. In any event, objectification per se does not necessarily entail dehumanization.

Finally, objectification can be consistent with kindness, even when there is special reason to fear manipulative control and exploitation. The incendiary power of sexuality is one such case. The language of lovers in the freshness of sexual discovery is replete with joyful objectification that, in turn, enhances and deepens the joy of that love. *The Song of Songs* is only one example, as when the groom sings:

> *How beautiful you are, how pleasing, my love my delight!*
> *Your very figure is like a palm tree, your breasts are like clusters.*
> *I said: I will climb the palm tree, I will take hold of its branches.*
> *Now let your breasts be like clusters of the vine and the fragrance of your*
> *   breath like apples,*
> *And your mouth like an excellent wine (7: 7–10),*

to which the bride responds:

> *that flows smoothly for my lover, spreading over the lips and teeth.*
> *I belong to my lover and for me he yearns (7: 10–11).*

Nussbaum is also interested in the phenomenon of objectification, both benign and unacceptable (1995b, 1999). Her distinctions between "Seven Ways to Treat a Person as a Thing" (1999, 218) detail the complexity of the phenomenon in ways that Marcel and Cox do not. In order, these "seven ways" are: (1) "*Instrumentality*"; (2) "*Denial of Autonomy*"; (3) "*Inertness*," that is, "The objectifier treats the object as lacking in agency, and perhaps also in activity"; (4) "*Fungibility*"; (5) "*Violability*"; (6) "*Ownership*"; and (7) "*Denial of subjectivity.*" Objectification means "treating a human being in one or more of these ways"

(1999, 219; emphasis in original). They are independent of each other but non-disjunctive: rather like Wittgenstein's notion of "family resemblances," they contingently overlap in different types of cases of objectification. It might be the case that each is a sufficient condition of objectification, but it is more likely that in any given context, more than one feature will be present.

However, despite the complexity inherent in the concept of objectification, Nussbaum appears to correlate morally unacceptable cases with the essentially Kantian position of denying one's own or another's autonomy and treating oneself or another as nothing but an instrument (1999, 223 ff.), and with Marcel's protest against reducing someone merely to sets of functions. Thus in terms of sexual morality, she argues that Kant misapplied his own moral criteria: to say that in merely "focusing on [body] parts there is denial of humanity seems quite wrong. Even the suggestion that [a couple] . . . are *reducing* one another to their bodily parts seems quite wrong" (ibid., 229).

Such is the case with the bride and groom in the *Song of Songs*. In fact, so far from being dehumanizing, this identification with one's bodily parts and the mutual sharing of that experience, are actually constitutive of the self's liberation in a joyous sexual union. For that self includes a dimension of animality, "complexly interwoven with individuality and personality" (ibid., 1999, 231). As such, this form of objectification in situations of this type can be an important ingredient in both kindnesses to oneself and to one's sexual partner, as in the passage from *Beloved*, in which Paul D.'s body becomes "an arc of kindness" as he leans over Sethe's back and holds her breasts in his hands. Perhaps the best description of this type of objectification in these two literary texts is that of an intensely high degree of aesthetic appreciation, in both senses of thankfulness and valuing up, of erotically stimulating observable features of a beloved partner. Also, Paul D.'s gesture is subtended by an infinite compassion for Sethe's long suffering.

Nussbaum makes two other points about objectification that are crucial for assessing its kindness or unkindness. First she notes that context is decisive for whether particular sexual (and other) objectifications are benign or immoral (1999, 227). Second, in human sexuality the temptation to dehumanizing objectification is particularly seductive. It is especially "sexy" to treat a human being rather than a thing as a thing because, like sex itself, "it is a dizzying experience of power" (ibid., 233). Male competition for status in part turns on this fact. Women can be dominated, but a car, say, cannot be, so a trophy wife will always tend to be more exciting than an automobile. Perhaps it was Nietzsche (1966) who best captured the difference between benign and morally objectionable sexual objectification when he wrote, "The chastest words I have heard: *Dans le véritable amour c'est l'âme qui enveloppe le corps.* ["In true love it is the soul that envelops the body"] "Epigrams and Interludes" § 142, 89).

Generosity

This brief, critical assessment of some aspects of Marcel's thought has already brought to light, mainly in terms of Native American thought, the third essential characteristic of personal kindness, which is warm generosity. This is what Kant referred to as the "good-natured temperament," "love out of inclination," or "pathological love." It has for him, contrary to Marcel and Native American cultures, no moral value as opposed to the "worth of character" that can be shaped by a good will acting out of respect for duty. The latter, stripped of all feeling, is, as noted in the Introduction, "kindness done from duty" (benevolence), which is "practical" love" (1964a, 66, 67).

"Warm" generosity does not necessarily imply being "effusive," "gushing," or any other predicate indicative of a saccharine sentimentality or similar styles of behavior associated with certain personality types, cultural subgroups, or even whole cultures. Rather, "warm" here refers to the genuineness of feeling inscribed in a commitment of service to the other. Since, as Merleau-Ponty observed, there are many ways to be a body-consciousness, and no one natural or correct way, it follows that there is no one right or best way of expressing a warm generosity.

Recall again from Chapter 1 the case of the unsmiling Korean grocer whose cool demeanor was misunderstood by his African-American neighbors as hostility. The "cool" grocer may or may not have been a kind person. As noted above, one can be kind and not appear so, and vice versa. Satisfying different cultural expectations for appropriate behavior can mask one's kindness, just as can living in chronic pain or suffering a disproportionate share of tragedies, injuries, or illnesses, which makes kindness struggle for existence on a meagre enjoyment of life. However, if the grocer were a kind person, he would have to have some type of warm generosity, however it might be appropriate for him to express it, and he could not be perceived as a kind person unless at least other members of his subcultural group could understand it as an appropriate expression.

The many kindnesses shown to me in Taipei and Hong Kong, for example, certainly communicated a spirit of warm generosity, but the way in which that generosity was conveyed was quite different from that to which I was accustomed. It did not take the form of effusive cordiality, congenial, affable smiles, and compliant bodily gestures. Rather, it consisted of an intensity and almost single-minded devotion to my welfare. Yet just because such generosity can take unfamiliar forms, this does not mean that we cannot come to understand it. There is a type of intersubjective understanding grounded in feeling, as Marx and Marcel have noted, and, as Dufrenne points out, "We come to perceive this sort of meaning . . . by means of the emotion which it arouses in us. . . . Like motor activity, emotivity is knowledge" (1973, 384).

The warmth of generosity, of whatever intensity, is an essential quality of personal kindness because, as we have seen, how acts of kindness are performed is as important as what is done. Those driven by guilt or fear—say, obsequious employees or those who dread being downsized—may constantly and sincerely do things for us, and we may be tempted to take them as acts of kindness. Such individuals may also be constantly at our disposition. Thus they might embody perfectly the first two essential qualities of kindness, and yet at the least, there would still be room for doubt about personal kindness. They might not really be at my disposal, but only, as Marcel argued, partially and temporarily (and fearfully) on loan. In contrast, a sense of warm generosity conveys a real presence, a strong impression of the persons themselves embodied in the act.

In Western philosophy, it was perhaps Aristotle who most completely addressed the virtue of generosity, but that which characterizes a kind person surpasses his picture of liberality in money matters and his related treatment of gentleness. Personal kindness also transcends Aristotle's ethics of internal self-governance. The generosity of personal kindness is more closely associated with benevolence—although, as we saw in the Introduction, they are not identical—and with love, in which we recognize that other people have claims on our freedom.[30] It is the sort of generosity that, as Levinas says, in following Marcel, makes people feel "at home" (1979, 37). The warmth involved shows the manner in which we can be tempered—in the double sense of a knife or other tool readied to perform correctly and, as Marx would express it, in terms of attuning our moods to the welfare of the other. The kind person lives in this state of feeling attunement, and so we can easily believe that kind acts really come from her. The tempering process produces magnanimity—the thoughtfulness, in both senses, of the *magna anima*.

In conveying the readiness of kind people to be at the service of others, their *prêt à servir*, warm generosity manifests the thought*ful* in both senses as dynamic—as tending to be expressed in concernful action. Another way of saying this is that warm generosity gives us the impression of what is sometimes called "simple kindness." "Simple" in this context does not necessarily mean to be without calculation or strategy, nor must it be naive. It is probably what Blake had in mind in supposing the impossibility of our failure to respond to another's woe, and it is reflected in an illuminating contrast in Eliot's *Middlemarch* when Dorothea Brooke visits Dr. Lydgate's bride, Rosamond. She "put out her hand with her usual simple kindness, and looked admiringly at Lydgate's lovely bride." Rosamond, on the other hand, bedecked in stunning dress and jewels, possessed that "controlled self-consciousness of manner which is the expensive substitute for simplicity" (Eliot 1965, 470, 471).[31]

The warm generosity characteristic of personal kindness distinguishes genuine concern from several facsimile (im) postures. (All postures of kindness are impostures.) Familiar cases include superficially assuaging feelings, even when harmful in the long run; plastic "care" trumpeted in advertising ("We really care about *you!*"), and institutional postures toward customers *de convenance*—as when banks make loans in inner-city neighborhoods only under the threat of lawsuits and civil rights complaints.[32] There are also the artificial smiles to which the Dalai Lama referred—say, those of landlords, bureaucrats, and salespeople— that sometimes leave their faces even before the end of the particular transaction. There is also the attitude of "metallic" charity in which the presence of the other is acknowledged grudgingly as an unwelcome burden,[33] and what Charlotte Brontë complained of in her life as a governess, her employers' compulsion disguised as kindness. There are also acts sometimes described as "prosocial behavior" that, unlike acts of kindness, are done with some expectation of avoiding pain and suffering and/or reward (Baron and Byrne 1987, 260ff.).

Along a different line, there are equally neurotic do-gooders who show us that "open" and "closed" are distinguishable from "warm" and "cold." As noted above, such types are always open to us (around the clock), ever alert to intervene in our lives, but without the warm generosity of personal kindness. That is because, as noted in the previous chapter, they really intend their own welfare rather than that of the objects of their ministrations. All of these posturing gestures of false kindness attempt the self-contradiction of trying to force an unforced appearance, and so are usually self-revealing and self-parodying.[34]

Probably Marcel believed that warmth of generosity is inscribed in *disponibilité* but if so, he left it unstated.[35] Levinas, on the contrary, makes the connection explicit. His principal moral concern is justice (1979, 303), but because of the way he conceives of justice, much of his work is relevant to kindness as well.

Focusing very narrowly—only on what is relevant in Levinas' writings for understanding the warmth of generosity in personal kindness—one must begin with his primordial notion of the face. It is not a mere "plastic form, which is already deserted, betrayed, by the being it reveals" (1987, 55). In its "epiphany the face is not resplendent as a form clothing a content, as an *image.*" It is, in fact, the "dead face [that] becomes a form, a mortuary mask" (Levinas 1979, 262). Rather, the face is "a living presence; it is expression" (ibid., 66).[36] This expression for Levinas is visual, just as it was for the doctor in Josephine Hart's *Damage*: "The eyes break through the mask—the language of the eyes, impossible to dissemble. The eye does not shine; it speaks" (Levinas 1979, 66). The expression is also linguistic: "Speech cuts across vision" (ibid., 195), hence, "The manifestation of the face is already discourse" (ibid., 66).[37]

In both look and word, the face of the kind other expresses warm generosity in terms of welcome, peace, and hospitality, a good example of which may be found in Frederick Douglass' moving account of his encounter with Robert Ingersoll. After traveling all night, Douglass arrived at the Ingersoll residence in Peoria, Illinois. He writes that Mr. Ingersoll had "real living human sunshine in his face, and honest, manly kindness in his voice," and he tells us that his welcome "would have been a cordial to the bruised heart of any proscribed and storm-beaten stranger, and one which I can never forget or fail to appreciate" (1962, 462).

Expression in the face of the Other is "appeal and teaching, *entry into relation with me*—the ethical relation" (Levinas 1979, 181). The moral life, for Levinas, presupposes the irreducible and illimitable otherness of the Other, but Western philosophy has persistently attempted to reduce that otherness to a product of reason (or Reason). My thinking the Other rationally—a "representation"—attempts to capture the Other in concepts and categories as a totality of interpretation. Thus the alterity of the Other gets "reabsorbed into my own identity as a thinker or possessor" (ibid., 33) by making her (1) a mere negation of myself; (2) at the other extreme, a mere extension of myself; (3) an object to be manipulated; or (4) by any other totalizing act ("the objectivism of war" [Levinas 1979, 25]), an object captured in my categories.

There is no better illustration, literally, of what Levinas protests against than René Magritte's drawing (actually done several times), *Le Viol* (*Rape*). The drawing likewise illustrates Bartky's notion of psychological oppression, Marcel's picture of human degradation into a mere assemblage of functions, and several, if not all, of Nussbaum's senses of objectification, and perhaps Kant's as well. When we look at the drawing, we are directly facing the head of a woman. We see her face, surrounding hair, neck, and the beginnings of her shoulders. But her face is really her torso: her breasts take the place of her eyes, her navel serves as her nose, and her pubic hair and beginnings of her legs become her mouth and chin. This drawing, which still has the capacity to shock, unsettles us precisely to the degree that it conveys so vividly the violence of manipulating someone as an object, of attempting to capture her in categories, and finally of the subject's internalized self-image of a violated (totalized) object. For this is no longer a full-fledged Other facing us. The anonymity of anatomy has replaced the individuality of the face. She has been reduced for herself and us to the way that others objectify and want to possess her.

For Levinas, on the contrary, following Buber and Marcel, the "you must" of moral obligation can be directly experienced only because the Other is not an object but a free, independent subject,[38] and it is the face of the Other that prevents me from denying her reality as other. The face manifests the absolute otherness of the Other as an infinity that overflows all attempts at capture in a totality of concepts and categories. Such attempts do violence to this Other, or deface her. In contrast, the concern of the kind person is, as noted above, both to remedy needs and to express a positive desire to enhance the Other's flourishing. The expression of the face bids me not to kill or otherwise harm but rather to experience a kinship and responsibility through welcome and peace. In assuming this responsibility, borrowing Marcel's language, I "participate" in the being of the Other (Levinas 1979, 61) to make the stranger, the widow, the orphan—in brief, the injurable Other—"at home" (ibid., 156).

The Other imposes herself on me in her weakness, and this imposition—far from not rising to the level of the moral life, as Kant would have it—is a "privileged heteronomy" (Levinas 1979, 88) that is the origin of the ethical. The latter does not begin with me and stream out toward the other. The origin of the prescriptive lies, rather, in the Other's ability to interrupt the spontaneity of my freedom and make me pay heed: "Morality begins when freedom, instead of being justified by itself, feels itself to be arbitrary and violent" (ibid., 84). Hospitality to the Other is conscience itself.

This conception of conscience means that Levinas also rejects, as do Marcel and Buber, a self who is centered in the subject. Rather, the moral conception of a self is one whose center is elsewhere, "otherwise" than its own interiority. The authentic self is centered on others to whom, and for whom, it finds itself responsible. In contrast, the egoist is centered on her own interiority, even when that interiority is mediated by external things. For example, Madame Merle, in *The Portrait of a Lady*, muses to Isabel Archer, "What shall we call our 'self'? Where does it begin? Where does it end? It overflows into everything that belongs to us—and then it flows back again" (James 1986, 253). For the egoist, it all "flows back again" to the inevitable self-reflexive center of reference and enjoyment.

A corollary of the replacement of egocentricity by heterocentricity is that Levinas, along with Marcel and Buber as well, would reject an ethics of internal self-governance, good intentions, and the primacy of, or exclusive focus on, individual rights,[39] in favor of concrete action. Thus Levinas would say, with William James, "Take any demand, however slight, which any creature, however weak, may make. Ought it not, for its own sole sake, to be satisfied? If not, prove why not" (1911, 195).

However, in his earlier writings, Levinas' reasons for agreeing with (William) James in fact mark one of the most important ways that his work differs from Buber's and Marcel's, namely, that my relationship with the Other is asymmetrical: unequal and irreversible. For Levinas, "Goodness consists in taking up a position in being such that the other counts more than myself" (1979, 247). Reversibility, the sense of being the equal of the Other, is derivative from this fundamental inequality, because it implies a third-person point of view in which I and the other both count the same. Hence, morality cannot begin from the experience of equality but from the immeasurable demands made on me by the widow, the stranger, the orphan, and the poor. We receive our freedom from this responsibility imposed by the Other. As Jacques Derrida puts it, this responsibility "is assigned to us by the other, from the other, before any hope of reappropriation permits us to assume this responsibility in the face of what could be called *autonomy*" (1988, 634; emphasis in original). Since my responsibility comes from the Other, I essentially experience that command of the Other in the accusative mode (in both senses).

In *Totality and Infinity*, Levinas expresses this irreversibility by saying that the Other has a dimension of "height" or "verticality," an inequality invisible "to the third party who would count us" (1979, 251). This dimension of height is what gives the Other the capacity to put my liberty in question, and what gives her face an ethical teaching role. Correlatively, equality alone is unable to lay claim to my freedom and make me put it and myself in question.

In Levinas' later writings, chiefly *Otherwise than Being*, his account of my relations with the Other becomes quite different, if more obscure. Some remnant of verticality appears to survive, as when the author writes, "In the accusative form, which is a modification of no nominative form . . . I approach the neighbor for whom, without having wished it, I have to answer" (1981, 124). Even so, in the later writings the language of verticality gives way to that of the "trace." I bear the trace of the Other within me (and vice versa)—in my flesh, Merleau-Ponty would say—in a manner that is more primordial than can be captured through the constitutive activities of consciousness or the formation of any explicit knowledge. As David Levin points out, the trace marks the inscription of my responsibility to the Other in bodily feelings that are prior to any activities of a constitutive consciousness (1998, 349).

The notion of height, or verticality, is important for understanding the possibilities of personal kindness. Even if one could perform acts of kindness for others perceived immediately as equals, one can easily imagine Levinas arguing, equality by itself could not sufficiently fund the warmth of generosity and life of service required to be a kind person. Treating others as equals can ground respect and negative moral and legal rights—the rights not to be killed, injured, or have one's freedom unjustifiably infringed. However, equality by itself cannot motivate one to a life of service—Hallie's "positive" as opposed to a "negative" morality. What is needed for a life of service, Levinas would likely conclude, is a perception of the Other—the stranger, the widow, the orphan, the poverty-stricken migrant worker, and the like—as counting *more than* the agent. This alone would suffice to impose a burden of responsibility capable of interrupting the spontaneity of freedom and thus create a disposition of being-for-the-Other.

It is not certain whether Levinas would advance the above argument, but he does maintain, at least in his earlier writings, that verticality is a necessary condition of nonviolative encounters with the Other. That is because this view appears to follow from two others discussed above—that my relationships with the Other are those of remoteness, and that the other imposes moral responsibility on me. Only in this way can the face block the possession and colonization of totalizers. Totalizers are indifferent egoists, but their indifference is more complicated than what Schlick referred as "inconsiderateness." Totalizers are indifferent to the Other's real welfare or "illfare," but they are far from indifferent to their own constructions of the Other's welfare or "illfare." This is because they want to overflow and colonize others to possess them as extensions of their own identities. In such cases, where egoism equals egotism, it is a question of an aggressive, conquering egoism made all the more dangerous by such egoists' inability and/or unwillingness to recognize it as such.

Colonizers, such as the fictional Madame Merle, referred to above, are not encumbered by the self. Rather, they project it (often unconsciously) like a searchlight as the only source of illumination to guide them. To the degree that this source of light excludes all others, the result is an unavailability to, or an alienation from, the Other. Receptivity is closed off, and communication tends to take the form of one-way transmissions. They can take the form of preaching, literally and figuratively, set agendas masquerading (sometimes) as open discussions, questions that are only apparently genuine, but are actually posed only to give the speaker the opportunity to answer, and so forth.

It is a matter here of alienation through weakness rather than strength, of psychological rigidity as opposed to true resilience. Like the neurotic do-gooder who offers free advice when you do not want it—especially because you do not want it—such a person *needs* to possess you in order to reinforce his or her own deficient sense of self-worth. Such alienated individuals fit perfectly Nietzsche's descriptions of the morality of the weak, and one index to this need and the alienation that underlies it consists of how such people perceive obstacles to their efforts at colonization. Once their attempts to control are spurned, they often continue to identify themselves with their own rejected advice—that is, with their own conception of the identity of the other—and alienation only increases. They tend to be incapable of what Marcel referred to as "creative fidelity," because their fidelity has been distorted into exclusive allegiance to their own principles as principles—what Marcel called "idolatry."

Examples abound, both fictional and real, but we shall consider here only one transparent literary case. Gregers Werle, in Henrik Ibsen's *The Wild Duck*, gives us one of the clearest, most frightening pictures of the risk of unkindness embedded in constituting and assigning oneself responsibility for other people's lives. He has, as another character, Dr. Relling, observes, a bad case of "acute rectitudinal fever" (Ibsen 1984, 271).[40] His commitment to truth outdoes even that of Kant or Robbespierre, and with equally destructive consequences. He cannot abide the fact that the successful and happy marriage of two of his friends, Hjalmar and Gina Ekdal, rests on the husband's illusion that his daughter is his own. Werle insists on revealing the fact that his own father is also that of the girl and gets Hjalmar to tell Gina that he knows that she used to be Werle's father's mistress. Thus, in Werle's mind, all deception can be cleared away, and the marriage can have a new foundation in sincerity and veracity.[41] He appears genuinely shocked when he discovers that, from within the wreckage of their marriage, they do not share his passion for truth. George Eliot once wrote that, what Marcel, Levinas, and Ibsen surely would approve, "There is no general doctrine which is not capable of eating out our morality if unchecked by the deep-seated habit of direct fellow-feeling with individual fellow-men" (1965, 668).[42]

Having moral responsibility assigned to us, the second view underpinning Levinas' belief in the necessity of verticality that we are now analyzing, leads us to conceive of personal kindness as the fulfillment of the piety of acting to match a Heideggerean piety of thinking. It also directs us to consider personal kindness as the achievement of a certain type of innocence. There are two types of innocence, that which we lose and that which we can gain or, as Wittgenstein phrased it, "an innocence which comes from a natural absence of temptation" and "the innocence a man has fought for" (Malcolm 1972, 80). Levinas would certainly contend, and rightly, that perceiving the Other in the dimension of height requires some degree of success in the struggle to achieve this second type of innocence. For such an accomplishment demands resisting the centrifugal force of the temptation to totalize, and resistance in turn demands recognition of good and evil that is absent from the first sense of innocence.

The first sense of innocence means to be "*an* innocent," to be "free of a variety of unpleasant tendencies: envy, pride, jealousy, malice, suspicion are a few; and is free of the actions that often express these" (Wolgast 1993, 298). This sort of innocence is usually identified with children or child-like people such as (Wolgast's examples) Herman Melville's Billy Budd, Dostoevsky's Prince Myshkin, and May Welland in Edith Wharton's *The Age of Innocence*. This type of innocence implies ignorance rather than knowledge—the archetype of which is Adam and Eve before their fatal dose of cognition—and the absence of regret. Ignorance, and the innocence it produces, means never having to say you are sorry.[43]

As Wolgast points out, this first type of innocence is not morally commendable, because nothing has been done to earn it, and nothing tests it in order to perfect it. Far from being morally praiseworthy, it lies outside of the scope of virtue altogether. Hence, Montaigne's remark, "What good I have in me I have . . . by the chance of my birth. I have gotten it neither from law, nor from precept, nor from any other apprenticeship. The innocence that is in me is a childish innocence: little vigor and no art" (1958, II:11, p. 313).[44]

One should also note that the distinction of "kind" and "kindly" is closely connected to that between warmth of concern and cool indifference, at least in adults. Charlotte Brontë joins these two distinctions in *Shirley*, when Caroline describes her uncle, the Reverend Helstone, to the title character. For all of his generosity, Caroline confesses, her uncle "is simply a man who is rather liberal than good-natured." Shirley readily assents: "Oh! yes: good-nature implies indulgence, which he has not; geniality, warmth of heart, which he does not own;

and genuine justice is the offspring of sympathy and considerateness, of which, I can well conceive, my bronzed old friend is quite innocent" (in Wolgast's first sense of innocence) (Brontë 1974, 223).

We shall take up the connection between sympathy and justice in the following two chapters, but here let us note in passing a second famous literary illustration of Wolgast's first sense of innocence, namely, Charles Bovary. The fact that there is much to praise about Dorothea Brooke and almost nothing about Charles shows again that this first sense of innocence is pre-moral, and hence not subject to praise or blame. Charles is clueless, stupid, boring, supremely devoted to Emma, and easy to delude. That his romantic purity shows that his fellow citizens are much worse is irrelevant to his utter lack of practical wisdom. For his ignorance about his wife is complete: he never has the slightest idea that she can deviate from goodness. *She*, on the other hand, is the very picture of an anxiety-ridden Sartrean consciousness, a flight out of itself and away from the in-itself. For her, Flaubert tells us, "[E]verything was a lie. Each smile hid a yawn of boredom, each joy a curse, each pleasure its aftermath of disgust, and the best of kisses left on your lips only the unattainable desire for a higher delight" (Flaubert 1964, 267).

Charles is guileless, but it would make as little sense to congratulate him for it as it would to praise an infant for avoiding misspellings. In contrast, people who are innocent in the second sense—what one must struggle to attain—do deserve praise for being guileless, because they are capable of dishonesty. Balzac's country doctor is one such case. Monsieur Benassis has known and committed evil deeds, but he turns aside from self-destruction and harming others by sequestering himself in a poor village near Grenoble. He devotes himself to a life of anonymous service to the peasants' welfare, and in time he becomes the mayor of the village—now a prosperous town with triple the original population. The doctor, like the Bishop of Digne in Victor Hugo's *Les Misérables*, is not a dupe. Both are kindness personified, and they know evil. They have fulfilled the biblical injunction (Matthew 10:16) to be as wise as a serpent and as guileless as a dove.[45] Thus the good bishop gratuitously gives Jean Valjean the silver candlesticks to get rid of the gendarmes and even tells a lie to do so. At the same time, he contends for Valjean's soul by claiming—again, falsely—that he had promised "to use this silver to become an honest man" (Hugo 1987, 106). Levinas would surely argue that the doctor and the bishop accepted a responsibility imposed on them in a "privileged heteronomy," and that there is therefore a close connection between the acceptance of that responsibility and achieving the second sense of innocence described above.

For the last several pages we have been reflecting on Levinas' claim that verticality is a necessary condition of non-violative encounters with others, and especially on one premise of that claim, namely, that our responsibility to and for others comes from them rather than streams out from us to them. The view that I want to defend here as most phenomenologically accurate is that verticality is not a necessary condition of non-violative encounters with others, but it is a strong, contributory cause. Levinas' argument, as noted above, rests on two premises. The other premise, that our relationships with the Other are those of pure exteriority, is complicated by the uncertainty noted above about its fate in his later writings. The relationship between the "trace" of the Other within me and alterity is obscure at best. However, it is clear that any meaningful relationship of kindness and justice with a radically Other presupposes what it cannot explain, namely, an explanation of how that Other could break through the enclosure of my self without some cooperative *disponibilité* on my part. Thus Ricoeur is correct to argue against *that* view that what is needed is "the complicity of this movement of effacement by which the self makes itself available to others" (1992, 168), and if I can be complicit with the Other in welcoming her into myself, I cannot be exclusively exterior to the Other to begin with.

On the other hand, perhaps Levinas does not intend to provide us with a complete account of the genesis of intersubjectivity, as Ricoeur apparently takes him to be doing, but only to give us a description of one of its aspects. On this reading, Levinas' purpose would not be to construct intersubjectivity out of verticality but rather presuppose it in order to describe one of its strands. In support of this interpretation, it seems clear that verticality gets relegated to the background in Levinas' discussions of neutrality, commerce, and politics. If this interpretation is correct, it become difficult to see where the difference between Levinas and Ricoeur actually lies.

However this may be, Merleau-Ponty is more nearly correct to insist on the primacy of relatedness, and that the other expresses herself by disclosing her Otherness in and through the dynamics of our mutually intersecting lexicons of corporeity. "A good part of phenomenological or existential philosophy," he tells us, "consists of being astonished at this inherence of me in the world and of me in the other, of describing for us this paradox and this confusion" (1964c, 58). As a result, whatever the conundrums and ambiguities in my greeting the other, and however remote she may seem from me, those conundrums, ambiguities, and remotenesses all rest on, and presuppose, the inseparability of my being and that of the other. "[O]therness is not added on to selfhood from outside . . . [but] belongs instead to the tenor of meaning and to the ontological constitution of selfhood" (Ricoeur 1992, 317).

From this angle, difference is not radical alterity, because what is primary is the connection that supports and makes possible diverse interpretations of the lexicon of the other's corporeity. That is, we can find people remote and difficult to understand not because their being is wholly exterior to our own, but because their behavior consists of unknown or puzzling variations on common themes for which we do not yet have the key, although we are already marked by the "trace" of their presence. We should keep the *experience* of radical alterity an important part of moral experience, for the reasons given by Wild and Emerson, but also recognize that such experiences are parasitic on those of communication and communion.

It follows that Levinas' second premise, his view that responsibility is imposed on us, is not the entire story. He was certainly right to criticize Husserl's attempt to derive alterity from one's own consciousness—otherness from the same. It is also incontestably true that Levinas' account of responsibility does have a basis in experience. There are Levinasian moments *par excellence* in which we come face-to-face with victims of poverty, for example, and when eyes meet and cannot look away, one feels the power of Levinas' appeal to this "privileged heteronomy." Even so, the intimate dialectic of reciprocity between my self and the Other is equally impossible to comprehend exclusively through Levinas' model. Since the Other could not break through my exteriority unless I were complicit in welcoming her, there is already established in me a movement toward the Other of taking responsibility for that Other.

Ricoeur calls this movement "solicitude," and it is rooted in what he calls the "ethical aim of life": "aiming at the 'good life' with and for others, in just institutions" (1992, 172). Solicitude expresses the vector of "for others" in my sense of "self-esteem" that is embedded in this ethical aim. Solicitude is thus internal to self-esteem, because it "unfolds the dialogic dimension of self-esteem . . . self-esteem and solicitude cannot be experienced or reflected upon without the other" (ibid., 180). As a result, there is a dialectic between my own self-esteem and my ability to esteem others, and this creates an equivalence between "the esteem of the *other as a oneself* and the esteem of *oneself as an other*" (ibid., 194).

Ricoeur argues that, even though we have to do justice to Levinas' conception of responsibility (1992, 331), the latter's emphasis on "absolute otherness," with all of the consequences for responsibility that that view entails, "stems from the use of *hyperbole* . . . [i.e.,] the systematic practice of *excess* in philosophical argumentation" (ibid., 337). Perhaps this is so, but it is probably more instructive to contrast Ricoeur's emphasis on self-esteem, the ethical aim of life, and—as we shall see in the next chapter—on friendship, with Levinas' life that was shaped by so much appalling tragedy. I do not say that Ricoeur is unaware of these differences, and still less that he was insensitive to them. Nonetheless, they do not play as significant a role in his criticisms of Levinas as they should. Likewise, *Oneself as Another* does not devote nearly enough attention to those Levinasian moments *par excellence* that demand that we yield to the suffering Other. As a result of these differences, Levinas' view is much closer to that of Jean-François Lyotard (1988), who sees society as divided into plaintiffs and victims, than it is to an Aristotelian picture of solicitude and friendship. For this reason, it is disappointing as well that Lyotard's voice is absent from *Oneself as Another*.

Finally, Levinas is also mistaken in believing that verticality is a necessary condition of non-violative encounters with the Other. He is clearly right to worry about the otherness of the Other being "reabsorbed into my own identity as a thinker or possessor" (1979, 33), and he points to certain crucial experiences in which consciousness can overflow and dominate the Other. Certainly these possibilities are important and pose risks of dehumanization, and we should always be sensitive to the fact that they are frequently, if not always, on the social agenda. Likewise, we should keep in mind that, for Levinas, verticality subtracts nothing from our ability to judge the appeal of the Other and to decline the invitation to help in whatever ways are requested. In other words, verticality by itself does not imply a willingness to, say, subsidize drug addiction or other harmful habits just because we are asked to. Rather, verticality is about the *origin* of the ethical—where and how moral appeals enter our lives. For a phenomenology of kindness, there is a further question of sufficient motivation for being a kind person.

In terms of that motivation, it is crucial to realize that totalitarian temptations are always contingent, and they should not be erected in a general theory of intersubjectivity or morality. They are not primordial and so not that by which intersubjectivity—or intercorporeality, as I would prefer to express it in following Merleau-Ponty's ontology of the flesh—as such can be understood. Hence, the dignity and value of the Other are not necessarily at risk if we decline to adopt Levinas' interlaced views of exteriority, responsibility, and alterity.

Another way to say this is that the question of sufficient motivation to a life of generously warm service to others is an empirical rather than a conceptual claim. As a matter of contingent, empirical fact, there are quintessential Levinasian moments and dangers of totalizing and colonizing actions. There are also many experiences in which we respond to the Other's needs while perceiving her directly as an equal rather than someone given in height. In any event, through solicitude we actively seek her welfare.

However, even if Ricoeur is right, as I think he is, that solicitude is already inscribed in self-esteem and that friendship is its first spontaneous flowering, it remains true that reaching out to the other is vulnerable to all of the temptations of Nietzschean "human, all too human" uses of power. Such actions are also especially liable to the self-deception that afflicts sincere, neurotic do-gooders and other social pests—of which Nietzsche was far from the least skilled analyst. Therefore, it is not enough for a life of personal kindness to rest content with, and leave unexamined, expressions of kindness that originate in the agent's solicitude. Although verticality, even taken as only one strand of intersubjectivity, may not be necessary for a life of personal kindness, it is still a contributory cause. Verticality must be taken seriously as a challenge and checking device to purify the motives behind our desires in intervening in the Other's life.

For all of the differences between the two concepts, this revised conception of verticality has something in common with W. D. Ross' description of a "*prima facie* duty" (1930, 19). It is objective fact rather than subjective perception, non-arbitrary as opposed to being optional. Yet it is a "conditional" duty that may or may not turn out in the circumstances to be an actual duty (ibid., 19–21). To meet the challenge imposed by verticality, the kind person must be actively disposed (in Marcel's sense of *disponibilité*) to be of service to the other whose claims prima facie trump those of the agent. The agent should live "as if" the other were given in height, although so treating the Other is not necessary for personal kindness.

To understand fully how kind persons go about meeting the challenge of refraining from imposing themselves on the other and to maintain a disposition to perceive the other in a position of height, we must consider one other essential characteristic of personal kindness. This is self-restraint, which becomes visible when we turn to the agent's own point of view in doing kind acts, and that is the subject of the next chapter.

Chapter 3

The Agency Of Kindness

Love seeketh not Itself to please,
Nor for itself hath any care,
But for another gives its ease,
And builds a Heaven in Hell's despair.
—William Blake, *Songs of Experience*

Self-Withdrawal

The previous chapter described and illustrated three main qualities essential to being a kind person: habits of doing kind acts, an active disposition to perform them—one's *prêt à servir*—and a warm generosity transcending a perfunctory, "metallic" charity. There is at least one additional characteristic essential to personal kindness, self-withdrawal, which is best described from the agent's own point of view in performing kind deeds. Such a move—in Husserlian language, from the noematic to the noetic—will also enable us to investigate the particular types of feeling bonds that bind us to the Other who is the object of our kind acts, the notion of motivated freedom referred to earlier, and finally, the difficult but crucial topic of the relationship of feeling and judgment inscribed in kindness. The latter subject, in turn, will set the stage for the discussion of social kindness in Chapter 4 and for hermeneutic interpretation in Part 2.

The point of departure for understanding the meaning and necessity of self-withdrawal consists in the fact that acts of kindness, along with many other types of acts, consist of *interventions* in the lives of others. Kind interventions limit themselves to being—the literal meaning of the word—a "coming between" the individuals concerned and the world in which they are attempting to act. This is to say that kind interventions imply some necessary restraint in order to be distinguished from the acts of totalizers and colonizers. As Vincent

Descombes puts it, communication is more than a mere fact. It also "entails certain obligations and constraints" (1993, 26).

We have seen that unkind acts, as well as acts outside the scope of kindness and unkindness completely, do something *to* the other, but do not embody the quality of acting for the other. These may be the acts of, say, an IRS employee conducting an audit, a telephone solicitor, or someone carrying a placard in a political protest. In contrast, when I act for the other, when I intervene in her life for her sake, I take her place in order to help her complete her disrupted projects. My intervention does not make me, as it were, face toward her, but outward with her in the unity of a common project. If I am a kind person, I am actively disposed to be of help—my *prêt à servir*—motivated at best by the positivity of desire as diversely expressed by thinkers such as Levinas, Marcel, and (Werner) Marx.

When I attempt to take the other's place, I engage in what Herbert Spiegelberg called "self-transposal" (1986, 99).[1] Inspired in part by Adam Smith's notion of sympathy, Spiegelberg envisages self-transposal as an act of imaginative consciousness, albeit of a very special type. It is done with the clear recognition of its unreality and literal impossibility. Through "an imaginary rearrangement of reality" (ibid., 100), I pretend to be in the other's place—I willingly suspend my disbelief—so that my imagination can produce "a fiction deliberately flying in the face of the facts" (ibid., 100). I cannot really become the other without leaving off being "I." Thus when I attempt to take the other's place, my failure is already sketched out in advance. Imaginatively, therefore, the Kantian "ought" that implies "can" is inverted: I cannot actually take the other's place, but I ought to anyway.

When I put myself in the other's position, the "place" I attempt to occupy is not a region of objectively measured space and time but rather the other's lifeworld as she perceives it. On the objective side of the phenomena, it is the world and other people, including myself, spatially and temporally organized from the perspective of the other's bodily presence. On the subjective side, what we have to grasp is the other's "network of thinkings and feelings" that ties her to the Lifeworld (Spiegelberg 1986, 101). An actor who assumes many different roles on the stage knows well what such an imaginative connection implies. The accomplished actor who fills various roles is not identical to any of them but rather slips into each with as much grace, delicacy, and with as little artifice as possible. The agent must strive to take up the other's situation and become cognizant of all possible causes of suffering. As Smith puts it, "He must adopt the whole case of his companion, with all its minutest incidents" and describe as closely as possible the "imaginary change of situation upon which his sympathy is founded" (1976, 66).

With some acts of kindness, this is considerably easier than with others. Usually there is no difficulty adopting "the whole case" of someone struggling with crutches and trying to open a door at the same time. In a non-dominating, non-manipulative way, one can slip unobtrusively into the role of facilitating the project of the injured person. There are likewise no difficulties when one finds oneself in the "presence of a noble nature, generous in its wishes, ardent in its charity, [which] changes the lights for us" (Eliot 1965, 819). In *Tess of the D'Urbervilles*, for example, Angel Clare decamps to South America in a snit because of Tess' seduction. But his thoroughly negative view of his bride changes after he comes under the influence of a "large-minded stranger" whose criticisms of Clare were "sublimed by his [the stranger's] death, and influenced Clare more than all the reasoned ethics of the philosophers. His own parochialism made him ashamed in contrast" (Hardy 1978, 422).

Nevertheless, even in simple instances of adopting "the whole case" of another person, there are sometimes ambiguities and surprises. One of the most astonishing in my own experience occurred one winter morning when I was shoveling snow from the walks of an octogenarian neighbor. I could not have believed it possible that he would want to risk broken bones falling down icy steps or a heart attack while shoveling, or that he could even clear his walks (the snow was wet and heavy). Thus his torrent of abuse took me by surprise. His invectives clearly (and colorfully) displayed his belief that I falsely thought him incapable of shoveling for himself. (He later finished the job, very slowly.)

With this class of comparatively simple cases, despite the example of my prickly neighbor, the intervention recommended by the situation is usually obvious. The nonappearance of any contrary reasons for intervening—or, if there are contrary reasons, their comparatively trifling weight in the decision—is phenomenologically significant and often dispositive. But with more complex, ambiguity-laden cases of kindness, it becomes proportionately more difficult to take the other's place. The direction my generosity should take, therefore, becomes unclear; I do not know how, if at all, I should try to help.

One reason for such ambiguities and resultant uncertainties in taking the other's place is that I may not know enough about the person involved to be able to consider the "whole case," and thus the risks of doing harm and causing alienation correspondingly increase. For example, I may discover that an acquaintance is suicidal but gives every indication of being rational, autonomous, and not pressured by some immediate crisis. Or again, I might find out that her fiancé's previous sexual partner is HIV-positive. In each case, I am aware that failure to intervene could be interpreted later, if my knowledge of the facts is discovered, as callousness and cold-heartedness. On the other hand, if my lack of knowledge of the particular individual's beliefs and feelings is substantial enough, my interventions could backfire and cause both moral as well as legal problems.

A second reason for complex ambiguities and uncertainties in certain attempts at self-transposal is that the other, however familiar, can be situated in circumstances with which I do not know how to deal. When, for example, I am attempting for the first time to comfort someone dying, I may be aware of the fact that the sufferer is in denial and is indirectly and enigmatically attempting to get me to reveal the truth. I become acutely aware of the fact that, as Sartre said in another context, every gesture takes on the weight of commitment and that, consequently, one way or another, I will disclose *something*. I become equally cognizant of the agonizing facts that my imagination is too impoverished to allow me to occupy the patient's place, that any dissemblance will certainly be detected and despised and that, consequently, silence is no refuge. I also realize that, if I were to state the truth straightforwardly, it could plunge the patient into the agony of despair.

Care for the dying generates many other types of difficulties in imaginatively taking the place of the other, and these uncertainties have become the staple of well-known dilemmas in biomedical ethics. To take only one of a myriad of examples, should an ER team attempt to resuscitate an elderly patient in danger of dying of a heart attack whose only alternative is a largely non-sapient, vegetative condition?[2] In the absence of any written instructions, how can we be sure that we are taking the patient's position? If the uncertainties are so great, we may believe that the recommended course of action is a principled refusal to speak for the dying. Here our reluctance to act would amount to a concern for the patient rather than indifference, because we wish to avoid doing harm. Yet if we do not act, and the patient is resuscitated, only to be returned to an existence no one would wish, we may be doing harm anyway. That sort of life may be the very sort of existence that the patient wished to avoid at all costs, and may be (or have been) counting on me to save her from it by imagining myself in her unhappy situation.[3]

Unkind people, whether they are Schlick's sort of egoists or Levinas' totalizers, are unable and/or unwilling to act for the welfare of the other through imaginative self-transposal. They are both unconcerned, and totalizers add to that uninterest the wish not merely to take the place of the other but rather to take it over. However, the difficulties involved in morally ambiguous cases of self-transposal also show us that not all cases of such inabilities or unwillingness are instances of unkindness. They become unkind when acting was possible and the failure to act stemmed from indifference or hostility. Harmful consequences only make the experience worse, but they are not necessary for a failure to intervene to be seen as unkind. Even if there had been no Good Samaritan, the robbers' victim may have managed by himself, but his opinion of those who passed by would scarcely have been better.

With this brief sketch of self-transposal and its necessary constraints, we are now in a position to understand the fourth characteristic of personal kindness, that is, self-withdrawal. It is embedded in kind interventions in others' lives in the form of a double self-limitation: a refusal to carry over one's self as well as self-imposed limits on the "occupation" of the other's life. In the refusal to carry over one's self, Spiegelberg's second distinguishing characteristic of self-transposal, it is a question of what is *not* being transposed—my *self*, all of my own values, beliefs, experiences, frame of reference, and the like. All of that mental "baggage"—revealingly, *impedimenta* in Latin—prevents understanding the other as other. The other viewed through the prism of our own mental baggage is precisely the other whom totalizers de-face, the other to whom I do violence. As Spiegelberg phrases it, "[S]uch self-transposals have the character rather of invasions and occupations than of attempts to enter into the world and personality of the other; hence they do not stand a chance of giving us real understanding" (1986, 102).

In these "invasions and occupations," the violated other becomes the object of subtle or obvious coercion. Coercion, however closely it might resemble (mere) persuasion in certain cases, is distinguishably alien and intrusive. As Robert Sokolowski points out, "We are coerced into 'saying' another's 'speech'; his articulation is foisted on us" (1985, 123). It is true that, as we shall see in Part Two, not all coercion is perceived as such and therefore not seen as "intrusive and alien." But there are multiple and diverse instances that are so perceived and with which the contrast with genuine self-transposal is clear.

Consider, for example, parents who wish to relive their childhoods through their children and hence attempt to understand the latter in terms of their own criteria and expectations of happiness. Also, after several residents of Lockerbie were killed by the crash of Pan Am Flight 103, certain London psychotherapists were unhappy when they perceived the televised images of Scottish dour grief. In the absence of a healthy quantity of tears, the former sent psychologists to Lockerbie to teach the Scots how to grieve "properly." On this side of the Atlantic, the film *Dances with Wolves* generated considerable sympathy for Native Americans, the Lakota in particular, at the price of turning the latter into stylized images of whites. The film largely failed to understand cultural variances let alone respect them. It flattened and distorted the relevant differences between Native American and white cultures in order to make the characters resonate more sympathetically with mainstream American movie audiences.

There are also numerous literary examples of those who try to take over the other's place with their own mental baggage. One such case is Gregers Werle. Another is the aggressive colonizing cleric, the Reverend James Smith, in Chinua Achebe's *Things Fall Apart*. His uncompromising rigidity contrasts sharply with his humane, accommodating predecessor, the Reverend Brown, and with Althusser's country priest. Reverend Smith's dogmatic inflexibility led directly to the destruction of the Ibo culture in that sector of Nigeria, for he "saw things as black and white. And black was evil. He saw the world as a battlefield in which the children of light were locked in mortal conflict with the sons of darkness" (1992, 158).[4]

There is also a real-life counterpart of Reverend Smith, the Reverend Wiley Drake. Prosecuted for allowing homeless people to camp in the parking lot of his First Southern Baptist Church in Buena Park, California, he accused that city of intolerance toward the homeless. That charge brought a critical riposte that he himself was intolerant because he supported the boycott against the Walt Disney Company for its practice of providing medical benefits to partners of gay and lesbian employees. Disputing the comparison, Reverend Drake professed great tolerance for homosexuals—even those who might be sleeping in beat-up cars and mobile homes in his church parking lot. He distinguished his attitude toward homosexuals from Disney's, because "he embraced homosexuals with the idea of converting them."[5]

In genuine self-transposal, in contrast, the agent has to divest herself of all of the particular features of her life that are not central to her selfhood. This task of "radical and conscientious abstraction from one's own personality" is clearly difficult. It requires a "negative imagination" (Spiegelberg 1986, 102) which means coming to detach ourselves from the ways we normally live. However, such a move is as necessary for understanding the other as it is difficult. This is because we can fail in that understanding through becoming the other just as much as we can fail through indifference—the absence of meaningful contact. In either case, we would only understand ourselves.

Achebe's *Things Fall Apart* also provides us with an excellent example of failing to understand the other due to egoistic indifference. At the very end of the book, and at its most dramatically intense moment, the author describes the British district commissioner who has just refused to cut down Okonkwo's body from the tree from which he had hanged himself. Okonkwo is the protagonist of the novel, and his fate creates the fulcrum on which the story's action turns. His story *was* the story of his people, the Ibo. The commissioner was "a student of primitive customs" and planned to write a book about his experiences in trying "to bring civilization to different parts of Africa." As he walked back to court from the scene of the suicide, he thought of including Okonkwo in that book. In fact, he concluded that, "One could almost write a whole chapter on him. Perhaps not a whole chapter but a reasonable paragraph, at any rate. There was so much else to include, and one must be firm in cutting out details. He had already chosen the title of the book, after much thought: *The Pacification of the Primitive Tribes of the Lower Niger*" (Achebe 1992, 179).

Self-transposal demands an *appropriate* type of presence as well as absence of self. The totalizer, the colonizer, and the officious do-gooder all provide clear and familiar examples of an inappropriate presence of self, and the uninvolved, coldhearted egoist illustrates the inappropriate absence of self. In contrast, the truly kind person offers us a model of intervening in the lives of others while at the same time refusing to transfer her own mental baggage. Kindness is a way of knowing the other as other, because it requires both closeness and distance, proximity and tactful differentiation, compassionate intervention and appropriate withdrawal. It is what George Eliot described in *Middlemarch* as "self-forgetful goodness" (1965, 538), or what Thomas Hardy has Eustacia Vye wonder at in the unselfish love of the reddleman of *The Return of the Native*: "The reddleman's disinterestedness was so well deserving of respect that it overshot respect by being barely comprehended; and she almost thought it absurd" (1981, 208).

The appropriate presence and absence of self, the core of discretion, is also central to Annette Baier's analyses of trust. Good will, she notes, is not a sufficient condition of trust. Like the do-gooder, those whom we trust can also act with "interfering impertinence" and can betray our trust. For example, "[T]he babysitter who decides that the nursery would be improved if painted purple and sets to work to transform it, will have acted, as a babysitter, in an untrustworthy way, however great his good will" (1986, 236). Such people overstep their bounds that also define the limits of the trust we have in them.

The truly saintly among us may well be spontaneously inclined to an appropriate absence of self in their interventions in the lives of other people—they may not have the smallest desire to transpose all of their mental baggage into those lives. But for most of us, absenting ourselves from our taking other people's places is perceived as an imperative of self-restraint, success at which is a result of effort and discipline in resisting temptation. Its necessity and its usual perception as self-restraint reflect the fact that, as Hume said famously, "[T]here is some benevolence, however small, infused into our bosom; some spark of friendship for humankind; some particle of the dove kneaded into our frame, along with the elements of the wolf and serpent" (1957, 92).

This sense of self-restraint is both different from, and similar to, Aristotle's notion of self-control (*sophrosne*).[6] It is unlike the latter, in that it is not a mean between excess and deficiency in bodily pleasures that we share with other animals. Nor is self-restraint simply a principle of internal self-governance of a well-ordered soul. Like *sophrosne*, however, self-restraint, the appropriate absence of self in acts of kindness, also implies a positive sense of knowing one's own limitations and, as Nietzsche would remember, self-mastery. We shall return to this topic below in the context of practical wisdom.

We have already noticed that, in addition to a refusal to install one's mental baggage in the life of the other, self-withdrawal also consists of self-imposed limits on the "occupation" of the other's life. This aspect of self-withdrawal Spiegelberg takes to be the third distinguishing characteristic of self-transposal, namely, "the position occupied by this self after the performance of the transposal" (1986, 100). After taking up the position of the other, we should remain only for the time required to become acquainted with the way the other perceives her Lifeworld and to become cognizant of the ways that we relate to those perceptions. Furthermore, since we fail to understand the other if we attempt to become that other, it is critical to self-transposal that such cognizance be premised on our maintaining our own position beyond the other while imaginatively shifting back and forth between us.

Thus the first aspect of self-withdrawal, self-restraint from transposing our own selves into the lives of others, forbids us to be totalizers. The second aspect, self-imposed limits on the "occupation" of those lives, enjoins us from being colonizers. "Taking up" the Other's life is not equivalent to, and should not lead to, "taking over" that life. Even so, the temptations and dangers can be great, and recognizing this fact can teach us the socially beneficial lesson of "social humility and respect for others" (Spiegelberg 1986, 104). Certainly an important part of that lesson is that contingency inevitably qualifies self-transposal, and that all interventions in the lives of others, no matter how well intentioned, are unavoidably risky. If, as Malebranche thought, sensations always impinge "respectfully" (Merleau-Ponty 1962, 87), so much cannot be said for human beings, no matter what their intentions.

The necessity and difficulties of self-withdrawal in taking the place of the other also have interesting implications for the nature of virtues such as charity and justice. For example, Philippa Foot points out that some virtues are "corrective" in nature: "As with courage and temperance so with many other virtues: there is, for instance, a virtue of industriousness only because idleness is a temptation; and of humility only because despair too is a temptation" (1978, 9). But virtues such as charity and justice are different, "because they correspond not to any particular desire or tendency that has to be kept in check but rather to a deficiency of motivation; and it is this that they must make good" (ibid., 9).[7]

With kindness and charity, there plainly can be such a deficiency of motivation. However, kindness also corrects a "particular desire or tendency that has to be kept in check," namely, the Humean elements of the "wolf and the serpent." Another way to say this is to grant that "Charity is a virtue of attachment" (Foot 1978, 11), but that it is possible to be attached too much and to remain too long. In the case of such totalization and colonization, the ties no longer merely connect but also violently bind.

There is a particularly common and interesting type of unwillingness or inability to take the place of the other that differs in important ways from those cases already detailed above. It is the phenomenon of self-absorbed indifference referred to in Chapter 2 that prevents us from registering the other's presence. This is a familiar shortcoming, to which we all appear to fall prey at some times in our lives, and some of us at most times. I may, for example, arrive from out of town at a friend's house. It is late, and he has been waiting to eat until my arrival. He believes, falsely, that I have not yet eaten. I am so eager to show him the presents I have brought that I insist on doing so at once. I genuinely care about him, and that is part of the reason I am so eager to share my gifts.

Nevertheless, it does not register that he is desperately hungry, precisely because he has been waiting for me. Or, in a different sort of case, I may be so much taken with an argument I am propounding in a lecture that I do not notice that no one in the class comprehends or is even paying attention.

A famous, real-life instance of self-absorption consisted of an experiment at the Princeton Theological Seminary. Divinity students began the study in one building where questionnaires were filled out, and then they were assigned the task of giving a talk in another building. Some were asked to preach a sermon on the Good Samaritan, while others were asked to talk about what jobs were best for seminarians. The sort of talk and how fast the students were asked to hurry from one building to the next were the independent variables in the study. The experimenters had arranged to have a "victim" slumped in an alleyway through which the students had to walk in order to see how many students would stop to help—the dependent variable in the study. Few students did stop, and the fact that they were going to preach on the Good Samaritan made no difference in their behavior. However, what did make a difference was how much in a hurry they were: "Subjects in a hurry were likely to offer less help than were subjects not in a hurry. Whether the subject was going to give a speech on the parable of the Good Samaritan did not significantly affect his helping behavior on this analysis." Indeed, one seminarian "going to give his talk on the parable of the Good Samaritan literally stepped over the victim as he hurried on his way!"(Darley and Batson 1973, 199, 203).[8]

The failure represented by self-absorption is related to egoistic indifference, but it is also different. First, except for a minority of persons, it is not an enduring character trait but a momentary lapse. Second, in all of the above examples, there is no "cold" indifference. Although indifference to the welfare of others is the net result in each case, none is subtended by indifferent intent. The failure is to implement a concern for others because of another failure to appreciate the facts of the situation. As the examples in Chapter 1 showed, it is not a question of a perceptual failure; ignorance of the facts is not the problem. Rather, it is a matter of having those facts register correctly.

Thus self-absorption does not always imply distraction or modes of attunement to the world, such as fear or anger that can "blind us" so that we do not "see straight." While the seminary students could be distracted from the "victim" by a worrisome assignment and the desire to make a good impression, nothing suggests that they did not see him. After all, one even stepped over him. Also, nothing distracts the lecturer expounding the argument from the uncomprehending class or the guest from her famished hosts.

Rather, the blindness present here is the agent's inability to appreciate the significance of the facts because of that agent's inability to take the place of that Other. As noted in the previous chapter, we wrongly tend to label this failure to register as "thoughtlessness." Self-absorbed consciousness is not empty but rather too full of thought turned inward with the feeling—conscious or not—of self-sufficiency, self-satisfaction, and self-pleasure that masks everything else. The agent is absorbed in the thought of giving friends presents, for example, or introducing students to a certain argument, and it is only in its aftermath that she could guiltily say, "It did not occur to me that . . . ," "I did not realize that . . . ," or "I should have known better." Thus self-absorption represents narcissism, or at least a temptation to it, but of a very particular type. It is rather like Narcissus without a mirror image, as if enjoying more the experience itself than the image reflected. Or, if one prefers, it is as though the experience were self-mirroring and self-completing via the affectlessly present other who provides its occasion and ostensible justification.

This sort of narcissism presents phenomenologists in particular with an interesting phenomenon that is a counter-example to one of their stock-in-trade claims. Consistently since Husserl, they have correctly pointed out that perception gets absorbed in its intentional objects so effortlessly and invisibly that it is difficult to bring to explicit awareness the constitutive activities of consciousness that are presupposed in the experience. Self-absorption is the inverse of this normal state of affairs for the perception of things. It is the centripetal force of self-enjoyment that at first balances, and then overcomes and conceals, the centrifugal force of perception of the other. As a result, the self-absorbed agent sees and does not see, feels and does not feel, touches and does not touch. Reciprocally, the agent's experience of being looked at by the other approaches empty formality, because it is conjugated with self-satiety. This self-satiety is a pleasurable sort of anesthesia, and this anesthesia in turn creates the necessity for an *effort* to develop habits of being at the service of the other. This is just one instance of the fact that, as we shall see at various junctures in this book, there is an intimate connection between unkindness and alienation from the world of feelings.

Viewed from this angle, transcendence of self-absorption provides a very particular illustration of the notion of motivated freedom referred to above and that Paul Ricoeur first detailed in *The Voluntary and the Involuntary* (1966) and reprised most recently in *Oneself as Another* (1992). Let us recall very rapidly here from the former text the well-known triple cycle of reciprocities between the voluntary and the involuntary, in which the involuntary at each level both limits and funds the voluntary, and the voluntary gives shape and definition to the involuntary. In the first cycle of willing, decision, I decide that I shall do something. This decision is reflexive: I decide myself (*je me décide*) at the same time that my will is intentionally directed toward the world. The object of my willing is my project-in-the world, and my voluntary is funded by involuntary motivation. So, for example, I can decide to help the lost stranger or the weakened heart patient, and at the same time, I am deciding the shape of my own existence as someone who is willing to be of service to the other. The object of my willing is the whole ensemble of acts required to be of service, and my motivation may be a positive desire to enhance the other's flourishing.

My intention gets fulfilled in the second cycle of willing, action, in which my "empty" intention to act gets "filled in" through the mediation of the body. The involuntary is present to the willed action, both as obstacles in the world to be dealt with and as bodily resistance that requires effort to overcome it. Thus my act of kindness must negotiate an indifferent or a hostile environment, and I must overcome the resistance of centripetal force to rest content in myself.[9]

Finally, bodily mediation in my projects presupposes the third cycle of willing, consent to necessity, which, for Ricoeur, I can never quite do. "Necessity" here indicates three main facts about my existence that I cannot change. The first is my character—the particular style of my consciousness that differentiates it from everyone else's, and that is the fixed perspective from which all values manifest themselves to me. My unconscious and my life situation are also involved—how I am inevitably limited by where, when, and into what sort of personal and social history I am born. To these three necessities correspond my desires for totality, to overcome the partiality and particularity of my perspective on the world, self-clarity, or transparence—the idol of total self-knowledge—and self-completeness.

We shall return to the theme of character shortly, but let us first see how this phenomenology of the will helps us comprehend the phenomenon of self-absorption present in many cases of unkindness. At the first level of the will, the agent is engaged in some project in the world. That decision can be motivated by a desire to please which, in turn, is a light refracted from the deeper motive of giving herself pleasure. Then decision can give way to action. At this second stage of reciprocity between the voluntary and the involuntary, the act required to complete the project makes certain efforts to mobilize a bodily response to control the particular situation. In this way, the action can get carried forward under the impulse of the motive of self-pleasure present in the first cycle of the will. Depending on how complete the sense of self-satiety, there might also have to be some effort expended in order not to notice the sufferings of the other whom the agent wants to help. This effort in turn may involve unconsciousness at the third level of willing. The third level is also invoked in a very general sort of background sense of my character and unchangeable life situation.

In self-absorption, the will rests content in decision and action with an auto-masking pleasure that recognition of the suffering other cannot penetrate. As described above, the dimensions of the self that comprise communion with, and service to, others, get cloaked behind self-enjoyment. This is a self-enjoyment that can overlap a legitimate sense of pride in doing a good job or, say, smugness. But it is also different from these other senses of self-enjoyment, because it is not, or at least not necessarily, self-congratulatory. It is more nearly the state of being suffused with the pleasures of self.

There are also important implications for kindness in Ricoeur's revised view of character. In *Oneself as Another*, character is defined as "the set of distinctive marks which permit the reidentification of a human individual as being the same" (1992, 119) and "the set of lasting dispositions by which a person is recognized" (ibid., 121). This definition does not repudiate the earlier version, but it includes one significant difference. In the most recent account, the immutability of character is now called into question. This is because of a new emphasis on "the *temporal* dimension of character" that allows for "acquired dispositions" (ibid., 120). Acknowledging Aristotle's discussion of character (*êthos*) and habit (*éthos*), Ricoeur depicts acquired dispositions based on habits "being formed" as well as those "already acquired" (ibid.). He also analyzes dispositions in terms of "acquired identifications" (ibid., 121) through which we merge our identities with our communities in various ways. In so doing, some degree of loyalty gets embedded in character and points it toward "fidelity" and "maintaining the self" (ibid.).

One important implication of acquired dispositions is that they authorize us to supplement the claim in the last chapter that some people have more of a disposition to kindness than do others. Now we can say that even those less inclined to any "fellow feeling" can, at least up to a point, acquire contrary dispositions. In this regard, Scrooge is simply an extreme case of what is possible for all of us through more mundane sources of motivation. This is why, on the one hand, Sidgwick argues correctly the Kantian position that "it cannot be a strict duty to feel an emotion" of love or kindness to the degree that "it is not directly within the power of the Will to produce it at any given time" (1913, 239). One obstacle is the fact that, "some men are naturally so unattractive to others that the latter can feel no affection, though they may entertain benevolent dispositions, toward the former" (ibid.). Some real-life attitudes toward the obese, as well as fictional reactions to Dr. Frankenstein's creation, are cases in point, though without "benevolent dispositions." However, Sidgwick also rightly tells us that we have a duty to try anyway to perform kind actions toward the unattractive until we determine the effort to be "fruitless" (ibid.). The reason is that such acts raise "the mere beneficent disposition of the will to a higher degree of excellence" and make it more effective (ibid.).

A corollary of Sidgwick's observations is that kindness and duty are not necessarily disjuncts. As a regulative ideal, at any rate, kindness can be commanded and expected. This is not to deny that kindness and duty can sometimes be mutually incompatible and that, as already noted, it is sometimes difficult to tell whether a given action is one of kindness, duty, or both. This is particularly true in contexts where special relationships already create a probability of acting out of duty. So, for example, in *Nervous Conditions*, Tambudzai, the protagonist, is a poor country relation of her well-to-do uncle, Babamukuru. She goes to live with him, and she sees him as doing her a great kindness in finding her a job. But Babamukuru's daughter tells Tambudzai that she "had misjudged the situation. It was the obligation of all decent people in positions like Babamukuru's to do such things" (Dangarembga 1988, 159). The succeeding discussion leaves it open as to whether he acted out of duty, kindness, or both. Additional perplexities exist at the level of social justice, and we shall discuss those in Chapter 5.

It follows from Sidgwick's twin claims that acquiring dispositions itself involves all three levels of Ricoeur's earlier stages of reciprocity between the voluntary and the involuntary. An intention fulfills itself through decision, which also decides the shape of the freedom of the agent. Action struggles against bodily inertia, which perhaps implicates an unconscious, involuntary resistance. Likewise, since the formation of new dispositions is never a matter of purely voluntary decision making, it is not something that can be forced and shaped exclusively through commands or other similar interventions. This is why, for example, in James' *A Portrait of a Lady*, Ralph Touchett tells his cousin, Isabel Archer, "Don't try so much to form your character—it's like trying to pull open a tight, tender young rose" (James 1986, 273–74). People do not develop dispositions to kindness through willpower, decision making, and conscience alone but also under the influence of different types of possible motivations and through doing kind acts that eventually sediment themselves in this habitual character trait.

Fellow-Feeling: Empathy and Identification

Self-transposal and its necessary complement of self-withdrawal are also crucial in understanding the feeling bonds uniting the kind person with others. To understand these types of "fellow-feeling," we shall look first at some helpful and largely forgotten[10] distinctions borrowed from Max Scheler and Edith Stein. Together they will enable us to grasp what kind of feeling connections with the other can and cannot underwrite a life of kindness.

For Scheler, there are four main types of feeling that are often construed as fellow-feeling. The first is an "immediate community of feeling, e.g., of one and the same sorrow, 'with someone'" (1954, 12). For example, two parents can share the same joy (or sorrow) at their daughter's wedding or the same anguish over the body of their dead son. This "highest form of fellow-feeling" (ibid., 13) is non-sensory; it is limited to mental pain, because two people cannot share the same physical pain or sensory sensation.

In this first type of feeling, the suffering of one person and the sympathy of the other are joined together in one fact. In the second type, in contrast, suffering or rejoicing, and sympathy, are two distinct facts, and in the experience itself they are perceived as distinct. This is genuine "fellow-feeling 'about something'; rejoicing in his joy and commiseration with his sorrow" (ibid., 12). What one feels vicariously and participation in the other's feeling "are separately given and must be sharply distinguished" (ibid., 13, 14).

The third sort of feeling is "mere emotional infection" (ibid., 12). This is what happens when someone's grief provokes me to tears, or when I catch the contagion of laughter and start to laugh myself. Or, in a very different sort of case, consider Dickens' savage comment in *Hard Times*: "It was one of the most exasperating attributes of Bounderby, that he not only sang his own praises but stimulated other men to sing them. There was a moral infection of clap-trap in him" (1995, 49). For Scheler, emotional infection is not fellow-feeling at all, but their frequent confusion is responsible for a number of misguided genetic theories of fellow-feeling.[11] It is not genuine fellow-feeling, because there is no intentional directedness of feeling toward grief or joy of the other, and no participation in it. This is only an involuntary "transference of the *state* of feeling, and does *not* presuppose any sort of *knowledge* of the [for instance] joy which others feel" (Scheler 1954, 15).

There is, finally, authentic "emotional identification" (ibid., 12). This is the "act of identifying one's own self with that of another"; it is "only a heightened form, a limiting case as it were, of [emotional] infection" (ibid., 18). The limit is formed by the fact that, in this type of feeling, it is not simply the other's feeling that is appropriated, but "his self (in all its basic attitudes), that is identified with one's own self. Here too, the identification is as involuntary as it is unconscious" (ibid.).

Schopenhauer, for example, writes that the suffering of another person's moving me "necessarily presupposes that, in the case of his *woe* as such, I suffer directly with him, I feel *his* woe just as I ordinarily feel my own. . . . But this requires that I am in some way *identified with him.*" This is "*compassion,*" "immediate *participation* . . . in the *suffering* of another . . . that is the real basis of all *voluntary* justice and *genuine* loving-kindness" (1965, 143–44; emphasis in original). However, to say, "I feel *his* woe just as I ordinarily feel my own"—just as some politicians today say vainly (in both senses), "I feel your pain"—is much more like Scheler's sense of "emotional identification" than it is genuine "fellow-feeling" or, as we shall see, what Stein characterized as "empathy."

Authentic fellow-feeling embraces the other "as part of the object of commiseration or rejoicing" (Scheler 1954, 39), while at the same time keeping her and her experiences distinct from the person commiserating. True fellow-feeling grasps the other's feeling of, say, joy or grief, without getting into a joyful or sorrowful state itself (ibid., 42). This is why emotional identification and emotional infection can motivate one to perform a kind act, but they cannot provide any relationship with the other as other. Fellow-feeling is not emotional fusion. Persons, Scheler points out correctly, are "concrete centres of spiritual activity" (ibid., 75), not extensions of our own identities. Hence, the pity and compassion on which Marx rested his ethics[12] must likewise keep distinct boundaries between the self and the other.

Because the other is not another myself, the fact that she is like me is not a necessary (or sufficient) condition of my establishing fellow-feeling with her. True fellow-feeling is also possible with people from very different states in life. Thus Scheler points out that the Buddha gave up a life of wealth and luxury in the face of sickness and poverty in order "to discern and respond to all the pain and misery of the world" (ibid., 50). Similarly, our own lives provide evidence of, as Butler and Hume knew well, "a rhythmic alternation between the closed and the open viewpoint, between self-regarding aloofness and sympathetic interest in the lives of other people" (ibid.), many situated very differently than we.

Scheler does not discuss the difficulties for fellow-feeling involved in appreciating difference, such as the obstacles to *disponibilité*, described in the previous chapter, although there is no reason he could not acknowledge them. For every Buddha, there are thousands of people insulated in lives of privilege and wealth who, like Mr. Wilcox in *Howards End*, cannot come to see the poor as anything better than social nuisances. (Their usual response is to tell them to cut it out and get back to work.) This is one reason, as noted in the Introduction, politicians have been so successful in demonizing the poor. More generally, for every rare individual who can break down obstacles of racism, sexism, and homophobia, there are countless others incapable of it.

Scheler is also right that love and hate are not just responses to established values. Rather, they are "acts in which the value-realm accessible to the feeling of a being . . . is either *extended* or *narrowed*" (1973, 261). The act of love is a creative one, because it extends that value-realm to new, higher, and heretofore unknown values. The ability of the other to interrupt a person's life in this manner means then also the capacity "to generate unforeseen responses and to pry open her self-contained existence [that] points to a lively wellspring of fresh value disclosure" (Barber 1993, 100). This is to say that those who really lay themselves open to those who are different simultaneously commit themselves to a piety of action, rather than just of thinking, by learning from them rather than by dominating or dismissing them. Conversely, those who hate have their value-realms and range of appreciation of others contracted and their own being correspondingly diminished. If the news reports were correct, Barber's observation about hate aptly characterizes the killers at Columbine High School in Littleton, Colorado.

Just now, for instance, I am looking at another especially vile example of such value contraction—one that Edith Stein would find especially poignant and painful. It is a photograph of a shop window spray-painted with a lurid red Nazi swastika and the words "Juda verrecke" (roughly, "All the Jews should be exterminated"). The shop belongs to an uncle of an Austrian friend who sent me the photograph. She also sent me a variety of Nazi propaganda leaflets routinely affixed to the windshield of her car. But the photograph and propaganda date from 1987, not 1937. The obstacles to appreciating difference can indeed be formidable. Social conditioning steeped in suspicion, ignorance, distrust, and prejudice can destroy kindness at the root. However, it is also true that, where a small part of the root survives, great courage can be required to break through all of the barriers to realize an enriched life of kindness.[13]

Stein's On the Problem of Empathy (1964), a source of some of Scheler's revisions of The Nature of Sympathy (1954), provides us with an approach to fellow-feeling that is both similar to that taken by the latter text and also different from it. She agrees with Scheler's criticisms of an immediate community of feeling, emotional infection— which she calls "the contagion or transference of feeling" (Stein 1964, 22)—and true emotional identification as modes of knowing the other qua other. At the same time, she describes empathy (Einfühlung)[14] in much the same way that Scheler did fellow-feeling (Mitgefühl), or sympathy, and for her, fellow-feeling provides an experience of oneness that Scheler reserved for emotional identification.

What is most relevant to kindness in Stein's work is as follows. First, she sets out to account for empathy within a Husserlian framework of one ego coming into contact with another. This framework is inadequate for understanding how I live in the world with the other,[15] but that limitation does not diminish the philosophical value of her descriptions of empathy for understanding kindness. In empathy, as she sees it, I have a "non-primordial experience which announces a primordial one" (1964, 14). More exactly, "If I experience a feeling as that of another, I have it given twice: once primordially as my own and once non-primordially in empathy as originally foreign [i.e., not mine]" (ibid., 33). For example (Stein's), suppose someone reports passing an important examination. I can vicariously share her primordial joy as an experience she is having, but I am also given it as her experience, not mine. The object of my joy is not the other's joy, but (in the above example) the passing of the examination over which she is joyful. Empathy makes this feeling of oneness possible, and not the other way around.

Empathic experience, for Stein, creates a "we" as the subject of the experience. But at the same time—as in self-transposal for Spiegelberg and fellow-feeling for Scheler— the boundaries between the "I" and the other necessarily remain intact: "Not through the feeling of oneness, but through empathizing, do we experience others" (Stein 1964, 17). As we have already seen, we cannot understand others when we try to become them. Empathic connection with the other's experience does not and cannot mean appropriating that experience as our own.[16] In contrast, Spiegelberg once expressed one of the clearest examples of empathy when he scribbled on a file folder: "Empathy: Triumph of a Translator." The translator establishes a real connection with the author but understands her thought and words as hers, not as the translator's.

Kindness, like all forms of knowing the other as other, embodies and requires intelligently purposive feelings that conjugate similarity with difference, closeness with distance, proximity with tactful differentiation, unity with diversity, and compassionate intervention with appropriate withdrawal. Both halves of the dialectic are inscribed in empathy that, in our chiasmatic relationships with the other, is the crucial epistemological hinge on which kindness turns. As noted above, Stein situates her account of empathy within a Husserlian conception of consciousness as well as Husserl's distinction between the body as object (*Körper*) and one's own body (*Leib*), or flesh. Merleau-Ponty's ontology of flesh provides a foundation for this distinction and for empathy itself as one way in which the body's "corporeal schema" creates the fact that we are all "moments of the same syntax, we count in the same world, we belong to the same Being" (Merleau-Ponty 1968, 83). In empathic experience, self-transposal modulates activity and passivity as it moves between one half of the chiasm and the other. It does not follow, of course, that to say that the other's sensorality is implied in one's own implies that what is expressed is free of ambiguity or is self-interpreting. On the contrary, there is still work for consciousness to do in bringing their meanings to light, and as we shall now see, this interpretive work requires various types of judgments about others.

Judgment

Some people are persuaded that a deep sense of empathy for another's sorrow or joy and the acts of kindness that flow from that empathy preclude judgments about the other person's state of affairs. For example, Carol Gilligan and Grant Wiggins write that compassion, in the sense of "co-feeling," "depends on the ability to *participate* in another's feelings (in their terms), signifying an attitude of engagement rather than an attitude of judgment or observation" (1988, 122). Judgments in such cases are said to take on the appearance of intolerable intrusion in performing acts of kindness. Also, certain individuals are committed to a literal and an uncritical reading of the scriptural admonition to not judge in order to escape judgment themselves (Matthew 7:1), and from this nostrum they draw the conclusion that kindness and judgment are contradictories.

William H. Willimon, for example, a Methodist minister writing in *The Christian Century*, describes an ethics of kindness as limited to sincerity and good intentions, indifferent to the harm that our actions may involuntarily cause. "There was a time," he maintains, "when Christians wanted to be obedient and faithful. Lately we are content to be sensitive. Once we aspired to justice and righteousness. Our present ethical concern is that we be kind" (1982,

447). "The ethics of kindness," which he wishes to reject, "represents, for many of us, the slogans of our old Protestant pietism at their subjective worst: It Doesn't Matter What You Believe or What You Do as Long as You Are Sincere" (Ibid., 449). Thus kindness in Willimon's view, can allow or even encourage me to "pursue my illusions of self-interest [that] may inflict untold cruelty on others" (ibid., 449). Within an ethics of kindness, judgment, reflecting objective justice, equals cruelty, and so, "If kindness alone were enough, there would have been no cross" (ibid.).

Nevertheless, it is a serious confusion to hold that judgment is necessarily inconsistent with empathy and/or kindness. Empathy in fact requires judgment; it is not pure feeling. For one thing, there is no pure feeling devoid of all cognitive aspects—as Gestalt psychology has long since shown by a variety of experimental and experiential evidence. But even if we waive this point, empathy would require some types of judgment to be distinguished from emotional infection or identification. These types would include those involved in bracketing one's own frame of reference while opening oneself up to a foreign point of view. This opening up in turn presupposes interpretive judgments about that other person's Lifeworld and how that particular individual perceives it.

Equally importantly, however, if we really want to help other people, different types of judgments are necessary to supplement empathic understanding by assessing the *appropriateness* of another's joy, sorrow, anger, anxiety, and so on. This is why, for example, Emerson argued that friendship demands sincerity and a willingness to antagonize instead of just being a sycophant: the friend must "not cease an instant to be himself. The only joy I have in his being mine, is that the *not mine* is *mine*. . . . Better be a nettle in the side of your friend than his echo" (1937, 114). Similarly, Kant claimed that, "Morally considered, it is certainly one's duty to point out a friend's faults to him, for this is to his best interests and thus is a duty of love" (1964b, 136). Compassionate, kind response is based on reason, as well as on feeling, which, as the Dalai Lama points out, makes responsibility to and for another possible (1990, 121).

However, Kant goes too far when he adds that the corrected friend "sees therein a lack of the respect which he expects; and he believes either that he has already fallen in the former's respect or, since he is watched by him and secretly criticized, that he is in constant danger of losing it" (1964b, 136). This may or may not be true: the context is crucial. The friend's "watching" may amount to spying or protective oversight. The friend's secret criticisms may be made to others—behavior probably already inconsistent with friendship—or to the corrected party. Criticism by itself does not equal disrespect or lack of affection.[17] Also, it is one thing if the criticism is vicious and destructive but quite another if it is offered in a helpful, constructive way.

Adam Smith, with his notion of the "judicious spectator," has shown two ways that rational judgments function to supplement "sympathy" (empathy). In both cases, "sympathy" requires judgments about the reasonableness of the other's feelings. On the one hand, we can, via imaginative fancy, have a feeling that the other person does not have, but should have. For example, "We blush for the impudence and rudeness of another, though he himself appears to have no sense of the impropriety of his own behavior; because we cannot help feeling with what confusion we ourselves should be covered, had we behaved in so absurd a manner" (1976, 50). On the other hand, people can have certain feelings and be mistaken about the appropriateness of those feelings, and we cannot help by sympathizing with them. "If we hear a person loudly lamenting his misfortunes, which, however, upon bringing the case home to ourselves, we feel, can produce no such violent effect upon us, we are shocked at his grief; and, because we cannot enter into it, call it pusillanimity and weakness" (ibid., 57)[18] (whiners, take note).

To these claims Levinas might reply that at least some forms of judgment that filter the demands of responsibility imposed on me by the other constitute an invitation to totalization and colonization. From this angle, imposing judgment would be seen as a potential violation of, and violence done to, the other given in height. As noted in Chapter 2, Levinas does point out that I have the freedom to decide what to do with the appeal that the suffering other makes to me. Negative judgments are possible and sometimes legitimate responses. But what I think he would be worried about are filtering judgments that block that original appeal. Intolerance and prejudice provide ample examples and, as we have seen, the absence of any such filtering judgment was what Frederick Douglass most appreciated about Robert Ingersoll.

Similarly, Marcel might well see judgment as inextricably linked to objective, calculational thought that treats the other as object rather than as Thou. As we have seen, for Marcel, this view of human existence is not logically necessarily dehumanizing, but as a matter of contingent, empirical fact, it almost always is. Correlatively, at its best, such treatment of human beings fails to rise above a Kantian morality of general rules and duties that cannot find room for, or value, the *disponibilité* and creative fidelity essential to celebrating human being and being human. For this, as we have seen, what we need is a mode of thought that is close to Heidegger's conception of *Gelassenheit*.[19]

As an initial response to Levinas and Marcel, it is undeniable that there are judgments that are alienating, divisive, unkind, and inconsistent with empathy, because they block us from imaginatively taking the position of another person. In fact, there are at least six prominent, closely related types of such judgments. Perhaps most obviously, there are judgments made in the face of overwhelming need and suffering. One feels that there is literally no place for such judgments, that they constitute a grossly inappropriate response to the evidence. For example, one would be hard pressed to imagine a contemporary Good Samaritan standing by the broken, bleeding victim of an automobile accident or a mugging and making any judgments about whether the victim merited intervention. The sheer facticity of the suffering not only underscores this fact but also provides a rationale for "Bad Samaritan" laws in Continental legal systems.[20]

Second, there are judgments that convey insincerity and unavailability through the metallic charity referred to in Chapter 2, or what E. M. Forster once referred to as "mechanical cheerfulness" (1985, 112) and "barbed civilities" (1986, 14). Such judgments are embedded in empty, hypocritical social forms, among other places, of which we get an excellent picture in Isabel Archer's husband deceitfully engaging with her former suitor, Lord Warburton: "Nothing could have been more adequate, more nicely measured, than his courtesy to his wife's old friend. It was punctilious, it was explicit, it was everything but natural" (James 1986, 432).

Third, there are judgments that reflect decisions to follow rules with no accompanying sensitivity to the demands of the context of the action. Sometimes "going by the book" does have its value—for instance, when it is reasonable to lack confidence in alternative strategies with high stakes at serious risk. There is, after all, usually a good reason(s) for having a "book" in the first place. But from the point of view of kindness, blind obedience to the principle that "rules are rules" invites disaster. As John Lachs notes, moral reasoning is more offensive when it is abstract than when it is simply in error. For abstraction practically ensures error "by missing the human predicament that needs to be addressed, and worse, it is a sign that thought has failed to keep faith with its mission" (1994, 10).

Among other things, this principle inverts the importance of rules and persons subject to them and blinds actors to specific, context-dependent facts that practical wisdom must keep in view. Thus George Eliot observed correctly that moral judgments are empty and false in the absence of continual reference to individual, living circumstances: "All people of broad, strong sense have an instinctive repugnance to the men of maxims. . . . [Practical wisdom demands] a life vivid and intense enough to have created a wide fellow-feeling with all that is human" (1985, 628).[21] Likewise, Ricoeur notes that when respect for the law and respect for persons collide, practical wisdom may demand, allowing the latter to outweigh the former "in the name of the solicitude that is addressed to persons in their irreplaceable singularity" (1992, 262). This is certainly one lesson of Shakespeare's *Measure for Measure* and, in *The Merchant of Venice*, of Portia's counsel to Shylock that "[E]arthly power doth then show likest God's when mercy seasons justice" (1975, 222, Act IV, Scene 1).

Fourth, there are the *negative* judgments of the judicious spectator that, in the pursuit of truth and justice, are apparently inconsistent with kindness, and even with empathy—possibilities that Smith and Nussbaum do not discuss or perhaps even recognize. Spouses in divorce and domestic violence proceedings, for example, may correctly believe that acts of kindness toward the abuser, and even attempts to achieve an empathic understanding of him or her, will conflict with their legitimate self-interests and claims for justice.

The Mill on the Floss contains two different types of examples of such judgments. In the first case, Tom Tulliver upbraids his sister Maggie for her unwise behavior. Maggie ashamedly recognizes the truth of the judgment: "There was a terrible cutting truth in Tom's words—that hard rind of truth which is discerned by unimaginative, unsympathetic minds" (Eliot 1985, 504). In the second example, Mr. Tulliver loses a foolish lawsuit and his home, and in the wake of total ruin, "[T]here was a general family sense that a judgment had fallen on Mr. Tulliver, which it would be an impiety to counteract by too much kindness" (ibid., 279). Here the judgment is recognized as normative, and kindness—at least "too much" of it—would present itself as an attempt to escape justice.[22]

Fifth, there are judgments that reduce their objects to mere fungibility, one of Nussbaum's senses of objectification. One type, which has nothing to do with injustice, nevertheless can conflict with kindness in a different fashion. Consider, for instance, purported privileged relationships in which one party disappointingly treats the other in the same way she does anyone else. Tambudzai, in *Nervous Conditions*, depressively reflects that her uncle's kindness did not make her "anything special," for he would have been just as charitable to any poor relation, and she was the beneficiary of his largesse just because of their different economic strata (Dangarembga 1988, 65). Thus she perceives herself as substitutable for any of Babamukuru's impoverished relatives.

The sixth and most complex type of judgment that conflicts with empathy and kindness is that which, in a variety of ways, expresses, or at least suggests, inappropriate claims of superiority. Some of these inappropriate judgments reflect objectifications that, in Marcel's sense, privilege "having" over "being." A graphically clear example appeared recently on the front page of *The New York Times*:

Watching classmates strut past in designer clothes, Wendy Williams sat silently on the yellow school bus, wearing a cheap belt and rummage-sale slacks.

One boy stopped and yanked his thumb, demanding her seat.

"Move it, trailer girl," he sneered."[23]

Other examples of these unjustified judgments of power over inferiors involve "gaming" in the sense of Eric Berne's manipulative scenarios illustrated in *Games People Play* (1964). The full force of gaming is felt when we encounter its rare absence, as in the reddleman's disinterestedness or in the elder Mr. Emerson, a paragon of kindness in Forster's *A Room with a View*. The Reverend Beebe says, "He has the merit—if it is one—of saying exactly what he means. . . . It is so difficult—at least, I find it difficult—to understand people who speak the truth (Forster 1986, 10).

There is also Foucault's account in *The Birth of the Clinic* and elsewhere of the politics of the body that gets medically reduced to a number of interpretive schemes, plus the all-too-well-known interactions with physicians in which patients are seen as organs, symptoms, or systems and never acknowledged as persons.[24] Likewise relevant here are physicians' judgments that refuse to distinguish between disease—the objective bodily pathology—and illness, how the patient lives the disease (Kleinman 1988; Toombs 1987, 1988). Typical results include invalidating entirely the patients' Lifeworld perspectives in favor of pharmacological solutions to their problems and, as we shall see in the following chapter, medical practitioners being seduced by their own technology to pursue the riddle of the cure at the cost of needless pain and suffering in their patients.

Another kind of judgment that expresses superiority to those perceived as inferiors is that which gave rise to "politically correct" language. The deliberate use of non-inclusive language is an obvious case in point. Also, although it is wrong to substitute "challenged" for "handicapped," for the reasons given in Chapter 1, it is equally mistaken to refer to someone as "handicapped" if that word is meant to imply an irrebuttable presumption of a general inability to compete with the rest of the population.[25]

There are also judgments made *in situ* that focus undesirably on a given individual's disability. Such ill-advised judgments fail to appreciate the nature of the context and so end in poisoning kindness at the root. This is what happens, for example, in D. H. Lawrence's *Sons and Lovers*, when the well-intentioned Clara returns to Jordan's and encounters the female employees in her department who did not like her managerial style. She criticizes all but one of them, "coolly and with perfect politeness." Her single exception was a cripple, Fanny, and with her she "was unfailingly compassionate and gentle, as a result of which Fanny shed more bitter tears than ever the rough tongues of the other overseers had caused her" (1982, 263). This example links the distinction between challenges and handicaps and that between kindness and gentleness. For surely Fanny or any real-life counterpart would perceive such gentleness as patronizing and would much rather be seen as challenged and expected to meet those challenges as best she could. Therefore Fanny perceived Clara's actions as rubbing the salt of singular attention and special treatment into the wound of her own lack of able-bodiedness.

This fictional scenario contrasts strikingly with certain types of kind omissions to act that we also studied in Chapter 1. There we found that a cardiac patient, for example, may be struggling at rehabilitation, and others may witness her fear, tenuous motility, and diminished energy. When others see, but pointedly do not notice or comment, the patient becomes aware of their recognition and also of their kind omissions to call attention to it. Their not speaking is not egoistic indifference but rather an effort to bolster the patient's self-esteem to keep the bonds of intersubjectivity from being disrupted any further.

There are other types of judgments that falsely express superiority in equally well-known ways. For instance, we can debase the giving of gifts by embedding in the act assumptions of moral superiority. In Eliot's *Middlemarch*, for instance, Dorothea gives her sister, Celia, their mother's jewelry, because she (Dorothea) views it as morally corrupting. Celia is hurt by the "strong assumption of superiority in this Puritanic toleration" (Eliot 1965, 35). Some other expressions of false superiority are manifestations of pity masquerading as consolation to the vanquished—a hypocrisy of which Nietzsche was an unexcelled critic. Thus in *Middlemarch*, Mrs. Plymdale, whose son's offers of marriage Rosamond had rejected in favor of Dr. Lydgate's, rejoiced that her son had made a better match. Given this superiority, "Mrs Plymdale's maternal view was, that Rosamond might possibly now have retrospective glimpses of her own folly; and feeling the advantages to be at present all on the side of her son, was too kind a woman not to behave graciously" (ibid., 703). In these types of cases, as Ricoeur says in another context, "a sort of equalizing occurs, originating in the suffering other, thanks to which sympathy is kept distinct from simple pity, in which the self is secretly pleased to know it has been spared" (1992, 191). Sympathy here is "distinct from simple pity," but they are still intertwined to the degree that Mrs. Plymdale's pity is conjugated with revenge.

Other such alienating judgments originate in the look. In Richard Wright's *Native Son*, for example, Jan and Mary look at Bigger Thomas in ways that make him self-conscious about being Black. Bigger's reaction to this unwanted, gratuitous inspection was "a dumb, cold, and inarticulate hate" (1993, 76). Another clear example of an alienating look, which also embodies a case of pity (mixed with revenge) masquerading as compassion, occurs in Dickens' *Hard Times*, when Mrs. Sparsit pities Bounderby's choice of a wife by means of a destructive tenderness. Her very politeness and cheerfulness rub it in: "She had that tenderness for his melancholy fate, that his great red countenance used to break out into cold perspirations when she looked at him" (1995, 109).

Other alienating judicial looks occur independently of pity and even of compassion. One type can express a desire to measure and improve the object of those looks. We can have a "moral lantern" turned on us, as Eliot phrases it, but, "If you are not proud of your cellar, there is no thrill of satisfaction in seeing your guest hold up his wine-glass to the light and look judicial" (1965, 151). What Henry James called "stern justice" (1986, 133) is not what we seek in the other's gaze.[26]

Such judgments lead to the most deeply alienating type of all, namely, the judgment that does not merely leave us wanting but also finds us wanting. This type of judgment strikes at our sense of self-worth. One instructive example of the depths of such alienation occurs toward the end of Brontë's *Jane Eyre*. The protagonist's spurned suitor, St. John Rivers, casts on her much more than a mere judicial look, which signaled that he would never forget her words of rejection. He also bestows extra kindnesses on his sisters as a weapon to punish Jane, as though he were worried that "mere coldness" would not suffice to convey his displeasure (Brontë 1966, 437). In the face of such judgments and tactics, he appears to Jane as literally inhuman, "no longer flesh, but marble" (ibid., 436). As Ricoeur notes, "What is called humiliation—a horrible caricature of humility—is nothing else than the destruction of self-respect, beyond the destruction of the power-to-act" (1992, 220).

Such are, in brief summary, some of the main ways in which judgments can be alienating and divisive and hence block empathy and kindness from taking root. However, it still does not follow that all judgments must be this way, or that kindness and empathy do not require any judgments. As noted at the beginning of this section, there are many cases of judgments that are both consistent with empathy and kindness and essential to their proper functioning. It is not so much that a literal adherence to not judging would produce "an impoverished moral philosophy," as Michael Moore has stated (1987, 188), but rather no moral philosophy at all. We have already seen that, and how, benign manipulations can be necessary to perform acts of kindness. Such manipulations require judgments embedded in the calculational thought behind the strategies for such acts, as well as various judgments about what is, or seems to be, in the person's best interest while empathetically taking her point of view. One obvious function of such judgments, as noted above, is to distinguish between short-term benefits and long-term harms—as, for example, when we refuse to give an addict money for another hit or when employers decline to turn a blind eye to employees' drug use.

Sometimes failure to make such necessary judgments is attributable to the desire for self-gratification as much as it is to ignorance of the consequences. In these cases, caring for others turns into an imitation of the Los Angeles priest, Father Maurice Chase, whom the news media have described as "the minister of dollar handshakes." He attempted to help the poor on Skid Row by giving them a dollar bill along with a handshake. As one social worker described it, this mode of care "does nothing for the people but does a lot for Father Chase" (Wuthnow 1991, 105–106).

Moreover, a given individual can sometimes transcend her own suffering to consider impartially the other person's refusal to satisfy immediately her desires, and thus see the appropriateness of the other person's judgment (s) that led to that decision. For example, during one of Louis Althusser's psychiatric hospitalizations, his doctor refused to grant all of his requests or to yield to the "sometimes extravagant requests" from his friends to accord his famous patient special privileges. Althusser tells us that his physician "always stuck to principles he had adopted and never deviated . . . I considered his position both fair and unassailable" (1993, 266).

Judgments are also required to help troubled people work through problems of self-esteem and, in a Kantian sense, self-respect. These judgments include both those made about such people in our roles of judicious spectators as well as judgments we think it reasonable for those individuals to make about themselves and their Lifeworlds. For example, certain people are in therapy, and still others are in need of therapy, because of unjustifiably low senses of self-esteem attributable to their inability or unwillingness to make judgments that others are the source of their problems, and not they themselves.[27] They are so determined to think well of everyone—and not judge—that they falsely berate themselves for illusory failings. It has long been debated whether we have duties to ourselves, but it seems incontestable that we can be both kind and unkind to ourselves. As Montaigne observed, contempt for our lives "is ridiculous. . . . It is a malady peculiar to man, and not seen in any other creature, to hate and disdain himself" (1958, II:3, 254).

Conversely, some people, such as Mr. Tulliver in *The Mill on the Floss*, need the benefit of our judgments in order to help them accept responsibility for their actions. "There are people," Jane Austen tells us, "who the more you do for them, the less they will do for themselves" (1966, 115). In this light, let us observe that, although "politically correct" language, as noted above, does have the merit of avoiding giving gratuitous offense, such language is also abusive when it prevents, or tends to prevent, the assumption of responsibility. That is, it is one thing to say that a person is "auditorially inconvenienced" instead of "deaf," or "chronologically dated" in place of "old," but it is quite another thing to call someone "a client of the correctional system" instead of a "prisoner,"[28] or "chemically inconvenienced" instead of "stoned"(!).[29]

Finally, judgments are also necessary for kindness to underwrite a practical wisdom as an alternative to a Kantian morality of rules and to George Eliot's "men of maxims" generally. As Dr. Kay Holt writes of physician-assisted suicide:

> There are no easy solutions. Anyone who can easily take one side has probably never really dealt directly with an actual situation of a child or an adult who is suffering terribly, but is not going to die within minutes or hours. Fixed, rigid opinions about whether it is right or wrong to assist our patients in alleviating suffering are of little value." (Holt 1994, 23)

Such wisdom is intelligent and purposive. It is also, as described above, empathetically imaginative, judiciously speculative, and it requires calculative thought to accomplish its aims. It does not reduce to casuistry but rather provides space for rules that it both incarnates and supplements with an *inventive charity* that is context sensitive.[30] It describes a principled, coherent plan of life that surpasses "random acts of kindness" ("and senseless acts of beauty," whatever they might be) that bumper stickers urge us to perform.[31] As Sidgwick noted, "the benevolent impulse" may by itself produce some social good, as can "the habit of considering the complex consequences of different courses of action that may be presented as alternatives." However, contrary to Marcel's usually sharp opposition between *disponibilité* and calculative thought, Sidgwick correctly argues that, to the degree that there is "a certain natural incompatibility between this habit of calculation and comparison and the spontaneous fervour of kindly impulse," "Common Sense" seeks shelter in "an ideal that transcends this incompatibility and includes the two" (1913, 244, n. 1).[32] Both are required to become as wise as a serpent and as guileless as a dove—to achieve the second sense of innocence described in the previous chapter.[33]

Context sensitivity referred to above is also a necessary condition of inventive charity, or *effective* kindness. Clara's misreadings of Fanny's needs show how it is all too common to be misunderstood; because we do not take into account the unavoidable contextuality of our actions, speech acts, gestures, and facial expressions.[34] Kindness is an accomplishment rather than a given, because it requires not only the right sort of disposition but also a factual understanding of the external circumstances that we wish to arrange to our purposes. *Native Son* illustrates the same lesson when Bigger is telling his attorney, Max, that he hated Mary for getting in the front seat with him. Max tells him that she was being kind to him because she accepted Bigger as a human being. Bigger retorts, "What you say is kind ain't kind at all. I didn't know nothing about that woman. All I knew was that they kill us for women like her. We live apart. And then she comes and acts like that to me" (Wright 1993, 405). Max replies that Bigger should have tried to understand because she was acting toward him in the only way she knew how, but that was cold comfort to Bigger, who could not possibly have understood. Mary, like Clara, had the best of intentions, but her lack of context sensitivity undermined the possibility of practical wisdom.

The significance of context for practical wisdom also shows up clearly when we want to express some particular value but cannot because the context will inevitably color its appearance to the contrary. This is what happens to Dr. Lydgate in *Middlemarch* during a meeting of town leaders at which the past financial improprieties of Bulstrode, the banker, come to light. Lydgate was already under the suspicion that Bulstrode's loan had been a bribe. When Bulstrode is forced to leave the meeting, his reputation shattered, he finds that he cannot stand. Lydgate gave him his arm and helped him out of the room. But this act of being at the service of the other, normally one of "gentle duty and pure compassion, was at this moment unspeakably bitter to him" (Eliot 1965, 783). The context, of which he was perfectly well aware and which publicly qualified him, made the cost of kind rescue an apparent confirmation of people's false suspicions about him.

Judgment plays at least one other key role in practical wisdom, namely, the ways in which it prevents us from being too kind. However, there are multiple senses of being too kind, and not all of them are incompatible with practical wisdom. With those that are, there is, first, that of the unpraiseworthy child-hood innocence of an *ingénu* such as Charles Bovary. Judgment here leads us to conclude that, although he is a paragon of fidelity and has purity of heart, he is in no case a model of practical wisdom. Additionally, as described earlier in this section, there is the sense of being too kind to others by not judging them cor-rectly as the source of our problems—something for which certain people have to obtain therapeutic intervention. In a considerably different vein, there is also a sense of being too kind that is violative of justice, as, for example, in at-tempting to temper the harsh and deserved consequences of Mr. Tulliver's fool-ish behavior. Any such kindness would not only have failed to satisfy the requirements of justice but would actually have prevented their realization.

A non-literary and very peculiar variation on the same theme occurs in a let-ter written by Pope Gregory IX to the Archbishop of Santiago de Compostella on May 18, 1233, to complain about the intolerable comfort of Jews living in Santiago. " 'Since their own sin [of being Christ killers] consigned them to eternal slavery,' the Pope begins, 'the Jews ought to acknowledge as just the misery of their condition, and ought to live without troubling those who accept and tolerate them out of kindness alone' " (Hay 1960, 104). Here also, kindness is taken to lie outside of justice. But it does not do so as its perfection—as, say, exemplified by Portia's advice to Shylock or, as in the film, *Enchanted April*, by Lottie's transcending justice by taking back her cheating husband in a reconcil-iation beyond the level of rights and duties. Rather, what the Pope had in mind was a kindness falling short of justice and capable of frustrating it.

There are also at least two senses of being too kind that are consistent with practical wisdom. The first is what we perceive as undeserved favors to which we have embarrassed reactions. We may believe that we have never done our benefactors a single kindness, for example, or that, for other reasons, we do not merit their generosity. In extreme cases, we may even complain of being "killed with kindness." Or we may believe that such generosity implies an unjustified judgment of our own worth. Here also, kindness is taken to be outside of jus-tice, but in a different way. Justice is merely transcended rather than violated, and practical wisdom can continue to function unimpeded.[35]

The second sense of being too kind that is not inconsistent with practical wisdom is the meaning that comes closest to sanctity, because it embodies the life project of humility. For example, in *House of the Spirits*, the author tells us that Esteban's son, Jaime, "despite his peevish attitude . . . was generous and candid and had a tremendous capacity for kindness, which he tried in vain to cover up because it embarrassed him" (Allende 1986, 186). The reason for the embarrassment is that, as Michael Barber explains in a commentary on Scheler's ethics, when we are aware that we are trying to achieve a certain value, that very awareness can interfere with our submission to the value. Likewise,

"The truly humble person feels anxiety about the 'image' of herself as good and shows her true goodness in this very anxiety. The best people are those who do not know that they are the best, those who, in St. Paul's sense, do not even dare to pass judgment on themselves" (Barber 1993, 94).

The type of self-knowledge lacking here is radically distinct phenomenologically from that of an ingénue. Nor is it disingenuousness. It reflects, rather, a deliberate choice not to make use of self-objectification in the eyes of other people for fear that that knowledge would conflict with the value being pursued. As such, far from being inconsistent with practical wisdom, this pursuit of value is closely related to the second sense of innocence and becomes the culmination of practical wisdom and the perfection of justice.

Some instances of being too kind are, then, inconsistent with practical wisdom, and they need corrective judgments to shape commitment into effective help for others. Other cases in which being too kind does not interfere with practical wisdom do not require such judgments. However, for the reasons stated above, they do entail some judgments, albeit not corrective ones, which distinguish them from expressions of purely unreflective spontaneity. While there are, as described above, spontaneous, unreflective acts of kindness that reveal an unreserved *disponibilité*, these are very different from the deliberated, ingenious acts of kindness that James describes, or the artful tact of a judicious spectator, which many other sorts of kindness require.

It is also true that, in these latter instances of kindness, there can be a tension between practical wisdom and the warmth of generosity that people count as evidence of personal kindness. As we have seen, it may take a considerable amount of time before mediately presented kind acts can be seen as such, and in the interim, those who perform such acts are not likely to appear as interested in the welfare of the objects of those acts. But even if there is sometimes a tension between practical wisdom and presenting oneself to others as generously *disponible*, truly effective kindness requires, for all of the reasons given above, the types of judgments discussed here to become a coherent, intelligible life commitment. Conversely, as discussed above, unreflective, unrestrained satisfaction of other people's short-term needs—or what they perceive they need—can sometimes lead to substantial harm, however good it might make the agent of such misplaced generosity feel.

Another way to say this is to focus again on friendship as the first fruit of one's own self-esteem, which, as Emerson argued, sometimes requires tensions, dissonances, and conflicts in relationships. We have seen that, for Ricoeur, the "ethical aim of life" consists of "aiming at the 'good life' with and for others ["solicitude"], in just institutions" (1992, 172), and that solicitude is internal to self-esteem, because it "unfolds" its "dialogic structure" (ibid., 180). Furthermore, through solicitude, friendship is the "first unfolding of the wish to live well" (ibid., 183), and by friendship, Ricoeur also means the type based on a mutual pursuit of "the good." As such, he would regard it as providing a foundation for Hallie's "positive" or "maximal" ethics of hospitality.

Morality, in contrast, is a Kantian system of universal rules, and it has its analogue of self-esteem in the notion of self-respect as an end in oneself. Likewise, just as solicitude is not added to self-esteem, respect owed to others on the plane of universal rules does not stand outside of the autonomous self (Ricoeur 1992, 218). For Ricoeur, the Golden Rule is the "appropriate transitional formula between solicitude and the second Kantian imperative" (ibid., 219). That is, one side of the dialectic between ethics and morality is that the former has primacy over the latter, because a universalism of rules is anticipated in a teleological perspective. Furthermore, to achieve practical wisdom, as described above, we have to refer to "the ethical ground against which morality stands out" (ibid., 249) in order to resolve conflicts on the plane of morality. But the other half of the dialectic is that the ethical itself gives rises to inevitable conflicts because of the imprecise nature of justice. These conflicts cannot be resolved except by making the ethical submit itself to a *moral* critique—that is, subject itself to obligations imposed by the universalism of moral rules. Solicitude must become critical—the ethical aim must be filtered through morality—in order to achieve practical wisdom "in the region of interpersonal relations" (ibid., 273).

As a result, practical wisdom involves both ethics and morality in order "to shelter moral conviction from the ruinous alternatives of univocity or arbitrariness" (ibid., 249). This is what Dr. Holt sought in the context of physician-assisted suicide and what George Eliot argued for as an alternative to "men of maxims," on the one hand, and "casuistry," on the other hand. Ricoeur's own example is also situated within biomedical ethics, namely, whether to tell the truth to dying patients, and in fact, he comes close to the notion of kindness as inventive charity in claiming that, "Practical wisdom consists here in inventing just behavior suited to the singular nature of the case. But it is not, for all that, simply arbitrary. What practical wisdom most requires in these ambiguous cases is a meditation on the relation between happiness and suffering" (Ricoeur 1992, 269).

Nevertheless, just because practical wisdom requires that solicitude be filtered through morality, it follows that I and the other are brought under the same norms and rules as equals. The same judgments apply to us, because we are mutually enjoined through conscience, we are both called to be faithful to ideals of justice and morality, and we can both be actively engaged through *disponibilité* that is the "key that opens self-constancy to the dialogic structure of the Golden Rule" (Ricoeur 1992, 268). Practical wisdom, conceived as a dialectic of ethics and morality, keeps the way open for seeing empathy as normative to the extent that its absence is inhuman. Such an absence would be inhuman because it would amount to the self-refuting denial of already existing objective relationships such as those that the Lakota call "mitakuye oyasin." To this concept one can compare Norman Malcolm's comment that, "A characteristic remark that Wittgenstein would make when referring to someone who was notably generous or kind or honest was 'He is a *human being!*'—thus implying that most people fail even to be human" (Malcolm 1972, 61).

This is why we find examples of the complete absence of empathy essentially *chilling*. There is something fundamentally inhuman about them, whether they are literary cases, such as Dr. Frankenstein's creature, Jane Eyre's description of the inhuman appearance of St. John Rivers, Bitzer in Dickens' *Hard Times*, or non-fictional cases, such as Heinrich Himmler or participants in the infamous Unit 731 of the Japanese Imperial Army. Himmler "believed his task to be a necessary duty in which human feeling had no proper place" (Manvell & Fraenkel 1965, 51). As he said to his Death's Head SS units that staffed the death camps, "To have stuck it out and at the same time (apart from exceptions caused by human weakness) to have remained decent fellows, that is what has made us so hard. This is a page of glory in our history which has never been written and will never be written" (Manvell and Fraenkel 1965, 136).

Similarly, consider a certain ex-Japanese soldier from Unit 731. As described by *The New York Times* reporter who interviewed him, "He is a cheerful old farmer who jokes as he serves rice cakes made by his wife, and then he switches easily to explaining what it is like to cut open a 30-year-old man who is tied naked to a bed and dissect him alive, without anesthetic." The prisoner was Chinese, and the reason for the dissection was that he was a research subject for the development of plague viruses that the Japanese hoped to use during the war. (After the war, the U.S. Army granted immunity from prosecution to those involved in order to obtain the research data. For, as scholars have pointed out, "the research [like the Nazi concentration camps] was not contrived by mad scientists, and . . . was intelligently designed and carried out. The medical findings saved many Japanese lives.") In concluding the interview, the old man said with a congenial smile, "There's a possibility this could happen again. . . . Because in a war, you have to win."[36]

One could also contemplate here the Allen-Littlefield Collection of lynching photographs at Emory University, from which came the recent stunning exhibition at the Roth Horowitz Gallery in New York. The victims are horrific enough, perhaps especially Frank Embree of Missouri who, before his hanging, stands naked on a wagon after having been savagely whipped. Yet even more chilling is the affectless indifference on the faces of the victim's persecutors. Some appear proud and even smug. Others wear congenial smiles in the carnival-like atmosphere. The workers were given time off from their jobs, and the children were excused from classes for the festive occasion: what were they thinking as they morally stained themselves with innocent blood?

Whatever else we might learn from such psychopathological cases, they at least teach us that when we do not have the ability to reach out through caring to establish communication and community with others, we are in some way fundamentally damaged. It is another dimension of an oft-repeated theme in these pages, that there is an intimate relationship between unkindness and disconnection from the world of feelings. Humanity gets distorted when the chiasmatic exchange of offering help and being offered help is no longer operative. For the same reason, abused children have great difficulty in being moved empathically by the suffering of other children, and it is surely no coincidence that an enormously high percentage of child molesters—in the United States, better than 90 percent, by some estimates—have themselves been abused as children.

Accordingly, certain treatment programs have profitably concentrated on such offenders' lack of empathy for their victims by making their denial of their victims' pain more difficult. The offenders watch and read victims' accounts of molestations and then have to write about their own crimes from what they imagine to be the victims' point of view. Later, in group therapy, they are required to answer questions from the victims' perspective. Lastly, they have to act out the offense while assuming the victims' role. Sex offenders who have participated in this program have only half the rate of recidivism of offenders who did not receive such treatment (Goleman 1995, 107).[37]

These studies and treatment programs also show us that empathetic relationships with others cannot be reserved for intellectual constructs. One would be inclined to construe them as such only if one has already in some sense lost one's moorings in a more primordial physical and emotional well-being in which is already inscribed the presence of other people. Through the reversibilities that make up our intercorporeality, as Merleau-Ponty has pointed out, other people are already "flesh of my flesh" (1964b, 15); they are not the products of a constituting consciousness.

In the next two chapters, we will prolong and deepen these reflections in the wider context of society itself, as opposed to particular interpersonal relationships. This social context has been presupposed throughout Part One in the description of kind acts and omissions and personal kindness; it is distinguished here in separate chapters only for the sake of analysis.

Chapter 4

Social Atmospheres, Technology, and Nature

The past era has taught us, survivors of the totalitarian regime, one very good lesson. . . .
Man is not a nomnipotent master of the universe, allowed to do with impunity
whatever he thinks, or whatever suits him at the moment. The world we live in is made
of an immensely complex and mysterious tissue about which we know
very little and which we must treat with utmost humility.
—Václav Havel, *The New York Times*, June 3, 1992

Social Kindness

A descriptive phenomenology of kindness culminates with society itself, because individual acts and omissions and particular individuals in intimate, friendly, or casual relationships do not exhaust the ways in which the phenomenon of kindness appears to us. Accordingly, the following two chapters will attempt to provide an account of the main features of kindness as a social phenomenon. We shall see that kindness and unkindness manifest themselves in indeterminate atmospheres with deeply embedded values—particularly regarding technology and nature, which is the subject of this chapter. We shall also find in the following chapter that kindness and unkindness appear in various types of social structures, some of which are themselves intimately related to technology and nature, and in the presence or absence of community. We shall likewise see that kindness and unkindness at a social level are considerably more complex and ambiguous than they are in particular acts, non-acts, or persons.

The social aspects of the phenomenon of kindness can be considered both as the widest background context that conditions individual kind acts, omissions, and persons, and as a set of unique evidences that disclose more about the nature of kindness than can be revealed by individual acts and persons. It is in this latter sense that Robert Coles once wrote instructively of psychology in the sense of the word "perhaps best understood (and rendered) by novelists such as

George Eliot in *Middlemarch* and Tolstoy in *War and Peace*." Each writer, Coles points out, attempted to link the human self to "broad social and political events, even to the tides of history that bear down on all of us" (1992, 38). These are the compulsory social forces that condition our lives to which Auden (1979) gave such eloquent expression in *September 1, 1939*, and it is in studying these broader connections that we shall attempt to complete our descriptions of kindness.

Social Atmospheres

In a perceptual Gestalt, the background context, or horizon, conditions the presentation and therefore the experiential identity of the perceptual object. So also, any given aspect of the social world is presented to us within such a horizonal structure. One consequence of this fact is that, as (Karl) Marx and Max Weber, among many others, have pointed out, a society's economic system, religion(s), ethical and political commitments, and legal system do not exist in watertight compartments. Rather, they interpenetrate and mutually express each other—just as the various aspects of a perceptual Gestalt are internally related.[1] For any given aspect of the social world, there are multiple levels or concentric circles of such contexts: within certain institutions, such as families or corporate structures, particular subcultural groups, society at large, and the ways in which the society is itself inserted into the world community.

As also in the case of a perceptual Gestalt, the halo of a social atmosphere that rings the presentation of any feature of the social world is indeterminate, but it is not nothing. On the contrary, in both the perceptual and social worlds, the indeterminate is "a positive phenomenon" (Merleau-Ponty 1962, 6). In the social world, such atmospheres, or horizons of meaning, constitute themselves as *Zeitgeists*, climates of opinion that shape our perception of the social world. Some of these opinions we hold consciously, as does Franny in J. D. Salinger's *Franny and Zooey*, when she indicates her fear of engaging in competition. "Just because I'm so horribly conditioned to accept everybody else's values," she explains, "and just because I like applause and people to rave about me, doesn't make it right" (1991, 30). However, many values embedded in social atmospheres we subscribe to unsuspectingly and unconsciously, and these we shall study in Part Two.

Indeterminate social atmospheres, derived from various layers of meaning "sedimented" (Merleau-Ponty) over time, are themselves more or less kind in the ways in which they define our perceptions of ourselves and other people, and in the ways in which they create behavioral expectations of us all. They can be benign, thoughtful, and encouraging, or coercive, repressive, and exploitative. It can be a question of the nurturing culture of a good school, or whole system, or of companies that are known to be—have instituted a culture of being—worker friendly and "good places to work," or of what is usually referred to as a "bureaucratic mentality." Or it can be an example such as that cited in the Introduction about the mean-spirited capitalism of the 1980s, in which greed became acceptable again in America, and the poor were politically demonized. The same attitude persists vis-à-vis prisoners and hostility—or, sometimes, coldhearted indifference—toward poor children in inner-city schools (Kozol 1991), to which we shall return below.

To say that social atmospheres, as climates of opinion, are indeterminate means that they present themselves to us as *non-attributable*. That is, they are everywhere (accepted) and nowhere (explained or defended, except in times of social upheaval and crisis). We do not know their origins or authors. They are expressions of what George Herbert Mead called "the generalized other," "the attitude of the whole community" (1934, 154). The "other" is thus not necessarily a particular individual. As Alfred Schutz points out, "the generalized other" may "take the structure of an individual, a type, a collectivity, [or] an anonymous audience or public" (1962, 189).

Indeterminate atmospheres of varying degrees of kindness and unkindness abound. They attach to, among other things, politics and government, corporate cultures, the entertainment industry, and the ways in which institutions such as schools, hospitals, and homes for the elderly function. For example, Lt. Col. David Grossman, a military psychologist, argues that American children are trained to kill by the same kinds of conditioning techniques used in the military to brutalize recruits and desensitize them to violence. With children, it is primarily a function of repeated exposure to television and film violence and interactive video games in which point-and-shoot reflexes are developed.[2]

Some indeterminate atmospheres are so general and pervasive—for instance, those that get expressed in popular morality, traditions, customs, taboos, and so forth—that they transcend any given institution. But for all such atmospheres, it is usually impossible to attribute any of them to a particular individual or set of individuals. Rather, they get carried along anonymously, like the way Heidegger describes *Das Mann* ("the 'they' ") (1962, 149ff.), as in, "They say that . . ." They live as unseen presuppositions as, for example, when poor children have difficulty getting adequate dental care. Among other social obstacles is "an underlying sense among everyone from insurance planners to state officials to patients that dental care is somehow secondary, or optional."[3] It is this "underlying sense among everyone" that testifies to the social atmosphere through which the "generalized," anonymous other becomes manifest.

Heidegger stresses the inauthenticity of the "they" whose "idle talk" (1962, 211ff.) betrays a flight from our ownmost potentiality for death. For the phenomena with which we are concerned, language is only part of the story. Electronic images, chiefly those of television, powerfully convey beliefs and values embedded in our more or less kind social atmospheres. The less kind are usually the more noticeable. For example, they can generate visceral reactions against certain groups—say, against gays and lesbians, or the obese. The Duchess of Windsor said famously that in America one could never be too rich or too thin, and this is a message the media convey relentlessly. Before the recent introduction of American television programming to the Fiji Islands, "going thin" was a sign of ill health. Now young girls are falling victim to eating disorders.

There can also be something of an analogue in social atmospheres with *Das Mann's* flight of inauthenticity. It is found in the collective superficiality that masks and discourages reflective consideration of received cultural values as, for instance, in Edith Wharton's *The Age of Innocence.* "Does no one want to know the truth here, Mr. Archer?," the Countess Olenska asks her cousin. " 'The real loneliness is living among all these kind people who only ask one to pretend!' She lifted her hands to her face, and he saw her thin shoulders shaken by a sob" (1986, 77). Here the "kindness" of particular individuals and social groups rides on the surface of a dishonest, self-contradictory collective attempt to remain ignorant of their coercive, vicious tribal morality.

With this type of example, we reach the limits of a descriptive phenomenology. Further analysis must await the hermeneutic phenomenology to be developed in Part Two. Here, remaining within the descriptive as much as possible, let us first note that a special effort is necessary to see pervasive social atmospheres for what they are, because they are always with us. We tend to notice things only when they are absent, just as, in another context, Heidegger pointed out that we take equipment for granted as long as it preserves its character as "readiness-to-hand" (1962, 98). Special efforts are thus required for conscious awareness of social atmospheres, and there are several possible avenues to that end.

For example, through literature or other sources, we can *imagine* alternative modes of social conditioning and the various types of values embedded in them. Here imagination can take on a liberating function. Even more effectively, we can contrast our own social atmospheres with those of other contemporary cultures, as in the example of the French Alpine village, noted in Chapter 2. We can also contrast our own climates of opinion with past examples to appreciate the intervening sedimentations of meaning.

For instance, contemporary attitudes toward smoking show how the bounds of tolerance have shifted since the 1930s, 1940s, and 1950s. When I was young, the epitome of film noir romance was when *he* took *her* cigarette, lit it, took a puff, and then placed it between her lips. Such a romantic experience would be impossible today, and not just because of a long-past childhood. One can equally consider the contrast between the society-wide sexism in those same decades and contemporary values. It is usual to refer to this phenomenon as "institutional" or "systemic sexism," and it is not wrong to say that it applied across whole institutions. But it was much more than that. It was an indeterminate atmosphere that colored people's attitudes and made institutional or systemic sexism possible.

As an example, Rex Harrison's memorable "Hymn to Him" in *My Fair Lady* included the complaint that:

> *Why is thinking something women never do?*
> *Why is logic never even tried?*
> *Straightening up their hair is all they ever do.*
> *Why don't they straighten up the mess that's inside?*
> *Why can't a woman be more like a man?*

The usual reaction from both men and women in the 1950s consisted of polite chuckles, knowing smiles, and conspiratorial winks. Today, such lyrics would be tolerated by most men and women only as parody. But in the 1950s, it was surely no accident that Lucille Ball, whose screen persona came closest to embodying Henry Higgins' lament, had one of the most popular television programs on the air. Needless to say, the same social atmosphere that caused people to snicker at Henry Higgins and laugh at *I Love Lucy* was not unrelated to the deplorable gender tracking characteristic of both school and the workplace. We shall return to these subjects in Part Two.

Another even more striking example of the shifting bounds of tolerance and climates of opinion concerns human sexuality. I am not now referring to alternative lifestyles or to the greater prevalence of "adult themes" in films and television. What I mean is the publication of intimacy in television programs and in the mainstream periodicals that are unavoidable in supermarket checkout lanes. This week's are typical. *Glamour* offers its readers an "Orgasm Dos & Don'ts Survey," while *Mademoiselle* proffers an exposé of "Guys & Sex, What They Think about Foreplay, Experienced Women, and Lust vs. Love." *Cosmopolitan* features "Sex Tricks He's *Never* Seen Before" and "Guy Butt Watch '99," while *Redbook* reveals "His Secret Turn-Ons, Take our sex quiz and make him insane with desire tonight."

It would be easy to consign these and other salacious examples of illuminating journalism to mere titillation in the service of money ("sex sells"), but that would be to miss the deep unkindness in the social values behind such phenomena. The unkindness consists in the betrayal of intimacy, turning everything that should remain inside, outside. As we saw in Chapter 1 in terms of tact and discretion, there is a close link between the protection of intimacy and one's dignity as an individual. At one level, the lack of such protection is what is so abhorrent about totalitarianism. At another level, the failure to protect intimacy and human dignity destroys the privacy that we associate with, and legally protect in, personhood. To be completely transparent is to be completely a tool of others. And perhaps there is a deeper and more obscure link between the popularity of psychotherapy and our collective rush to surrender intimacy to voyeurs—indeed, to become voyeurs, as the Introduction noted about various television programs.

Such examples make the full meaning of our own social atmospheres stand out by contrasts through which we can measure both similarities and differences. Such contrasts also make us aware of our dialectical relationship with social atmospheres that parallels to some extent the dialectical relationship between the voluntary and the involuntary. On the one hand, social atmospheres condition us as we take them up and perpetuate them. On the other hand, we see that, even though they are anonymous, they are human creations. Therefore, once we become aware of them, we can also attempt the difficult task of changing them and modulating them to our own purposes. Such change, when possible, usually progresses by degrees and can provide for a creative advance of kindness in society in terms of increasing degrees of humaneness in public and private life. But it also makes possible regression into unkindness.

For instance, considering again the Duchess of Windsor's observations, it is still part of our pervasive social atmosphere that girls and women should hold themselves up to impossible ideals. Even in 1991, when Naomi Wolf wrote *The Beauty Myth*, almost one-third of cosmetic surgery procedures were for breast augmentations and liposuction. As Brown and Gilligan pointed out in part, teenage girls got not-so-subtle messages to be quiet, nice, thin, and, if possible, blond. These values found expression in massive commercial exploitation: billions of dollars a year spent for cosmetics, diets, cosmetic surgery, and pornography. Why should we be surprised that, even at the beginning of the 1990s, anorexia and bulimia were seen in eleven- and twelve-year-old girls and that, by the end of the decade, the American Anorexia Bulimia Assocation reported that one-third of girls ages twelve to thirteen are trying those deplorable means to weight loss?[4] It is the same social atmosphere that has begun to take hold in Fiji.

On the other hand, our awareness of the social atmosphere in which such values are embedded exposes them to criticism and creative change. Such resistance has already begun as plastic surgeons try to distinguish between those teenagers with true deformities and those who are driven by *Baywatch*, *Sports Illustrated* swimsuit pictorials, and *Victoria's Secret* catalogues. These surgeons "must decide whether to operate on patients who are too young to vote, but old enough to feel social pressures to be physically perfect."[5]

There are several other aspects of our pervasive social atmospheres that equally display varying degrees of kindness and unkindness—mostly unkindness—and of which conscious awareness has not led to appreciable amelioration. These include persisting American inabilities to achieve a balance of work and leisure, as opposed to European countries in which they are much more satisfactorily integrated. They also include the reification of workers as mere market commodities, and on the mistaken assumption that quantity is the same thing as quality, judging the value of educational institutions solely in terms of productivity. Similarly, much of education has been ruined by giving in to social pressures to treat students as consumers and faculty and staff as salespeople whose main object is to please their customers (Edmundson 1997).

The imbalance of work and leisure, and of treating employees as market commodities, are closely linked. Juliet Schor showed this at the beginning of the 1990s, when she described the causes of overwork and—the subtitle of her book—"The Unexpected Decline of Leisure." By leisure, she did not mean merely "free time" for relaxing or various self-improvement activities, but also all of the volunteer activities that keep society going. For Schor, the unexpected decline in leisure has been due to a number of factors. These include a decline in the power of unions to protect workers against long working hours and the fact that the market system itself is such that, the longer the hours and the fewer the employees, the less a particular employer must spend on training new workers and on fringe benefits. There is the fact that fringe benefits are more expensive than overtime costs for many employers. In addition, workers who opt for part-time work in order to have more satisfying leisure activities find themselves stigmatized at work as unserious workers. For example, women who seek time off to take care of children are often consigned to a "mommy track" instead of a "career track." Finally, low-end workers and their families are especially vulnerable to a cycle of "spend and work" supported by the mania of an acquisitive consciousness that is, in turn, driven by relentless advertising and other social pressures.

That mania we have known ever since (Karl) Marx to be a vicious circle in which desire leads to acquisition, acquisition in turn leads to increased desire, which leads to further acquisitions, and so on. So families go into debt to buy unneeded products, and then must work longer hours to pay for them. The satisfaction gained from the accumulation of material goods is ephemeral, so workers buy newer products, and the cycle begins all over again.

Schor opined that, during the 1990s, more people would opt for more leisure, even at the price of a reduced standard of living. But that did not happen. In fact, a recent study by the International Labor Organization shows that Americans are working more and more hours each year, while workers in other countries have been working less. In 1996, Americans were in first place in the number of hours worked each year, "surpassing even the Japanese by about 70 hours. On average, Americans work 350 hours more per year . . . than Europeans."[6] Corporate downsizings have become a routine aspect of American life, and most people who do have jobs are doing the work of three people. Further, most of the new jobs created by the booming economy pay so poorly that workers have to hold more than one just to survive, if barely. Most people seem to be afflicted with a pathological busy-ness, and the word "stress" has permanently worked its way into the language. And still, shopping remains our foremost cultural preoccupation, so much so that some art museums have been built with shopping malls. If shopping is what most Americans do with most of their scant leisure time, then they are trapped in the vicious circle that Marx outlined. Such widespread cultural values are deeply unkind in that they destroy human flourishing. In Marcel's language, such values stress the dehumanizing prevalence of "having" over "being." Conversely, the internal spiritual vacuum created is apparent in many different contexts. During lengthy flight delays, for example, as well as during flights themselves, it is not uncommon to observe the malaise of empty internality in certain passengers who cannot stand thinking quietly, who must have some distraction, and who would not possibly have thought of reading a book.

Overseas, there are also important examples of social atmospheres that have resisted attempts to leaven them with kindness. As indicated earlier, anti-Semitism and neo-Nazism have been on the rise, especially in the former East Germany, in the face of economic fear, high unemployment, social upheaval caused by unifying the former East and West, and increased immigration. Here, old values have allowed a regression into unkindness, to say the least. Other examples include the terrible social stigma attached to rape and adultery in Kosovo and in Islamic societies generally. In the case of rape, merely the rumor or likelihood of rape is enough to ruin a woman's reputation and bring shame not only to the innocent woman but to her whole family and village as well.[7] In the latter case, adultery, the male seducer usually suffers nothing more serious than a token imprisonment, if that. But the woman can be killed by her family, effectively with impunity, for having brought dishonor not only to herself, but to the whole family. Again, the mere rumor of adultery has led to such "honor killings."[8]

In what does the kindness, or unkindness, of social atmospheres consist, and how does it manifest itself to us? When we are presented with what we take to be an act of kindness, we believe that we perceive an act aimed both to and for us—underwritten by an intention to further our welfare. With social atmospheres, whether of the most pervasive types or those restricted to particular institutions, as noted above, the other is "generalized," anonymous, and unknowable. Therefore, we can have no information about motives and are left instead with effects. We assess the kindness or unkindness of the social atmospheres by how heavily they weigh on those conditioned by them. We ask whether they are liberating or repressive, enabling or burdensome, productive of human flourishing or harshly restrictive. Blame-the-rape-victim mentalities weigh very heavily indeed, as did society-wide sexism that artificially truncated the economic and personal enrichment of generations of women.[9]

There is also an analogue in social atmospheres to mediately presented acts and non-acts of kindness or unkindness, that is, those that appear only after the fact, in light of intervening experiences through which their meaning gets constituted. With social atmospheres also, their kindness and/or unkindness may appear only through subsequent sedimented layers of experience, here collective instead of merely individual. This means that the test of kindness, in terms of how heavily such atmospheres weigh on those subject to them, is not always a matter of present impressions.

Consider, for example, the "dumbing-down" of American education. Students may be quite happy in such an atmosphere—the author of *Generation X Goes to College* refers to his institution as the "A-Mart" (Sacks 1996, x)—but because it does a serious disservice to its participants, it is still deeply unkind. Just how much of a disservice and how unkind, many students will not discover until the post-graduation black coffee of realism begins to replace the undergraduate euphoria of easy A's.

The main features of this atmosphere are depressingly well known to almost all university instructors, even at elite universities. The root premise, borrowed from the destructive commercialization of education referred to above, is that students are consumers. This means that they feel a sense of entitlement to not only good, but very good, grades. Like the campers at Lake Woebegon, they all tend to see themselves as above average.

This sense of entitlement is, in turn, based on two facts. First, students have paid for the courses. As one of Sacks' students expresses it, "That's part of the consumer mentality—I paid for it, so I shouldn't have to work for it" (1996, 169).[10] And second, students believe that if they have made the strongest possible efforts to prepare for an examination or write a paper, regardless of the objective quality of the work produced, a high grade is the appropriate payoff. But "strongest possible efforts" themselves are defined only in terms of student-set priorities of work and leisure activities, and it is beyond dispute that students study much less these days than did previous generations. Hence, they entertain unreasonable expectations of success.

The final component of the consumerist premise is that students expect faculty to cater to, nurture, and entertain them. Paying for a course is no different logically than paying for a ticket to the theatre or, in the case of distance learning, a film. The expectation is, therefore, for instructors to be performers, to package their products in the most pleasing manner possible, and these expectations are duly noted and measured in course evaluation forms.

The visible outcroppings of a "dumbed-down" education are hardly difficult to locate. In class, students are bored—except when something entertaining happens— unmotivated, and unwilling (and sometimes unable) to read. They refuse to do assigned work and yet demand sterling grades. Their attention is keyed to humor and showmanship. Hence, it is hardly any surprise that many students today are more and more disconnected from anything akin to an intellectual life, and that a large number are enrolled in remedial courses at the cost of millions of dollars each year. But whether they are in remedial courses or not, it is typical to hear them blame everyone but themselves for their failures, complaints that are rooted in the fact that the social atmosphere that "dumbing down" expresses thoroughly infects K-12 education as well.[11]

On the side of faculty, the other side of the "dumbing down" phenomenon is equally visible. Instructors tend to pander to students' expectations in order to please administrators. The double and interrelated objectives are to keep enrollments high and to gain tenure. Also, many faculty, even if they do not wish to be a party to the slide into mediocrity, may perceive themselves as powerless as whole institutions to change, because "the cultural forces preventing change" are "too powerful" (Sacks 1996, xiii). Thus there is a short-term payoff in the game for everyone. Students get high grades with little effort or knowledge acquired, faculty get enthusiastic course evaluations, please administrators, and get tenure; and administrators get healthy enrollments. And that, of course, for public universities, pleases legislatures.

However, those students who discover after graduation that they have been ill prepared for life outside of the academy will have an experience that is the inverse of mediately presented acts of kindness studied in Chapter 1. They will come to perceive mediately presented acts and social practices as unkind. Even though as students they may believe in the kindness of their educational institutions and staff, in after years they will know better. Then they will blame (of course) their alma maters and refuse to support higher education.

Technology

We have seen that social atmospheres are value laden, and that most of these values have decisively important social and political consequences. Furthermore, we have earlier discussed, briefly, certain examples of science and technology that exemplify various degrees of kindness and unkindness. They also comprise some of the most important components in our own indeterminate social atmospheres, both as values and social practices.

Perhaps this is the case preeminently in the United States, but all societies are affected, whether they realize it or not. It is not just a question of the World Wide Web or other communications networks. Rather, as Václav Havel has noted, "The dizzying development of science, with its unconditional faith in objective reality and complete dependency on general and rationally knowable laws, led to the birth of modern technological civilization. It is the first civilization that spans the entire globe and binds together all societies."[12] Thus, for example, "The forester who, in the wood, measures the felled timber and to all appearances walks the same forest path in the same way as did his grandfather is today commanded by profit-making in the lumber industry, whether he knows it or not" (Heidegger 1977, 18).

Our civilization has also given birth to multinational corporations that span the globe and the technology of developed cultures dominating developing cultures. Even in the former, certain technologies have turned the lives of workers upside down. For instance, small-dairy farmers cannot compete with corporate dairy farms whose cows have been genetically engineered to overproduce milk, and the inability to compete does not stop with dairy farmers. Family farms in general are so threatened by huge corporate enterprises that the Secretary of Agriculture, Dan Glickman, recently said himself that, "There's a fear this will turn into fourteenth-century feudalism. Those farmers will turn into serfs."[13] This is just one example of the creative and destructive dialectic between capital and technological "advance." (Capital fuels research and development, which produces "improved" technology, which creates more capital, and so on.)

However, despite the destruction that capitalism can wreak with technology, not even Marx and Engels thought it evil per se. On the contrary, they considered that, at least in principle, machines could be used to help bring an ideal society into being. So Heidegger was also right that "What is dangerous is not technology. There is no demon of technology" (1977, 28). Technology by itself—inanimate things and unintelligent processes—can be neither moral nor immoral, kind nor unkind. Rather, that to which we do ascribe those predicates is the human use of technology, and we had the in twentieth century alone more than enough evidence of both its evil and good uses. At one end of the spectrum one finds Auschwitz, the Soviet Gulag, and the Japanese Army Group 731. Less spectacularly, but still in the negative range, there are many other more "banal" instances of unkind uses of technology. To consider again the tyranny of the perfect body image, for example, the cruelties of the weight loss industry generated some deplorable rationalizations on the part of those in the trade. The American Society of Plastic and Reconstructive Surgery argued for breast implants—or rather, "breast augmentations" and "enhancements," as the jargon went—"as a cure for the small breasts they described as 'deformities' that were 'really a disease.' "[14] On the positive side of the scale, dramatic technological advances such as word processors have replaced user-unfriendly typewriters, stunning genetic therapies exist now that were science fiction only two decades ago, and much less invasive and hence more successful cardiac surgeries are being performed. The central question here is how the use of technology manifests itself to us as kind and unkind.

We saw in Chapter 1 that kind actions at an interpersonal level present themselves as done not only *to* but also *for* us. They seek our good for our sake. A similar intentionality obtains with social practices such as multiple uses of technology, but there are important differences. For one thing, since we are part of the "generalized other" for technology providers, we do not perceive the kindness behind the technology as aimed at us particularly. Thus although it aims at our good, it does not do so to the exclusion of that of other people. In addition, I may be quite aware that a certain technology serves my good, but not my neighbor's, particularly when the technology in question confers economic advantages that *ipso facto* disadvantage others. In general, "good" here means increasing our convenience, competitive abilities, and time savings while reducing our burdens and not creating others gratuitously and making the carrying of necessary burdens easier. Success in this regard tends to be measured in terms of increased comfort, on the one hand, and decreased obstacles and encumbrances, on the other hand.

It is also difficult to assess intent to provide for our welfare because of the situation of technology providers. For one thing, they are for the most part also part of the anonymous "generalized other (s)," and thus little personal interaction obtains between recipients and providers. In addition, any manifestation of technology as an instrument of kindness is also conditioned on a recognition of an intent for the provider's own self-interest. Thus, for example, ATMs make our lives much easier in a number of obvious ways, but they also help banks keep old customers and attract new ones. Caller ID permits us to avoid unwanted calls but also makes money for the telephone company. Rural Internet users can make use of that communications technology in order to help overcome their isolation, further their education, and even receive emergency medical advice. But at the same time, they know that they are helping the service providers make money. The fact that a given action or social practice can serve both one's own enlightened self-interest and those of others creates an inevitable ambiguity about motivation.

As a result, the uses of technology present themselves to us as kind only in an extended sense, based almost exclusively on their ameliorative effects. We extrapolate to the providers' supposed "thoughtfulness," which constitutes an indirect presentation of intent. One common way in which this is done occurs when we extrapolate from the presence of intelligent design, durability, and quality of certain products to the conclusion that someone, even though self-interested, actually cared about the fate of those using the technology. Hence, we appreciate those rare, automated voice answering systems that actually make it easy to negotiate the menu of choices and, above all, to talk to a real human being. By the same token, we impute a degree of thoughtful care to those rare architects who design buildings that make us believe that they actually considered what it might be like for people to work or live in them. Conversely, we count cheap quality, poor reliability of products, and bad design as evidence of a lack of care and maximization of self-interest—as, for instance, with the flimsy, substandard housing that cost so many thousands of lives in the 1999 earthquake in Turkey.

Nevertheless, when we perceive a particular use of technology as unkind, we cannot always extrapolate to intent. Even in the technological exploitation of developing nations, there is still room for ambiguity. In part, this is because science is inherently experimental, and one cannot foresee all of the consequences of any new technology. DDT, for example, worked wonders against mosquitoes, but it also severely endangered peregrine falcons and bald eagles in this country and other animal life, including human beings, in other countries. Second, when we are inclined to ascribe a degree of kindness to the use of a certain technology, we are also aware of the fact that the harmful effects are not especially meant for us, and also that we may benefit while others may suffer. Thus, although, as noted above, we do tend to judge the kindness or unkindness of technologies based on their ameliorative effects, we must also remain sensitive to the fact that there are always mixed effects.

Therefore, in a recent heated debate about a proposal before the United Nations (UN) to ban DDT entirely, environmentalists and some scientists and physicians argued for this plan because of the chemical's destructive environmental impact, while other physicians pleaded for at least a moderate use of the chemical as a way to fight malaria in poor, undeveloped countries, where a child dies of the disease every twelve seconds. The phenomenon of mixed effects thus greatly complicates judgments about the overall kindness or unkindness of technology.

Still, even given the ambiguity and uncertainty of intent, it appears that, in general, various uses of technology appear to us as unkind when their effects either cause harm or take a substantial risk of doing so. That the latter qualification is important may be seen in the case of genetically engineered plants that, while less controversial in this country, have caused a huge row overseas. Yet even if such plants turn out to be harmless to the environment, many people will still see the experiments as fundamentally unkind, because they will believe that the companies (and governments) at issue negligently, or even recklessly, rolled the dice with their environment.

There is a broad array of contexts in which uses of technology appear to us as unkind, because they either cause harm or negligently risk doing so to either human beings or nature as a whole. However, one factor that all of these contexts have in common is that technology has achieved hegemony that we cannot escape, so that the harm caused is usually a product of exploitation, coercion, duress, or some combination of these abuses of power. For instance, those small-dairy farmers referred to above cannot escape the economic pressure of genetically engineered cows in corporate mega-dairy farms any more than can Heidegger's solitary forester evade the economic pressures of the lumber industry. Likewise, organic farmers have considerable difficulty protecting their growing fields against chemicals blown from nearby fields and pollen from their neighbors' genetically engineered crops.

In a different sort of context, the hegemony of computer and related electronic technology can appear as unkind to the degree that it leads to a collapse in the boundaries between professional and personal life. Thus students can expect professors to be available to answer e-mail at all hours, and managers can find that the convenience and ubiquity of the technology make it difficult to detach themselves from the office. Furthermore, employees are expected to do several things at a time. The label for this expectation, "multitasking," is revealing. Originally a computer term, it is now used to set norms for human beings. People also take cell phones and pagers everywhere, even to films and dinner, where beeps routinely disturb the peace of other patrons and diners. The 1990s attitude, which shows no sign of abating, was that the true work heroes are those who are super-busy, who work and live in the office. Some companies worry about new hires not getting up to speed because of "drag coefficient." A husband, wife, or child, each constitutes one drag.[15]

This situation is a clear case of what Marcel meant when he claimed that, "Man is *at the mercy of his technics.* This must be understood to mean that he is increasingly incapable of controlling his technics, or rather of *controlling his own control*" (1964b, 31; emphasis in original). We can control neither the speed of technological progress nor the allure of its products, so the engineer ends up becoming the engineered. Few things can strike us as more empty and more "thoroughly manipulated by the technology that we ourselves have devised" (Marcel 1967, 41) than conceptualizing a spouse or child as a "drag coefficient."

A very different but related example of technological hegemony consists of our constant tendency to rely on pills for solutions to personal and social problems. Sometimes this can entail unkindness to oneself, as when one can depend on pills to lose weight in order to avoid the self-discipline of eating the right amounts of sensible foods and getting appropriate exercise. At other times, this technique of medicalizing the body can lead to unkindness to others. For instance, pharmaceutical companies are now spending billions of dollars to technologize aphrodisiacs. The aim is to guarantee great sex, even if—perhaps, especially if—the participants do not feel like it. The objective is not, as in the case of Viagra, to improve performance but rather to change women's desires and to increase feelings of arousal (Hitt 2000, 40). The new pills, creams, suppositories, and other nondrug technologies would remedy these deficiencies for women—and, in the case of some drugs, for men as well—by manipulating hormones and genital blood flow.

From the point of view of kindness, there are several reasons to be hesitant about medicalizing sexuality. In the first place, there is the obvious question of whether there is such a thing as female sexual dysfunction, or whether it is simply a convenient, pharmacological, social construction. Changes in desire are one thing, but making it a problem is another.[16] This objection mirrors the discussion in Chapter 1 in terms of the body's natural and cultural realities. I argued that Carol Bigwood was correct to defend the natural aspects against a view of the body as simply the intersection of multiple cultural discourses. The application of that view here is that because of gynecological surgeries and the consequent absence of sufficient vaginal blood flow, some women need these sorts of therapeutic interventions for enjoyable sexuality. At the same time, however, the body is inevitably both natural and cultural, from which it follows that not every claim about nature is true. It is logically possible that any particular claim, such as widespread female sexual dysfunction, may be more nearly social construction with a tenuous connection to nature. Particular claims cannot be settled without more scientific evidence of the effectiveness of the drugs and other remedies under consideration so that we can judge the tenability of the social construction hypothesis.[17]

Beyond this theoretical dispute, medicalized sexuality risks unkindness as an instrument of duress or outright coercion if one were to pressure one's partner into a mood that he or she did not want. As we have seen, moods are basic states of being that reflect complex relationships with others in one's Lifeworld. Sometimes, of course, people fall into moods that they do not want, such as depression, and from which they may try to be rescued. But sexual mood is quite different. It reflects a delicate equilibrium, or lack thereof, of complex variables such as social relationships, body image, hormonal (im) balance, and so forth. Sexual moods should thus reflect how we want to live our bodies and, other things being equal, there would be no dehumanization when taking such pills represents an informed, voluntary decision. Such remedies would be on the same logical plane as all the other things we use to put ourselves in the right mood, such as flowers, chocolates, dim lighting, and perfume. Here there is only an *appeal* that inherently provides for a free response.

However, other things are not equal in many people's lives, and technological aphrodisiacs could be used to force sexual response into the frenetic timetable of modern life. As Hitt puts it, "With couples holding down two jobs and the enraged pace of modern life, who doubts that a drug-enhanced four-minute sexual encounter among harried day traders could become the norm?" (2000, 41). In Marcel's terms, sexuality would become degraded to one (fast-paced) function among others. Correlatively, there is a risk of unkind objectification, in that sexuality could be reduced to performance judged quantitatively: duration, numbers of orgasms, how fast, how slow, and so forth.

Beyond the context of medicalized sexuality, there are other types of actually or potentially unkind technological hegemony. One of them consists of the use of medical technology to enforce a paternalistic vision of our welfare. In this context, Sherwin Nuland gives us a set of illuminating examples of unkindness that shows how physicians' use of such technology can be a powerful contributory cause of abusing terminally ill patients with unnecessary, painful, and expensive treatments. The reason is that, at the end of the patient's life, there is an inevitable divergence in the physician's normally congruent roles of healer and comforter, on the one hand, and, on the other hand, "biomedical problem-solver" of the "riddle" of finding a cure (Nuland 1994, 247). In the world of high-tech medicine, the doctor can come to be dominated by the challenges to solve the riddle and thus push false hopes and unnecessary, futile treatments on the patient.

As Nuland sees it, the physician "allows himself to push his kindness aside because the seduction of The Riddle is so strong and the failure to solve it renders him so weak" (1994, 249). Instead of humility in the face of nature that characterized previous generations of medical practice, medical *hubris* dictates that, "Since we can do so much, there is no limit to what should be attempted—*today*, and for *this patient!*" (ibid., 259; emphasis in original). Or, as Thomas Laqueur phrases it, "The battle is joined: scientist v. cell, with a human being as battleground. . . . Dignity, we should note, was threatened not by nature's cruelties, beserk cells, and such like, but by lies, false hopes, and chemical warfare" (1994, 8).

Two types of fallacies underlie such unkind hubris. The first mistake, which is sometimes called the "capacity fallacy," states that if one can do X, one ought to do it. The second error, occasionally called the "necessity fallacy," asserts that if one can do X, one will or must do it. The language typically used for its description includes statements such as, "We have the knowledge, and it would be wrong not to use it," and "Now that we can control, treat, etc. . . . we must no longer submit to nature."[18]

Nuland's argument is not that the power of high-tech medicine should go unused. Indeed, to it, in his view, can be attributed "the great clinical advances of which all patients are beneficiaries" (1994, 259). Nor does he deny the reality, power, or desirability of hope. Rather, he wishes to bring both of these phenomena into a sort of stereoscopic vision of the humane use of medical power. The latter must include compassion and humility, "without which compassion is undoubtedly impossible. Where pride reigns, there is no room for mercy" (Marcel 1973, 95). Doctors have to learn when, with certain patients, enough is enough, and when it is wiser to let nature "take its course." Also, when disease is advanced enough, doctors, patients, and their families will all achieve a greater kindness when they learn how to hope more realistically rather than pursue "elusive and danger-filled cures" (Nuland 1994, 233).

We can also perceive the uses of technology as unkind when they debase human dignity by commercializing it. There is, unfortunately, a broad spectrum of examples. In certain parts of the world, there is an open market in transplantable body parts, and the same kinds of dehumanizing pressures are now being felt here. But there is another medical illustration that is singularly interesting, because on the surface it bears a deceptive appearance of kindness. It is the practice of human egg donation, which is sometimes the last resort for women who wish to become pregnant but cannot because of damaged fallopian tubes and/or ovaries. If the woman herself can carry a pregnancy to term, the eggs donated in this assisted reproductive technique will be fertilized with her husband's sperm and then implanted in her uterus. If she is not able to sustain a pregnancy, she will require a surrogate birth mother as well.

In theory, eggs are never bought or sold.[19] Rather, they are said to be "donated," and the fee paid to the donor is supposed to be compensation for time, effort, physical discomfort and, sometimes, extreme pain. Correspondingly, the official motive is the altruistic act of helping someone have a child. The realities of the trade, however, belie the appearance of such kindness. For one thing, ours is the only country in the world that has an open market in human eggs (and sperm too, for that matter). This has caused no great alarm in the United States, as it has overseas. Rather, most of the critical discussion has focused on—of course!—how much donors should be paid. For instance, in February 1999, an advertisement appeared in "several Ivy League school newspapers offering fifty thousand dollars to a donor who was athletic, had S.A.T. scores of 1400 or more, and was at least five feet ten inches tall." But the clients of the attorney who placed the ad were not the only ones seeking "high-end eggs": in 1998, a Los Angeles egg donor was paid $35,000 for her eggs (Mead 1999, 58–59). And donors do not receive just cash; they also receive expensive gifts that have included cruises, a year of college tuition, and other upscale incentives.

Recipients of donated eggs vehemently reject the accusation that they are merely shopping for high-end genes, but the egg as merchandise and the ideal of genetic upgrades essentially comprise the message of all of the literature about potential donors given to would-be recipients. Certainly egg donation can be an altruistic act of kindness, and it is equally clear that women who are truly desperate for a child benefit from the practice. Even so, the practice still has unkind effects for both donors and recipients, and perhaps for the eventual child(ren) as well. Potential donors who are immature, poor, or vulnerable for other reasons are exploitable to the degree that the pressure of so much money can prevent them from making informed, responsible decisions about such serious matters. Potential recipients who happen to be poor, or at least not the high rollers who place ads of the type described above, risk being priced out of the market, while those who are financially well off get exclusive access to the "high-end eggs." The result is a two-tiered scale of human value with literally a price on their genetic endowments. Such practices also implicitly reinforce racism to the extent that the "high-end eggs" usually come from, and are "donated" to, white women.

The practice of egg donation is also unkind to the degree that it threatens to dehumanize the child to the status of a "product," or "merchandise." Love for a child is supposedly undiminished by a child's "imperfections." It is tragic enough when children's "imperfections" that consist of objective disabilities prevent parents from loving them. But it is even worse when the "imperfection" is measured solely in terms of the unfulfilled expectations of egg recipients who have had donors screened so assiduously.

Such degradation to the status of a product and the services to produce it can also take place even when the child is not loved. With abortion rates dropping nationally, certain abortion clinics in cities that contain too many for the local trade are now seeking an edge over the fierce competition by offering amenities such as spa-like atmospheres with "low light in the rooms, aromatherapy, candles, and relaxing music."[20] Regardless of one's beliefs about the morality of abortion, not many are likely to think of it simply as a positive option for commercial exploitation. Whatever else it is, abortion is killing, and killing requires a type of justification that most other business ventures do not.

There is at least one other, and considerably different, example of how the uses of technology can be unkind. This is when technology conceals and alienates us from nature. In such cases, technology prevents our appreciation of nature—in both senses of valuing up and being thankful for—and fulfillment within it. This alienation in turn leads to the serious moral and sociopolitical consequences of the destruction of nature. Here we return to a Heideggerean *Gelassenheit* and again to Marcel's criticisms of technology.

Heidegger's highest sense of what he calls *poiesis*, "bringing forth," is *physis*, for "what presences by means of *physis* has the bursting open belonging to bringing-forth, e.g., the bursting of a blossom into bloom, in itself" (1977, 10). In contrast, an artwork, such as a silver chalice, "has the bursting open belonging to bringing-forth not in itself, but in another, in the craftsman or artist" (ibid., 11). Both kinds of "bringing-forth," including the nuances of producing, generating, begetting, and eliciting" (ibid., 10, n. 9), function by revealing what had been concealed.[21] Poiesis is a revelation of truth, and techné is, for Heidegger, sometimes a part of poiesis. Thus techné "is the name not only for the activities and skills of the craftsman, but also for the arts of the mind and the fine arts. *Techné* belongs to bringing-forth, to *poiesis*; it is something poietic" (ibid., 13).

For Heidegger, the usual definition of technology as instrumental, means-end thinking is not false, but it is not what is most central to modern technology. The type of revealing of nature characteristic of "modern machine-powered technology" is not poiesis. It is, rather, a "challenging" of nature to "supply energy that can be extracted and stored as such" (1977, 14). The peasant's field once tended with care gets revealed as a "coal mining district, the soil as a mineral deposit" (ibid., 14–15). Coal gets stockpiled. It is "on call, ready to deliver the sun's warmth that is stored in it"; the stockpile becomes a "standing-reserve" (ibid., 15, 17). In other words, nature now appears only as its use-value. The same is also true of plants and animals that our technology circumscribes. We neither gather nor hunt them. Rather, they are "bred and harvested in huge, mechanized farms. 'Nature,' it would seem, has become simply a stock of 'resources' for human civilization" (Abram 1996, 28). Similarly, the dammed-up Rhine appears as a *"power* works," instead of the way it is described in the *"art* work, in Hölderlin's hymn." Just as all of nature in modern technology, the river becomes the energy released, transformed, stored up, and distributed (Heidegger 1977, 16).

Heidegger designates this way of viewing nature as "enframing," or *Ge-stell* (1977, 19), and enframing poses a double danger to truth: it blocks us from other modes of revelation of nature, particularly from the poietic, and it conceals itself in the sense that we are not aware of how our relationships with nature have been thus restricted. As a result, the dominance of enframing threatens to cut us off from "a more original revealing and hence to experience the call of a more primal truth" (ibid., 28), what it means to dwell on the earth. That is the insight open to the poietic, the piety of thought that, as we have seen, Marcel contrasted favorably to the "attitude of the pure technician."

Enframing has important implications for kindness, because modern technology's reduction of nature to use-value conceals the poietic insight of nature as object of appreciation—in both senses of valuing up and being thankful for. The sense of valuing up encompasses nature as a unity of fact and value, an artwork in Hölderlin's sense. The poet's language is only a highly visible variation on the way that all speech, as Merleau-Ponty has shown, rooted as it is in bodily gesture, bears an affective meaning that lays the foundation for later conceptual elaboration. Bodily gesture creates a flesh of language that "sing[s] the world's praises" (Merleau-Ponty 1962, 187); language becomes "the very voice of the things, the waves, and the forests" (Merleau-Ponty, 1968, 155). Hölderlin and poets such as Gerard Manley Hopkins have provided us with masterful descriptions of this *evocative* power of nature.

Some examples of traditional Irish music also serve as excellent illustrations of the unity of flesh singing the world's praise and nature as object of appreciation. It is no accident that such music is performance oriented and invokes bodily appreciation through gesture and, above all, dancing—what for Nietzsche was the epitome of joy. Conversely, passive audiences who limit themselves to polite applause create an impression that the music has "fallen flat." Then there are the ethereal Gaelic songs—hymns, really—of almost mystical attachment to the land. They do not express a sense of land belonging to human beings as possessions—and still less as raw materials for technological exploitation—but rather of human beings belonging to the land.[22]

The second sense of appreciation—being thankful for, which Hopkins' poetry and certain Gaelic songs also exemplify—incorporates a piety of thought that includes the humble acknowledgment of our dependence on other organisms. This sense of appreciation also rests on the perception that we could not be the creatures of flesh that we are without those relationships to the non-human. One finds this sense of appreciation endorsed by a broad range of thinkers, including Heidegger, Marcel, Ricoeur, Merleau-Ponty, and Havel (see the epigraph for this chapter). Central to the sense of appreciation as thankfulness is the insight that, as we have seen with Merleau-Ponty, our bodies are part of the flesh of the world, and our flesh is adapted for relationships. My life and the rest of nature intertwine in one tissue of flesh, and it is the primitive knowledge of that intertwining that underlies and makes possible abstract thought that diverts us from this basic recognition. Technologies that distract and insulate us from nature make it "all too easy for us to forget our carnal inherence in a more-than-human matrix of sensations and sensibilities" (Abram 1996, 22). We become fully human only through relationships with the nonhuman.[23] Kindness here in the natural sense is closely linked to kindness as a moral quality, as Rabindranath Tagore shows. He wrote that, ever since infancy, he had a "deep sense" of "nature, a feeling of intimate companionship with the trees and clouds, and the touch of the seasons," and simultaneously "a peculiar susceptibility to human kindness" (Chakravarty 1961, 84).

Thus the body has its "silent conversations with things," while scientific discourse misses the fact that both our flesh and the flesh of the world are just dual aspects of the same fundamental reality. My body's chiasmatic reversibilities engage other entities, especially other animal intelligences that break the normal way I look at things and open me to a world "all alive, awake, and aware" (Abram 1996, 19).

How exactly does the reduction of nature to use-value conceal nature and end up serving as a mirror for our own images and desires instead of enhancing our poietic appreciation of it? The answer lies in objectifying thought, which is common to both instrumental thinking and enframing. That is, technology abstracts from the richness and complexity of nature to the concept of nature as pure object. The forest is reduced to materials for lumber mills, the high meadow to space for building another sprawl of condos, the deer or the marlin to the trophy mounted over the mantel, the coral reef to potential souvenirs, and so on. Heidegger pointed out that, as noted above, enframing contains a double concealment—of nature and of itself. But within the technological concealment of nature, there is also a double concealment. We lose sight of living nature and the ways in which it resonates in our own actively participatory flesh.

In *The Grapes of Wrath*, John Steinbeck elegantly captures both senses of concealment of, and disconnection from, nature. He describes the "tractor man" who lives far from the land he plows, and whose work the tractor makes so "easy and efficient" that it empties all of the wonder out of the work and the land. He understand the chemicals with which he fertilizes the land, but the land, just as the tractor man himself, is much more than the product of a chemical analysis. The one who understands this irreducibility is the farmer who walks the land and knows it intimately, who eats his lunch close to the earth that he plows. But for the tractor man, "his home is not the land" (1976, 148–49).

This sense of alienated disconnection from nature is often marked by illusions of domination and control and intolerance for the involuntary and unmanageable. Thus just as land for the tractor man, human eggs come to be seen as manageable and manipulatable resources, stockpiles of genes, a practice that also reflects the use of technology as a mirror of our own image. Here the enframing at issue imposes quality controls as it sorts the resources into "high-end eggs" and others, including the logically implied "low-end" varieties. Prospective parents apply the same calculative mentality to these resources, as we have seen actual parents do in paying for Little League baseball lessons. Children, potential or actual, are managed as "growth stocks" according to accepted market strategies. Such thinking instantiates Marcel's view of an empty, functional world dominated by fear and desire: "Every technique serves, or can be made to serve, some desire or some fear; conversely, every desire as every fear tends to invent its appropriate technique" (1964b, 30). A "poietic" revelation of a child, on the contrary, would reveal her as a work of art, treasured for herself rather than because she satisfies parental product specifications.

This dialectic of fear and desire is clearly present in the human egg market, the medicalization of sexuality, the portrayal of small breasts as "defects" and "diseases," as well as in the workplace, where employees cannot free themselves from the demands of a fast-paced technology. A world centered on functions and "technics" is one of "having" rather than "being," of "problems" to be solved instead of mysteries (of love, hope, and the like) to be celebrated. Since technology consists of the manipulative control of what functions we "have," the success of technology will always be only partial. There is a close dialectical connection between "the optimism of technical progress and the philosophy of despair which seems inevitably to emerge from it" (Marcel 1964b, 31–32). The sadness of the onlooker joins itself to the *malaise* of the actor herself whose life is reduced to performing functions.

Marcel has considerable evidence at his disposal to harbor such misgivings about the unkindness of technology, but we also need to keep in mind that, although he tells us that there are, in principle, humanizing uses of technology, all of his examples are quite to the contrary.[24] Clearly a more balanced picture is required, not only to take account of the kindness in technology described above but also for at least three other reasons. Marcel tends to conflate manipulation with dehumanization, and they are distinct logically, if not always in fact. On an interpersonal level, we have already seen a number of cases in which strategic manipulation is not only consistent with doing acts of kindness but is actually necessary. Thus just because the uses of technology are manipulative, it does not follow that they must be unkind. Second, as we have seen, objectifications can sometimes be benign. This means also, finally, that instrumental reasoning is not inherently destructive and morally corrupt.

Disjunction and alienation from nature are not necessarily part of the human condition. Abram, for instance, notes that Merleau-Ponty's notion of the flesh has a "startling consonance with the worldviews of many indigenous, oral cultures" (1996, 69). This is certainly the case with the Dakota, whose forms of social communion, as we have seen, rested squarely on a metaphysical unity with nature, plunging "purposively deeper into the relatedness of all things" (Lee 1959, 61). In this organic view of nature, all forms of life are related and holy. As Black Elk phrased it, "us two-leggeds sharing in it with the four-leggeds and the wings of the air and all green things; for these are children of one mother and their father is one Spirit" (Neihardt 1961, 1). The living center consisted of the people themselves among "all good things in the sacred hoop of the world" (ibid., 277).

Within hostile external conditions, the Dakota inhabited a personalized tribal space. It was a space that Marcel would describe as contributing the feeling of being "at home." It was a space "which by its very nature was socializing. The Dakota inhabited a space where he belonged" (Linden 1977, 21). It was a space that created a harmony of self-fulfillment with nature as well as home.[25] This space was also temporalized not by clocks but by happenings and events that gave their names to the months of the year. In terms of Marcel's critique of functions and Goodman's remarks about the fast-forward office, it is instructive to realize that Dakota time-consciousness, like that of other tribes, was not frenzied busy work. Normal time was not quick time, so whites came to see Native Americans as "unmotivated and lazy. This was a mistake. Dakota time was not lazy time. It was leisure time. Such time converts labor into work and work into serious play" (Linden 1977, 22).

The sense of fundamental, ontological relatedness, coupled with a high moral sense of responsibility, reinforced the Dakota concept of centering, of being grounded in nature. Chief Luther Standing Bear phrased it this way: "The man who sat on the ground in his tipi meditating on life and its meaning, accepting the kinship of all creatures and acknowledging unity with the universe of things was infusing into his being the true essence of civilization" (Linden 1977, 23).

Similarly, but in a completely different context, St. Francis of Assisi shared this fundamental identification with nature. What was really novel about his view of nature was that, as Scheler points out, "natural objects and processes take on an expressive significance of *their own*, without any parabolic reference to man or to human relationships generally" (1954, 89; emphasis in original). Further, just as with Native Americans, St. Francis' sympathetic insight into the heart of a creature gave insight into the unity of divine life incarnated in all things that drove his social mission. Conversely, both for St. Francis and for Native Americans, alienation from this elemental centering in being would have been a very deep unkindness to others and to oneself.

There is another aspect of St. Francis' view of our unity with nature that has important implications for kindness. In the nineteenth century, Paul Sabatier contended, and Scheler accepts his arguments as dispositive, that the source of St. Francis' identification with nature lay in Eros, in his youthful devotion to the "*Provencal cult of chivalrous love*" (Scheler 1954, 91; emphasis in original). This aspect of St. Francis' life, woven together with the others, created a singular convergence of Eros and agape.

Today one sees the same confluence, in different social forms, in the art of Marc Chagall. The recurrent symbols in his paintings, sculptures, and glass windows all testify to his desire to achieve a unity of Earth and Heaven, Eros, and agape. Goats, chickens, amorous couples, and scenes of birth and death mingle in glorious profusion with angels and menorahs. For example, in *The Bride and Groom of the Eiffel Tower* (*Les Mariés de la Tour Eiffel*) (1938–1939), the body of the goat is actually a string bass, and the hoof of the ebullient animal holds a conductor's baton over the heads of the couple to orchestrate this exuberant unity of Heaven and Earth. Chagall's work likewise overcomes the alienation of nature from grace in another way, through its depictions of the kinship of Eros and Thanatos that has had a long history. In so doing, it has also illustrated the reality of death as part of the spiritual life, a reality that, as we have seen, the Dakota recognized and that Marcel endorsed in opposition to its functional degradation as the failure of the machine.

To this synthesis of nature and grace should be compared the stark picture of their alienation that one finds in the Lowood school for poor girls in *Jane Eyre*. The clergyman, Mr. Brocklehurst, upbraids the school's director, Miss Temple, for feeding the children decent food. Preferring the discipline of hunger over the kindness of loving care, he says, "Oh, madam, when you put bread and cheese, instead of burnt porridge, into these children's mouths, you may indeed feed their vile bodies, but you little think how you starve their immortal souls!" (Brontë 1966, 95).

The same alienation of nature from grace appears in the real schools depicted in Kozol's horrifying stories. For example, a young African American in Boston became a teenage alcoholic and a battered veteran of mean streets. He ended up with a twenty-year prison sentence for murder. Kozol knew him when he was eight years old. He talked to himself in class but was never offered any help. Instead, he was taken to the basement to be whipped. A small person with a very hard life, "shy and still quite gentle," "He has one gift: He draws delightful childish pictures, but the art instructor says he 'muddies his paints.'" She shreds his work in front of the class. Watching this, he stabs a pencil point into his hand" (Kozol 1991, 194).

Scheler argues (1954, 82) that the unity of the cosmos presupposes an organic view of nature that has been accepted in all cultures except in the West because of the mechanistic worldview that emerged in the seventeenth century.

To this worldview we owe, as he sees it, a cleavage of human beings from nature and from each other.[26] He points out that the organic view of nature still coexists with scientific materialism, and that it is the task of "philosophical metaphysics" to bring them together in some form of unity. Doing so will entail, among other things, jettisoning our "one-sided conception of Nature as a mere instrument of human domination" (ibid., 104–105). Reciprocally, we must revitalize our ability to identify with "the life of the universe" (ibid., 105).

Scheler also anticipates Chief Luther Standing Bear and Abram in his diagnosis of the disastrously unkind consequences that flow from losing this identification with nature. All would argue that, in the absence of this unity with nature, we are alienated from our "eternal mother" in a way that violates our nature (Scheler 1954, 106). Scheler then states that, as a result of this cleavage, in a capitalist, industrial era, we will come to love only humanity as divorced from all other forms of life. Further, this exclusive affection will be expressed in "an arbitrarily destructive attitude toward the whole of organic Nature," including cruelty to animals and the scandalous destruction of natural resources (ibid.).

Scheler is right as far as he goes, but it is not simply a question of a destructive attitude toward nature but also toward humanity. Black Elk expressed this very well when he described his impressions of New York when visiting as part of Buffalo Bill's Wild West show. He could tell that the Wasichus [the Dakota word for "white man"] were, unlike his own people "before the nation's hoop was broken," indifferent to each other's welfare. "They would take everything from each other if they could, and so there were some who had more of everything than they could use, while crowds of people had nothing at all and maybe were starving. They had forgotten that the earth was their mother" (Neihardt 1961, 221).[27] In our own day, Kristen Monroe's study of altruism, to which we shall return in the following chapter, bears out the close connection between an identification with all living things and a disposition to kindness that Native American thinkers, Scheler, Francis, and Tagore, all defend. Of the various classes of altruists she studied, she found such identification common among rescuers and present by degrees in philanthropists (Monroe 1996, 83, 123–24).

In his writings on sympathy, Scheler does not discuss capitalist exploitation of developing nations, colonialism, or Joseph Conrad, but all would have been appropriate. Furthermore, had he not died so young (at age fifty-four, in 1928), he would have lived to see many other destructively unkind consequences of the mechanist view of nature and instrumental thinking—and not only in the spectacular example of the Holocaust. He would have seen the beginnings of what are now entrenched social practices between developed and developing countries, and within developed countries. On both levels, wealthy elites refuse to make meaningful changes in their lifestyles and patterns of consuming energy resources. These patterns take different social forms; some obvious examples are the continual and consistent destruction of rain forests, industrial waste contamination of ground water, industrial farming techniques of destroying topsoil, and the accelerating loss of other species.

In terms of energy consumption, the United States is by far the greatest offender. A child born in the United States will eventually place six times the burden on planetary resources as will a child born in the developing world. Indeed, the United States appears to be getting worse in terms of the average number of barrels of oil used per citizen and the amount of energy used to generate goods and services. New homes tend to be ever larger, have higher ceilings and thus more space to heat, and are equipped with a greater number of luxury appliances. In fact, although the average American family size has decreased by 20 percent since 1970, in that same time period the average new American home size has increased by 50 percent.[28] Outsized sport utility vehicles and what are conveniently named "full-sized" vehicles—a specious norm—have achieved a great degree of popularity. Few people remember, let alone take seriously, the 1973 "energy crisis." In short, by whatever measure, the United States remains the greatest energy glutton in the world. This lamentable fact is reflected in Congress' hostility to the Kyoto Accords and the likelihood that, despite government promises to reduce emissions of greenhouse gases by 7 percent from 1990 to 2010, those emissions will continue to increase.[29]

Perhaps it was such destructive consequences of a mechanistic worldview that Václav Havel had in mind when he argued that any contemporary defense of individual rights, on the one hand, and a search for world peace, on the other hand, must overcome this fissure between ourselves and nature. As the epigraph of this chapter indicates, Havel argues for the realization that we enigmatically mirror the universe, and vice versa. A scientific acknowledgment of this fact restores human integrity, in the sense of wholeness, by securing our moorings in nature. This is indeed what makes the "Gaia hypothesis" so attractive to Havel. The hypothesis proposes that the Earth is a single, interconnected network of organic and inorganic relationships that form a living organism. For Havel, the hypothesis reminds us of the ways in which we are a central part of "higher, mysterious entities against whom it is not advisable to blaspheme. This forgotten awareness is encoded in all religions."[30]

Similarly, Scheler argues correctly that a revival of our sense of unity with the cosmos goes hand in hand with practical consequences such as caring for animals, demonstrating against vivisection, and forest conservation. Our unity with nature also implicates kindness to oneself in terms of healing. This healing comes from listening to the wisdom of the body in its relations with its natural and social worlds, rather than unilaterally imposing demands on it as an instrument in the various production processes that make up the social world—the ubiquitous corollary of which is stress. Such listening not only provides a sense of mental well-being but also has substantial health-protective benefits, perhaps most visibly in the prevention of heart attacks and strokes.[31] In contrast, the reversal of these values in favor of accumulating as much wealth as possible is "the product of *ill-feeling toward the weak and helpless* and betrays a corrupted morality" (Scheler 1954, 108; emphasis in original).

For the sense of the organic unity of nature to come to life again, certain conditions have to be fulfilled. Absent a thermonuclear war and unlikely survivors left to start over, modern industrial technology will not change essentially. It will still be what Heidegger calls "enframing." But the ways in which we use it must change. Charles Taylor states that what Heidegger really seeks is an "alternative enframing" (1992, 106). So, in fact, do Havel and Marcel. The latter argued as far back as 1933 that despair stems from the acknowledgment of all "technics" as ultimately insufficient, coupled with the unwillingness or inability to reassess the meaning of technology in light of the "fundamental nature of being" (Marcel 1964b, 30). More recently, Havel has ventured the hypothesis that "the revolt of the masses," as Ortega y Gasset described it, along with "the intellectual, moral, political, and social misery in the world today," is "merely an aspect of the deep crisis in which humanity, dragged helplessly along by the automatism of global technological civilization, finds itself" (Havel 1991, 207).

It is not merely a question of trying to escape the hegemony of technology, because that would be to remain trapped within a dyadic opposition of domination and non-domination. Rather, we must step outside of this opposition entirely by finding other, more poietic ways that technology can challenge nature. Or, what is the same thing, an alternative enframing is necessary to appreciate (in both senses) nature, to avoid the pitfalls of alienation from it, and to maximize our humanness in kinder relationships toward both other people, external nature, and ourselves. This is why Havel contrasts the intimate connection of nature and *Lebenswelt,* in which we are "at home" and for which we are responsible, with the world of science and industry. Atmospheric pollution, for example, is not just an instance of correctable anti-ecological industrial practices. It also has a metaphysical significance as "the symbol of an age which seeks to transcend the boundaries of the natural world and its norms and to make it into a merely private concern" (Havel 1991, 251).

It is likewise difficult to imagine kindness flourishing in families whose members are seen as "drag coefficients" and whose children are conceptualized as investments, or "stockpiles," of "high-end" genes. Similarly, it is also hard to envisage a society as both kind and systematically destructive and gluttonous in using up natural resources and in causing other animals unnecessary pain and suffering to support its own luxuries. Also, to the degree that a life centered on technological thinking is caught up in a dialectic of fear and desire, in the spiral of having and wanting (more), the less such a life is open to others, the less it will be able to manifest the *disponibilité* characteristic of kindness. Fear leads to self-contraction and desire to increased competition for scarce goods. Both, albeit in different ways, underwrite an egoism of indifference or hostility that we can easily grasp not only from experience but also by performing the Hobbesian experiment.

Thus in our dealings with human beings, other sentient life, and external nature, we must transcend a purely technical attitude and come to see them as something more than *manipulanda* in the double sense of having no inherent value and as a mere means to our ends. The illusions of domination, control, and unlimited power must give way to a more humble approach to nature. This means that our alternative enframing will continue to be a challenging of nature, in Heidegger's sense, but at the same time will have to be a respectful one. That is, we will continue to confront nature in terms of its use-value, as stockpiles of resources, but at the same time, we must do so appreciatively (in both senses) and invest much care in return. It is also worth noting in passing that domination and control have had as their object that part of our environment that is our immediate habitat, namely, the land. It appears that familiarity breeds, if not contempt, at least the illusions of pride. But such attitudes in the uncertain milieu of the sea constitute the folly of the uninitiated. Sailors quickly learn what we all should know, even on land, namely, that we must acknowledge nature on its own terms while we make thankful use of it.

These revised attitudes toward nature and their enhanced potential for kindness imply also that an alternative enframing not only transcends Marcel's view of technology but also Heidegger's conception of *poiesis* as excluding all modernist rationality. It is true that the latter has led to Auschwitz, nuclear weapons, and a rapacious capitalist destruction of the earth. Nevertheless, it does not follow that modernist rationality has no constructive, redemptive possibilities. Thus Heidegger's desire to replace modernist rationality *tout court* with *poiesis* is mistaken. For that reason, overcoming this false dichotomy underlies Taylor's own conception of an alternative enframing, which he sees as "Technology in the service of an ethic of benevolence toward real flesh and blood people; technological, calculative thinking as a rare and admirable achievement of a being who lives in the medium of a quite different kind of thinking: to live instrumental reason from out of these frameworks would be to live our technology very differently" (Taylor 1992, 107).

Living "instrumental reason from out of these frameworks" implies that such instrumental reason is no more necessarily morally corrupt than is technology necessarily evil. In fact, the instrumental thinking that underlies the uses of technology itself emerges from a moral background. Francis Bacon, its progenitor, conceived that the new science of his day would have a moral in addition to an obvious epistemological value. It would, he wrote, unlike previous science based on Aristotelian method, "relieve the condition of mankind" (Taylor 1992, 104). As Taylor goes on to point out, recovery of this moral background can demonstrate that technology not only does not have to lead to increased control and domination, but also that such domination would betray that moral background. This is precisely the misuse of instrumental thinking that Nuland described.

This revised sense of instrumental thinking is also consistent with both senses of the appreciation of nature. Indeed, appreciative instrumentalism comes close to expressing the ideal of scientific wonder that drives curiosity. It is also the same attitude that characterizes what Marcel calls "sanctity." A "saint," in his view, is precisely the person who manages to overcome her alienation from nature and, on an ontological level, the contemporary saint is the naturalist. "For him, the word 'insignificant' has no sense. In the passionate study of a particular species he has triumphed for all time over such reactions . . . the naturalist experiences a kind of wonder before the fineness and the complexity of the structure he observes" (Marcel 1973, 117). As Scheler, St. Francis of Assisi, Native American thinkers, and Tagore pointed out, there is a close relationship between our unity with nature and kindness in both its senses of achievement and of being part of humankind.

Marcel does not say so, but the difference between what he calls the "profane and ignorant" view of nature and that of the naturalist is similar to the difference that phenomenologists ever since Husserl have described as that between the "world of the natural attitude" and the changed attitude introduced by the epoché (see the Introduction). Here it is the naturalist who provides us with what Fink described as an "astonishment" in the face of the world. We need a phenomenological *epoché* of the natural attitude with which we perceive nature itself and a changed attitude that would flow from that suspension of belief—including our own mastery. Marcel's conception of such a changed attitude, as previously noted, is that which "implies a gift of self, a reverential attitude designated by the term 'piety' " (1973, 114). As such, it closely resembles Taylor's notion of an alternative enframing. It is the *Gelassenheit* that the poet ably represents as an alternative to exploitation, along with the altered conception of instrumental reason, described above.

Such a technology must be put to use at the interpersonal level, to be sure, but clearly it will not be effective unless it is given institutional sponsorship and sheltered by institutional protection. Again, as Heidegger pointed out correctly, "It is only as protected and preserved—and that means enclosed and secure—that anything is set free to endure" (1977, 11, n. 10). Individuals by themselves cannot change social atmospheres or the values underlying the current *Zeitgeist*. Thus one physician merely, or a cluster of them here and there, will not be sufficient to change the dehumanizing excesses of medical practice, but "topdown" institutional enforcement can. We shall return to this theme in the following chapter, because both Heidegger and Marcel prolong their reflections on nature and technology in the context of community.

Since Heidegger's and Marcel's writings on technology appeared, there have been scattered successes in establishing an alternative enframing. In this country we now at least pay lip service to conservation, and we have the Environmental Protection Agency (EPA). The field of environmental ethics, which did not even exist thirty years ago, is now one of the most popular parts of the university curriculum. There is also a spreading consciousness of the need to restore nature as well as take from it. For example, during Heidegger's and Marcel's lifetimes, recycling was no more than a fringe-group fad; now it is an important part of mainstream culture. Further, strip mining is no longer practiced in the United States, and some modest steps have been taken to do something about global warming, the greenhouse effect, and the destruction of the ozone layer. Moreover, many once-dead rivers and streams again host fish and other forms of life and, as noted above, with DDT banned, certain endangered species such as peregrine falcons and bald eagles either have been, or soon will be, removed from the endangered species list.

But these are only meagre beginnings. Locked in a global dialectic of fear and desire, our multiple unkindnesses are still very far from an alternate Gestell that would incarnate the "reverential attitude designated by the term 'piety' " that Marcel recommends toward nature, and which makes possible the type of appreciation that Hopkins expressed when he wrote that, for all the human degradation of the earth, "There lives the dearest freshness deep down things."[32] The challenge for us in the third millenium is to reach that freshness respectfully and appreciatively—poietically.[33] In this way, like the Dakota, we will grow into the responsibility that we already have. It is the responsibility about which the Dalai Lama asks rhetorically if we will be to blame for exploiting all natural resources available to us and leaving nothing for succeeding generations. If, on the contrary, we live up to this responsibility, we will achieve a healthy equilibrium in the way in which we relate to the environment. In the end, he concludes, "the decision to save the environment must come from the human heart" (Dalai Lama 1990, 116). Hans Jonas has expressed the same thought as a novel categorical imperative, "that of acting in such a way that a future humanity will still exist after us, in the environment of a habitable earth" (Ricoeur 1992, 295).

Nature

The previous section dealt with certain major ways in which kindness and unkindness are embedded in our technological manipulations of nature, including the human body. But our relations with nature also raise questions of kindness that transcend technology. We have already ventured on some of these questions in terms of character development, the fact that some people have less of a disposition to kindness than others, the involuntary dimensions of the will, and the difficulties of acquired dispositions. However, kindness has other relationships with the will not yet discussed here. These include our treatment of other forms of sentient life, including our eating habits; the ways in which nature provokes involuntary unkindness, and, finally, the penchant by some to appeal to nature as a (or the) norm for human moral development.

The previous section presented a picture of humanness increasing in relation to what is non-human and that, as Scheler and Abram argue, kindness as a moral achievement similarly enlarges as the reversibilities of our flesh dispose us to an active, participatory perception of other sentient creatures. The two senses of kindness merge in that our kindness in a moral sense expands in tandem with the augmentation of our natural kindness, as part of the world of flesh. But since the objectification inherent in instrumental thinking conceals those other natural voices, the separation that results—as Scheler, Chief Luther Standing Bear, and Abram point out—diminishes our humanness. We are likely to miss, for example, the way in which certain other animals are capable either of language, or of something very like it, of social feelings and compassion, of forming friendships, and of manifesting a sense of responsibility in their relationships with other creatures. As noted earlier, Darwin claimed in *The Descent of Man and Selection in Relation to Sex* (1898, 98–129) that compassion and altruism are not unique to our species.[34]

But separation from other species is only one way to lose a degree of humanness in relation to the non-human. Another and much more morally serious means is through cruelty to other animals, a subject that both transcends and overlaps technology. It transcends it because, either on an individual or a societal level, we can be cruel to animals without technological manipulation. There are sadists who torture animals, as we have seen in Hogarth's *The Four Stages of Cruelty*. Communities can also be cruel to animals (and the rest of nature) by, say, allowing pollution to destroy forests, or by permitting suburban sprawl to destroy habitats. The overlapping consists in the fact that it presents us with another interesting and important case of technological concealment of both nature and our fleshly participation with it.

In our previous chapters, for the most part, the others who comprised the objects of the acts and habits of kindness described were human beings. One exception was Uncle Toby's act (in *Tristram Shandy*) of putting a fly outside rather than killing it. Had he been a real person, we would have said that his flesh resonated with the creature's helplessness—just as our flesh can respond to various forms of sentient life as members of the moral community.

What one will believe can stand in this relation to us is variable from one society to another. In the type of society in which we live, most people would not hesitate to swat an unwelcome fly or mosquito. Yet most people would shrink from doing the same thing to cats or dogs, and not just because it would violate laws against cruelty to animals. It is part of the social atmosphere currently prevailing in our society that most people abhor cruelty. However, it is also the case that most people appear to have a sliding scale of compassion for nonhuman life depending on, among other things, their beliefs about the degree of consciousness and pain present.[35]

With whatever life-form, the general value here inscribed in our social atmosphere is that we have a nonoptional duty to some, if not all, other forms of sentient life. Montaigne expressed this value as follows: "[T]here is a certain respect, and a general duty of humanity, that attaches us not only to animals, who have life and feeling, but even to trees and plants. We owe justice to men, and mercy and kindness to other creatures that may be capable of receiving it. There is some relationship between them and us, and some mutual obligation" (1958, II:11, 318). However, in our own day, we no longer draw such a sharp line between justice and kindness. In our own social atmosphere, we tend to see cruelty to animals as unjust as well as unkind. Thus, for example, Peter Singer's *Animal Liberation* and People for the Ethical Treatment of Animals (PETA) do not condemn cruelly painful laboratory experiments just on the basis of their unkindness, but rather on the grounds that the victims have the same negative rights that we do not to be tortured.

It is also part of the values that inform our own social atmosphere that we argue for the obligation to avoid cruelty on the basis of the animal's interests rather than our own. That is, we base this duty on the animal's pain and suffering rather than on human-interested reasons. We believe with Sidgwick and Bentham that, as the former expresses it, common sense dictates that "the pain of animals is *per se* to be avoided" (Sidgwick 1913, 241).

But while most people would refuse to participate in conscious, intentional cruelty to animals, an equal number are unknowingly complicit with invisible, unintended cruelties. As the Society of Friends states in writing about a duty of kindness to animals, "Suffering can be caused through callousness and carelessness based often upon ignorance, and we must testify against such cruelty wherever we find it. Kindness therefore requires knowledge and understanding as well as good will" (Society of Friends 1960, 480). Technology plays a major role in concealing our complicity with cruelty to animals, because it blocks our exposure to those practices as well as our sensitivities to the victims.

Unfortunately, there are a great many examples. A rapid survey of just a few includes puppy mills, agribusiness techniques of cruel and painful confinement of calves for more tender meat, and gorging the livers of ducks and geese to produce *foie gras*. Other examples include greyhound racing, vivisection, monkeys with smashed skulls in head injury clinics and, in others, eyes stitched closed. There are also inhumane traps and clothing and other food products that are produced with cruelty. Sometimes, media exposés raise one or another of these practices to the level of conscious awareness, but we rarely become cognizant of the ways that animals have been cruelly abused in testing cosmetics and household products such as shampoos, detergents, or soaps. The technology of product production, distribution, and sales blocks customers from not only the pain and death of the victims but also from their abilities to be sensitized to their torment.

These experiments return us again to the complexities of intent and effect with kindness at a social, as opposed to an interpersonal, level, as well as to the ways in which kindness interlocks in a Gestalt of other social values. Those that perform these experiments and test the products referred to above are not necessarily sadistic. The purpose of the research is to develop drugs, vehicles, and household products that are safe for human beings, or that are safer than those now available. Further, some researchers at least do take steps to alleviate suffering unnecessary for the research. Conversely, the price of not doing the experiments would be the unkindness of placing human lives at risk with a much higher probability of injury, or even death. Thus, on a social level, pursuing a policy of kindness toward one constituency can have the effect of unkindness toward another. Also, in terms of interlocking social values, there are at least three underlying value judgments in these experiments and product testings. At least in some laboratories, there is a commitment to causing as little pain and suffering as possible. There is also the belief that human life is worth more than nonhuman life—what Peter Singer (1990) has termed "speciesism"—as well as the correlative view that nonhuman life should pay the price required for enhancing the welfare of our species.

In turn, these values clash with other perceptions outside of the laboratory. In addition to factual questions about the necessity of the experiments, products tested, and the availability of cruelty-free alternatives, we are aware of different levels of comparative value judgments about whether the goals of the experiments and product testing are worth the cost of the suffering to produce them. For example, should we use a particular hair spray that has been tested by spraying it into the eyes of terrified rabbits in order to verify that it will not harm a child who inadvertently does the same thing? More generally, should we use hair sprays at all if cruelty is a necessary condition of producing them? All such questions involve competing values, but not all values weigh equally in the scale. No one has to eat *foie gras*, just as nobody has to use shampoos produced through torture.

Hunting and fishing are other social practices that, in terms of kindness, display ambiguities about intent and have conflicting results. Conflicting results emerge with the disturbance of the balance of nature. Thus, for example, in the absence of wolves and other predators, deer herds will tend to increase fairly quickly beyond the carrying capacity of their habitats. Without hunting, many deer will die of starvation which, proponents of the sport argue, is much more unkind than being dispatched with a high-powered hunting rifle. (This claim obviously does not extend to those who hunt deer and other animals with automatic weapons.) Hence, those who see recreational hunting as cruel are forced into a dilemma of having to choose between two unkindnesses. Ambiguities about intent persist, because there are multiple, non-disjunctive possibilities. Hunting and fishing can be motivated by survival, both personal and as a way of making a living, but also by the desire for non-necessary food as well as for the thrill of the catch or shot and possession of displayable trophies.

Killing out of necessity does not by itself distance or alienate one from nature. One can still maintain a consciousness of a unity with nature while attempting to survive in it. Both possibilities are prominent aspects of Native American oral and written histories, myths, symbols, and religion. They testify to life situated in a harsh environment that simultaneously maintained a respectful, appreciative unity with the cosmos while killing for food, clothing, and shelter. But killing for excitement is inconsistent with such an attitude and its attendant kindnesses, because it is grounded in an instrumental thinking that takes other sentient creatures as pure objects, mere means to human pleasures. The excitement depends on an alienation from the target and would quickly wither if hunters and fishers saw their actions from the perspective of the victim. If they permitted these chiasmatic reversibilities of flesh to allow the resonance of suffering that they were about to cause, then only the extremely masochistic would take any pleasure in it.

Hunting and fishing, even out of necessity, also point to another important aspect of the relation of nature and kindness, namely, involuntary unkindness. Consider again Montaigne's condemnation of cruelty to animals. "I do not see a chicken's neck wrung without distress," he tells us, "and I cannot bear to hear the scream of a hare in the teeth of my dogs, *although the chase is a violent pleasure*" (1958, II:11, p. 313; emphasis added). This is to say that nature itself has the capacity to play upon our fleshly reciprocities in such a way as to contribute to our alienation from it. Even those most respectful of nature and other forms of sentient life are subject to these unwanted resonances that produce unkindness in both senses.

Montaigne's aversion to suffering has another implication in terms of the rejection of that torment being grounded on the animal's plight rather than human revulsion. Scheler rejects as "spurious" cases of fellow-feeling in which one utters words similar to those of Montaigne cited in the previous paragraph. He writes: "The really instructive feature here is the way the agent brings his own pleasure or pain into the foreground of attention, so as to *mask* their presence in the other person, and concentrates upon these obtrusive feelings of his own . . . genuine instances of commiseration or rejoicing are never self-regarding states of feeling" (Scheler 1954, 41; emphasis in original). Montaigne gives no indication whether his objections are based on the animal's or his own suffering, but if his only reason were the latter, Scheler would be correct.

Montaigne's resonances of "violent pleasure" not only constitute much of the appeal for recreational hunting and fishing but also provide a bodily explanation for the popularity of guns. Guns themselves, as well as the act of firing them, as even certain strong proponents of gun control have admitted, have a fundamentally visceral appeal to pleasure, power, and the pleasure of having power. Another dimension to the naturalist's state of "sanctity" that Marcel describes could well consist in resisting the temptations of pleasure that would alienate us from nature and lead us to be agents of its gratuitous destruction. A helpful first step in that direction would be, as proposed above, a phenomenological *epoché* of the natural attitude with which we perceive nature itself, and a resulting changed attitude that would flow from that suspension of belief—including our own unbridled mastery.

Nature also confronts us with instances of involuntary unkindness in very different sorts of situations. These are cases in which kindness in the sense of nature provokes unkindness, or at least blocks the emergence of kindness, in a moral sense. One unremarkable type of such experiences occurs when we encounter people who grate against all of our sensitivities. They "get on our nerves," we "can't stand them," even while we can recognize at an intellectual level that there is not only no rational basis for our reaction, but that the individuals in question are perfectly decent, good people. So we say, frustrated with our failure, that "there is just something about them" that we cannot abide. This is what happened to Lucy Honeychurch in Forster's *A Room with a View*. She has tried repeatedly to like her cousin, Charlotte Bartlett, but to no avail: "One might lay up treasure in heaven by the attempt, but one enriched neither Miss Bartlett, nor any one else upon earth. She was reduced to saying: 'I can't help it, mother. I don't like Charlotte. I admit it's horrid of me" (Forster 1986, 162).

Even though nature and culture are inextricably woven together in human existence, it is difficult to believe that the socialization process plays a significant role in such familiar aversions. One reason is that these reactions can occur almost instantaneously and can coexist with conscious recognition of their irrationality. On the other hand, there are at least two cases of visceral antipathy that do owe as much to culture as to nature. One is racism which, as noted earlier, does not survive today as an intellectual construct. An instructive contrast may be found in the free and easy acceptance—not mere tolerance—of mixed racial couples and their children in the French West Indies and elsewhere. Racial aversions therefore cannot show by themselves that flesh has within it reciprocities of irreducible animosities. However, the fictional example of Jane Eyre, discussed in Chapter 2, comes nearer the mark, because she differed from her aunt and cousins only in terms of family complexion. She was perceived as "alien" because of the absence of "blood-ties" and because she, unlike her blonde and fair cousins, was "dark." Similar considerations apply to the previously mentioned fact that, in the United States, the number of minority children awaiting adoption far exceeds the supply of adoptive families and that, in contrast, a lucrative black market exists for (healthy) Caucasian children.

The second example of visceral antipathy that is just as culturally as naturally formed consists of homophobia. It is not a question of reasoned criticisms of homosexuality which, whatever one makes of them, are not, like those supporting racism, confined to the lunatic fringe. Rather, what I have in mind is a visceral response that resembles that which is inscribed in racism. Perhaps it is true that, as Michael Moore (1987) following Nietzsche, has suggested, the violence of the reaction increases in direct proportion to the strength of the desire that the agent is attempting to repress—a fact graphically portrayed in the film *American Beauty*. In that case, reciprocities of animosity embedded in the flesh would be self-referential enough to plunge masochism into self-loathing. In any event, the acceptance of homosexuality in other cultures itself shows the significant role of the socialization process in homophobia.

These cases also illustrate one other example of the relations of kindness and nature that is irrelevant to technology. This is when people make normative claims about human nature that are based on, and placed in the services of, essentialism. In the past, almost all such claims have been used to defend beliefs about morality and acceptable gender roles in society and to provide a basis for political systems and law. Usually such interpretations have reinforced patriarchy and hierarchy. Accordingly, in avoiding the snare of essentialism, as in the case of medicalized sexuality, poststructuralist thought has favored a non-normative constructivism that has allowed for a variety of discourses about the self. None of these discourses is said to have any privileged truth-value, let alone a grounding in natural law theory.

As indicated above, on a descriptive level, I take Merleau-Ponty's phenomenology of the body and perception to provide a compelling refutation of the diametrically opposed positions that there is an immutable substratum of human nature for which culture serves as a changeable veneer, and that we can eliminate all references to nature in favor of social constructionism. At the same time, however, a descriptive answer is not enough to resolve the difficult questions involved in essentialism. They must be postponed to Part Two because, as we shall see, a good deal of the debate will turn on unconscious meanings and unseen power struggles that lie beyond the scope of a descriptive phenomenology of kindness.

However, before undertaking the hermeneutics of kindness required to answer those questions, one more chapter of the descriptive phenomenology is necessary to complete our account of social kindness. The subject of that chapter consists of institutions and communities. Both are crucial to social kindness in their own right, but also because, as Heidegger pointed out, poietic flourishing requires shelter and protection. Thus, in their severe environment, the Dakota knew that merely living close to, or in accordance with, nature was not enough to guarantee survival, let alone a robust sense of human flourishing. They knew that in the harsh life on the plains, life could very frequently be, in Hobbesian terms, "nasty, brutish, and short." What was also needed for both survival and well-being was social defense. To that subject, therefore, we now turn.

Chapter 5

Institutions and Community

I wouldn't give you two cents for all your fancy rules if behind them they didn't have a little bit of plain, ordinary kindness and a little looking' out for the other fella.
—Jimmy Stewart, in *Mr. Smith Goes to Washington*

Institutions

In any given society, the values embedded in indeterminate social atmospheres take determinate forms of customs, traditions, taboos, and the like. They are also inscribed in social institutions through their procedures, rules, policies, and own traditions and customs. These diverse phenomena can present themselves with varying degrees of kindness or unkindness for reasons analogous to those that make a given social atmosphere in some degree kind or unkind. Furthermore, as the previous chapter suggested, a significant dimension of their kindness is the degree to which they provide an umbrella of protection for humane values.

Institutions perform a contextualizing function for kind acts and persons just as do social atmospheres, which themselves condition our perceptions of institutions. Many, if not most, of the acts of kindness and unkindness and kind and unkind people we encounter on a daily basis are to be found in institutions—store clerks, airline gate agents, post office employees, and the like. Some may treat us with insufferable tactlessness and arrogance, care-full kindness, or a certain degree of kindness between these extremes.

Furthermore, institutional contexts create ambiguities about the meanings of actions. It is at least sometimes difficult to determine whether an act is a true expression of the person herself, or whether she is simply acting "in an institutional capacity," "in her role as . . . ," and so on. One type of this ambiguity occurs when institutional demands, stresses, and frustrations lie behind the particular act that we witness. The surly airline gate agent, for instance, may have had a thoroughly rotten day dealing with flight delays and irascible, contentious passengers before

I reach her. Sometimes, of course, there may be no ambiguities, as in racist policies and actions against African Americans at the Denny's restaurants that refused to serve African-American FBI agents, or at the highest management levels of Texaco.

A second type of this ambiguity occurs when the employee may, for whatever reason, feel called upon to represent the institution to the exclusion of all of her personal feelings. Thus Dorothy Day says somewhere that once the highly offensive customs agent took off his uniform and became a human being again, his behavior would perhaps change accordingly. Here the institutional shaping of identity interferes with their members' abilities to perform acts of kindness and become kind persons. This was the Tsar's problem in Tolstoy's "The Forged Coupon," and it is equally a problem for many contemporary CEOs.

Lawrence's *Women in Love* dramatically expresses a variant on this same theme. A wealthy mine owner, Thomas Crich, belongs to a group of mine owners called "the Masters' Federation." For the sake of the industry, Crich and his fellow owners sought a pay reduction from the miners. When the latter refused, the Federation called for a lockout. Since Mr. Crich belonged to the Federation, he considered himself honor bound to close his pits. But Mr. Crich also desired to be a Christian, equal to all other people. He even wanted to share all of his wealth with the poor. But, Lawrence tells us, he could not do it, because he knew that he had to maintain his power and authority, and he believed that a strong industry was good for society (1985, 255). Torn between the two ideals, Mr. Crich was broken.

Conflict between personal and institutional identities manifests itself not just in public or private enterprise but equally in institutions such as families. These institutions also function as forms of social activity that mold individual and collective experience and identities. They shape their members by regulating conduct, both positively and negatively. They form character "by assigning responsibility, demanding accountability, and providing the standards in terms of which each person recognizes the excellence of his or her achievements" (Bellah et al. 1992, 40). Thus parents sometimes have to act *as parents* rather than in the ways they would wish to, for the good of their children, by imposing rules and discipline and by deciding on punishments. These obligations lead to a large number of mediately presented acts of kindness, as described in Chapter 1.

Any mature society possesses the widest variety of institutions. In addition to families—traditional and nontraditional, immediate and extended—there are also ethnic groups, churches, and the like. These fall under the first half of Ferdinand Tönnies' classic distinction between *Gemeinschaft* (community) and *Gesellschaft* (association). Under the latter half of the distinction are private-sector businesses, political and legal institutions, educational and health care institutions, the armed forces, and so on. Whatever the type, institutions' rules, procedures, policies, and customs, along with their own indeterminate social atmospheres, govern normal daily operations and provide a recognized means of settling disputes. In this way, institutions function as structures "held together" by a "bond of common *mores*" (Ricoeur 1992, 194).

Sometimes we know the authors and origins of rules, procedures, policies, and the like. For example, in terms of the law of equity, we know the cases that established it and even, in many cases, the names of the judges. But often we have no such knowledge; it is once again a question of "generalized" others. In the absence of direct information about the intentions and concerns of our predecessors, we have to hypothesize in terms of a means-end rationality, and of what we have seen that Schutz calls "because" and "in order to" motives. Thus we come to judge the kindness of rules, procedures, social policies, and so forth in terms of their impact on us. Similar to the way that we extrapolate an intent of kindness from intelligent product designs, as discussed in the previous chapter, we can work out, for example, that a particular employee or rule maker anticipated our steps and took measures to lessen our burdens or to avoid imposing them. We can also infer that they wished to guide us toward a fulfillment that we might not have grasped by ourselves. But in such cases we inevitably lack certainty about "the degree of congruity between the scheme of expression which determined my predecessor's communicative acts and my scheme of interpretation" (Schutz 1964, 60–61). In the absence of direct evidence of motives and concerns, we have only the historical record, the objective effects of their actions.

Even in the present, the anonymity of the actors involved and lack of information about their motives are common features of contemporary institutional life. Just as with the background values of social atmospheres, present institutional rules, policies, procedures, and so on are usually given as non-attributable. Steinbeck's *The Grapes of Wrath* (1976) offers an especially clear example, and one that also shows how institutions can be interrelated and responsibility therefore more and more diffuse. At a certain point of the novel, a sharecropper is defending his house against a man on a tractor who has been told to destroy it for non-payment of debts. The farmer threatens to shoot the would-be destroyer, but the latter explains that he will lose his job if he does not do it. He then tells the farmer that he is shooting the wrong person. The farmer agrees and asks, "Who gave you orders? I'll go after him. He's the one to kill." The tractor driver says that he still has not got it right, because the bank ordered his boss to, "Clear those people out or it's your job." The farmer then thinks he could kill the president and board of directors of the bank. But the driver responded, "Fellow was telling me the bank gets orders from the East. The orders were, 'Make the land show profit or we'll close you up.'" The farmer then fairly wails, "But where does it stop? Who can we shoot? I don't aim to starve to death before I kill the man that's starving me." The driver answers, "I don't know. Maybe there's nobody to shoot. Maybe the thing isn't men at all. Maybe, like you said, the property's doing it. Anyway I told you my orders" (Steinbeck 1976, 49).

Rules, procedures, policies, and the like join social atmospheres in exhibiting varying degrees of kindness and unkindness in terms of the ways in which they facilitate the flourishing of those who live in or are subject to a given institution. Such kindness is reflected in, among other things, a constant attention to relevance—say, in replacing outmoded and obsolete rules and regulations. In cases in which that is not possible, kindness becomes evident in sensitive interpretations by those currently in charge of institutions. Here the kindness of the functioning institution itself depends on the practical wisdom of current administrators. This is true not only of institutions that are part of a society's *Gemeinschaft*, such as families or churches, but also of those which make up *Gesellschaft* as well. Legal institutions are obvious examples. If such adjustments could not be made, law would quickly become the dead weight of the past crystallizing into tyranny.

On the other hand, there is a signal difference in the way that the two different types of institutions manifest kindness. With families, for example, we expect functioning relationships to be underwritten by commitments of love, because membership in the institution consists of occupying a non-voluntary, unique, non-substitutable position. This premise is obviously missing in institutions such as government or private-sector businesses in which downsizings underscore the fungibility of employees, though even here, as noted previously, we expect some dedication to the welfare of members of the institution. Further, in the case of private-sector businesses, we generally have no expectation of special acts of kindness toward their customers. We recognize that such institutions have their own legitimate self-interests, and kindness manifested to customers appears as a surplus over and above the performance of institutional duties. Hence, there is a powerful ambiguity built into the phrase, "health care industry," at least with regard to its private sector.

Nevertheless, to say that we have no legitimate expectation of kindnesses from such institutions does not imply that we should expect unkindness. Unhappily, though, the markers of the unkindness of procedures, traditions, rules, policies, and so forth in all types of institutions are only too plain. One is unintelligibility in the sense of objective unjustifiability. A rule or policy, say, appears as unjustifiable when no intelligible motive can be hypothesized, and the rule or policy does not serve as a means to any institutional purpose. In law, for example, one instance of this unintelligibility consists of a statute's failing what is known as the "rational basis" test of being a means to a proper state objective.

Sometimes the unintelligibility of rules, policies, procedures, and the like extends only to those outside of a particular institution, but in other cases, such rules, policies, and procedures can also appear unintelligible to those who work (and live) within the institution. H.L.A. Hart's distinction between the "internal" and "external" aspects of rules in a legal system explains why this is so in any given institutional context. The external aspects of rules are those that appear to an observer to be outside of the system and also to the minority of dissident participants within the system. This perspective is limited to those who correlate regularities in participants' behavior and, without necessarily accepting or even understanding the meaning of the behavior, would be able to predict correctly the existence of rules that influence the behavior. The observer could inductively arrive at the conclusion that such and such a rule merely exists in that legal system and could predict the existence of such a rule merely on the basis of observed behavior.

In contrast, the internal aspects of rules express the point of view of participants who do accept the rules and give them as reasons for their behavior, "as a standard for all who play the game" (Hart 1961, 55). For game players, rules are not merely predictions that people will behave in certain ways, but explanations for their behavior. A red light, say, is not a prediction that drivers will stop, but a reason for them to do so. Correlatively, "the violation of a rule is not merely a basis for the prediction that a hostile reaction will follow but a *reason* for hostility" (ibid., 88; emphasis in original).[1]

The distinction between the internal and external aspects of rules also applies to non-legal institutions, because procedures, rules, and practices can all look unintelligible to those outside of institutions—clients, customers, patients in hospitals, students, and so forth—but can be explained along the lines sketched above by those within the system. Then the appearance of unkindness tends to disappear or at least tends to soften. On the other hand, there are clearly cases in which those phenomena manifest themselves as unintelligible, even to those within a certain institution. They make no sense, because they do not appear to have any rational relationship to the institution's purpose (s) and objective (s). They tend to rest on the thin rationale of past practice ("We've always done it this way"), and in some cases they may appear as internally unintelligible, because they resemble "Catch 22's."

In these and a plethora of other examples, we perceive unintelligible rules, procedures, practices, customs, and so on as unkind because they manifest themselves to us as needless restrictions on our freedom. They are perceived as needless, because we believe that, with unhampered rational scrutiny, they would disappear. This is just another way of appreciating the enduring value of Mill's observation in *On Liberty* (1956), that one of the pernicious effects of not being allowed to question truth claims is eventually to lose sight of their very meanings. Closely related to this fact is Nussbaum's observation that "a supposed organic unit such as the family has constructed unequal capabilities for various types of functioning" (1999, 34), and that tradition is one of the principal causes of such inequalities.

There are many other ways besides unintelligibility that rules, procedures, practices, and other institutional phenomena can be unkind—in all "the stupidity[2] and heartlessness that present themselves daily in the world in forms that command respect" (Malcolm 1972, 32), about which Wittgenstein worried so much. Such "heartlessness" can take a number of diverse and overlapping forms. The four most important ones appear to be malice, the abuse of power, neglect, and the imposition of inappropriate values.

Malice provides all too many examples from the historically prominent—such as the genocide of Native Americans or the Holocaust—to less noticeable, local, and more banal cases. One common example consists of prejudice against the poor and/or immigrants. In one case, a poor immigrant couple, not long in the United States, took their critically ill nine-month-old son to a hospital. The hospital demanded $100 in cash before treating the child. By midnight, frantic phone calls to a number of friends finally produced the needed amount. The medical staff then informed the desperate parents that they "had lost valuable time" and that the odds of recovery were no better than 50-50. The staff then ordered the parents out of the hospital, because they were "in the way." Four hours later, the hospital telephoned to say that their son had died, and that they had to collect the body as soon as possible. Upon their arrival at the hospital, they were given a bill for $99.99. This happened in (of all places) Valley Forge.[3]

Another appalling example of institutional cruelty based on malice, conjoined with ignorance and greed, consists of juvenile prisons. The one at Tallulah, Louisiana, was especially heinous, but in general form not unrepresentative. Until a settlement of several lawsuits in the federal district court in Baton Rouge forced the state to make sweeping changes and effectively close its private youth prisons,[4] the Tallulah institution was privately run and dreadfully overcrowded. Fighting and serious injuries were common, with injuries often attributable to beatings administered by the badly paid and trained guards themselves. The fights occurred over, among other things, scarce clothing and food. In addition, there was little education, and up to 25 percent of the prisoners were mentally retarded. Psychiatric visits were rare, and therapy was non-existent. Emotionally disturbed boys were put in isolation cells for weeks on end. But even though Tallulah was closed, officials of the correctional system said that the social forces that created the prison—putting ever more mentally ill young people in jail, politicians in a hurry to build new prisons with no provision for education or mental health needs, and privatizing prisons to save money—"have caused the deterioration of juvenile prisons across the country."[5] Such penal institutions provide a vivid example of the fact that "punishment in general and prison in particular belong to a political technology of the body" (Foucault 1977, 30). In these and other cases, punishment becomes a political game to be deciphered.

However, in this and in certain other examples of institutional abuses of power conjoined with malice, the decoding is not at all difficult. These cases include courts turned into death mills in the service of an unconscionably flawed system of capital punishment,[6] as well as colonialism and the exploitation of nature, of which Conrad's *The Heart of Darkness* gives us an unforgettable portrait. Its primal metaphoric contrasts of white and black and light and dark at first stand for Europeans and Africans, respectively, but then get inverted when ivory, as the symbol of evil, is contrasted with the darkness of the jungle. "The word 'ivory' rang in the air," Conrad writes, "was whispered, was sighed. You would think they were praying to it. A taint of imbecile rapacity blew through it all, like a whiff from some corpse" (Conrad 1985, 52).

Other sorts of examples of institutional abuse of power consist of various unkindnesses in the ways in which public utilities, such as the public health care system, treat the poor. It is true that some people, somewhere, have to bear the operating costs, and it is also true that there are deadbeats who cannot and will not pay their utility bills. But it is equally undeniable that poor people in this country who are not deadbeats have had their heat cut off in the winter only for lack of ability to pay—which is illegal in, for example, France and Sweden.

Yet a different sort of institutional abuse of power consists of coercive environments, rather like Foucault's examples of prisons, but in some ways distinct from it. The *Miranda* decision, briefly described in Chapter 1, and which is now under review, demonstrated this in terms of custodial atmospheres. The U.S. Supreme Court held that it was not simply imprisonment that was coercive and intimidating but the very fact of being in custody: "[T]he modern practice of in-custody interrogation is psychologically rather than physically oriented. As we stated before, 'Since *Chambers v. Florida*, 309 U.S. 227, this Court has recognized that coercion can be mental as well as physical'" (384 U.S. 436 [1966], at 448).

The third form of institutional cruelty, neglect, often overlaps both malice and abuse of power. And even when institutional policies wear the label of "benign neglect," they sometimes have cruel consequences. Certainly this has been the case with Native Americans for most of the twentieth century, and reservations that struggle with astronomical rates of alcoholism, unemployment, and violence bear grim testimony to governmental and wider societal indifference. In addition, wherever Native Americans have tried to make economic gains—say, through casinos or insisting on fishing rights guaranteed by treaties that were usually the object of cynical disregard—the white establishment has fought contentiously in court (and sometimes out of it) to stop them.

Neglect can intersect the abuse of power in different ways. One of them shows up in Kozol's blistering indictment of hostility or indifference toward inner-city schoolchildren, which the previous chapter briefly described. He tells the story of "the lifelong deformation of poor children by their own society and government" (1991, 191).[7] He does this by describing the hellish conditions in a number of inner-city schools across the country and the difficulties—in most cases, impossibilities—that those schools face in providing their children with anything akin to an education equal to that enjoyed by most white (and wealthy) suburban schools. Kozol shows how the institutional cruelty unfolds in a rigged system that considers poor children inferior and a waste of money, and so funds are severely reduced. Then, when in the midst of such a deprived, miserable atmosphere many poor children do not do well, the critics and the social planners say, "I told you so." In short, the children's lack of success becomes a self-fulfilling, planned prophecy.

Of course, most children are unaware of the game in which they are the pawns, and we shall go into that aspect of Kozol's work in Part Two. But not so much can be said for the victimizers. As one New York City principal said of them, "You cannot issue an appeal to conscience in New York today" (Kozol 1991, 89). His reason was that the people in a position to help poor children had an infinite capacity not to notice them—in the sense of not registering, described in Chapter 3. If anything, wealthy suburbanites showed themselves much more willing to pay for more prisons to deal with the effects of poor education and crime than they were to fix the educational system.

Kozol did find some children, rich and poor, who were able to discuss the merits and demerits of equalized funding for schools.[8] In the wealthy school district of Rye, New York, one child, perhaps after having read Marx, noted that giving every student an equal chance at a good education would amount to "changing the whole economic system" (Kozol 1991, 128), which she thought impossible. Another student objected that "Money comes from taxes. If we have it, we should pay it." But a third student replied, "I don't earn the money. I don't need to be conservative until I do. I can be as open-minded and unrealistic as I want to be. You can be a liberal until you have a mortgage" (ibid., 129).

Kozol found that both rich and poor children were able to articulate judgments about fairness by insulating themselves from their feelings. The linguistic games were played only after the insulation was in place. The same thing could be said of their parents' rationalizations and defense mechanisms against too close a scrutiny of their children's (and their own) privileges. This reaction leads us back to Moritz Schlick's notion of inconsiderateness at the heart of egoism, and the principal cause of this "cold indifference"—our oft-repeated theme of insulation from the world of feelings—is the same in institutions as it is for individual actions. We have already seen that institutional representatives sometimes have to deliberately set aside their feelings in order to do their jobs properly. But the insulation meant here is quite different. It is not the product of reflective acts but rather a *loss* of contact with the world of feelings. Paralleling Laing's comment about the lack of a word in the psychiatric literature for "disturbing," as opposed to "disturbed," people, Kozol points out that there is no academic study of the pathological detachment of the very rich, although it would be useful to society to have some understanding of these matters" (1991, 193).

It would indeed. However, even when it is not a question of the very rich, separation from the world of feelings is at least a strong contributory cause of all of the different types of institutional cruelties that we have been studying here, and more.[9] It is one of the main themes of Charlotte Brontë's *Shirley*, which, written during the Industrial Revolution, tells a story of individual lives against the backdrop of powerful economic, religious, and political forces shaking up England—the "tides of history," of which Coles wrote. As its editor states in his "Introduction," the book shows that pathological detachment causes the suffering of particular individuals and social groups, and that it constitutes "the source of that bitterness and hatred which is on the point of tearing the whole fabric of English society violently apart" (1974, 25).

The primary cause of these ruptures was the creation of barriers that segregated the haves from the have-nots. As Kozol understands perfectly well, these barriers consist largely of the ownership of property. Thus, in *Shirley*, Robert Moore, the mill owner—unlike his foreman, Hiram Yorke, referred to earlier—is detached from the world of his workers. He does not come from the neighborhood, and he feels no kinship with its families. His only concern is for profit and loss figures. But then he sees in London and Birmingham the misery and despair of impoverished workers, and he learns the lesson of what, as we saw in the Introduction, Hallie terms "positive ethics": "I have seen the necessity of doing good: I have learned the downright folly of being selfish" (Brontë 1974, 597).

The capacity of ownership of property to insulate us from the world of feelings returns us to Marcel's anxieties about "having" overcoming "being," a solidary being with others. As the narrator of *The Grapes of Wrath* forcefully warns its readers, "If you who own the things people must have could understand this, you might preserve yourself. . . . But that you cannot know. For the quality of owning freezes you forever into 'I,' and cuts you off forever from the 'we' " (Steinbeck 1976, 194). It will perhaps be the destiny of the young man in Rye, New York, who said, "You can be a liberal until you have a mortgage." It is also the fate of certain pro-life movement members from a wealthy suburb in our community who have no feeling connections with poor women seeking abortions. They will probably never know what Hallie called the "dark space that separates intimate knowledge from smug gentility."

However, in some institutions, such as certain private-sector businesses in which "ownership" is collective rather than individual, the connection between ownership and insulation from the world of feelings gets transmuted, and the beneficiaries have always been more than the owners. For example, over the last few years, we have witnessed the demise of a considerable number of independent bookstores that could not compete with chain mega-stores. In terms of institutional kindness, the impact of these displacements is ambiguous. On the one hand, superstores of whatever type offer consumers more goods and services and lower prices than can most small businesses. On the other hand, they have destroyed livelihoods, the quality of the lives of those most directly affected, and they have had unhappy civic consequences—for example, damaging the economic life of those downtown areas that consist mostly of smaller shops.

In contrast, the related phenomenon of mergers of large corporations is much more serious and less ambiguous. Here, unkindness will likely greatly outweigh kindness, because the promises of consumer benefits are much more apt to be fraudulent. Once competition is eliminated or seriously diminished in a particular market, no incentive will exist to keep prices at existing levels, and still less to lower them. This will be true not only of prices but also of the range and quality of goods and services available.

There is at least one other way that institutional cruelty comes about, and one that overlaps those that stem from malice, the abuse of power, and neglect. Here, also, detachment from the world of feelings lies at the root of many examples. It is the misapplication of values that is appropriate in one sort of context to very different types of contexts in which they cause harm. In institutions as well as in interpersonal relationships, as we have seen, context sensitivity is a necessary condition of practical wisdom. One of the most serious examples, discussed briefly in the last chapter, is the exclusive, or almost exclusive, reliance on the productivity model to evaluate the quality of a university education. (Many aspects of the argument also apply to K-12 education, as well as to the health care industry.)

There is nothing inherently unkind about using productivity as one tool among others for assessing university education. There are at least two important reasons for this. One is the need for accountability in the distribution of resources—say, in the case of public institutions—tax monies. Another stems from the nature of tenure. Tenure provides lifetime job security, and, like water or electricity, most people sometimes follow the path of least resistance. Some people, unfortunately, tend to do so most of the time. Therefore, it is for the good of the faculty, students, and university as a whole that there be some internal system of checks and balances. Productivity is one of them, both in decisions to grant tenure and in salary decisions after tenure is awarded.

However, considerable unkindness emerges when productivity becomes the sole criterion by which to assess academic quality. Colleges and universities do not sell ideas or degrees the way other stores sell shoes or plumbing supplies. The relationships that exist, or should exist, between faculty and students are significantly different in kind from those that obtain in commercial relationships between salespeople and customers. This is partly what is so wrongheaded about students' consumer mentality that, as Ursula Brangwen discovers in D. H. Lawrence's *The Rainbow* (1983), can be encouraged by the faculty as well. She has become disillusioned with the university, because everything has been assigned a cash value. The professors "were only middle-men handling wares they had become so accustomed to that they were oblivious of them"; they "offered commercial commodity that could be turned to good account in the examination room; ready-made stuff too" (Lawrence 1983, 484, 486). It is true that faculty and students happen to fill economic roles, but that fact is neither primary nor that by which the rest of their relationships should be understood. Commercializing education flattens and distorts faculty-student relationships and fractures academic community.

Yet even despite the manifold ways in which institutions can perpetuate cruelty and unhappiness, it remains true that they are necessary for social kindness to become effective. Without the objective, enduring protection that institutions can provide, acts of kindness would have to depend for support on an environment of spontaneous good will. Except for *Gemeinschaft* sorts of institutions such as families—or at least some of them—this is not likely to be the case, because there are inevitable shortages of goods and legitimate conflicts of interests in the competitive pursuit of power, money, privilege, status, and so forth. The synonymy of "rationality" and "self-interest" in economics and psychology testifies to this fact. Therefore, acts of social kindness need the protection against hostile interests that institutions can provide, and only such an objective structure can provide social kindness with the temporal thickness and durability necessary in order to have a lasting effect on society.

This is perhaps preeminently true of legal institutions. For, as Blandine Kriegel points out, "[W]ithout a political guarantee of legal recourse, there are no individual rights but only pious professions of the value of human beings. Without the rule of law, there are no human rights. It is, indeed, only in those states committed to the rule of law that liberal democracy has taken root" (Kriegel 1995, 5). Nussbaum expresses the same truth when she observes that, "Legal guarantees do not erode agency: They create a framework within which people can develop and exercise agency" (1999, 19).

Now postmodern thinkers have long expressed considerable suspicion about institutions and the reason that they claim to embody. This is because, in their view, the "Enlightenment project" has actually degenerated into ideological, totalitarian "emancipation narratives" such as "Marxism-Leninism, fascism, apartheid, and colonial oppression as well as the suppression of sexual, ethnic, and political difference" (Hammer 1995, 120). Yet Havel's political writings underwrite the validity of Kriegel's observations and validate the necessity of social institutions for the protection of kindness and other humane values.

Havel is just as suspicious of "utopian rationality" and ideologies as are postmodern thinkers. The former is dangerous, because it sets itself above everything else and abolishes everything that is inconsistent with its plans. Ideologies, whether of the left or right, are closed systems of thought that fail to achieve the status of utopias, because they do not necessarily point to world harmony. Whereas ideologies are attacks on life itself, Havel, along with post-modernists and philosophers such as Merleau-Ponty, sees life as more ambiguous, pluralistic, open, and contingent than any given ideology can hope to capture. The point here, on a social plane, is the same as George Eliot sought to make in her attack on "men of maxims."

Thus both Havel and postmodernists seek a politics that is open, tolerant of diversity, and not resting on truth claims in any Enlightenment sense of certainty. For postmodernists, "Politics appears as a form of ongoing critique; discourse, as it inherently participates in power, is to be distrusted; and institutions, as they become formal instances of power, are always to be questioned" (Hammer 1995, 123–24). However, such a view of politics and political discourse provides no help in deciding how a given political community should be organized or what it should do, and this is exactly what Havel had to do in Czechoslovakia. He had to build up social institutions that were broken down, begin a political discourse where its predecessor had already dissolved, and reestablish beliefs and traditions where the previous order had collapsed. Thus his task actually began where that of the postmodernist ended. Impatient with narrow-minded, naive political opportunism on the left and the right, Havel envisioned the political world as the matrix for public discussion of the current state of his society and an assessment of their opportunities and future direction.

Moreover, political life in his view requires a continual emphasis on morality. Politics' "deepest roots," Havel notes, "are moral because it is a responsibility, expressed through action, to and for the whole." Furthermore, these roots go deeper than politics itself to "a metaphysical grounding" in the cosmos (Havel 1993, 6), as described in the last chapter. Therefore, he argues for the creation of political institutions as protection against both utopian and ideological discourses that threaten to deprive individual citizens of the freedom necessary for moral and political responsibility. By the same token, as he sees it, citizens should realize that their responsibility for the preservation of the institutions that help safeguard their liberties bars them from concealing their responsibility beneath ideological defenses.

Whether legal or non-legal, institutions, unlike abstract notions of "right," or "contracts," have the ability to link individuals in organic relationships, a linkage that is vital for human flourishing. It is part of that organic relationship that institutions furnish an objective structure and a temporal thickness for the creation of acts and habits of kindness. Institutions thus mediate human freedom; third parties, known and anonymous, inevitably impose a limit on all of our attempts to conceptualize social bonds as extensions of diadic dialogues. As Descombes points out, "The crucial point is that societies acquire a *collective identity* [which] . . . provides a coherence that no intersubjectivity can" (1993, 151; emphasis in original).

So, for example, institutions allow us to make bequests under wills. They also provide a framework for distributing charitable contributions effectively in ways that would be impossible on an individual basis. They permit the investment of individual time and labor within an organization, such as Habitat for Humanity, which can help people efficiently and practically. Or, to take a very different kind of example, Marcel Gauchet and Gladys Swain (1980, 103–47) have described well the efforts of eighteenth-century doctors after the French Revolution who tried to revise the understanding of madness. Mental asylums had a political character: to produce the new human being. Psychiatrists wanted to cure madness by eliminating social alienation and isolation. Previously, the mad person was excluded as the absolutely other (i.e., non-human), tied to beds and abandoned as incurable. But the revolution sought to valorize everyone. Doctors tried to reach each patient in his or her own kind of madness and encouraged social interaction among the inmates.[10]

Institutions are, therefore, ambiguous mediators of acts of social kindness. On the one hand, they are capable of expressing and indeed forcing their members into unkindnesses. On the other hand, they form a necessary, protective structure for what are, by themselves, fragile flowers. Nussbaum is right to call for the use of compassionate imagination to create more humane institutions (1995a, xviii)—not least in the legal world, which is the immediate object of her comment, but in all institutions in both the *Gemeinschaft* and *Gesellschaft* sides of society.

This does not mean that the label of compassion alone can make, say, political or legal institutions more humane. The concept of "compassionate conservatism" is not without serious problems—not to say, intelligibility[11]— but it is precisely its problems that point directly to a necessary condition of making institutions more humane. Those problems, along with the possibilities of, and obstacles to, institutional kindness, which we have been discussing here, strongly suggest that reducing insulation from the world of feelings of those within and outside of institutions is key to their humanization. Across diverse contexts, struggling against this insulation is tightly linked to sensitizing the members of institutions to the plight of those ill served by it as well as within it. This struggle also has the potentiality of increasing the bounds of tolerance—say, for the sake of permitting same-sex marriages, furthering the welfare of inner-city school children, or reducing the political demonization of the poor.

Furthermore, it seems clear that reducing institutional detachment from the world of feelings requires the support and vigilance of the entire society. Living institutions, as Merleau-Ponty pointed out in *Signs* (1964b) and elsewhere, are always open and incomplete, meanings to be created. Just as origin-al speech takes up a given linguistic apparatus and breathes new life into it so that creative expression makes us take a new step, so also are we capable of creating new institutions and adapting others in order to show that they are capable of greater humaneness than previously thought possible. Conversely, of course, we are eminently capable of the reverse: we can make use of institutions to express intolerance and exclusion of difference and, in general, cruel abuse of fellow creatures.

Social Justice

In Chapter 3, we considered some main, interpersonal relationships between kindness and justice. We looked at cases in which kindness was both consistent and inconsistent with justice and transcended it entirely by perfecting it. The subject of this section is institutional relationships between kindness and justice, and we shall examine similar kinds of cases. However, it should be emphasized at the outset that the subject here is not a theory of justice or political theory or their social and historical implications. Alisdair MacIntyre (1988) was certainly correct to observe that the literature on justice is intimidatingly large, even before his capacious additions. Therefore, this section will focus narrowly on the phenomenon of kindness and discuss how just institutions can embody it.

Chapter 3 noted that, for Ricoeur, the "ethical aim of life" consists of a "solicitude" for the welfare of others that comes to fruition within the framework of just institutions. As Ricoeur observes in his "Intellectual Biography, " "this three-cornered definition unites the self in its original capacity of esteem to the other, made manifest by his face, and to the third party who is the bearer of rights on the juridical, social, and political plane," a distinction that permits "the passage from ethics to politics" (Hahn 1995, 51–52). What is particular about institutions, held together as they are by "bonds of common *mores*," as noted above, is collective and collaborative power, action, and life. Sometimes this collaboration can bring the "ethical aim of life" to completion in justice.

This completion, along with the necessity for institutional protection for acts of kindness, as described in the previous section, yields the conclusion that the flourishing of kindness on a social level is in some sense parasitic on justice. This necessary dependence is the lesson embedded in the powerful, un-Hollywood ending of Steinbeck's *Grapes of Wrath*. The Joads are cold, starving, penniless, and are trapped in the barn around which floodwaters are rising. In the face of their own imminent deaths, they find a man lying in the straw who is too weak to take any nourishment except a little milk. The Joad daughter, Rose of Sharon, offers him her breast. The breast is a symbol of life and hope against the crushing background of oppressive evil reflected not only in the Joads' imminent deaths, but also in the system that has displaced them from their homes. As Wuthnow points out, "The warm nourishment from a female breast stands only to emphasize the harsh, masculine cruelty of a society that pursues nothing other than power and wealth. . . . [People] must be more than compassionate. They must also work for social justice" (Wuthnow 1991, 245).

From an ethical perspective, justice has bi-directional vectors. The first is "toward the *good*, with respect to which it marks the extension of interpersonal relationships in institutions." The second direction, given the dialectical relationship of ethics and morality, as described in Chapter 3, is "toward the *legal*, the judicial system conferring upon the law coherence and the right of constraint" (Ricoeur 1992, 197). As we saw in the previous section, effective social justice is required to transform "pious professions of the value of human beings" into "individual rights" (Kriegel 1995, 50).

Whether it is a question of distributive or reparative justice, the common core is equality, and so justice in institutions transforms the solicitude characteristic of interpersonal relationships into a concern for equality. The concern for equality does not diminish interpersonal solicitude. On the contrary, as Ricoeur observes, borrowing from Marcel, equality presupposes such solicitude "to the extent that it holds persons to be irreplaceable" (1992, 202). Justice supplements solicitude by applying equality to humankind in general.

Kindness, whether interpersonal or institutional, begins with the recognition of need. But in the pursuit of equality, as Hume, Mill, and other thinkers have pointed out, justice originates in and therefore presupposes conflicts of interest, whether legitimate or illegitimate. Justice emerges only when there is a necessity of treating all parties to the dispute equally. Otherwise, as Charlotte Brontë had Jane Eyre articulate it, and as Thucydides' account of the Athenians' cynical destruction of the Melians amply illustrates, some people dominate, or attempt to dominate, and others are forced to submit. "[Y]ou know as well as we do," the Athenians put it bluntly, "that right, as the world goes, is only in question between equals in power, while the strong do what they can and the weak suffer what they must" (Thucydides 1951, 331).

More completely, justice enters in when it is not only necessary to treat people as equals but also when achieving equality becomes *problematic*. The accomplishment becomes problematic because of social conditions that are both objective and subjective, conditions that make collaborative efforts possible as well as necessary. The conditions of external objects include what Hume called "their *easy change*, join'd to their *scarcity* in comparison of the wants and desires of men" (Hume 1967, 494; emphasis in original) as well as things such as institutional demands that some members, but not all, must bear certain burdens. Subjective conditions, as Hume also pointed out, include "*selfishness* and *limited generosity*" (ibid.; emphasis in original) and the inherent limits of good will to adjudicate disputes. They also embody the fact that each person has "different interests and ends," "a distinctive life plan, or conception of the good, which he regards as worthy of advancement" (Sandel 1998, 29).

Hume also argues, and Sandel agrees, that justice begins at the limits of benevolence and, in general, the "enlarged affections" (Hume 1957, 17) under which he would surely include kindness. In addition, both view families as institutions generally governed by "enlarged affections," in which justice would have little place. Hume focuses the issue of justice in terms of the lack of necessity of establishing property rights in marriage: "Between married persons, the cement of friendship is by the laws supposed so strong as to abolish all division of possessions, and has often, in reality, the force ascribed to it" (ibid.). Similarly, Sandel considers that in "a more or less ideal family situation, where relations are governed in large part by spontaneous affection," appeals to justice are "pre-empted by a spirit of generosity." In this generosity, particular family members might receive what they are owed under the relevant principle (s) of justice. They might also get more or less than what they are owed. However, the main point is not so much what they receive, or how spontaneously, but rather that a consciousness of what they get or what they are owed does not figure very importantly in that type of life (Sandel 1998, 33).

For similar reasons, justice emerges at the limits of friendship, and not just the marital version to which Hume refers. Friendship is centered in "spontaneous affection" and presupposes the equality that justice seeks. Therefore, "esteem of the *other as a oneself*" is equivalent to "esteem of *oneself as another*" (Ricoeur 1992, 194; emphasis in original).[12] By the same token, given that justice comes into being at the limits of generosity, it also follows that, although social kindness is parasitic upon justice as described above, kindness and what Hume calls "enlarged affection" generally have a primacy that justice does not. As Hume noted, if the sphere of benevolence were sufficiently widened, and if there were no scarcities of goods, justice would be useless, and so not exist.

As different as justice is from friendship, both Hume's and Sandel's remarks about justice and the institution of marriage require correction. It is true that the conditions of benevolence, kindness, and in general "enlarged affection" "prevail in so far as the circumstances of justice do not prevail" (Sandel 1998, 32). But this does not mean that there is no place for justice in even ideal, or nearly ideal, marriages. Not only are "spontaneous affection" and justice not contradictories, but justice, in the sense of procedural fairness rather than division of shares of property, is necessary for maintaining the spontaneity itself. In part, this is because partners in even the best of relationships can have legitimate conflicts of interests, and because they are legitimate, they do not present themselves as the expression of selfishness. These conflicts threaten commitments to child care and the performance of other expected tasks.

Justice is also necessary, because most spouses are not completely free of the temptations of selfishness, and so rules governing the fair distribution of burdens have the same corrective function that they do in social morality generally. Having rules in place that embody respect for both parties provides a structure on which they can rely as protection against exploitation, while they unreservedly share their affection with each other. This is just another example of the ways in which institutions are necessary to preserve acts of kindness and of our continuing dispositions to perform them.

Justice differs from kindness in terms of function as well as origins. Whether distributive or reparative, as Luc Boltanski points out, justice "doesn't become less a dispute" about equality. It is only a dispute substituted for violence (1990, 138). Moreover, for the sake of impartiality, this dispute is located at a second level, detached from the particularity of the persons involved. Justice "stands detached and aloof, as a fair decision procedure stands aloof from the claims of the disputants before it" (Sandel 1998, 16). In contrast, when kindness becomes "detached and aloof" for the sake of impartiality, it loses its anchorage in feeling and its experiential identity.

Furthermore, disputes of justice are always in the argumentative mode. We expect, even if we do not always get, reasoned and reasonable arguments to defend different sides of a particular *case*. We stand behind arguments, used as verbal weapons to defend ourselves, to seek justification for a claim to some good or to avoid some burden—in the case of distributive justice—or to defend past conduct in questions about reparative or retributive justice. Judgments that are finally rendered, either formally or informally, are divisive in nature.

Kindness, however, at institutional as well as interpersonal levels, does not have *cases* as its object. Rather, dehumanization is marked by the degree to which an individual is reduced to a "case." For example, as painfully described in Kozol's grim writings, school officials sometimes cannot hear the child pleading for help behind the "case" of disruptive behavior with which they have to deal, or they respond by providing psychologists or social workers to make the student accept the status quo.[13] Also, the anonymous, faceless officials of HMOs sometimes cause the needless deaths of patients by deciding that their "cases" do not warrant physician-recommended tests. It is true that that some medical tests are unnecessary, just as are some operations—as has been known ever since the Code of Hamuravi, c. 2500 B.C.E. Even so, no serious student of the American and other health care systems today really doubts that lives have been lost because of cost-cutting initiatives.

In addition to not being based on "cases," kindness also differs from justice by its tendency to unite rather than to divide. Instead of standing behind arguments, it opens up and out to embrace others—figuratively and sometimes literally. Boltanski notes that critical questioning and justification, perfectly appropriate in justice disputes, have no place in spiritual love ("agape") (1990, 238). Nor can they, therefore, in that part of it that kindness overlaps. As for kindness outside of the scope of agape, critical questioning and justification are, as we have seen in Chapters 1–3, appropriate when, and only when, they are essential for coming to the aid of the other.

Boltanski has, in fact, provided a comprehensive, clear account of a variety of ways in which agape and justice differ functionally, and certain points in his discussion apply to kindness as well. A second contrast is that justice and agape, like kindness, are both alternatives to violence, but in different ways (Boltanski 1990, 142). Because justice cannot mediate disputes of self-interest from within, it can put an end to such disputes only by imposing a judgment on them from the outside. In this way, as Hannah Arendt noted, justice canalizes and turns aside violence but cannot destroy the impulse (Boltanski 1990, 178). As a result, justice by itself cannot lead to peace. Thus the Psalmist's utopian vision: Kindness and truth shall meet; justice and peace shall kiss (Psalm 84:11). Kindness, in contrast, seeks peace through synthesis and internal resolution of problems. Its solutions are subtended by the desire to seek the good of everyone involved in a particular situation rather than by a decision about whose interests should prevail.

Closely related to this contrast, disputes about justice can be driven by the desire for possession, won by willpower and calculation, and they are based on calculations about the value or merit of their objects. But the only desire that kindness, like agape, contains within it, whether on interpersonal or institutional levels, is "the desire to give" (Boltanski 1990, 236), that is, to seek the welfare of others. Here nothing is forced or enforced (ibid., 239). We have also seen in our studies of alienating objectifications and judgments in Chapter 3 that kindness excludes calculations about the value or merit of persons who comprise the objects of kind actions. The same conclusion also obtains at the institutional level when it is a question of policies, procedures, customs, and so forth, hence the viciousness of expressions such as "the deserving poor," when that phrase is used to distinguish members of the moral community from those who are not. Yet it does not follow that institutional any more than interpersonal kindness excludes all calculation. In institutions as well as in interpersonal acts, there can exist strategies of inventive charity for the benefit of their clientele and/or members. Kindness at whatever level does not rest on willpower and calculation alone, but the latter can certainly be part of such kindness.

Boltanski points out that agape's indifference to calculations of value and merit gives it the quality of gratuity (1990, 172) and places it beyond justice. Some "simple" acts of kindness are likewise gratuitous, as when a friend needs sunglasses and I just lend her mine without any thought of justice, moral duties, consequences, or social utility. However, even though kindness can be at odds with justice, duty, and calculations, we have seen at several junctures over the last three chapters that they are not necessarily disjuncts. And this is true, even under the traditional Western ethical concept of "duties *to*" some person or group instead of Marcel's, (Werner) Marx's, or Levinas' conception of "duties" or "responsibilities *for*" other people. However, at a social rather than an interpersonal level, difficulties of interpretation are multiplied.

Dangarembga's *Nervous Conditions* (1988) provides a simple example, but one that is not unusual in terms of the complexities involved. Dressed in rags that reflect her poverty, the protagonist of the novel is standing on a city sidewalk selling maize so that she can earn her school fees for the following year. An elderly white woman, Doris, and her husband happen by. At first she takes Tambudzai's male chaperone to task for "child labor" and "slavery," but when the latter speaks "most sorrowfully and most beseechingly" on the child's behalf, "Doris darkened like a chameleon [!]. Money changed hands" and Doris patted her on the head and called her a "plucky piccannin" (ibid., 28, 29). In fact, Doris gave her ten pounds, which was an astronomical sum. At that, some members of the black crowd that had gathered "cheered, saying she was more human than most of her kind. Others muttered that white people could afford to be, in fact ought to be, generous" (ibid., 29).

These different responses mirror the social ambiguities of the episode. The first reaction, which repeats Wittgenstein's equation of humanness with kindness, effectively construed Doris' donation as a gratuitous act of kindness flowing from the empathic bond that she formed with the girl as her chaperone spoke in her behalf. On the other hand, it is not that simple, as the second sort of reaction shows. The novel is set in colonial Rhodesia in the 1960s, and the social background of exploitation and racism inevitably shapes the perception of such actions. From this angle, Doris is no longer simply Doris but is *representative* of the colonial masters. Thus as certain members of the crowd effectively argued, Doris' act was nothing more than the acknowledgment of a minimal duty that oppressors have to the oppressed. (Of course, oppressors also have a deeper, more fundamental duty not to be oppressors at all, but that criticism does not get advanced in the passage under discussion.)

Closely related to this functional difference between justice and kindness is the fact that kindness, just as agape, is forgetful of injuries suffered and benefits that it has accomplished (Boltanski 1990, 177). Kindness is, in George Eliot's idiom, which we encountered earlier, "self-forgetful goodness" (1965, 538). Justice, on the other hand, is characterized by vigilance rather than forgetfulness, and justice disputes can always be reopened through discussion and argumentation (ibid., 237). Wherever justice is a possibility—whether in families, labor organizations, private-sector corporations, public health care facilities and educational institutions, or law—rules can always be questioned, decisions appealed, individual players' stakes in the game argued, obligations incurred as part of the functioning of the institution renegotiated, and so on.

Given these possibilities, it is clear that the integrity and the preservation of institutions depend on the creation and maintenance of cultures that emphasize, among other things, procedural fairness in the application of rules, procedures, policies, and the like, and on their general acceptance. Sometimes even the preservation of an institution from outside threats may depend on such vigilance. At the interpersonal level, acting contrary to private rules of conduct yields inconsistencies and, depending on the extent of the lapse, perhaps puzzled reinterpretations of the agent's actions. At the institutional level, however, permitting exceptions cannot only cause injustice but also can wreak havoc among purportedly equal participants.

These requirements of institutional integrity also can create conflicts between kindness and justice, in the sense of procedural fairness in the application of rules, and some of these antagonisms are irresolvable. Such conflicts occur when institutions are unable to respond to the recognized needs of their members and/or those they serve, because doing so would place the entire institution in jeopardy. Thus the individuals at issue are sacrificed to institutional well-being.

For example, in the many years that I participated in the Philosophy for Children program in schools, it was not, and perhaps still is not, unusual in lower grades to encounter lonely, insecure children whose greatest need appeared to be an encouraging hug. It was not simply a matter of my limited experience or untutored eye, since the regular classroom teachers with whom I worked routinely confirmed my hypothesis. But whereas elementary schoolteachers regularly used to provide comforting touches in the classroom, it is clearly now impossible in the litigious social atmosphere created by the actual and imagined sexual abuse of children. This change is of serious concern to teachers and it is perhaps in some way connected to the previously observed fact that increasing numbers of children require psychiatric help.

However, when institutions are not caught up in irresolvable conflicts between justice and kindness, they express kindness in at least two interrelated ways. The first is the maximization of inclusion rather than exclusion of its members and the institution's clientele, if any. There are multiple layers and forms of such inclusion. Toward members it minimally entails a concern for the rights of affected individuals to fair shares of goods and services, and to a fair sharing in the burdens associated with institutional membership. More expansively, such inclusion also involves as wide as possible a sharing of benefits and help. Such concern for inclusion can manifest itself either as the direction of institutional management or, less formally, among groups of members of a given institution.

As an example of the latter, a 1995 study at Bell Laboratories near Princeton, N.J., showed that the electrical engineers who were most valued and productive were not those who had the highest IQ scores, college grades, or achievement test scores; rather, they were those who were most concerned about the welfare of their co-workers. Their congeniality positioned them at the center of communications networks, which would spontaneously come to life when crises emerged or during periods of great creativity. They, as well as institutional managers who had the same qualities, expressed kindness by inclusively encouraging trust, loyalty, strength, and institutional consistency.[14] In contrast, those whose interpersonal skills needed a great deal of improvement had to wait days or even weeks for answers.[15]

Toward the institution's clientele a similar vector of care expresses kindness by treating them in ways that transcend duties listed in a given job description. Such actions present themselves as kind, because they have the qualities of kindness described in Chapter 1, but also because they express the exceptional *disponibilité* of an individual within an institutional context or an entire institution that invests extraordinary effort in its service mission. Thus, paradoxically, although it can be a duty to perform acts of kindness, in such contexts they will not be recognized as such unless they can appear as more than a duty.

An instructive example of institutional care for clients consists of the "holistic law" movement founded by Bill Van Zyverden, which aims to replace the zealously combative, vengeful courtroom behavior of lawyers seen as adversaries with an approach that emphasizes shared responsibility, equitable resolution of the case at hand, and civility in the administration of justice. Van Zyverden has been criticized by fellow attorneys as a "wimpy lawyer," but he has struck a sensitive nerve. The Boston Bar Association released a study in 1997 that showed that uncivil behavior among lawyers is an important factor in attorneys' sense of increasing lack of professional fulfillment. Exposure to conflict and aggression clearly takes its toll, and this is as true for many clients as well.[16] It is not clear whether Van Zyverden would argue that every legal case is amenable to a holistic approach. Perhaps the cases of spousal abuse discussed in Chapter 3 would not and should not be. But it is also clear that there are important lessons here for law students, such as those who orchestrated the cruel and macabre *Harvard Law Review* parody.

The second way in which institutions can express kindness is closely related to the quest for inclusiveness. It is a preservation of the dignity of its members and clientele, and "dignity" here means much more than a Kantian respect for persons as ends in themselves. It also includes an active acknowledgment of and assistance in their flourishing—the multiple dimensions of the "I can" which, as we have seen, Ricoeur is correct to locate at the heart of human worth. Institutional relationships, such as those enjoyed by the Bell engineers, provide a framework for this flourishing.

For example, Hewlett-Packard has addressed the connection between its employees' happiness and productivity and the impact of work demands on their family life. Employees are encouraged "to adjust their workweeks, arrange flexible work schedules, work at home if necessary, and even share jobs—all so that they could meet their personal responsibilities." They are even able to take unquestioned, year-long, unpaid, sabbatical leave.[17] Several companies offer these possibilities, but Hewlett-Packard appears to be one of the very few that actively encourages them.

It is a question here of a much richer institutional solicitude than Ricoeur's own conception of seeking equality, though not inconsistent with it. Kind institutional relationships create support frameworks that provide those affected with core values of institutional stability, coherence, and consistency. In turn, as any academic seeking tenure knows, these qualities inspire trust, loyalty, and a sense of safety and also lead to the flourishing of enhanced creativity in the freedom of self-development. Conversely, as employees know who are systemically exploited and/or live in constant fear of downsizing, when those qualities are absent, the freedom of individual development contracts into fear. People are no longer willing to take risks to find new ways of doing things. Institutional atmospheres turn poisonous and cutthroat, and desperation can shrink into despair.

Another way to say this is to rework and expand Ricoeur's observation, noted earlier, that the search for equality presupposes interpersonal solicitude "to the extent that it holds persons to be irreplaceable" (1992, 202). First, simply on the plane of equality, very few members of institutions that make up *Gesellschaft* are irreplaceable. (It is probably only in institutions such as families that Ricoeur's statement is true without serious qualification.) Indeed, most live continually with the self-consciousness of being eminently replaceable. Almost all university professors, for example, know that on any given day, at least 200 highly qualified and desperate applicants would line up to take their places. But institutional solicitude in the more robust sense that includes kindness amounts to treating members of the institution as well as their clientele, if any, *as if* they were irreplaceable. This solicitude for their flourishing does not imply pampering but only a concern for their dignity as human beings. As we have seen, when members of institutions are treated as mere "snap-on" tools, that fungibility becomes one of the dehumanizing senses of objectification.

Community

Institutions exist in a dialectical relationship with the society in which they exist, and they both reflect and contribute to the values of that society. A crucial dimension of those values is the sense of community that the society supports, and community itself manifests kindness and unkindness in a variety of ways, including particular acts and non-acts, with which this book began. With this base in community, our descriptive phenomenology will come full circle and reach its limits.

Community is not grafted onto individuals conceived as isolable monads. Rather, community consists first of certain possibilities inscribed in the reversibilities of our flesh, as Merleau-Ponty described them. Those possibilities are there for us in outline, to make something of them if we are motivated to do so. A sense of community requires, therefore, "myself as both partially constituted by and partially constitutive of the generalized other . . . in the dynamic and changing manner of ongoing social adjustment" (Rosenthal 1996, 109).

Since the possibilities for community are schematized in our flesh, they also constitute the groundwork, or bodywork, for Habermas' ideal communicative situations (Levin 1985). Equally important, Merleau-Ponty's view also underpins Habermas' rejection of an isolated, deliberating subject as the cornerstone of discourse ethics, although Habermas failed to recognize the support that Merleau-Ponty's phenomenology of the flesh could have provided him. (See, for example, Habermas 1987, 317). For both thinkers, subjectivity is social. Subjectivity is intersubjectivity, the embodiment of sociality and the sociality of embodiment.

Our fleshly schemata simultaneously open us to different types of overlapping communities, with different subgroups in each category, and with similarly altered meanings. There are natural communities, based on ethnicity. There are neighborhoods as well as cities or groups of farmers or ranchers in rural areas. There are also provinces, regions, states, countries, and transnational groups such as the European Community. Michel Henry even speaks of a "feeling with" (*pathos avec*) in which we participate in a community with the dead (1990, 154).

Furthermore, the meanings change in each context. For example, it is one thing to live immediately in a community with particular individuals, and I can identify with an ethnic group given as an "immediate datum." On the other hand, my participation in the academic community becomes more and more diffuse the farther I get from its local representatives. Similarly, my participation in the life of the nation as a whole is comparatively empty and a "rupture with the given" (Schnapper 1994, 95). This is just another application of the distinction between the personally known versus the generalized other, and it will be important later in understanding how limits to empathy create obstacles to communal kindness.

For a sense of community to come into existence, at whatever level, certain conditions have to obtain. As John Smith notes, I must acknowledge myself and other people "as continuing or enduring agents answerable individually for our deeds." In addition, unlike my relationships with collectives and associations that I jettison when they are no longer useful, communal relationships must not be merely cognitive. Rather, they "must include love, loyalty, and concern" (Smith 1984, 341). This condition also provides me with an alternative between being lost and degraded in an anonymous mass of people and withdrawing into myself to stand against the masses.

A feeling of community does not require that "love, loyalty, and concern" must *all* be involved, though at least one must be. In some communities, such as families, all three will no doubt often be present. But, for the reason that Schnapper gives, as one widens out in concentric circles, the less likely it will be that "love" will be present. Or, if it is, it will have a different meaning in the way that, for instance, love of family members differs from love of country. This difference is also related to Harvey Cox's distinction of "I-you" relationships, which constitute a third possibility between the extremes of completely objectified, degraded existence and the intimacy of "I-Thou" relationships.

A third condition of community is that its members must focus both love and knowledge on the community's basic concerns. Community is thus not so much a set of "horizontal relations between pairs of members—myself and the other" (Smith 1984, 341) as it is a common, vertical relationship of dedication to those basic concerns through which community members create nonindividualistic relationships.

Thus with a family, the purpose usually consists of the stability and endurance of the family unit as well as the flourishing of its individual members. With a nation, on the other hand, the purpose consists of successful existence as a community of citizens. As a functioning principle and common ideal, it legitimates government power, regulates conflicts, rules divisions of goods, and affirms "the independence of the will of the nation among other political entities" (Schnapper 1994, 96). Beyond the limits of nationalism, such as in the European Community, the purpose is, among other things, the maximally advantageous coexistence of trading partners.

Smith's second and third characteristics of community reflect its solidarity. They recall the idyllic scriptural exclamation, "How good it is, how wonderful, wherever people dwell as one" (Psalm 133). Similarly, Hallie points out that the German root for "good" is "Gath," which means "gathering" and "unity" (1997, 29). And in a letter of August 20, 1993, he joins together his admiration for solidarity and community with what is not very different from Merleau-Ponty's reversibilities of the flesh: "Only acts of help and, in short, communion deeply move me to joyous tears . . . my work on cruelty and then Chambon showing me that my deepest yearning was for communion.[18] OUTTHERENESS is *outhereness*, communion. Exteriority is internal, or could be or should be" (Hallie 1997, 213; capital letters and emphasis in original). For the same reasons, Loewy argues correctly that the "cement of beneficence" holds society together and that future communities should be based "on a vision that sees social contract as originating in nurture and, therefore, community as necessarily dedicated to the prevention and amelioration of suffering" (1991, 132).

At the same time, however, since members of communities do have legitimate conflicts of interests, there are always tensions between goals of community and liberty, identity and difference, and justice and peace. But as Smith points out, community exists to the degree that the common purpose that transcends us can also lead us to set aside those tensions and conflicts of interests for the sake of what binds us together in a higher loyalty to the community.

Such transcendence finds excellent expression in Steinbeck's descriptions of the genesis of community in the migrant camps of those fleeing the Dust Bowl in *The Grapes of Wrath*. At night, desperate and fearful families huddled together for mutual support and protection. The common cause or purpose that held them together was both fear because of their extreme needs and their dream of a new life in California. Thus in their camps, community emerged as "the twenty families became one family, the children were the children of all. The loss of home became one loss, and the golden time in the West was one dream" (Steinbeck 1976, 249). This passage effectively focuses our attention on the process of building community and its dynamic functioning. Community is made up of and grows through a continual dialectic between novel individual efforts and the entire group. Insofar as the community can increase in kindness, the aim of the dialectic is, as the Dalai Lama put it, to "build closer relationships of mutual trust, understanding, respect, and help, irrespective of differences of culture,[19] philosophy, religion, or faith" (1990, 53).

In sharp contrast, the tribal mentality of old New York society that Edith Wharton described scathingly in *The Age of Innocence* (1986) made them savagely intolerant of outsiders with different values, yet that society did possess all three community-creating conditions noted above. We must therefore distinguish clearly between factual and normative senses of solidarity. Those community-creating conditions are value-neutral in that they apply equally to the types of community sought by, say, the Dalai Lama or Native Americans, and to communities with immoral moralities—for instance, those of Nazi Germany or the antebellum South. Or again, it may take a village to raise a child, but those villages may also practice genital mutilation. Communities can vigilantly protect the moral welfare of their citizens, but, like the Puritans and those Levinas meant to characterize as totalizers and colonizers, they can also manifest an exceptional "predilection for minding other people's business" (Miller 1976, 1).

Detachment from feelings and the indifference of egoism are perhaps the two principal factors that exploitatively split communities. It is illuminating to contrast characters such as Ma Joad in *The Grapes of Wrath*, who fed all of the hungry children, with real-life people who embody spurious senses of community by plastic friendliness, superficial smiles, metallic charity, and other modes of alienated unavailability. In the migrant camps, communities formed in the face of calamities, desperate poverty, and urgent need. In those contexts, failure to respond to such needs would have been shameful. What was at issue was Levinas' "privileged heteronomy" of the suffering Other. In *A Streetcar Named Desire*, Blanche Dubois said famously "Whoever you are—I have always depended on the kindness of strangers" (Williams 1972, 142). It is singularly appropriate that the set direction for this scene includes the following instruction: "*Blanche* . . . [manifests] *a look of sorrowful perplexity as though all human experience shows on her face*" (ibid., 134; emphasis in original).

What then are the phenomenological evidences of increases in kindness in existing communities? As with institutions, the results of communal action are diffuse and ambiguous, especially in large, pluralistic societies. Civic action, public policy making and implementation, and legislation may all have the effect of increasing kindness for a subset of a particular community at the price of diminishing it for other (s). Furthermore, even if a particular civic action benefited everyone in a given community, it may be at the cost of other communities, and since we belong simultaneously to more than one community, the same action can both benefit us at one level and work against us at another level.

One consequence of these uncertain results and of the contrast of our large, pluralistic society with small towns earlier twentieth century and in the nineteenth century as well, is a certain nostalgia for "a simpler time" in which questions about societal foundations, values, and criteria for community acceptability and membership usually did not arise. This fact by itself makes intelligible why Americans continually wax nostalgic over "a simpler time" and a "kinder, gentler" one as well. As Thomas Bridges notes, modern political life has forever broken open "the tranquil world of monocultural solidarity" of small-town America, and it has exposed those who once lived in it "to a whole new range of problems focusing precisely on questions of meaning, purpose, and value" (1994, 169–170).

Nonetheless, such nostalgia is misplaced because of the usual problems of selective memory. Small towns can also harbor petty jealousies, intrigues, and acts of revenge driven by murderous hatred. Even so, Bridges argues that, "[C]ivic friendship exists only as a modification of communitarian solidarity. The very possibility of civic friendship therefore depends upon strong communitarian identity." Likewise, having this sense of identity is a necessary condition of understanding and appreciating civility (1994, 240–241). However, the distinction between factual and normative solidarity carries over to the concept of communitarian identity as well. In a repressive society, such as that of the antebellum South, "civic friendship" can be equally odious.

As a result, a first minimal step toward increasing kindness, at whatever level of community, would consist in increasing the range of toleration. We can do this in one of two ways. We can show respect for others' moral and political beliefs either by ignoring them—say, in the context of political decision making—or we can deliberately and deliberatively build them into public discussions "sometimes by challenging and contesting them, sometimes by listening and learning from them" (Sandel 1998, 217). It is impossible to predict *a priori* whether we will come to like or dislike these convictions, but the latter option—what Sandel calls "the deliberative view"—embodies the additional kindness of being more inclusive.

The deliberative view thus resists marginalization and exclusivity. Yet because toleration, like kindness, is only one of many civic virtues, kindness will be maximized here to the degree that the toleration sought is consistent with justice and, following the deliberative view, allows for the freedom to criticize. George Santayana once remarked that, "The virtue of liberalism is a sort of intellectual kindness or courtesy to all possible wills" (1964, 282). This is a virtue not only of liberalism, but it must be balanced by the assertion that the "intellectual kindness or courtesy" that he had in mind provides for respectful critical response. For, among other reasons, it has to confront the difficult problem of the tolerance of intolerance, which is one of the most vexing problems in freedom-loving, democratic societies.

Toleration by itself is only a first step in the struggle of kindness for a more inclusive community. It can break down barriers or penetrate them without outbreaks of violence by at least minimizing them. In any democratic society, there are always thorny problems associated with establishing limits to toleration. In some cases, this will be much easier than in others. As noted earlier, only the lunatic fringe defends racism these days, but many people across all social and economic strata are homophobic and present more or less reasoned arguments in defense of their intolerance.

Thus Bridges goes too far when he says, "Liberal political communities *encourage* the cultivation of a multiplicity of diverse and conflicting concepts of the good, among which citizens may choose" (1994, 183; emphasis added). Sometimes this is the case, but not always. For example, a former Makah chief defended his tribe's controversial killing of a gray whale with the claim that, "[T]he hunt reaffirms the vitally important traditional male role in Makah society at a particularly difficult time for the people." The lack of such hunts, he argued, disempowered males from traditional ways of providing for their families, with the subsequent results of alcoholism, drugs, unemployment, and despair. The hunt thus constituted a means of healing the tribe's broken communities.[20] Nevertheless, there are many who would count themselves as members in good standing in the contemporary liberal political community who would never encourage killing whales for the sake of male power and authority, or for any other reason.

There are similar values clashes and problems of toleration as diverse immigrant cultures are absorbed into American society. Bilingual education, compulsory linguistic exclusion (English-only laws), and genital mutilation are familiar examples, but there are others that are less well known. In Maine, for example, an Afghan refugee welcomed his newborn son to the world with a traditional greeting of kissing the baby's penis. To the police, however, this action looked like child abuse, and the baby was removed from the family.

Especially with regard to customs such as genital mutilation, the question becomes, "How do democratic, pluralistic societies like the United States, based
on religious and cultural tolerance, respond to customs and rituals that may be
repellant to the majority?"[21]

Barber recalls for us Scheler's view that phenomenology is the guardian of
dialogue with those very different from us (Barber 1993, 164–65). This dialogue must obviously be based in part on toleration. Nevertheless, it is equally
clear that toleration by itself is not enough for a maximum increase of communal kindness and the struggle against marginalization and exclusivity that
kindness requires, for toleration always bears some censure within it. Toleration
is always *only* toleration; it is never approbation.

What is required for the inclusiveness characteristic of kindness is, rather,
acceptance. That was what Frederick Douglass found in Robert Ingersoll's radiant good will, and Jean Valjean likewise discovered in the good bishop of
Digne. Radiating a spirit of good will is also at the heart of Boltanski's conception of the socialization of agape and Havel's definition of our role as
"ambassadors of trust in a fearful world" (Bellah et al. 1992, 286). At an institutional level also kindness increases to the degree that more people can be
brought within the umbrella of the values common to the society, to make
them feel, using Marcel's phrase, "at home" in their community (ies) and in society at large.

Achieving this feeling of being "at home" in community (ies) and in society
was crucial to Richard Wright's objectives in writing *Native Son*. It was also the
object of Hallie's positive ethics of hospitality as epitomized by the Trocmés and
the other Chambonnais who rescued Jews hiding from the Gestapo. Whereas
Nussbaum argues that literature sensitizes people to individuals, Wright reverses
this view in order to help us comprehend *systemic* exploitation. He wants to lead
us to understand "twelve million Negroes" "struggling within unbelievably nar-
row limits to achieve that feeling of at-home-ness for which we once strove so
ardently" (Wright 1993, 464). The Chambonnais also sought inclusiveness, because they tried to stop the killing for the sake of both victims as well as victimizers. They dedicated themselves to "an active gentleness" of compassion that
Tocqueville argued for in a quite different context, namely, substituting it for the
gentleness of indifference in democracy (Manent 1994, 111).

The twin themes of making people feel "at home" in their community (ies)
and the assumption of responsibility create an instructive generalization of the
Greek concept of the reciprocity and reversibility of guest-host (*xenia*). "In
Greek thought 'guest' and 'host' were indistinguishable in word and concept,
since playing one role carried with it entitlement or obligation to eventually
perform the other. This reciprocal system of welcoming and being welcomed
was under the protection of Zeus *Xenios* ('of guests/hosts')" (Martin 1991, 42).
Persons such as Robert Ingersoll, the Chambonnais, and fictional characters

such as the good bishop of Digne performed the duties of *xenia* in an exemplary manner. They show that individuals have a crucial role to play in maximizing the kindness of making others feel "at home" in their community (ies), especially as social life becomes more and more bureaucratized, and members of various communities come to regard governmental institutions as being less and less capable of social beneficence.

Detective K. Skip Mannain of Poughkeepsie, N.Y., is a paradigm case. When a certain Mexican immigrant worker was killed by a hit-and-run driver and left a widow and four children in Oaxaca, the widow insisted on getting the body back for burial. He could have just told her that it was not his job, but he went looking for funds to pay for the transport. A newspaper article provoked contributions from Hispanics as well as non-Hispanics totaling $22,583. After the body had been shipped home, he flew to Mexico to deliver the money. He met and befriended the widow and her children, and he saw to it that the money—a gigantic sum locally—was invested in a trustworthy bank. Then the *Poughkeepsie Journal* sent a team of reporters to Oaxaca to report on local poverty. They informed "comparatively comfortable Poughkeepsians why at any time one-quarter of the men in certain villages are in Poughkeepsie."[22] Due to this publicity as well as Detective Mannain's slide show in local schools and his descriptions of Mexican poverty, attitudes toward immigrant workers have largely changed from hostility and indifference to curiosity and warmth.

There are, of course, countless individual efforts to increase kindness within communities that go unreported and even unnoticed. Eldora Spiegelberg, to whom in part this book is affectionately dedicated, provides an ever-instructive example of what Kristen Monroe calls the "important quiet, hidden, quality of much altruism" (1996, 150). Such people manage to free themselves from the bonds of egoism into the sort of life of fellow-feeling and active hospitality for which several thinkers cited in this book argue. Their lack of aggression and demonstrativeness makes them difficult to notice. Thomas Hardy, in *Far From the Maddening Crowd*, expressed this inconvenience clearly in the following perceptual analogy: "We learn that it is not the rays [of light] which bodies absorb, but those which they reject, that give them the colours they are known by; and in the same way people are specialized by their likes and dislikes and antagonisms, whilst their goodwill is looked upon as no attribute at all" (1982, 201).

Such people also constitute an entirely convincing reply to Robert Solomon's approval of Nietzsche's view that it is pointless to discuss the ordinary, good person "who breaks no rules or laws, offends no one, and interests no one, except moral philosophers." The obedient *hoi-polloi* "who serve their city-state well and honor their superiors appropriately" are too banal to notice. Rather, it is their leaders whom we should discuss, because they are "the models from whom the vision of humanity is conceived" (Solomon 1985, 261). It is not entirely clear for what purpose (s) Solomon thinks that it is not worthwhile discussing merely good people. He suggests that it is a question of seeking moral exemplars. If so, however, the last sentence of *Middlemarch* is much wiser: "[T]he growing good of the world is partly dependent on unhistoric acts; and that things are not so ill with you and me as they might have been, is half owing to the number who lived faithfully a hidden life, and rest in unvisited tombs" (Eliot 1965, 896).

Even though individuals can do much to increase kindness within communities and society at large, it also appears that those efforts will not be sufficient unless they can also lead to changes in social institutions. For the same reasons already noted about the inadequacy of spontaneous good will and for institutional protections for an alternate enframing of technology, here also many of the problems to be solved and obstacles to be overcome are systemic. Volunteering will always have a limited social efficacy without structural changes. As Bellah et al. remark, it is a question of "the difficulty of being a good person in the absence of a good society." In choosing whether or not to give spare change to a homeless panhandler, we know that neither is the right answer. The problem lies deeper in the "failures of the larger institutions on which our common life depends" (1992, 4).

One hopeful counter-example occurred in December 1996 in Malden, Massachusetts, when Malden Mills sustained serious fire damage. In fact, the disaster struck only two weeks before Christmas. Three-fourths of the employees were thrown out of work, more than 1,400 workers. The owner, Aaron Feuerstein, could easily have closed the mill and rebuilt in another country with lower operating costs. Instead, he chose to rebuild the mill because, unlike Brontë's character, Robert Moore, he had a commitment to his employees and to the people of the area in which it was located. He said that he thought the average American wanted corporate executives to treat workers as human beings, and that is what he decided to do. Feuerstein's decision attracted long letters from workers in other corporations who complained about downsizings, how they were unable to obtain other jobs, and how their children's hopes for college were ruined.

Feuerstein has clearly connected the world of business to the world of feeling and community in a way that the authors of *Howards End* and *Shirley* would have greatly admired. Forster argues for this connection in the symbolic marriage of the elder Mr. Wilcox and Margaret Schlegel. In part, that is why the epigraph of the book is "Only connect!" And Brontë would have praised Feuerstein's exceptional ability to escape the way that economic and political forces deny the world of feeling and alienate the haves from the have-nots behind barriers of possessions.

Yet as splendid as Feuerstein's actions were, they do not argue against the necessity for institutional change in order to maximize communal kindness. If Malden Mills had been publicly traded, then regardless of its owner's goodness, it could have been taken over anyway, the workers fired, and their jobs given to *maquiladora* (foreign-owned factory) workers in Central America or the Caribbean who make designer clothes for upwardly mobile Americans. Young girls are the workers of choice in these textile factories, ostensibly because of their hand-eye coordination, but also because they are the most docile workers and are easy to discourage from defending their rights. Most are so young that they are driven to the factories in yellow school buses. They make thirty-eight cents an hour working brutal shifts of fifteen hours (at least).[23]

Forster, for his part, was a cautious realist about uniting the worlds of business and feelings. He knew that the odds were against him (and us). Writing about the same time as John Dewey, Forster shared Dewey's concerns about "the impoverished character of public life" (Sandel 1996, 37). For Dewey, this barrenness was due to the incongruity between the impersonal organization in modern economic life and the ways in which citizens had defined themselves as autonomous, free individuals, "even as the huge scale of economic life dominated by large corporations undermined their capacity to direct their own lives." Dewey worried about, just as did Forster, "[m]echanical forces and vast impersonal organizations" that did away with local community organizations formed throughout the nineteenth century without substituting another form of community (Sandel 1996, 37–38). These concerns echo Charlotte Brontë's fears in *Shirley*, as well as what Coles (1992) described as the "the tides of history that bear down on all of us."

In Dewey's civic liberalism, the revival of democracy depended on reclaiming public life, and this in turn depended on "creating new communitarian institutions, especially schools,[24] that could equip citizens to act effectively within the modern economy.... Community would take the form of a national community" (Sandel 1996, 38). But by then the country was much too large and diverse for anything like a national community to emerge. Similarly, in our own days, corporations exert their power to wring concessions from municipalities to get tax reductions, environmental protection waivers, and changes in zoning regulations. They are successful, because the communities at issue, as well as the states in which they are located, are desperate for jobs. Large, mostly American hotel chains do the same thing to Caribbean islands. They provide jobs, for which local governments are frantic, but at the unconscionable cost of contributing nothing to the local tax base.

Thus part of the challenge to maximizing communal kindness on a global scale is to enable local governments to protect the welfare of their citizens against the power of transnational corporations. Given the above arguments about the necessity of institutions for the protection of kindness, at whatever level of community, enabling local governments in this way means that we must strengthen present institutions and create new ones where necessary in order to pursue the welfare of the whole planet.

At the international level of community, additional complexities and ambiguities in the kindness of institutional acts and policies exist. At one level, there are dilemmas in providing humanitarian aid to countries such as Bosnia, Somalia, Rwanda, or Liberia, because such action unfortunately has generated war economies, refugees, and games of playing off aid agencies against each other.[25] Further, just as kindness toward a particular local community can result in unkindness to another (s), similarly those expressed toward one nation—say, in terms of economic preferences—may disadvantage others. Equally, a country that tries to stay out of the economic fray to preserve a modicum of kindness and civility may find itself with serious economic disparities. Such is apparently the case with Japan. To become more aggressively competitive in the world market, the Japanese are being encouraged to become nastier by jettisoning their traditional "civility and egalitarianism [which] shape just about every aspect of life." Companies these days are much more interested in cutting costs and prices of their stock than they are with the welfare of their employees.[26]

Finally, as a very different type of example, several nations and cultures across national boundaries view as deeply unkind the hegemony of American culture, because it threatens certain basic cultural values. Their resentment is directed against different types of phenomena. It may be McDonald's in France, fear of genetically modified foods throughout Europe and the United Kingdom, or the media presentations of American sexual mores throughout the Islamic world.

Examples such as these return us once again to the theme that one main obstacle to kindness, on a social as well as on an interpersonal level, is a disconnection from the world of feeling. There is a consequent loss of a sense of community and of an ability to appreciate—or, in some cases, even tolerate—those who are different. The limits to empathy discussed in Chapter 3, along with the social barriers to kindness noted above, raise obvious questions about the possibilities of social kindness having any sweep and effectiveness wider than very narrowly circumscribed communities.

Hume (1967, 581), Adam Smith (1976, 68), and Sidgwick (1913, 246) all pointed out that we are much more inclined to sympathize with those closest to us, our acquaintances, and our own compatriots than we are with those in remote lands, strangers, and foreigners. We have already encountered one result of this fact, that civic participation becomes more diffuse and harder to motivate the farther the objects of our concern are from us. (All politics is in some sense local.) Hence, we are much more likely to have some feeling connection with our next-door neighbors and perhaps with those neighbors one or two houses away than we are with those farther along the block, on the next street, in the next community, in other cities, and so on. In addition, recent psychological research confirms this tendency to bias in empathy. Martin Hoffman (1987) has shown that we tend to be much more sympathetic toward victims that resemble us than we are to those who are very different. As Nietzsche observes at §162 of *The Gay Science*: *"Egoism.*—Egoism is the law of perspective applied to feelings: what is closest appears large and weighty, and as one moves farther away size and weight decrease" (1974, 199). This is why, at least in my area, charitable appeals that feature pictures of hungry children almost always show Caucasian children who look as acceptably bourgeois and white as their likely benefactors, whereas most of those who are hungry are neither. As we have seen, physical difference can be a serious impediment to *disponibilité.*

Hoffman also points out that people are much more likely to be empathic toward someone who is actually in distress than by the suffering that they know is taking place in some other locality. For example, as Curley noted apropos of American indifference to Iraqi lives lost in the Gulf War, our "orgy of self-congratulation on the 'successful' conclusion of a war in which a great many people died" rested on a convenient inability to identify with "the suffering of others not connected to us by ties of family, religion, nationality, or political alliance" (1991, 36). Hence, there would seem to be considerable difficulty in implementing Solon's nostrum for ending injustice, cited in Chapter 2, to make bystanders feel "the same resentment with those that suffer wrong" (Hay 1960, 4).

Nevertheless, it is not impossible. As Alvin Goldman points out, as a matter of normative ethical theory, an empathy- or sympathy-based universalist theory is not a self-contradiction (1993, 92). Hume himself and R. M. Hare (1963) provide notable attempts. Thus although we might be inclined to construe an empathy-based view of morality as very likely to reinforce the interests of particular people or sets of people with whom those formulating or following the morality most closely identify—as Lawrence Blum (1987) suggests—this is not necessarily the case.

Monroe's research on altruism also provides some interesting counterexamples. She studied entrepreneurs who were self-interest maximizers, philanthropists who were more altruistic than entrepreneurs, but who still based their charity on self-interested considerations; heroes and heroines, and certain rescuers of Jews in Nazi-occupied Europe. What she found was that of the four classes of people, only entrepreneurs and, to a certain degree, philanthropists, evidenced the favoritism that Hume, say, would predict. Heroes and heroines, as well as the rescuers of Jews, thought of rescue as normal behavior. Conversely, they regarded failure to render aid as abnormal. Over and over again, they said that they had no choice in rescuing their victims. "Humanity plus need: This is the only moral reasoning, the only calculus for altruism" (Monroe 1996, 212). They made something out of their connections with suffering others no matter how different they were, and that difference (s) made no difference, because they believed in the bond of a "common humanity" that constituted "the bonding that goes on in affective empathy" (ibid., 264, n. 29). One merit of Monroe's research is to point out the counter-examples required for the plausibility of altruistic perspectives. As noted in the previous chapter in terms of evolutionary psychology, kindness on both the interpersonal and social levels has to take into account the legitimacy of both self-interested and altruistic perspectives and find a way of integrating them so that neither will define the other out of existence.

There is one other factor that argues in favor of the possibility of a universalist, empathy-based approach to morality, and to the possibility that kindness can prevail over an attitude of pure self-interest. That is an appeal to what is common to everyone on the planet, a common dwelling and rootedness in nature. As Havel puts it succinctly, "The only real hope of people today is probably a renewal of our certainty that we are rooted in the Earth and at the same time, the cosmos. This awareness endows us with the capacity for self-transcendence."[27]

Along the same lines, Marcel reflects on the implications of Heidegger's verb, "to dwell," in his *Vorträge und Aufsätze*. He focuses on "the initially disconcerting formula, '*Die Sterblichen wohnen, insofern sie die Erde retten,*'" "Mortals dwell insofar as they redeem the earth" (1973, 152). He could add that, from the point of view of kindness, they also redeem themselves because, conversely, when a dwelling loses its anthropocosmic value, human beings are degraded. For Marcel, the prevalence of this loss and degradation increasingly defines contemporary society. As he sees it, it is the contractors more than the architects who control the style of people's dwellings today. Thinking of huge blocks of apartments, he says that in those "huge barracks where the people of tomorrow will be huddled . . . one no longer finds that essential concern for knowing *what kind of humanity* is being prepared for, and yet no one can deny that a man's existence is molded by his dwelling" (1973, 153). Moreover, it is not just a question of individual apartment buildings or houses but the style of one's broader Lifeworld as well that shapes our existence.

In contrast, the Dakota, as we have seen, maintained a tight link between metaphysical communion and social community. They designed their dwellings in round shapes to mirror this connection with the universe and the web of life, because, as Black Elk explained, all of life is a circle. The sky, stars, Earth, changing seasons, whirling of the winds, and shapes of bird nests were all round or revolved around them in circular motions. Thus the "Power of the World always works in circles" (Neihardt 1961, 198). The Dakota did not just live but dwelled on the earth.

In the previous chapter we looked at the ways in which the architectural styles of our dwellings—homes, businesses, schools, and the like—present themselves to us as kind or unkind, according to their livability. We infer this kindness or unkindness from the thoughtfulness of the design. That is not the issue here, however, though it is related to it. Rather, we are now interested in the ways in which the construction and styles of our dwellings can reinforce or conceal our connections to nature.

First, the construction of our dwellings can be carried out in such a way that they fit into their natural settings with a minimum of destruction, or the construction process can be dominated by the goals of possessiveness, greed, appropriation, and destruction. In the one case nature is the object of respect, and in the other case it is solely a *manipulandum*. Communities differ widely in the protection of nature that they are willing to enforce. In some, every effort must be made to preserve each tree on the developed terrain. In others, developers can destroy everything living and pave over the landscape with asphalt. Some communities have strict zoning regulations to avoid overdeveloping certain areas, whereas others take a laissez-faire approach that leads to severe overcrowding and to too-heavy burdens imposed on water and energy resources.

Second, in terms of community design, some communities preserve green spaces and make those natural presences easily accessible, but in other communities these are lamentably absent. Furthermore, to the degree that most people's enjoyment of nature tends to be confined to leisure time rather than to work, some communities and whole cities are organized in ways that allow working and leisure time to be integrated successfully. We say that such cities are more "livable" than those in which home and office are spatially and temporally discrete and often separated by great distances.

There is little redemption of the earth in suburban sprawls paradoxically destroying the very nature that was supposedly enjoyable only outside of the confining limits of inner-city life. Not all suburbs do this, but many do. They also tend to contribute to the destruction of city centers from which many of the suburbanites have fled. In addition, suburban sprawl has increased commuting times and distances, energy use, and the number of cars, and the vast majority of commuters still do not carpool. All of these facts contribute to increased pollution, time wasted in traffic jams, and deterioration of roads—in general, much more a sense of life merely being lived than any sense of dwelling.

The design and location of suburban homes also contribute to an insulation from nature that is correlated with indifference and unkindness. As we have seen, new homes now, most of which are in the suburbs, contain more luxury appliances and higher ceilings than in previous years, thus contributing to our extravagant use of energy. In terms of location, suburbs once built with isolation in mind that are now impacted, and still more those that are gated communities with twenty-four-hour security protection, mold the existence of their inhabitants in such a way that both nature and the opportunities and problems of the city are farther away psychologically than they are physically. The common good and the affective bonds that relate us to it tend to get lost in such settings in lieu of fear and possessiveness of private goods and pleasures.[28]

Alienation from nature represented in outsized homes and extravagant energy usage, whether in cities or suburbs, is only a part of the current *Zeitgeist* of those comfortable Americans who are riding the wave of the current stock market explosion. The possessiveness of creature comforts extends to mutual funds, gourmet coffees, designer clothes, appalling credit card debt, and the like. Here also there are dangers of being cut off from the world of feelings, which includes those of the suffering others to whom we should respond. Moreover, these same phenomena tend to reinforce a certain type of liberalism that converges with what Schlick meant by egoistic indifference.

The current debate between libertarians and communitarians, to which these phenomena also point, raises broadly sweeping issues, just as the subjects of justice and sociopolitical theory did with the notion of kindness also interwoven. As with these latter topics, there is not enough space here for even a rapid discussion of the main issues, relevant positions, and criticisms thereof. However, since I have already referred to some thinkers who play roles in the debate, I shall bring this chapter to a conclusion with a very brief sketch of what in their positions is most relevant to communal kindness.

From that angle, the liberalism that descended from John Locke to Stephen Holmes, Nussbaum, and John Rawls, passing by way of Constant, Tocqueville, and Mill, is correct to stress the precious achievement of personal freedoms. People do not give their lives in war so that other citizens might be more exhaustively defined by society, and no inmate in a Chinese prison or alumnus of the Soviet gulag needs any lessons on this score. There is truth also in the Lockean view that property (in a pre-Marxist sense) brings freedom to its owner. Even Sandel, usually identified as a "hard communitarian," notes at one point that possession is bound up with a sense of empowerment and dispossession with disempowerment (1998, 56-57). This observation is closely related to the sense that Merleau-Ponty gave to the body's "I can" and that Ricoeur extended to the ethical realm. It would be deeply unkind to deny these two truths of liberalism because they are necessary conditions of human flourishing.

Correlatively, not all aspects of capitalism are inconsistent with kindness, and not all features of socialisms are consistent with kindness. The test in both cases is the respect for and protection of individual freedoms, competitive initiatives, dignity, and the abilities of individuals to use property (in pre- or post-Marxist senses) as safeguards for freedom, happiness, and well-being. Market investments make it possible to buy a home, send one's children to a university, and provide for retirement. That said, it is also true that possession is not equivalent to possessiveness. The latter exposes the agent to the danger of socially destructive selfishness—egoistic indifference, or worse. As described above more than once, an unrestrained market economy has had several socially unkind consequences, to put it mildly, that work against even the self-interest maximizers who benefit in the short term.

Nevertheless, libertarians are still correct that the society into which we grow, and which grows through us, is not all that we are. We are not subordinated to society, as "hard" communitarianism has it—that which is usually identified with the thought of Sandel, Taylor, and MacIntyre. Pushed to its logical limits, that doctrine too easily slides into totalitarianism. Perhaps this is part of what Nussbaum is worried about when she stresses "the equal importance of each life, seen on its own terms rather than as part of a larger organic or corporate whole. Each human being should be regarded as an end rather than as a [mere] means to the ends of others" (1999, 10), and what troubles Rawls in the threat of "autocratic state power" (1996, 303–304). An important part of us is our self-interests that only we should be allowed to define and pursue as we think best. And, as noted several times before in this book, in the type of world in which we live, we do have legitimate conflicts of interests and "incommensurable and irreconcilable conceptions of the good" (ibid., 303). Even so, the type of liberalism defended by Rawls and Nussbaum does not argue that egoism is a necessary consequence. They also are sensitive to the fact that people do have fundamental needs for one another. From their perspective, liberalism is just as consistent with kindness, compassion, and care for others as are communitarianisms. The difference between them, rather, is about the nature of the self.

In terms of the self, the view defended here is that communitarianisms, whether "soft"—a position usually identified with Bellah and Amitai Etzioni—or "hard," do have something important to tell us. That is, the self is solidary rather than solitary, and in terms of social consequences, it is equally unkind to us to deny our inherent connection to the common good, not simply as something that we should feel or something to which we should, as isolable individuals, contribute from time to time, but rather as something we *are*.[29] For the reasons given above, there is a close link between communal identity (ies) and our ability to flourish. Furthermore, since the solidarity of the self is underwritten by our connection to nature, the natural and moral senses of kindness finally converge—as we have learned from thinkers as diverse as Native Americans,[30] Marcel, Heidegger, and Havel. It is doubly unfortunate, therefore, that contemporary American society tends to live more in disjunction from, than unity with, nature.

In addition, communitarians, or anyone else, can point out that in Nussbaum's concerns about "the equal importance of each life, seen on its own terms rather than as part of a larger organic or corporate whole," the phrase "in part of" is crucially ambiguous. There are many senses of belonging. Not all invoke the dangers of what Rawls called "autocratic state control" or its analogue at the level of communities. Hence, her following explanatory statement, "Each human being should be regarded as an end rather than as a [mere] means to the ends of others," unnecessarily narrows the meaning of "in part of" to its dehumanizing sense. Sandel's "constitutive" view of the self—defended by most, if not all, of the people and groups cited in this book—is not vulnerable to the charges that Nussbaum would level against it.

Therefore, a socially responsible view that seeks to maximize social kindness does not throw out either liberal or communitarian ideals *tout court* but rather argues that we should attempt to find ways to connect those ideals with flourishing communities. Better, it should seek to show how, in Kant's sense, their connection is analytic rather than synthetic. There are perennial tensions between liberty and community, just as, on another plane, there will always be those between love and justice. The corresponding political challenge, for which there is no solution on the order of the Pythagorean theorem, is to find humane and politically effective ways to hold both ends of the chain together at the same time. It is a question of developing an "inventive charity" on a communal level to extend and deepen its interpersonal counterpart.

PART II

Now I believe I can hear the philosophers protesting that it can only be misery to live in folly, illusion, deception, and ignorance. But it isn't—it's human.
—Erasmus, *Praise of Folly*

Chapter 6

The Hermeneutic Challenge

The proficiency of our finest scholars, their heedless industry, their heads smoking day and night, their very craftsmanship—how often the real meaning of all this lies in the desire to keep something hidden from oneself! . . . . [They are] drugged and heedless men who fear only one thing: regaining consciousness.
—Friedrich Nietzsche, *On the Genealogy of Morals*

False Consciousness

The aim of the first part of this book has been to describe and understand the meanings of all the types of kindness of which we are conscious in the social world. Accordingly, at the interpersonal level, we examined acts and non-acts of kindness as well as kind persons. At the social level, we considered indeterminate social atmospheres, technology, and our relationships with nature, institutions, and community. The objective has been to present the evidence in a non-normative fashion, as far as possible, in order to keep within the limits of the epoché, as described in the Introduction.

Nevertheless, the normative emerged at several junctures and not only as a datum that could itself be described. Finally, it broke into the open at the end of the last chapter because description, when driven to the limit, cracks up and yields to normative interpretation. This is one reason phenomenology must become hermeneutic in order to complete its mission of accounting for the phenomena. Ricoeur is correct that, "[W]hat hermeneutics destroyed was not phenomenology but the idealist interpretation that Husserl gave of it in his *Ideen I* and in the *Cartesian Meditations.*" Non-idealistic phenomenology "remains the unsurpassable presupposition of hermeneutics" (Hahn 1995, 34).

The second reason hermeneutic scrutiny must supplement and build on a descriptive phenomenology is that the latter treats what is openly available to

171

conscious awareness, whereas the former deals with what is hidden and, as Nietzsche knew well (see the epigraph of this chapter), often unsuspected. As such, scrutiny disrupts uncritical acceptance and, in the case of kindness, naïve public praise, by prying out those hidden meanings and making trouble for them. For example, the Dalai Lama states, "*Whether one believes in a religion or not, and whether one believes in rebirth or not, there isn't anyone who doesn't appreciate kindness and compassion*" (1990, 52; emphasis in original).

However, Frederick Douglass shows us that we have to be more suspicious. He recalls in his autobiography that, "[T]he kindness of the slave-master only gilded the chain. It detracted nothing from its weight or strength. The thought that men are made for other and better uses than slavery throve best under the gentle treatment of a kind master" (1962, 155). Similarly, the scene in *Huckleberry Finn*, in which Jim has been captured and is in jail, underlines the same need for suspicion. The local doctor describes Jim to his friends as follows: "I never see a nigger that was a better nuss or faithfuler, and yet he was risking his freedom to do it, and was all tired out too, and I see plain enough he'd be working main hard lately. I liked the nigger for that; I tell you, gentlemen, a nigger like that is worth a thousand dollars—and kind treatment, too" (Twain 1959, 276).

In the context of sexism rather than racism, at the end of Henrik Ibsen's *A Doll's House*, when the scales fall from Nora's eyes, she says to her husband, "You and Daddy did me a great wrong. It's your fault that I've never made anything of my life. . . . I'm desperately sorry, Torvald. Because you have always been so kind to me. But I can't help it. I don't love you anymore" (Ibsen 1981, 80, 83). Nora is in the same situation as is Edna in Kate Chopin's *The Awakening*. She "continues to admire her husband's many fine qualities—his generosity, kindness, business skill—to the very end, even while realizing that he can never possibly understand or accept her as an individual human being, a person as well as a wife and mother" (Skaggs 1985, 105). Nora and Edna are, it scarcely needs to be added, only fictional embodiments of the dominant view of women in American and other societies down to the rise of the modern women's movement, which still prevails in some parts of the world.

Finally, in a very different sort of context, R. D. Laing and A. Esterton showed that the mental illness of the schizophrenic children they studied is at least in part "intelligible in the light of the praxis and process of his or her family nexus" (1964, 27). As I have described more fully elsewhere (Hamrick 1983), one of the main features common to all the cases studied consisted of conflict between the blossoming autonomy and freedom of the child and the beliefs, rules, practices, and expectations of parents and occasionally other adult family members. These conflicts centered on what is socially acceptable behavior, religious and moral values, the "correct" role of women in society, and the like. In the interlocking relationships between parents, aunts and uncles, grandparents, and so on, these families turned in on themselves and became "relatively closed system[s]" in which the patient was "particularly enclosed within" them (1964, 224–25).

There was very little, if any, outright coercion in these family situations. Rather, the coercion was hidden, both from the child and the adults. The latter honestly believed that they wanted what the previous chapter described as the usual purpose of the family—the stability and endurance of the family unity and the flourishing of its individual members. Accordingly, they regarded their behavior toward their children as loving kindness, and they were mystified when the latter suddenly, inexplicably, became ill. However, the children were equally baffled, because when they were sane in their own eyes, they were ill from the point of view of their parents and other adults in the family. Conversely, when their parents took them to be sane, they were then in their own eyes ill. In short, when the children attempted to live both for their parents and other adult family members as well as for themselves, they were tied up in knots.

These skeptical replies obviously contradict the way in which kind acts and persons were described in Chapters 1 and 2, respectively. They also appear to conflict with the claim in Chapter 4 that kindness must be parasitic in some sense on justice in order to flourish. All of the acts and non-acts of kindness, as well as other social phenomena that embodied kindness, as described in Part One, consisted of cases of which we would approve. However, the acts described above are equally motivated by the desire to seek the good of the other and are fully consistent with justice and respect for rights, *but as defined by the agent.* Since we do not agree with the definition, we would say that such acts produce cruelty rather than kindness, harm rather than compassion, totalizing oppression instead of empathy. In short, all of the instances cited above involve victims and victimizers.

Perhaps, though, the flaw is much more fundamental: conceivably, kindness might lend itself to cruelty and injustice in a much more basic and sinister way. Do not the examples cited above show us that kindness itself can be infected by surrounding social values and corrupted by them? This possibility is similar to, but also different than, what we saw on a descriptive level, namely, that kindness takes its place in a constellation of other values and reflects them. Tolstoy's revolutionary, for example, was unfailingly kind and considerate with children and the elderly, but she also cheerfully murdered all of the aristocrats she could get her hands on. Here, rather, it is a question of suspicion that what seems to the agent to be kindness is actually illusion or delusion. Therefore, hermeneutic suspicion is required to distinguish appearance from reality.[1]

A hermeneutics of suspicion, as Ricoeur points out, functions as "demystification," as a "reduction of illusion" (1970, 27). Negatively, as described in the previous paragraph, it shatters naïve (uncritical) self-assurance by illuminating the reality "behind," or "beneath" the appearances. By "disclosing," "unveiling," or "revealing" hidden meanings of which we are unconscious, hermeneutics pushes beyond and destabilizes overt evidence for consciousness. It is therefore a creator of discord necessary for philosophical completeness. Its positive function, on the other hand, is redemptive, namely, to lay the groundwork for a more adequate understanding of the phenomena. In this and the next chapter, we will follow its negative impact on the descriptive phenomenology of kindness in Part One, and in the last chapter we will focus on its positive role.

As noted in the Introduction, Ricoeur takes Nietzsche, Marx, and Freud as the three "masters of the school of suspicion." What these thinkers had in common, he tells us, is that they viewed all of consciousness as a "false consciousness." They all tried "to make their 'conscious methods' of deciphering" carry out "in reverse the work of falsification of the man of guile" (Ricoeur 1970, 33–34).

Following the contours of this mental archaeology, the present chapter will first critically analyze Hallie's and Douglass' observations about kindness and cruelty, and then will take up the Nietzschean challenge to kindness. The following chapter will deal with Marx and also Carol Gilligan. Both chapters will consider Freud's significance for understanding kindness, though to a much lesser extent. That significance will consist first of his reflections on "civilized" behavior—where he would undoubtedly locate kindness—as the fruit of repression and sublimation, and productive of neurosis, and then his sense of self and moral development. As for the first dimension of relevance here, Nietzsche discussed most of it first, for which reason Freud stopped reading his discerning predecessor. Therefore, the arguments advanced against Nietzsche will count against Freud as well. As for the second area of Freud's significance here, those arguments will be best discussed in the context of ideologies of patriarchy and Carol Gilligan's alternative voice. Finally, although there are still multiple dissatisfactions both about civilization and sexuality, our own society could scarcely differ more in that context from the late Victorian civilization plagued by Freudian discontents. For, among other things, sexuality is no longer bound to the model of normative heterosexuality as the only socially acceptable form. In addition, a plethora of postmodern and poststructuralist discourses and more than twenty-five years of the women's movement have created a wide awareness and discussions of the distinction between sex and gender. Also, less social repression follows naturally in the wake of less dogmatic certainty about sexual identity and difference. These subjects are openly discussable in ways about which Freud could have only dreamed. His principal obstacle, as with Nietzsche, was with a century that refused to face reality and honestly describe sexual desire and dysfunction.

The first step in this analysis consists of discovering what "false consciousness" in regard to kindness can mean, and in what sense someone who suffers from it is a "man of guile." To begin with, the evidence that displays this falsity shows that, in all of the real and fictional cases noted above, the agents' consciousnesses are not necessarily false in the sense of insincerity. Such victimizers can genuinely mean what they say and do; none must be conceived as lying or dissembling, though they sometimes can be. Therefore, none must be a "man of guile" in the usual sense of being malicious, of having a conscious intent to deceive or harm.

Thus Douglass' owners, just as the accountant in *Heart of Darkness*, could have honestly believed him to be non-human, or not fully human—in the sense of not having equal membership in the moral community—and therefore to have no more rights than animals. By their own lights, dim as they were, their kindnesses to him could have satisfied all of their moral obligations. The doctor in *Huckleberry Finn* had precisely the same view of Jim, and Douglass' own description of a slave auction provides us with a graphically clear picture of this objectifying mentality: "What an assemblage! Men and women, young and old, married and single; moral and thinking beings, in open contempt of their humanity, leveled at a blow with horses, sheep, horned cattle, and swine" (Douglass 1962, 96).

Similarly, Nora's and Edna's husbands, as well as their numerous real-life counterparts, believed that they were acting in their wives' best interests, and that their kindnesses were part of a coherent and an appropriate way of treating them, just as did the parents of the schizophrenic children studied by Laing and Esterton. Again, by their own lights, their conduct has not only not been morally wrong but actually praiseworthy. That is why they are shocked at the disintegrating marriages and relationships with their children, respectively.

The absence of any conscious intent to harm also displays itself in the reactions of many such victimizers when they realize, if they ever do, that they have harmed the very people whom they thought they were protecting. The immediate response is typically expressed in language such as, "I had no idea," "I never meant to hurt her" (confusing or conflating harming and hurting), and the like. The case of slavery is much more complicated than the cases of the parents of the schizophrenic children or patriarchal husbands because of systemic immorality and different types of slave owners (see note 4 in this chapter). Even here, though, it is not impossible to imagine benighted slaveholders who really did believe that their kindnessness to their slaves satisfied all of their moral obligations to them.

Nevertheless, the consciousnesses of all of these victimizers were false in the sense of being deceived, and their deception was caused by a particular sort of blindness—blindness that, as we shall see, many real-life victims of scenarios such as those sketched above shared. To lay hands on this type of blindness, we will begin with the simpler types of examples presented above and finish with the more complex case of slavery.

The statements that the abusive adult relatives of the schizophrenic children made to Laing and Esterton show that they did not really perceive their own children as they existed in and of themselves, but rather as extensions of their own values and identities. Thus they equated diversion from their control with unbearable rejection. Since they could not endure it, they non-consciously concealed it from themselves by labeling their children as "sick"—and so unable consciously to reject their parents. In a later text, Laing describes the children's perspective of their parents as "playing a game. They are playing at not playing a game. If I show them I see they are, I shall break the rules and they will punish me. I must play their game, of not seeing I see the game" (Laing 1971, 1). But we must be cautious about using such language. For the reasons given above, this description is true of most, if not all, the parents (and other complicit adult family members) only on condition that "playing a game" occurs non-consciously.

Nora's and Edna's husbands, as well as the legions of real-life men for whom they stand, resemble these parents. The armature of the motor of their blindness, as in fact in all of the scenarios sketched above, consists of non-conscious possessiveness. Each of these two fictional characters, as well as certain other male characters in Chopin's mature writings, is a kind, decent individual who "believes that the woman he marries should be, like the largest and brightest jewel ornamenting a monarch's crown, his most prized possession" (Skaggs 1985, 22). Such beliefs exemplify the discussion in Chapter 2 of the closely interwoven themes of objectification, "trophy wives," and Marcel's distinction between "being" and "having."

This attitude is one of possessiveness rather than mere possession, because these men are not neutral or indifferent about the fate of the "objects" at issue, and because they see their wives as mentally and physically dependent on them in a strong sense, as derivative from their own identities. Torvald expresses this attitude exactly when he says to Nora, "No, no, you just lean on me, I shall give you all the advice and guidance you need. I wouldn't be a proper man if I didn't find a woman doubly attractive for being so obviously helpless" (Ibsen 1981, 78). Edna's husband, Léonce Pontellier, likewise believes that his kindness and generosity demonstrate that he loves his wife. Although he follows what he thinks is the best advice he can get[2] to deal with the confusion of his disintegrating marriage, his "immersion in the culture that idolizes the 'mother-woman' precludes his ever understanding his wife's awakening need for autonomy" (Skaggs 1985, 100).

However, the parents studied by Laing and Esterton, on the one hand, and Léonce, Torvald, and their real-life counterparts, on the other hand, diverge in one major respect, namely, the causes of their respective blindnesses. With the latter, the principal cause consists of a lifetime of successful, unseen, and hence unchallenged social conditioning. A propos of Léonce, for example, Skaggs writes that, "[A]ll the thought patterns of his forty years, his entire way of looking at life, blind him to the fact that a woman may properly have a 'position in the universe as a human being' [*The Awakening*] . . . apart from her place as wife and mother" (1985, 101). Because social conditioning contributes powerfully to the values inherent in social atmospheres, we must be careful here also in describing behavior attributed to it in game-playing language that suggests or implies a conscious possessiveness or posturing. They were not playing roles or "games" as distinguishable from their lives. The victimizers could see neither the harm that they caused nor the fact that they were playing a game.[3] Thus both the parents of the schizophrenic children as well as the patriarchal husbands were not necessarily malicious, but they were tragically misguided.

With the considerably more complex case of slavery, on the other hand, it is not only a question of particular acts or attitudes that we would label immoral but, as noted above, a systemic immoral morality that forms the conditioning matrix. Slavery, like the Nazi concentration camps or those in the Soviet Gulag, consisted of a vast assortment of individual and collective acts of harm causing through diverse types of coercion and exploitation. It also provided for, as well as provoked, different types of kindnesses as well as alleged kindnesses, and both the harms and kindnesses, real and alleged, will be subjected to hermeneutic scrutiny below. Here our concern is with the false consciousness of the slave owner.

The blindness of the slave owner appears to have consisted of three interlocking premises. First and foremost, there was the belief noted above, that slaves were not, or not fully, human beings, in the sense of being equal members of the moral community. Their only social value consisted of being *manipulanda*. It is the same objectifying view that many whites took toward Blacks in America until the 1960s, and some still hold today—as the recent horrifying examples of racist killings demonstrate. Second, it followed from this that moral obligations toward slaves, such as they were, consisted at most of the sort of kind treatment—the same obligations, and for the same reasons—that Montaigne held to be appropriate for animals. Thus what Joel Feinberg says of animals the prudential and sincere[4] slave owner would have said of his slaves: "It would be good business as well as good morals to treat them kindly (so long as they are obedient), for that way one can get more labor out of them in the long run" (1973, 97). Third, given the first two premises, slaves were possessions—though unlike the cases of possessive husbands and Laing's and Esterton's parents of schizophrenic children, this was true by definition. However, slave owners were equally possessive, because the number and condition of their slaves contributed substantially to their own social and economic status.

In the case of slaveholders, no matter how benign, as well as in the cases of all of the other victimizers described above, what blinds them is principle, dogma, or another cultural belief. The slaveholder can be convinced that his slaves are not (fully) human. Torvald, Léonce, and their real-life counterparts believe firmly in patriarchy and in the concept of wife as property. The parents of Laing's and Esterton's schizophrenic children who are in some way implicated in their children's mental illness[5] hold to a vision of the latter as extensions of themselves and regard diversion as treason. Such intellectual commitments drive a wedge between victim and victimizer and fatally separate the latter from the world of feelings—again, the cause of so much unkindness. Therefore, at one level, we can praise the goodness of an individual for having certain principles, a devotion to duty, self-sacrifice, and so on. But at another level, and a more profound one, such praise must be conditioned on knowing whether that commitment is grounded in feeling and authentic kindness.

Dogmatic blindness may be observed in many more real-life contexts as well, but the following instances are most pertinent to the cases cited above. The first example concerns, of all people, Gandhi. " 'I was,' said Gandhi, 'a cruelly kind husband. I regarded myself as her teacher and so harassed her out of my blind love for her.' " Gandhi rejected the cogency of his wife's objections to opening her home to strangers. He also turned a blind eye to the differences between adolescent and adult sexuality. Thus he "compromised in his everyday life the ethic of nonviolence to which, in principle and in public, he steadfastly adhered. The blind willingness to sacrifice people to truth, however, has always been the danger of an ethics abstracted from life" (Gilligan 1982, 1993 printing, 104, citing Erikson 1969, 233). By "truth" here, Gilligan means "principle," but the harm that blind victimizers cause divides the two, and it is therefore equally appropriate to speak of a blind willingness to sacrifice people to avoid seeing the truth. Like the fictional characters, Torvald and Léonce, Gandhi had no intention to harm his wife, but his actions were cruel nonetheless. He loved her, but wrongly.

The second example is also a case of loving wrongly, but in the context of slavery, and in a radically different manner. In the summer of 1998 on the island of Martinique, there was an exhibition dedicated to the 150th anniversary of the end of slavery in the French West Indies. The exhibition was located at La Pagerie, the Empress Josephine's former plantation. Among the artifacts on display was a photograph of an iron used to brand slaves. There was nothing unusual about that, but what was appalling was the design. It consisted of the letters "S V," and above and between them a valentine-shaped heart. In the absence of any accompanying explanation, the brand suggested that S was giving to V the slave into whose flesh was seared this image of love, or V to S, or that the recipient of this burning icon incarnated S' and V's love for each other.

Third, Reverend Cyprian Davis, O.S.B., has documented a number of depressing instances of American slaveholding religious institutions. Religious leaders and religious orders were just as blind to human suffering as were most other members and sectors of the white majority. Many American Catholic bishops owned slaves, including the first one, John Carroll, and Louis William DuBourg, the first bishop of New Orleans, who used his slaves "as collateral to borrow money and as investments for other financial ventures" (Davis 1990, 43). Many more bishops, even if they were not slave owners themselves, defended the institution, despite the fact that Pope Gregory XVI condemned it in 1839. For William Henry Elder, when he was bishop of Natchez, "[T]he African American slave was part child, part animal, part saint" (ibid.). John England, bishop of Charleston, South Carolina, and a born "spin doctor," responded to slave owners' criticisms of the Pope's condemnation by assuring them that the Pope had in mind the Spanish and Portuguese slave trade and not the domestic variety (!). In a number of public letters, he argued eloquently from Scripture, history, church councils, canon law, and Roman law, that slavery had always existed and was moral under certain circumstances. But, as Bishop England knew very well, even the moral minimum he defended did not exist for slaves in South Carolina. Francis Patrick Kenrick, the Archbishop of Baltimore, wrote a manual of theology in which he took an excruciatingly legalistic attitude toward slavery. Slaves, he opined solemnly, should venerate God by being good servants of their masters. The whips and chains, he perhaps thought, were just punishment for not rising to the prescribed level of goodness. Kenrick's priorities were "tranquility of civil society first, then the good of the slaveholders who were Catholic, and finally the well-being of the slaves" (ibid., 49). Lastly, Bishop Auguste-Marie Martin of Natchitoches, Louisiana, was such an enthusiastic supporter of slavery that even Rome cracked down. He offered a "theological justification for slavery—it was something noble because it was God's plan for the conversion of the black race, who were dependent on the white race" (ibid., 52).

Fourth are Rev. Niall O'Brien's reflections (1988) on the evil that good people do. The context was the shocking institutional injustice on the island of Negros in the Philippines, on which he served as a missionary. One case he recounted concerned a certain hacienda owner who fretted to the point of tears about not being able to receive Communion but was entirely unbothered by the impoverished, dying peasant children on her ranch. In the same way, Douglass recounts that, when he belonged to Mr. and Mrs. Thomas Auld, the slaves were starving, while "meat and bread were mouldering under lock and key." Even when Mrs. Auld knew that their slaves were "nearly half-starved," "with a saintly air she would each morning kneel with her husband and pray that a merciful God would 'bless them in basket and store, and save them at last in His kingdom'" (Douglass 1962, 105).

There is a final religious example, this time from the Inquisition, on which Douglass himself gives us a remarkable commentary. Visiting the prison in the palace of the popes at Avignon, he states that no great imagination was needed "to see the terror-stricken faces, the tottering forms, and pleading tears of the accused, and the saintly satisfaction of the inquisitors while ridding the world of the representatives of unbelief and misbelief." He then expressed his incredulity that "men could from innocent motives thus punish their fellows, but such is, no doubt, the fact. They were conscientious, and felt that they were doing righteous service unto the Lord. . . . They could smile when they heard bones crack in the stocks and saw the maiden's flesh torn from her bones. It is only the best things that serve the worst perversions. Many pious souls today hate the Negro while they think they love the Lord" (ibid., 566).

Some still do, alas, so it is more than a matter of mere historical curiosity to discover just how it is that principle overrides feelings and brings on this false consciousness—and then to consider the consequences for the moral value of kindness itself. In distinguishing various layers of meaning in such experiences, let us first note that both commitment to principle and feelings coexist in the way that cognitive and affective awareness are usually intertwined—*Ineinander*, as Merleau-Ponty often expresses their relationship. Further, these feelings are fully intentional; they have as their objects the suffering other. However, the class of sadists apart, empathic response to this suffering, and even emotional infection, is blocked. Slave owners were fully aware of the bloody whips and chains and the groaning sufferings of their victims, but few were ever motivated to free them. Likewise, the inquisitor remained unmoved, except perhaps in pleasure, when he saw the tortured body on the rack or the wheel and heard the screams of innocent victims.

This is to say that in some sense the victim's suffering does not register in such people. This sense is related to, but also different from that of Schlick's indifferent egoist. Both groups had, in Stanley Kubrick's admirable phrase, "eyes wide shut." However, here it is not a question of self-satiety but of an attitude more difficult to name. It combines the notions of self-defense, self-justification, and self-ratification in a rigid self-image. Once again, this is not to say that these notions normally rise to the level of conscious awareness. Usually they do not, for that would expose them to debate and critical attack. Rather, everything conspires to keep them safely buried so that they can be maximally effective.

Beyond the slave owner, ordinary racists, and inquisitors, the same phenomenon can be detected in our other cases of victimization as well. Independent schizophrenic children threaten the self-images of controlling parents who desire them to duplicate their own values. It is much easier to label children "sick" rather than face the incipient challenge. Something of the same self-defensive, self-justificatory scenario gets played out in many schools in which student criticism or "non-standard" behavior is labeled as "deviant" and, as we saw in Kozol's descriptions, the miscreants tend to be punished or sent to psychologists who encourage happy conformity.[6]

However, when that is not possible, or when it is too expensive for HMOs, there is a growing preference for the often misguided, cheaper solution of medicalizing "problem cases." Not only does this decision substitute pharmacological solutions for the patient's Lifeworld, as we saw in Chapter 3, but the same ambiguities about nature and social construction emerge here as well. As one psychotherapist indicates, "Ritalin's production alone is up 700 percent since 1990. . . . Some children need medication; others don't. The real trouble lies in how we make that assessment" (Bloom 2000, 24). As Bloom goes on to explain, handing out pills with school lunches is much simpler than creating exciting classrooms that will constructively channel children's energies. "Most of all," she adds, "we prescribe medications for children who don't need them because the medications are available, and a cure for parental vanity and irresponsibility— along with the single-minded greed of HMOs—is not" (ibid.).

The emerging freedom of the schizophrenic children and of those who are medicated in school threatens the possessive, dominating self-images of their adult family members and teachers. Their respective "illnesses" are thus convenient mystifications. Similarly, the "awakening" independence that Chopin describes, and which Edna and Nora undergo, alarms their husbands. The latter take passive obedience and dependence as evidence of moral rectitude, devotion, and self-worth. On the other hand, they view active independence and autonomy as an attack on their manhood and social status, a wedge driven between the self (image) they wish to have their spouses ratify and the self that serves as the object of their wives' conflicting intentions. Thus as with the parents of the schizophrenic children, Torvald could not face Nora's challenge directly, but rather perceived her as deviant—as silly, stupid, and having taken leave of her senses—and so (conveniently) not responsible for her behavior.

Hume's argument that reason by itself cannot motivate us to act implies that commitments to principle and dogma that override empathic feelings of kindness cannot themselves be wholly rational. They must be underwritten, at some level and at least in part, by another sort of affectivity. What type has the capacity to block the force of empathic feelings, to induce otherwise rational people, when they are rational, not to recognize the harm they cause as harm? The most likely answer appears to be what Douglass referred to in the case of slavery as "the fatal poison of irresponsible power" (1962, 78). As Ricoeur notes (1965), our frightening history, which has led to the Nazi concentration camps, totalitarian violence, and the danger of nuclear destruction, leaves no doubt about the connection between, on the one hand, the problematic of evil and power and, on the other hand, the theme of alienation in eighteenth- and nineteenth-century philosophy and the criticisms of Old Testament prophets.

The context of Douglass' remark is instructive. It concerned his master's wife, Mrs. Sophia Auld. At first, Douglass tells us, she was "kind, gentle, and cheerful"; she had a "natural goodness of heart" (1962, 76). She was the very reverse of Schlick's indifferent egoist: "She had bread for the hungry, clothes for the naked, and comfort for every mourner who came within her reach" (ibid.,

82). When Douglass first moved into her home, she treated him "as she supposed one human being ought to treat another" (ibid., 81). She even started to teach him how to read, but ceased in the face of her husband's violently angry reaction. At that, she sought to "justify herself to herself. . . . One needs very little knowledge of moral philosophy to see where she inevitably landed. She finally became even more violent in her opposition to my learning to read than was Mr. Auld himself" (ibid., 82).[7]

Similarly, Hallie argues that cruelty and kindness are not opposites, and cites, beside Douglass himself, Wilbur J. Cash's *The Mind of the South* as support for his argument. In relevant part, Cash noted that the institution of slavery brutalized whites: "virtually unlimited power" inexorably provoked, "in the coarser sort of master," a sadism that "bred angry impatience and a taste for cruelty for its own sake." Further, these responses were invariably strong enough to prevail against "kindliness"—which "continued frequently to exist unimpaired side by side, and in the same man," with his sadistic behavior—and "notions of honor" (Hallie 1982, 106, citing Cash 1941, 84).

The diagnosis of corrupting power also fits well with our other illustrations of principle-blind victimizers. The parents of Laing's and Esterton's schizophrenic children would not have resented their progeny's emerging independence and autonomy if it had not threatened their power over them. Unable to admit their tyrannical control to themselves, they repressed and transmuted it into the explanation of sickness that would leave their power unchallenged. When Torvald and Léonce were confronted with their wives' "awakening," they could not see it as such, because it would have undermined their power as males and husbands. In the absence of a convenient rationalization, they could not understand what had gone wrong in their marriages. Likewise, as his wife's teacher, Gandhi could not understand his wife's objections to his notions of hospitality and adolescent sexuality. He was blind to both, because admitting them openly would have threatened his teaching role and exposed the great power he exercised as a public advocate of non-violence to the charge of hypocrisy.

The bishops to whom Father Davis refers were also driven by power, though in diverse ways. For Bishop Elder, it was the power that comes from successful evangelization. Bishops England and Kenrick appeared to have been moved by the power of institutional influence, the fear of social unrest, and the consequent unwillingness to disturb the *status quo ante*. Bishop Martin was overwhelmed—there appears to be no other way to describe it correctly—by a powerful, megalomaniac self-image of saving the souls of an entire race.

Father O'Brien's hacienda owner, in contrast, appears to be engaged in a struggle to maintain power over her own salvation, which she pursues with a purely formal approach to religion. That is, she must receive the sacraments, and it is in fulfilling the outer forms of religion that she will be saved. Conversely, not fulfilling these forms endangers her spiritual welfare. Her obsession with form is, therefore, an effect of her fear and struggle for eternal happiness, and her obsessive fear blinds her to the misery of others that it has caused. It is a classic case of grasping the shell and missing the kernel.

The inquisitors for their part could not respond to their victims in the way that we think any sane human being ought to, because they were seduced by the power of acting *in loco Dei*. "Heaven and hell were alike under their control," as Douglass put it. Their "saintly satisfaction" derived from identifying with their sacred mission of purifying society of heresy: "They believed that they had the keys [to the kingdom], and they lived up to their convictions" (1962, 566). The inquisitors also show us, in a peculiarly vivid manner, how *intoxicating* the irresponsible use of power can be. They remind us of the ancient saying that those whom the gods would destroy they first make drunk with power. But with the inquisitors and, *mutatis mutandis*, our other victimizers discussed above, it is more a question of early rather than celestial revenge of their devastation of innocent lives rather than the divine ruin of their own.

Finally, with "S" and "V," if my hypothesis about the meaning of the branding iron is correct, we have another example of irresponsible power in the service of love. Love is not only blind but blinds as well. The power that comes from the dialectic of being swept away, and sweeping away the beloved, in the service of the mutual commitment to fuse two lives into one, would have been, with this hypothesis, sufficient not to be bothered by the suffering of the slave. It is highly regrettable that we have no literary or artistic account of this gift of burned flesh. It would be instructive to know how the lover presented the gift and how the beloved received it. Did the former look on the newly burned flesh with pride? Did the beloved, in adoration of the lover, ignore and repress the reality of the cruelly maimed slave? Was the slave coerced into stifling all cries of pain and tears before assuming the form of a gift? Was he or she beaten later for not being able to? Did the beloved ever grasp Levinas' "privileged heteronomy" through a face-to-face confrontation with the slave? Or was it the case that both lovers looked upon the victim in no way logically different than, say, a newly branded cow or sheep?

The first key aspect of false consciousness consisted of the agent's being deceived about harm causing because of principle blindness. The preceding discussion has advanced a causal explanation for that blindness, the seduction of irresponsible power that blocks empathic feelings. In and through such power, non-conscious rationalization turns deception into self-deception. It is hardly likely that, though not logically impossible, slave owners were not self-deceived, and it is in the sense of self-deception that the agent can be a "man of guile," as Ricoeur phrases it—though of course not necessarily or even usually in a conscious manner. Self-deception is culpable even so, because it consists of ignoring rather than pure ignorance and surely suppressing doubts as well. One cannot ignore something without having recognized it, even if non-consciously. One wonders how many slave owners voiced to themselves the narrator's doubt in *Heart of Darkness*: "No, they were not inhuman. Well, you know, that was the worst of it—this suspicion of their not being inhuman, it would come slowly to one" (Conrad 1985, 69). However, even if it would "come slowly," it was surely repressed quickly. Therefore, the self-deceived agent is not innocent in either of the two senses described in Chapter 2—that from childhood, which a person loses, or that which she can struggle to attain.

The interpretation of kindness has so far yielded only a contrast with dogma blindness, because we have been considering the alleged kindness of the victimizers alongside their harm causing. We must now ask whether kindness itself can cause harm. Chapter 1 maintained that kindness could hurt but not intend to harm. However, at the descriptive level, the question has to be left open. We need to plunge deeper to see if our interpretive unveilings will force a revision in our provisional conclusion.

No recent writer has confronted this question more directly than Hallie in his reflections on cruelty, so I shall use his arguments to clarify the relationship between kindness and harm causing. We have already seen one example of Hallie's more general claim that kindness could not only cause harm but also intend to cause it. He bases this conclusion on his close studies of Gothic horror tales, the institution of American slavery—particularly through Douglass' writings—and Holocaust concentration camps. Even though the Chambonnais eventually taught him that he had "left out goodness" (Hallie 1982, 168), and that goodness and hospitality, rather than power or freedom, are the true opposite of cruelty, he continued to subscribe to Douglass' claim that the kindness of the slave master only "gilded the chain." Both on plantations and in the concentration camps "kindness could be the ultimate cruelty" because, "A kind overseer or a kind camp guard can exacerbate cruelty, can remind his victim that there are other relationships than the relationship of cruelty, and can make the victim deeply bitter, especially when he sees the self-satisfied smile of his victimizer." As a result, the victim "is being cruelly treated when he is given a penny or a bun after having endured the crushing and grinding of his mental and bodily well-being" (Hallie 1981, 35). This is a theme to which Hallie returns again and again, right down to his posthumously published writings.

However, across Douglass' long autobiography, it becomes clear that things were much more complex. He groups kindnesses within the slave-owning system in more or less three classes. To do so, he appeals to intention—malevolent or benign—and to consequences—those that cause harm and those that do not. Further, in terms of both measures, he assesses the kindness of his master relative to others in his area (1962, 64). The first class consists of those acts, customs, and social practices that deceptively pretended to be kind but that were malevolent and caused harm. They consisted of conscious attempts to manipulate and control slaves. Hence, they were not really kind after all; their "kindness" was but a façade that slave owners hoped would fool gullible slaves. So even the partially enlightened slave could distinguish between appearance and reality and detect what the slave owners already knew, namely, that the "kindness" in question was spurious and fraudulent.

For example, on holidays, and particularly at Christmas, owners invited their slaves to drink all the liquor they could. They sponsored contests to see which slave could drink the most. They hoped that the slaves would see this largesse as a great kindness. However, the real aim was to get the latter as drunk as possible and, later, disgusted with their "temporary freedom," to make them glad to return to the protection of the good, kind-hearted slave masters who would take care of them (Douglass 1962, 148). Thus although ostensibly "a custom established by the benevolence of the slave-holders," it was actually "one of the grossest frauds committed upon the down-trodden slave" (Douglass 1988, 115). The true aim of such customs was to root out all semblance of reasoning on the slave's part because, "It was the sober, thoughtful slave who was dangerous and needed the vigilance of his master to keep him a slave" (Douglass 1962, 148).

All of this was in the name of "love" for the slaves and kind attention to their welfare. It was the kind of "love" that Hallie had in mind before he discovered the Chambonnais. Douglass shows us, for Hallie, that "the opposite of cruelty is not kindness; nor is it Christian love (except if that word is subjected to what Montaigne would call 'a long interpretation,' an interpretation entirely in terms of the victim's point of view)" (Hallie 1982, 159).

Richard Wright gives us an updated version of such false kindness in terms of rich whites who would donate games and sports equipment, such as ping-pong tables, to the South Side Boys' Club where he worked. In his essay, "How 'Bigger' Was Born," Wright says that their kindness was pure self-interest. They were really paying Wright to keep actual and potential Biggers off the streets and away from white neighborhoods. Wright notes, "I felt that I was doing a kind of dressed-up police work, and I hated it" (1993, 530).

Douglass' second class of kindnesses consisted of well-intentioned, harm-causing acts. Unlike the acts, customs, and social practices in the previous class, these were not self-contradictory frauds. They comprised meagre, ameliorative pleasures, such as an extra bit of food, or at least having enough to eat—not starving while "meat and bread were mouldering under lock and key" (1962, 105). Such pleasures also included a few pennies from the sale of goods that the slave helped produce and occasional improvements in working conditions—as in the rare permissions not to have to be in the fields at sunrise, a permission "that gives to him that gives it the proud name of being a kind master" (1988, 48). Non-acts counted as well, such as lack of exploitation in fornication and adultery and in the low number and frequency of whippings.

These acts and non-acts were both ameliorative and harm causing at the same time. With unenlightened slaves, such acts harmed on a personal level by lessening their victims' resistance to their servitude. On a systemic level, the acts at issue harmed by facilitating the functioning of the machine—not only on a particular plantation, but indirectly the slave-owning system itself. And with even partially enlightened slaves, such acts caused an additional sort of harm. They were like salt rubbed in the wound without recognizing either that there was a wound or that the slaveholder's action was responsible for keeping it open. Therefore, Hallie notes correctly that, "What is well-intentioned kindness to the victimizer can be torture to the victim" (1982, 160–61), particularly the victimizer's "self-satisfied smile" (1981, 35). For it is precisely in this class of kindnesses that we find the dogma blindness at the heart of a false consciousness—a blindness that the awakened slave did not share. Hence, Douglass tells us that this type of kindness wore "a grim visage [that] could assume no smiles able to fascinate the partially enlightened slave into a forgetfulness of his bondage, or the desirableness of liberty" (1962, 155).

Hallie and Douglass are correct here, but it also follows that the object of their criticisms is not authentic acts of kindness. For we have already seen on a purely descriptive level that good intentions are not a sufficient condition of performing acts of kindness. Hence, a "well-intentioned kindness" and "self-satisfied smile" cannot be the measure of the kindness of the action. Real avoidance of harm is also necessary. Moreover, even though the harm caused here would have appeared to the alert slave as the product of the master's blindness, the harmful consequences consisted precisely in the master's blindness underwriting and making the institution of slavery more effective by "not seeing" his role in perpetuating it. It is this self-deception itself that "gilded the chain" of slavery.

The same conclusion applies, *mutatis mutandis*, for "cruelly kind" husbands and other well-intentioned victimizers. Therefore, what Nora should have said to Torvald was, "You think that you were kind to me, but you really were not." It is not thus authentic kindness that wears a "grim visage" but the acts that the victimizer wants the victim to believe are those of kindness. Douglass shows us that knowledge could pierce the façade and disrupt the power of the fascination—which is what happens to Nora at the end of *A Doll's House*.

Authentic acts of kindness comprise Douglass' third class of kindnesses, and they were such that he remembered them with great satisfaction after the war (1962, 391). The instances that he describes are cases in which the wives of his owners bound up his wounds after he had been severely injured in diverse attacks. Lucretia Auld, for example, cleaned the blood from his face and head and brought him her own bottle of balsam and bandages. Douglass writes, "The balsam was not more healing to the wounds in my head, than her kindness was in healing to the wounds in my spirit." He thought of these actions as "sunbeams of humane treatment" (ibid., 71).

On another occasion, after Douglass had been beaten by the white shipyard apprentices, Ms. Sophia Auld—she who had been poisoned by "irresponsible power"—recovered something of her old self and performed the same healing offices for him as had Lucretia. Recovering briefly her connection with a world of feelings, she was moved to tears and bound up his wounds. He notes, "It was almost compensation for all that I suffered, that it occasioned the manifestation once more of the originally characteristic kindness of my mistress. Her affectionate heart was not yet dead, though much hardened by time and circumstances" (ibid., 183). Her husband's reaction, typically, was quite different. He was outraged, not by Douglass' suffering, but because his property interests in him had been abused.

These acts do conform to the descriptions of kind acts described in Part One. They are distinguishable from those in the first two classes above, because they do not form parts of projects of conscious (or even unconscious) manipulation. There is nothing to unveil in order to reveal cruel underpinnings of intent to maim and destroy; there is no exploitation and coercion to unmask. These acts are the opposite of cruelty, even if they take place within a cruel system, just as were the unusual acts of kindness by concentration camp guards. They are rare and extremely delicate flowers that manage to bloom in a hostile, alien environment.

Nevertheless, even if such actions do not harm, they have the capacity to hurt because of the way in which they contrast with the immoral morality in which they are situated. This is how they can be what Hallie called the "ultimate cruelty." Genuine acts of kindness could remind victims of their imprisonment and degradation only on condition that such acts are informed with the respect and care that Part 1 illustrated is necessary for such acts. Those acts do not impeach the value of kindness or show that it is itself cruel. Rather, their rarity in plantation or concentration-camp situations honors kindness and casts shame on the immoral context.

The Case of Nietzsche

Although Douglass clearly does regard kindness as easily misled and betrayed, his third class of kindnesses shows that he does not reject its value completely. Hence, one gets the impression from reading his heartrending narratives that there was just the faintest possibility that Lucretia's and Sophia Auld's compassion could have been redemptive. If not, he certainly would have placed the blame on the external realities of a slave-owning system rather than on kindness itself. Nietzsche, on the other hand, invites us to take a more cynical view of even such acts of kindness as these, namely, that they are internally morally corrupt. In the context of his well-known distinction between "master" and "slave" moralities, he would simply have prolonged the destructive analysis that he began with pity to embrace not only kindness but also its allied supporting phenomena of empathy, sympathy, fellow feeling, and altruism generally.

The exuberant joy of the masters, let us recall, drives them to live life self-interestedly and unself-consciously to the fullest. Their morality begins positively with the perception of "good" as power and self-fulfillment, whereas "bad" means the absence of power. In reaction, slave morality begins negatively with the perception of the power of the masters as "evil" and their own impotence as "good." Hypocritically, though, they still desire power, but since they are weak, they must be clever about seeking it. Given that they cannot attack the powerful directly, they must do so indirectly; since they cannot overcome the masters, they attempt to undermine them. Therefore, Nietzsche says, "While the noble man lives in trust and openness with himself . . . the man of *ressentiment* is neither upright nor naive nor honest and straightforward with himself. His soul *squints*" (1969, 38; emphasis in original).

Christianity both springs from and incarnates *ressentiment*—as do, on an interpersonal level—acts of kindness, love, and altruism generally, whether within or outside of any particular religious commitment. In turn, these acts and Christianity itself function as tools of revenge in order to obtain whatever power is available. Nietzsche, of course, would also train his suspicious glare on any putative claim not to want power over others, and this would include Gandhi's politics of non-violence, the Hindu practice of *ahimsa*, and the Chambonnais rescuers. Kindness, in his view, would therefore be a strategem born out of envy and hatred of the powerful and would reduce to acts of spiritual vengeance.

However, to keep this recognition from breaking through the placid surface of consciousness, as the epigraph of this chapter indicates, various cognate acts and dispositions are baptized with names of appropriate virtues. Suffering and poverty are dignified as self-sacrifice. Pity and the acts that it produces are rewarded, or at least praised, as charity. Hate becomes (in Christianity, a religion of) love. In fact, for Nietzsche, these are all ignoble attempts to gain power over others stronger than the agents are. Forgiveness and pity, particularly, are underhanded attempts to gain power over the powerful when no other power is available to the agent. They constitute attempts to drag the strong down into the well of the suffering weak.[8] Ibsen, whose theatre of truth constituted the dramatic counterpart to Nietzsche's solitary meditations, captured the same phenomenon in *A Doll's House* when Torvald forgave Nora for her forgery. Torvald expresses his satisfaction at this forgiveness, a transparent will to power and domination, as follows: "It's as though it made her his [the husband's] property in a double sense: he has, as it were, given her a new life, and she becomes in a way both his wife and at the same time his child" (1981, 78).

Zarathustra's last temptation, having gotten over his nausea at the masses, is precisely pity. Thus the later *On the Genealogy of Morals* will recommend a remedy of "fresh air! fresh air! and keep clear of the madhouses and hospitals of culture . . . [and guard against] the two worst contagions that may be reserved just for us—against the *great nausea at man! against great pity for man!*" (Nietzsche 1969, Third Essay, §14, 125; emphasis in original). In *Beyond Good and Evil*, Nietzsche links pity to self-contempt (1966, §222, 149-50) and in *The Gay Science* claims that resentment and desire for revenge are grounded in self-dissatisfaction: "Whoever is dissatisfied with himself is continually ready for revenge, and we others will be his victims, if only by having to endure his ugly sight. For the sight of what is ugly makes one bad and gloomy" (Nietzsche 1974, §290, 233).

In contrast, the French Revolutionary writer Mirabeau is a good example of those who have "strong, full natures in whom there is an excess of power to form, to mold, to recuperate, and to forget." He had "no memory for insults and vile actions done him and was unable to forgive simply because he—forgot." As opposed to those wallowing in self-pity, "Such a man shakes off with a *single* shrug much vermin that eats deep into others; here alone genuine "love of one's enemies" is possible—supposing it to be possible at all on earth (Nietzsche 1969, First Essay, §10, 39; emphasis in original).[9]

Nietzsche is not the only one to notice the connection between resentment and revenge, on the one hand, and self-contempt or dissatisfaction, on the other hand. Nor was he the sole thinker to observe that the strong cannot cure the sick, because—it is a telling index to their hypocrisy—they resist being cured. For example, George Eliot pointed out that, "People who seem to enjoy their ill-temper have a way of keeping it in fine condition by inflicting privations on themselves" (1985, 190)—virtuously, of course. More recently, Florence King has noted that, "Insecurity breeds treachery: if you are kind to people who hate themselves, they will hate you as well. It does no good to try to help them because they never really change no matter how long they stay in therapy" (1992, 158).

In reply to Nietzsche, it is true that, as we saw earlier, Scheler underscored a key weakness in his indictment of kindness and other altruistic values by pointing out that he confused genuine fellow-feeling with emotional infection. It is also true that his categories of "master" and "slave" moralities are, to say the least, highly dubious. Nevertheless, his critique of kindness is still worth taking seriously for four closely related reasons. His masterful psychological diagnoses point to well-known non-moral cases of the "slaves," if not the "masters" as well. In terms of the former, the neurotic do-gooders and other similar social pests referred to earlier are easy examples. In addition, Nietzsche argues that, for the reasons given above, kindness is internally inconsistent—the wolf of self-interested power in the altruistic sheep's clothing. Like the evolutionary psychologists referred to in Chapter 4, his psychological egoism wants to explain away all forms of altruism. Also, his moral psychology is hermeneutically sensitive, because it revolves around power and self-deception, and lastly, strength and weakness have a primordial importance in understanding kindness, though not in the way he interprets them.

Nietzsche's contention that kindness is a tool of the weak to gain power over the strong, a device of the sick to infect the healthy, is, in fact, backwards. On the contrary, genuine kindness requires strength to come into being. This is so because: (1) it takes power to control power—that is, to resist the "human, all too human" uses of power. This type of power is essential for achieving and maintaining an appropriate absence from people's lives, which is one of the necessary conditions of personal kindness; (2) The *disponibilité* characteristic of kindness requires courage to the degree that it makes the agent vulnerable, at least in many contexts; and (3), as Scheler points out, leading your own life and believing it worth living are necessary conditions of sacrificing yourself for others (1954, 44). Or, as Douglass puts it, "A man without force is without the essential dignity of humanity. Human nature is so constituted that it cannot honor a helpless man, though it can pity him, and even this it cannot do long if signs of power do not arise" (1962, 143). This fundamental truth also explains our recoil from the poor—as in the exchange between Clara and Fanny in *Sons and Lovers*, and in those that Eliot described so well in *The Mill on the Floss*.

Self-neglecting and self-despising, which Montaigne observed is peculiar to humanity, no matter how well intentioned and socially useful they might seem, almost invariably culminate in hatred. This is so in direct proportion to our determination to throw ourselves away, because it is "the very opposite of really meritorious self-*devotion*." Self-awareness and self-respect "not derived from the effect produced on others" are necessary conditions of living morally (Scheler 1954, 44; emphasis in original). Ricoeur argues the same way while speaking of Levinas rather than of Scheler. He states that what is required for us to receive any "instruction" from the face of the suffering other is that we have "a capacity for giving in return" that is liberated by the other person's suffering. This capacity, these resources, are those "of *goodness* which could spring forth only from a being who does not detest itself to the point of being unable to hear the injunction coming from the other" (Ricoeur 1992, 189). This strength to which Scheler and Ricoeur refer is diametrically opposed to what Nietzsche meant by it. It is not a joy of strength placed in the service of self-interestedly, unself-consciously enjoying life but rather the celebration of being human in a life of ennobling service.

This is why weakness produces only specious acts of kindness—for example, in taking the path of least resistance to avoid giving offense, entanglements, public scrutiny, and the like. We recognize the speciousness, because we do not prize it or praise the agent. It may be service, but it is not ennobling. The following fictional and real examples illustrate this very clearly, as well as what Douglass, Scheler, and Ricoeur had in mind.

In a certain passage in *Sons and Lovers*, Lawrence describes a dinner in the Leivers household. Mrs. Leivers' consistent attitude toward her family, especially her sons, is one of apology, unflinching gentleness, and silent suffering under the lash of their reproaches. She lives as a sacrificial victim. In this passage, the lateness of the dinner and the potatoes being slightly burned triggered the usual barrage of criticisms: "The meal went rather brutally. The over-gentleness and apologetic tone of the mother brought out all the brutality of manners in the sons" (1982, 146).

Mrs. Leivers has multiple real-life counterparts. One was Dostoevsky's wife, Anna. She used to put some of her housekeeping money in reserve to support her husband's gambling habit. After losing whatever she gave to him, he would also return saying that he realized he was unworthy of her, that she was an angel and he a brute, but that he had to get more money. Usually she gave it to him for fear that an argument would throw him into one of his fits. Her mild attempts to take the path of least resistance were completely ineffective, and Dostoevsky in fact protested "that he would be better off with a scold for a wife. 'It was positively painful to him the way I was so sweet' [she wrote in her diary]. (Frank [1995] notes that the inhuman sweetness of Prince Myshkin in *The Idiot*, which Dostoevsky was writing at this time, produces the same exasperating effect on the people around him)" (Coetzee 1995, 14).

Robert Bellah, et al., discuss other instances of specious kindnesses and the lesson that a person cannot love others if she or he does not know and respect herself or himself. The pattern that emerges in the stories they relate consists of wives whose marriages are in trouble because they have lost themselves. This is because they have adopted as the one principle of daily living the belief that their love for their husbands meant an unconditional desire to please them. Typically, one of these women "had 'put aside' . . . her willingness to express her own opinions and act on her own judgment, even about how best to please her husband. . . . 'The very things I was doing to get his approval were causing him to view me less favorably'" (Bellah et al. 1985, 92–93). As Nussbaum indicates, a woman's inclination to care for others can deviate "into an undignified self-abnegation" in which she "subordinates her humanity utterly to the needs of another or others" (1999, 13).

In contrast, the strength that underlies genuine kindness reflects at least enough self-reliance, self-assurance, and security to enable the agent both to risk involving herself in other people's sorrows and to function as an autonomous being. This is what we sense in Eliot's *The Mill on the Floss*, for example, when the clergyman, Dr. Kenn, looked at Maggie Tulliver in the booth at the fair. Maggie feels "a child-like, instinctive relief" when she finds herself looking into Dr. Kenn's face: "[T]hat plain, middle-aged face, with a grave penetrating kindness in it, seeming to tell of a human being who had reached a firm, safe strand, but was looking with helpful pity towards the strugglers still tossed by the waves" (Eliot 1985, 553). The kindness that rests on such strength is not corrupted by a desire to achieve power over someone, is not self-deceived about hidden weaknesses and desires for revenge, and is, therefore, not internally inconsistent in the way that Nietzsche would claim.

Moreover, something else was present in Dr. Kenn's face: the elusive virtue of peace. It was not "anæsthesia" but rather "a positive feeling which crowns the 'life and motion of the soul' " (Whitehead 1933, 367). Peace is usually discussed as a by-product of justice, or at least seeking the latter, it is said, is necessary for achieving the former. Doubtless, there can be little peace in the absence of justice, but justice is not at issue in the kind of experience that Eliot describes here. This sense of peace derives from feelings that are both negative and positive. Negatively, there is the feeling that the agent's gaze bears no evidence of a desire to harm, that his strength is no threat. Positively, Dr. Kenn's face offers the miserable girl three closely related benefits. There is the understanding inscribed in its "deep, penetrating kindness." It is a discernment which accounts for the fact that, "There is always this possibility of a word or look from a stranger to keep alive the sense of human brotherhood" (Eliot 1985, 554). In addition, Dr. Kenn's face offers her security and shelter. It is the face of someone "who had reached a firm, safe strand" after weathering the storms of life. The strength of the face offers a lifeline to the suffering and a reason to hope. This hopefulness is in turn reinforced by the third benefit, a positive disposition to help, which serves as the armature of the motor of the experience.

Specifically how, in practical terms, are we to recognize and understand this strength and the support it offers to those in need? How does it express itself? The key is the *capable body*, the corporeal "I can" discussed in Part One that Ricoeur appropriates from Merleau-Ponty. Through its fleshly reversibilities, as Merleau-Ponty described them, it responds empathically to those in need, and in the "solicitude" (Ricoeur) of its ethical life, it mobilizes responses to that suffering with an inventive charity. Ricoeur observed after having written *Oneself as Another* that he had "given even greater force to this notion of being-able-to-do, in view of providing a basis for a political philosophy. I therefore speak of *capable man*, as the primary object of esteem and respect and even as the primary subject of law"[10] (Hahn 1995, 367). Underlying this "esteem and respect" is what Ricoeur calls "attestation," which is "the practical modality of belief, of the confidence I have in my being-capable, the opposite of which is not doubt but suspicion. To believe, here, is to have confidence that I can" (Hahn 1995, 367).

This is exactly what Dr. Kenn offers Maggie through the sharing of memory and experience. This is crucial because, as Whitehead observed, "Youth is not peaceful in any ordinary sense of that term," to say nothing of the sufferings of someone in Maggie's position. "In youth, despair is overwhelming. There is then no tomorrow, no memory of disasters survived" (Whitehead 1933, 370). Dr. Kenn has that experience and those memories with which he can attempt to shore up Maggie's determination, and he has the self-assurance required to suggest to her that he had "reached a firm, safe strand" from which he was throwing her a lifeline.

The notion of the capable body leads to two other, closely related similarities between Nussbaum and Ricoeur, and impliedly Merleau-Ponty as well. It will also lead us to a defense of some universal moral values against the way it is fashionable to use Nietzsche in defense of relativism. In turn, that discussion will return us to his moral psychology. The first chapter of Nussbaum's *Sex and Social Justice* takes capabilities as its main theme and argues for their provision for women just as they have been traditionally provided for "the capable man." Rather than focus on human well-being in terms of "goods," "items," or "things," as Rawls tends to do, she defends the view that we should focus on people's capabilities and functioning. We need to know "how each and every individual is doing with respect to all the functions deemed important" (Nussbaum 1999, 34).[11]

However, it is not just any "capabilities and functions" that should interest us, but rather those that are "more central, more at the core of human life, than others" (ibid.). It is here that Nussbaum wants to defend, just as Ricoeur did much earlier,[12] a type of "cultural universalism" against those who would deny us any "privileged place" (ibid., 35) from which we can make such judgments. For the latter, such judgments are disreputable exercises in colonialism that reflect "Western essentialist values" and hence fail to respect the "difference" and "otherness" of foreign cultures. Thus one "elegant French anthropologist," at a conference on "Values and Technology," sought to drive this point home by decrying the British smallpox vaccination program in India because it destroyed the "cult of Sittala Devi, the goddess to whom one used to pray to avert smallpox." In response to the criticism that it was better to be alive and well than sick or dead, even if religiously compliant, the unnamed *anthropologiste* replied that this Western binary logic of opposing life to death and health to disease is precisely what blocks us from understanding "the otherness of Indian traditions" (ibid., 35).

A suitable reply would have been that without the smallpox vaccination program, many fewer Indians would have been left to worship the goddess. Instead, Eric Hobsbawm took the philosophical high road that Nussbaum records and defends. His "blistering indictment of the traditionalism and relativism" at the conference provided a number of examples of "the ways in which appeals to tradition have been politically engineered to support oppression and violence" (ibid., 35), ending with National Socialism. For Nussbaum, such relativism is part of the problem, not the solution, of oppressed women: "Under the banner of their fashionable opposition to universalism march ancient religious taboos, the luxury of the pampered husband, educational deprivation, unequal health care, and premature death" (ibid., 36).

Nussbaum's answer to the relativists is both negative and positive. The negative part consists first in acknowledging the unhappy persistence of colonialist repudiation of cultural differences as "morally retrograde" (ibid., 30). Criticism does take the risk of not respecting "difference," by overriding local judgments of what is right and wrong. It is also the case that the "circumstances of justice" (Hume) will vary from one society and culture to another; solutions to problems of justice therefore will differ accordingly. However, it does not follow from these facts that strong factual and normative cultural relativism can discredit every external criticism, and that "the ultimate standard of what is right for an individual or group must derive from that group's internal traditions" (ibid., 8). This is another case of the fact that judgment does not always amount to unkindness, for there is no reason to think that customs may not be evil as well as good, and as a matter of incontestable fact, women throughout the world suffer under traditions and social structures that are unjust. Also, external critical voices may even be essential for providing a voice to those marginalized in a particular society. For example, when Arthur Miller visited the People's Republic of China, a former political prisoner told him how shocked she was to learn that *The Crucible* had been written by a foreigner. She was certain, she told him, that a fellow inmate was the author, because the play expressed so well the suffering of Chinese political prisoners. Thus if we believe that local acceptance constitutes a sufficient condition of a given practice's being morally right, we shall also risk the loss of appropriate judgment in cases in which real evil is present. It would be illuminating to witness a conversation between the French anthropologist and Frederick Douglass.

Thus it is not a colonial imposition of external values to provide the "basic capacities and opportunities that are involved in the selection of any flourishing life and then leaving people to choose for themselves how they will pursue flourishing" (Nussbaum 1999, 9). If that view entails criticizing any social traditions, so be it, because the traditions are unjust. "Or, as a young Bangladeshi wife said when local religious leaders threatened to break the legs of women who went to the literacy classes conducted by a local NGO (nongovernmental organization), 'We do not listen to the *mullahs* any more. They did not give us even a quarter kilo of rice'" (ibid., 30). Analogous to Wittgenstein's challenge that we should just try to deny the reality of the other person's pain, we can equally well say: just hear the story of the Bangladeshi wife, or read Douglass' soul-rending accounts of the horrors of slavery—and try to deny the social evil under which she or he labors. Just talk to the faultless rape victim, or a woman only rumored to have been raped, and attempt to deny the evil of her punishment. For those who were murdered, stand over their graves and try to deny the evil of their undeserved deaths.

The positive part of Nussbaum's answer to the relativist consists of fashioning a tentative and revisable list of ten human capacities and functions that "are so central that they seem definitive of a life that is truly human" (1999, 39). The list is based empirically on "a broad and ongoing cross-cultural inquiry" (ibid., 40). These capacities, which, when actualized, will yield a flourishing life, all express different aspects of the capable body and effectively refer in a summary fashion to much of the present book. They are: (1) "*Life*," which includes a "normal" life span rather than premature death; (2) "*Bodily health and integrity*," which includes not only adequate nutrition but also shelter; (3) "*Bodily integrity*," in the sense of unrestricted geographical movement, negative rights to be protected from violence, and the abilities to enjoy one's own body; (4) "*Senses, imagination, thought*," which entail the unrestricted use of one's senses, imagination, and cognition. This requirement also implies unrestricted access to education and freedom of expression; (5) "*Emotions*," that is, the capacity to be attached to and care for things and other persons, "being able to love those who love and care for us." This capability also requires the appropriate social structures and traditions that will enable it; (6) "*Practical reason*," the ability to frame, critically discuss, and follow one's own notion of the good life; (7) "*Affiliation*," which means "Being able to live for and in relation to others," which likewise requires imaginative, compassionate self-transposal into the lives of others who suffer, as well as institutional protections necessary for social relationships. Also necessary are "Having the social bases of self-respect and nonhumiliation"—being treated as an end in oneself with a dignity and value equal to everyone else's—as well as societal protections against discrimination [that] are similarly implied; (8) "*Other species*," that is, "Being able to live with concern for and in relation to animals, plants, and the world of nature"; (9) "*Play*," that is, the capacity for recreation, laughter, and playing; and (10), "*Control over one's environment*," both political and material. The former refers to the capacity to participate fully in the political process, and the latter indicates, among other things, equal rights to own property and to look for employment without the artificial encumbrance of discrimination (Nussbaum 1999, 41–42; emphasis in original). What these ten characteristics of basic human well-being provide is compendious specificity about the socially enabled capable body, the body that enjoys self-attestation.

Ricoeur's sense of attestation of capability and self-confidence is also closely linked to Monroe's studies of differences between altruists and self-interested entrepreneurs. Those studies illuminate fundamental behavioral differences between the two groups, which in turn provide further details about how the strength that makes kindness possible expresses itself. In their active care of those around them, rescuers, for example, are more likely to take charge of situations. They also accept greater personal responsibility, which displays itself in more substantial dedication to completing tasks. Rescuers are also more willing to keep promises, to become involved in the problems of friends, and to engage in civic virtue by donating some of their time to the welfare of their communities. Moreover, they do not commit themselves to these activities out of a feeling of weakness and vulnerability, since they had greater confidence in their abilities "to control and shape their own destinies" (Monroe 1996, 263, n. 25, citing the Oliners 1988).

These facts enable us, finally, to glimpse part of the outline of a new moral psychology to replace Nietzsche's negative hermeneutics of suspicion. It is, in fact, a moral psychology that is much more consistent with the positive part of Nietzsche's vision, what he envisaged for the "Overman." However, there is certainly one crucial difference. Kindness is not dismissive, let alone contemptuous, of the masses. Kindness is, as we have seen in Part One, inclusive by nature, not elitist and exclusive. Even so, there are at least three important similarities. First, the Overman also represents a triumph over the weakness of yielding to the "human, all too human" uses of power that people "the madhouses and hospitals of culture." Kindness similarly flourishes in the "fresh air" beyond festering resentment, pity, and revenge, and, as noted above, kindness also requires the power to resist "power over" others. Second, Nietzsche thought the Overman to be intrinsically valuable because her spiritual accomplishments created truth, beauty, and the advance of authentic culture. In the following chapter, we shall see that there is a close analogue of these goals in a life of kindness. Third, the moral psychology envisaged here can also adopt the Nietzschean *Aufhebung* and adapt it to its own purposes for understanding moral decision making in regard to kindness.

In terms of decision making, in the first "moment" of the *Aufhebung*, the passion and energy of involvement in other people's lives are preserved along with the power of the capable body to betray or fulfill that commitment embedded in that involvement (Ricoeur's notion of solicitude). The energy of the passions is, as Nietzsche himself pointed out, essential for creating value. It is true that, without the passions, we would not be tempted to abuse others in the "human, all too human" uses of power. Nonetheless, we could transcend all such temptation only at the price of giving up our humanness. Since we are only human, no more and no less, intervention in the lives of others inevitably brings along with it these enticements to gain power over the other—in short, colonization and totalization. Those possibilities remain on the agenda, even if damped to the fringes of our consciousness, because acts of kindness take place in situations of power imbalances created first by the other's need and then by her project of spiritual fulfillment which we may be inclined to assist. The strength of the temptation to abuse in any particular situation will depend in large part on the moral development of the agent. However, we all possess, as Hume pointed out, some "elements of the wolf and serpent" (1957, 92).

In the second "moment" of the *Aufhebung*, when the commitment is fulfilled, there is a "canceling out" of the temptation. The strength of the kind agent, which is manifested here as self-control and self-limitation in appropriately absenting oneself from the Other's life, overrides the inducement to colonize the weaker other. This strength, the resources of solicitude necessary to respond helpfully to the other person's suffering, also blocks the enticement of an enhanced self-image of director and controller of other people's lives. Conversely, when the commitment is not fulfilled, when the agent gives in to the temptation of power over the other, a double sense of failure attaches to the results. The agent has failed both the object of her kindness as well as herself in not developing, or continuing to develop, a life of virtue. This is the case whether the "power over" takes the form of outright domination or control by gaining ingratiating influence through establishing a dependency relationship.

In the final stage of the *Aufhebung*, the "lifting up" itself into a new and better form, passions and energy are rechanneled and placed in the ennobling service of an inventive charity. In giving new form to the body's energetic intervention in other people's lives, kindness becomes an achievement. It becomes an *honorable* acceptance of responsibility and thus can fund a given individual's self-attestation.

Further, a crucial dialectic operative at this stage accounts for the development of the virtue of kindness. On the one hand, the more that the virtue of kindness gets instantiated through such a process of making moral decisions, the more assured becomes the individual's self-attestation. On the other hand, the more confident the individual becomes in the truth of the belief about her own capabilities for kind interventions in the lives of others, the greater the development of the virtue. This is crucial for a life of *effective* kindness, because it requires not just the capability of the body to mobilize its forces to come to the aid of others, but the continuing ability to give this commitment the temporal thickness of duration that the habitual body provides. As the Oliners point out, rescuers are more likely than non-rescuers "to get involved and to stay involved, because of their general sense of responsibility and tendency to make [long-term] commitments" (Monroe 1996, 263, n. 25).

Lastly, habits of kindness can also break down, and virtues can be lost as well as developed. Similarly, a given individual's sense of self-attestation can atrophy and die out. There are, of course, multiple reasons for such moral pathology, but surely one of the most crucial is a hostile environment. Individuals do not develop lives of virtue or the lack thereof, in isolation from others and from the influence of society generally. Under the system of slavery, for example, Lucretia and Sophia Auld were severely limited in their abilities to develop dispositions to kindness. The "broad social and political events, even to the tides of history that bear down on all of us" (Coles 1992, 38), were sufficient to allow the infection of "irresponsible power," as Douglass put it, to poison their life of virtue at the root. The following chapter will return to those "broad social and political events" and "tides of history" in order to expose the virtue of kindness to its second major hermeneutic challenge.

Chapter 7

Ideologies

My task which I am trying to achieve is, by the power of the written word
to make you hear, to make you feel—it is, before all, to make you see.
—Joseph Conrad, *The Heart of Darkness*

Marxist Critique

The object of this chapter is to resume and extend the analysis of false consciousness in terms of self-deception, dogma, or principle blindness, and the
desire for power. Marx's word for dogma, or principle blindness, is, of course,
ideology. In the same light, I will extend his analysis to the work of Carol
Gilligan, who has also effectively advanced a hermeneutics of suspicion about
the false consciousness of women. I will attempt to buttress her arguments
with a sketch of a phenomenology of boyhood and manhood to match her descriptions of girlhood and womanhood. I will then conclude by defending the
moral psychology begun in the last chapter against certain criticisms of it,
chiefly with regard to certain radical feminist attacks on the notions of care,
sympathy, and trust.

As with Nietzsche, our concern with Marx is narrowly focused in a specialized context. Our only interest in his voluminous reflections lies in what those
reflections can tell us about a hermeneutic suspicion of kindness. Further, like
Nietzsche, Marx is worth studying these days more for his criticisms than for
his solutions. The worldwide success of capitalism has apparently eliminated
the viability of any other economic system or ideology. It is the only game in
town; even the Chinese are enthusiastic players. However, even though the
ideal of a free market is alternately appealed to as mantra or shibboleth, either
way it continues to be risible for individuals, social groups and classes, and
whole nations that do not have the resources to compete. Those who are excluded from the game can easily grasp that much of what Hallie and Douglass

said of the slave owner Marx would ascribe to the capitalist as well. Yet with slavery, there was only one clear remedy, whereas with capitalism, there are several alternatives, each of which has been defended and criticized at length in terms of its alleged economic, political, and moral advantages and its practicality. As a result, twenty-first-century debate will revolve around government restraints and interventions in a free market rather than whether there will be one. From all that appears, this debate will concentrate on two major issues: the familiar tensions between individual freedoms, and the needs of communities and conflicts between local communities and corporate power— particularly in regard to mergers, corporate ability to coerce and exploit local government and subvert local autonomy, and the preservation of local, and even national, culture.

Despite its global triumph, though, capitalism will never lose its inherent injustices, even if it can shed its worst abuses, and so, as Lyotard says somewhere, Marxist criticisms of capitalism will always be privileged. Similarly, as another writer notes, "All decent social theory is a footnote to Marx, because the capitalism that Marx criticized has now become almost worldwide, with terrible, destructive impact on the world's poor, workers, and environment" (Marsh 1999, 177).[1] However, even if the untenability of Marx's solutions leaves us unconvinced that his work is the source of all "decent social theory," it remains true that the reason given for that conclusion does prove that no responsible social theory can ignore Marx. For, as is clear from Part One, capitalism harmfully impacts both developed and undeveloped societies through its use of nature and human beings as mere means to ends of exploitation and greed.

This exploitation falls especially hard on the developing world, which is plundered for cheap labor, as in the *maquiladora* factories discussed earlier, and for raw materials. It is also plagued by crushing debt, massive unemployment, illiteracy, the arms trade, and a class system of a powerful, privileged elite set of landowners oppressing the impoverished mass of citizens. Corporate exploitation, aided by World Trade Organization (WTO) rules, even imperils their infants.[2] These are the types of facts that have driven Derrida to exclaim, "[I]t must be cried out, at a time when some have the audacity to neo-evangelize in the name of the ideal of a liberal democracy that has finally realized itself as the ideal of human history: never have violence, inequality, exclusion, famine, and thus economic oppression affected as many human beings in the history of the earth and of humanity" (1994, 85).

Nonetheless, there are evangelizations and evangelizations, and Marx's thought remains exceptionally useful in detecting the hypocrisy beneath the developed world's "concern" for workers in developing countries. It is not that Marx would think any better of child labor, the inability to unionize, and other forms of exploitation such as those described above—no matter who does it and where, but not all criticisms of it are honest. On the surface, such concern on the part of the developed world appears to be a transparent desire for justice, if not kindness, toward the exploited. And one might think that everyone would have endorsed President Clinton's desire for the WTO to link trade agreements with those on workers' rights and the environment (as a common wealth). However, as the Egyptian trade minister to the WTO, Youssef Boutros-Ghali, correctly pointed out, even here there is room for suspicion. "The question is why all of a sudden, when third world labor has proved to be competitive, why do industrial countries start feeling concerned about our workers? When all of a sudden there is concern about the welfare of our workers, it is suspicious."[3] The fate of the *maquiladora* workers and the debacle of the WTO meeting in Seattle in December 1999 demonstrate in part that Boutros-Ghali was not alone in his suspicions.

In fact, a number of developing nations explicitly rejected President Clinton's claim that they "have no choice but to live with the new global economy . . . so they would be wise to try to shape it, making environmental standards and workers' rights part of every future trade agreement." For nations such as India, Brazil, and Egypt, this smacked of "an ever-more-powerful, American-dominated trade organization that would begin dictating how much they paid their workers, or what kind of fuels they could burn, or what kind of magazines and films they had to let into the country."[4] They also pointed out that it is the United States that brings the most trade complaints to the WTO court.

Marx's detection of spuriously kind acts, policies, and laws has another type of utility for a hermeneutics of kindness. Within a given capitalist system, he would almost certainly join what was to become the standard Marxist objection to charity as insufficient, palliative efforts to remedy the injustices of the economic system that make those efforts necessary in the first place. Volunteering, for example, will always have a limited efficacy without systemic, structural changes. Thus such charitable efforts become almost cynical gestures around major holidays, when the capitalist conscience appears to be at its uneasiest. We are obsessed with the homeless having traditional Thanksgiving and Christmas dinners, but in general, we care if they starve for the remainder of the year only if they are likely to disturb our peace. On, say, February 26, July 18, or October 10, how many well-fed Americans really think about, let alone care, what the homeless eat?

On its face it is remarkable how many people indulge themselves in the illusion of goodness for pitifully small, "token" efforts. Marx, however, shows us why such astonishment can exist only on a superficial and thus a naïve level. Below the surface there is a straightforward explanation: capitalism makes such gestures of kindness necessary in the deeper and more powerful sense of providing a too-convenient rationalization for not pursuing—or even seeing—the necessity of systemic reform. That is, self-satisfaction of the peculiar type studied in the previous chapter creates a dogma or principle blindness, or ideology.

This is the third, and most important, reason for situating Marxist thought within a hermeneutics of kindness.

For Marx, ideologies are particular types of concealing ideas that emerge on a social plane to reflect and defend prevailing interests, or ideas whose advocates want them to prevail. They are ideas in the defense of power that perform the dual functions of "exalting oneself but also of acting as weapons *to cloak one's interests in an ideal form* and to gain deference for them" (Collins 1994, 66; emphasis added). In the Middle Ages, for instance, the aristocracy upheld the ideals of loyalty and honor, because these virtues mirrored their social positions as warriors and also by inference supported their hereditary prerogatives to own land and to obtain the humble acquiescence of their serfs. Honor signaled courage in battle and "chivalrous politeness to 'honorable' opponents of the same class." Honor also implied the pedigree of good breeding, and this nobility of family stood against the artisans' and merchants' (mere) profit-making work as well as the "dirty, unproductive work like that of the peasants who supported them" (ibid.).

In reactive contrast, doctrines of freedom, equality, and enduring human rights came into being as the bourgeoisie exerted its revolutionary power of commerce and improved social position through the acquisition of money. The universality of the declaration concealed its rejection of the aristocratic class and, by exalting the general rule of class-less money, "tried to keep the workers in their place by holding out the abstract notion of equality without mentioning that the competition of the marketplace was stacked against them" (ibid.).

From the perspective of institutional kindness and ideologies, one interesting aspect of this repression consisted in the way in which attitudes toward welfare took shape. In Charlotte Brontë's *Shirley*, for example, one of the characters declares that he would be too ashamed to seek welfare ("poor-relief"). The editor remarks that this feeling of resolute independence, an estimation of shame entailed in becoming poor, was more common in the 1840s, when the book was written, than it was in 1811–1812, the dramatic time period of the novel. Then, people generally saw obtaining "poor-relief" in bad times in the parish in which one was born "as a *right*. It was middle-class attitudes toward poverty, born of the rising costs of poor-relief, which gradually made the labourer ashamed of claiming what had always traditionally been his" (1974, 612, n. 4). This is an attitude that survives today, while reciprocally the idea of welfare as a right of any sort has practically disappeared in the United States, though not yet in certain Western European countries. This ideational shift is also an example of Marx's claim in *The German Ideology* that "The ideas of the ruling class are in every epoch the ruling ideas: i.e., the class which is the ruling *material* force of society, is at the same time its ruling *intellectual* force" (Tucker 1978, 172).

Ideologies are thus ideas that hypocritically present themselves as neutral, impartial, and independent of special pleading. They are devices for gaining power over others, consolidating the power of one's own group or class, "reflecting, legitimizing, and covering up class or group domination" (Marsh 1995, 308). Moreover, they not only cover up the act of domination but are vehicles of self-concealment as well. That is, their success depends largely on their ability to hide both their provenance and process of formation. To protect the interests concealed, the most successful ideologies are those that are concealed both from those who dominate as well as those who are dominated. As noted in the previous chapter, such hiddenness insulates power and privilege from conscious scrutiny, either from those who have it or those who are subject to it. Within the institution of slavery, the ideology of the "white man's burden," or "taking care of (what was conveniently seen as) an inferior race," served well, if not wholly successfully, to neutralize the slave owner's conscience and the slave's consciousness. And in terms of sexual relationships, the ideal of the "passionless woman" emerged to provide a convenient rationalization for women's social inequality in the face of the French Revolution's attempt to equally valorize all citizens.[5]

Successful ideologies thus become mechanisms for both facilitating and masking the multiple unkindnesses and injustices detailed above. That fact by itself is enough to cast an aura of suspicion around acts of kindness within the economic world. However, would Marx argue that all such actions and business practices are ideologically contaminated and untrustworthy, the products of self-denying power which claims to take the moral high road while aiming at our systemic disadvantage? Perhaps he could not have conceived of industrialists engaging in any type of altruistic behavior toward their employees, just as he probably would not have believed that labor unions or employee-owned companies were possible in a capitalist system. Whatever his likely answer, the arguments advanced in Chapter 6 vis-à-vis slavery apply here as well, *mutatis mutandis*, so that within a capitalist system, we can distinguish three classes of acts and practices that appear to be those of kindness. First, even if capitalism were an unmitigated evil, which it is not, the actions and practices of Lewis Platt at Hewlett-Packard and Aaron Feuerstein at Malden Mills show that there can still be genuine managerial acts or practices of kindness in the workplace or in a corporation's relationships with its community, even though the system within which these acts and practices take place is otherwise exploitative. Nevertheless, a capitalist system dedicated to an unrestricted free market, or one with as few restrictions as possible, does set severe limits on the range and efficacy of possible kindness.

Second, there can also be deceptive acts and practices of unkindness under the guise of kindness—those that are neither well intentioned nor for the good of their objects. Like their counterparts under the regime of slavery, they masquerade as kindness simply as a means to secure more compliant victims, and they obtain and maintain their experiential identity within such projects. It is not difficult to imagine such exploitative persuasion inscribed in employers' inducements to migrant and *maquiladora* workers, or in conversations between the representatives of corporate hotel owners and local officials of impoverished Caribbean islands.

Finally, as in the case of slavery, there can also be well-intentioned but spurious acts of kindness that are the products of a self-deceived, false consciousness. Particular employers as well as directors of entire corporations might believe sincerely that imposing free markets and corporate control of homogenized culture really benefits all those affected by them. They might actually be able to blink away rain forest destruction and the habitats of many species by focusing intensely (and conveniently) on the mantra of satisfying customer demand and duties to stockholders. There might exist also the benighted who really believe that they are doing impoverished workers a great favor in making them toil like demons all day long for thirty-eight cents an hour. They never honestly ask themselves, adapting a phrase from the Vietnam era, whether it is really necessary to destroy children in order to save them.

Thus it seems clear that Hallie's and Douglass' argument about kindness not being the opposite of cruelty—invidious exploitation—in the sense that it can exist within it, applies here as well. In capitalism as in slavery, this is true both of fraudulent "kindnesses" driven either by malice or self-deception, as well as of genuinely kind acts, policies, procedures, and the like, which can exist within an exploitative system. Capitalism itself does not impugn the value of acts and practices of true kindness taking shape within it, but, like slavery, it does create a fertile field for their abuse and illusions of goodness and, as noted above, it severely limits their scope and effectiveness.

This similarity notwithstanding, slavery and capitalism are disanalogous in terms of the way in which hermeneutic suspicion would function within them. The object of the slave's suspicion is that the putative kindness is simply a veiled tool to secure her compliant obedience. The slave owner's interest is *only* the passive, docile slave. Now when companies provide benefits such as flex time, child care facilities, and public recognition for meeting family obligations, management's self-interest in a more productive workforce is only one layer of meaning. There does not appear to be any other reason to be suspicious of the acts and policies of Hewlett-Packard or Malden Mills, referred to earlier. Absent other compelling evidence, the kindness of the managerial directives does not seem to be in doubt. There exists an inevitable ambiguity about motivation in such cases, but that ambiguity entails that suspicion is not dispositive. It may or may not turn out that the kindness of a corporate policy or practice is genuine.

Kindness is also not the opposite of cruelty within capitalism in the additional sense that it does not have the power to stop it. The opposite of cruelty here is not individual freedom, as Hallie argued before discovering the Chambonnais; nor is it, for the reasons given in Chapter 5, spontaneous good will. It is, rather, structural change. Thus the Chambonnais rescued hundreds of Jewish refuges, but they could not possibly have disabled the evil system from which the latter fled. Their enterprise depended on a great deal of luck in avoiding detection and capture by the Gestapo, and Pastor Trocmé in fact had some very near misses. Aaron Feuerstein kept his mill open, but he and his workers are powerless against market forces that will ultimately determine the viability of his business, just as the life of Heidegger's naïve woodcutter is shaped by the lumber industry.

Therefore, both goodness and freedom are necessary to combat cruelty, along with the protection of national and international institutions required to support them. Goodness without institutional freedom is fragile and easily destroyed. Institutional freedom without goodness is corrupting and destructive. The power of the goodness such as the Chambonnais incarnated comes from its appeal, not from its ability to be self-enforcing. They point to heaven, but we also have to keep our feet on the ground. As Chapter 5 argued in relevant part, kindness as a practical, inventive goodness must secure institutional validation to be truly effective.

The Hermeneutics of Gender

We have already encountered some of the results of Carol Gilligan's well-known research on the voices of girls and boys, women and men. That research belongs to the tradition of a hermeneutics of suspicion, because it also pries out ideologies and makes trouble for them. Looking back on *In a Different Voice* in her "Letter to Readers, 1993," Gilligan states that the book is located at the intersection of two lies, one theoretical and the other factual. The first is a lie in psychological theories that have taken men "as representing all humans." The second is to be found in the psychological development of women "in which girls and women alter their voices to fit themselves into images of relationships and goodness carried by false feminine voices" (1982, 1993 printing, xxvi). The first lie is closer to the surface of conscious awareness than the second, which is usually non-conscious and carefully concealed. From this angle, the type of "kindnesses" to which her work is most relevant is that which stems from a false consciousness and causes harm. However, as we shall see, she adds empirical completeness to this type of "kindness" by extending the false consciousness to the victim as well as to the victimizer.

The second lie entails that, as we saw in Chapter 1, women adopt false voices of passive dependency to replace those of the active self-confidence of girlhood in order to please powerful men who dominate the world of adulthood that girls enter. Initiation into that world signals the origin of self-doubt and the emergence of the awareness, however transient, that womanhood will demand a "dissociative split" between women's experiences of relationships and the significance of those relationships for their own self-identities, and a contradictory "social construction of reality" (ibid., xxi).

The "working theory" of *In a Different Voice* was that both boys and girls undergo relational crises in separation from women, "which is essential to the perpetuation of patriarchal societies" (ibid., xxiii). For boys, this disconnection occurs early in childhood, but for girls it takes place in adolescence. In resisting the loss of their own voices and consequent self-alienation, girls "become the carriers of unvoiced desires and unrealized possibilities [for relationships], [and therefore] they are inevitably placed at considerable risk and even in danger" (ibid.). For girls and women, a sense of gender identity does not depend on separation from their mothers or on the degree to which individuation has been attained. For boys and men, however, gender identity is defined in terms of separation. As a result, "[M]ales tend to have difficulty with relationships, while females tend to have problems with individuation. . . . Women's failure to separate then becomes by definition a failure to develop" (ibid., 8–9).

Whether disjunction or connection is primary has immediate consequences for different genderized conceptions of the self and the relationships of that self with others. Separation is closely linked in the process of psychological and moral development to autonomy and self-determination. When this is the principal constituent of self-identity, as it usually is for men, development would consist in an exploration of the possibility of relationships, working toward the perception of the other as equal, and the fact that relationships are safe. In contrast, when connection is primary, as generally is the case for women, development would consist of coming to see separation as non-threatening and not necessarily isolating. Women's sense of self thus is more consistent with Sandel's "constitutive" view of the self than the self as described in various liberalisms. Also, as against Freud's descriptions of the self in *Civilization and Its Discontents*, women's sense of self demonstrates "a continuing sense of connection in the face of separation and loss," and "does not appear to have separation and aggression as its base" (ibid., 47).

For Gilligan, these contentions have the status of empirical generalizations; they are not conceptual claims about male and female gender as such. Rather, she is prepared to find various degrees of emphasis on separation and connections represented in men and women. Therefore, not all men have problems with relationships, and not all women find separation threatening. Rather, these are "two different ways of viewing the world," she will write later, like the alternative organizational meanings of a Gestalt figure. Just as its ambiguous shape can be seen as a vase or faces, a duck or a rabbit, "there appear to be two ways of perceiving self in relation to others, both grounded in reality, but each imposing on that reality a different organization" (Gilligan, 8–9). Further, as one meaning organizes our perceptual field, the other temporarily slips away.

Gilligan's position is essentially same one that Nussbaum defends, namely, that society cannot hope to achieve a complete view of the self by merely adding one way of perceiving it to the other, and that society should attempt to develop in each of its members the complete array of capacities described in the previous chapter.

These different images of relationships and their significance for the notion of self-identity lead directly to Gilligan's celebrated distinction between an ethics of justice and an ethics of care. The former focuses on justice, rules, duties, rights, and dispute settling, and it describes moral actors as equal, rational, and separated contractors. This is the standard account of moral development advanced by Freud, Piaget, and Kohlberg, and it is Gilligan's well-known criticism that it takes the experiences of boys and men as normative. In contrast, female connectedness views moral experience in terms of care, is sensitive to conflicting obligations, and reflects a concern for synthesis, that is, to satisfy as many people's needs as possible. Instead of focusing on dispute settling according to rules, and thus deciding who will be winners and losers, the concern is for creating as many winners as possible. In Kohlberg's stage-based theory of moral development, then, girls' development will appear as arrested.

For Gilligan, Martin Hoffman's research on empathy, referred to in Part One, effectively challenges such cognitive theories of moral development by showing that they ask the wrong question. Instead of inquiring about how children develop a moral orientation from an "a-moral" or "a-social" infancy, researchers should look at what Hoffman and others have shown to be the very young child's capacities for "social responsiveness" and concern and should ask, has "the child's capacities for relationship been diminished or lost?" (Gilligan 1988, ix–x). Girls more nearly than boys maintain those capacities, so instead of seeing girls as " 'stuck' at some earlier or lower stage" (ibid., ix), we should see boys as endangered through loss.

The study of girls' and women's voices therefore allows another theory of moral development to emerge, under which conflicting responsibilities rather than rationally constructed duties generate moral problems, and to resolve, which requires sensitive, context-dependent thought along the lines defended by Eliot, (Henry) James, and Nussbaum, rather than abstractly formal reasoning. While an ethics of justice and rights rests on respect for others as equals, ends in themselves, and adjudicates conflicts between the self and those others, the ethics of responsibility "rests on an understanding that gives rise to compassion and care" (Gilligan 1982, 1993 printing, 164).

Writing some time after her earlier work, Gilligan added the qualification that the ethics of care and justice do not correlate perfectly with women and men, respectively. Rather, she asserts, *In a Different Voice* advanced an empirical generalization about a tendency that, "although not gender specific, was gender related" (1988, 8). Nor, she tells us, are the ethics of justice and care disjuncts.

Both are necessary for a complete moral life, which means that both detachment and attachment are important ingredients in the moral life. As Boltanski effectively argued in terms of justice and agape, detachment typifies developed moral judgments in justice orientations, but "becomes in the care framework a sign of moral danger, a loss of connection with others" (Gilligan 1988, 120). Marginalization, isolation, and alienation all testify to the fact that, "Moral outrage can be provoked not only by oppression and injustice but also by abandonment or loss of attachment or the failure of others to respond" (ibid., 120).

Even though justice and care perspectives are not disjuncts, as we have seen in Part One, they are different enough to generate tension and necessary choices between them. For example, and one that is tied closely to the possibilities of institutional kindness, for those for whom justice and separation are primary, usually men, "rule-bound competitive achievement situations" "provide a mode of connection that establishes clear boundaries and limits aggression, and thus appears comparatively safe." For those for whom care and connection are primary, mostly women, such situations "threaten the web of connection." Thus while women "try to change the rules in order to preserve relationships, men, in abiding by these rules, depict relationships as easily replaced" (Gilligan 1982, 1993 printing, 44). It is a question of "two different moralities whose complementarity is the discovery of maturity" (ibid., 164). Their exact working relationship is ambiguous but, like the two images of self, both must be kept instead of ruling one or another out of existence.

As far as a hermeneutics of kindness is concerned, Gilligan's research raises both empirical and normative questions. On the empirical side, she has been challenged about gender differences in empathy and moral reasoning.[6] Regardless of these studies, however, a telling number of childhood and adult experiences testify to certain significant differences between justice and care perspectives in ethics, and between the ways in which boys and girls are socialized in terms of basic feeling connections that create our intersubjectivity. One of these experiences concerns the difficulties women have in finding themselves—that is, as noted in Chapter 2, their true voices. Gilligan approaches this subject from two different, but related, angles: Nora's crisis in *A Doll's House* and her subsequent determination to look for her identity and moral beliefs, as well as women's traditionally limited options for controlling conception and childbirth by withholding themselves at the cost of either denying or sacrificing their own sexual needs.

Gilligan notes appreciatively Freud's discussion of the connection between the energy that must be expended for such "sexual suppression" and women's diminished intelligence,[7] and she herself likens the "strategies of withholding and denial" in sexual politics to women's "evasion or withholding of judgment in the moral realm" (1982, 1993 printing, 68). In terms of the notion of strength inscribed in the new moral psychology, which the previous chapter began to sketch, she observes that women who cannot find their true voices end up with a self unsure of its own power and disinclined to make choices and confront others. This silence of incertitude is not one of attestation and self-confidence but of diffidence and inability. It does not characterize the capable body but rather one that is accommodatingly submissive.

A different perspective on sexual suppression and the incapable body—and one that is more illuminative of its times—can be found in the writings of, of all people, Freud's ever-present precursor. In Book II, §71 of *The Gay Science*, titled "*On female chastity*," Nietzsche writes about women's "paradoxical" education in which they are supposed to remain ignorant of the erotic, not even "in their hearts" suspecting its existence. Then they marry and are "hurled, as by a gruesome lightning bolt, into reality and knowledge," which previously had been considered evil incarnate—and "precisely by the man they love and esteem most!" (1974, 127). They are tied in a "psychic knot" *sans pareil*: "To catch love and shame in a contradiction and to be forced to experience at the same time delight, surrender, duty, pity, terror, and who knows what else, in the face of the unexpected neighborliness of god and beast!" (ibid., 127–28). As Nietzsche sees it, not even the "compassionate curiosity of the wisest student of humanity" will suffice to unravel how she will manage to untie the knot. In her subsequent profound silence aimed both at her husband and often at herself as well, "She closes her eyes to herself." From the depths of this stillness, which is anything but serenity, "Women easily experience their husbands as a question mark concerning their honor, and their children as an apology or atonement. They need children and wish for them in a way that is altogether different from that in which a man may wish for children. In sum, one cannot be too kind about women" (ibid., 128).[8]

In contrast, in our own as well as in former times, for a woman who finds her voice, strength that comes from self-attestation is crucial for the courage to be countercultural. She must choose the authenticity of her own voice over the false consciousness of self-deception, the societal construction of the "good woman." As we have seen in examples cited in the previous chapter, the latter conceals affirmation in avoidance, repudiating responsibility by alleging the desire only to satisfy other people's needs. The woman who does achieve self-attestation must therefore try to resolve the struggle between autonomy and compassion to maximize as many people's interests as possible while minimizing harm.

In discussing this dilemma, Gilligan returns us to the literary examples described in the previous chapter, to Nora's moral crisis and to Maggie Tulliver's tumultuous struggles between feelings of justice and duties, on the one hand, and mercy and compassion, on the other hand. Her discussions open the way to understanding the greatest significance that her work has for a hermeneutics of kindness, namely, that false consciousness must be studied not only from the perspective of the victimizer, as in Chapter 6, but also from that of the victim.

As we have seen, Gilligan has argued that a girl's entry into womanhood is characterized by the awareness, however transitory, of a "dissociative split" required between her feelings and the social construction of reality according to gender. Her likely response will be to accede nonconsciously to this dissociation because of the socialization process that will be powerful and effective enough to conceal what she has to give up, as well as the fact that she is giving it up. In this case, she will unknowingly play the role of the "good woman": through repressing her self by unconscious self-deception, her acclimation to the adult world will be (relatively) untroubled. She may also more consciously accede to the dissociation, or she may consciously reject it by becoming the "bad woman" who recognizes what sacrifice is asked of her and rejects it as well as the game being played.

In terms of kindness, the most interesting cases fall under the first and more prevalent possible reaction, that in which not only the victimizer (s) but also the victim herself may suffer from the blindness of self-deception. These are instances of what Alan Wertheimer calls the controversial argument that "a person's objective interests can be harmed even if she does not now and never will regard these interests as her interests. She may suffer from false consciousness" (1996, 101). This sense of false consciousness, which itself facilitates the process of victimization, also applies to our other types of victims, described in the previous chapter. Thus children in several of Laing's and Esterton's families never realized what was done to them, just as there were passively compliant slaves who were happy to be taken care of. Like Nora, and Edna in *The Awakening*, before their marriages destabilized, they willingly played their parts as unsuspecting victims in uncritical passivity. Reciprocally, their parents, just as Torvald and Léonce before the destabilization of their marriages and a good part of real-life men in similar situations, maintained a "good conscience" and would have found no grounds for suspicion in their dependents' conduct.

Wertheimer further specifies two general forms of a victim's false consciousness in and through which she may not regard her objective interests as hers, mistakes about "the *substance* of one's beliefs" and "the *authenticity*" of one's beliefs"—that is, that the agent does not really hold the beliefs that she thinks she does (Wertheimer 1996, 258; emphasis in original). For the types of experiences Gilligan describes, it is "substantive false consciousness" that is more important, and this sort of false consciousness itself can take two forms. In the first, the victim is mistaken about the means to particular ends. This mistake is a factual one about whether a given course of action will really lead to the desired goal. In the second, people make normative mistakes about ends themselves by consciously pursuing and defending those that are objectively bad for them. It is this second type that is most central to the exploitation described in Gilligan's research, as well as to that of the other types of victims described above.

Thus Laing's and Esterton's schizophrenic children can be wrongly convinced that the sort of life they should lead is what is best for them, even though the only reason they hold such a view is their parents' successful mind control. The successfully conditioned slave can likewise mistakenly believe in the kindness of her master who protects her from a hostile, external world and from the insupportable burden of her own freedom. Women may sacrifice potential careers for family and household labor, because they erroneously believe that they should, and the reason they believe this is that a welter of conscious and non-conscious social messages has reinforced it throughout their lives.

In truth, Wertheimer holds, there is a "suggestion" that "the problem may be deeper," that a woman will actually "not fully develop an independent conception of her own interests, values, and ideals, and that she counts her own interests as fundamentally of less importance than the interest of her family" (1996, 260). There is much more than a suggestion, for Gilligan and others have argued this explicitly, and Bellah et al., as we saw in the previous chapter, offer concrete examples. The difficulty for women and other victims in similar situations is that, in these "double-blind" situations, they are naïve pawns in a game without realizing that they are pawns, that there is a game being played, and still less, how it is being played. In other words, they function naïvely within an interpretive framework without being able to see it as an interpretive framework, let alone how to step out of it. After the passage just cited, Wertheimer adds that, "of greater relevance to the problem of false consciousness, 'the person who would *allow* this exploitation in the name of love or duty is failing to respect [her] own value and importance.' She sacrifices her self-esteem"[9] (1996, 260).

But this is too quick. To speak of women (or other victims) allowing themselves to be exploited suggests a much too conscious recognition of the problem and response to it, or perhaps rests implicitly on a conflation of consciousness and voluntariness. Just as Marx argued correctly that alienation is independent of its irruption into conscious awareness, so also can women and other victims be coerced and exploited without knowing it. Psychological disposition is not dispositive, because their exploitation is one thing, and their false consciousness of it, when it exists, is another. Coercion and exploitation can be unseen and unsuspected, but nevertheless present, even though they produce voluntary commitments to, say, systemically unfair marital arrangements.

The reason is that, as Jeffrey Reiman explains apropos of Marxist criticisms of capitalism, it is possible to manipulate people into doing voluntarily what you desire of them by arranging a situation in which what you want is what that person will see as her most rational choice—even when other acceptable, but less rational, possibilities exist. A person's fate can be forced when a free choice constitutes the last link in a chain binding her to it. This fact, for Reiman, is easy to miss, because when an agent performs an action because it appears rational, rather than because it looks to be the only acceptable choice, it seems to be a free choice. To some extent it is, but instead of demonstrating that she is not forced to choose X rather than Y, what it does show is that force can work through her choices. "[S]ocial structures," for Reiman, thus "force fates on people while appearing to leave their fates up to them" (1987, 16).

In fact, Reiman, Wertheimer, Marx, and Gilligan herself—as well as Douglass and Hallie—all argue that the test of exploitation and coercion is not subjective. No defect in consent is necessary (or sufficient) for exploitation and coercion to occur. Wertheimer, for instance, states, "I simply do not see why B cannot legitimately complain about or resent A's exploitation just because she agreed to the transaction and even if she is bound (and regards herself as bound) to the terms of the transaction" (1996, 252). This is exactly the marital situation that Ibsen describes for his protagonist in *A Doll's House*.

However, to say that the "substance of the transaction is unfair to B" requires a means of assessing unfairness, and Wertheimer's method is to focus almost exclusively on objective gains. Thus a false consciousness of "objectively bad" ends that one pursues will itself turn out to be illusory if B gains from the transaction. So, for example, a marital arrangement might be unfair yet materially advantageous for a certain woman compared to her life if she had not married at all. In this case, for Wertheimer, she will not have been harmfully exploited (1996, 260).

This conclusion goes too far. A rich bachelor might offer marriage to a desperately poor refugee that she would otherwise turn down, yet voluntarily accept in order to escape her grinding poverty and to help the rest of her family. Regardless of the subsequent material advantages, the offensive bachelor will have (factually) exploited her weakness and (normatively) her. Harm-causing exploitation is not limited to what is "relative to a resource base" because, as we have also seen in terms of Nussbaum's and Ricoeur's analyses of self-attestation, women can be exploited when they are dealt with in a manner that makes it impossible for them to cultivate their individual abilities, no matter what financial advantages they derive from such arrangements (Sensat 1984, 32). Likewise, slaves would still be the objects of harmful exploitation, even if we could agree that, all things considered, their material welfare was more advantageous than before their enslavement.

Sensat describes the inappropriate use of someone or a group, harmful exploitation, as acting "contrary to [that person or group's] nature." This will occur when one of two conditions is satisfied. The first is that, "The principles governing the process establish an incompatibility between the realization of [end] e and the realization of [the exploitee] y's nature." The second condition is present when, "The principles governing the process render the process itself, irrespective of the degree of realization of e, incompatible with the realization of y's nature" (1984, 34). Both possibilities seem to obtain in the social conditioning that leads to the harmful exploitation with which Gilligan is concerned. In terms of the first condition, the principles governing the social conditioning process are such that the process has traditionally served the interests of patriarchy in ways that are clearly incompatible with the nature of women as autonomous, independent, self-actualizing beings. As for the second condition, the process itself, no matter how successful, is incompatible with the nature of women because of the way in which it has attempted to discourage girls from developing abilities and pursuing lifestyles inconsistent with a narrowly construed role of wife and mother. And, of course, this process will be most effective when girls are also blinded by received dogma and become non-consciously compliant.

Evidence of such systemic unkindnesses is present in small as well as large aspects of childhood training. One of the more revealing sources of evidence is in childhood games. Just as Junior Achievement school programs trained children to be successful capitalists, card games such as Old Maid constituted not-so-subtle attempts to coerce girls into finding husbands. For the Old Maid herself was (at least in our deck of cards) a hideously ugly figure dressed in garish clothes. There was no logic internal to the game that dictated such an appearance. She might have been a very attractive woman dressed in an upscale, bourgeois outfit. But her appearance was dictated by another game prescribed by the adult world. She was a tangible, visible warning about the dangers of the independent life.

Awakening

It is easy to recognize such stratagems once one has stepped out of the game and recognized the framework of interpretation for what it is. However, when both the victimizer and the victim are self-deceived—which is the most interesting case of self-deception for a hermeneutics of kindness—how can they break through the psychic barriers of false consciousness? Given their "double-blind" situation, that they are both naïve players in a game without recognizing that a game is being played or what it is, how can they awaken to the evils of exploitation? The power relationships at issue, along with their coercive and exploitative aspects that take such a psychic toll and inflict deep unkindnesses on self and others, are hidden from the participants. How can they be made visible?

We will divide these questions by considering victimizers in this section and victims in the next section. How is it that we want victimizers to change? What do we believe they must become in order to awaken their self-consciousness as victimizers? To begin with, there is clearly a cognitive dimension of what we would take to be their moral enlightenment. We want men, dominating parents, capitalists—and would have wanted slave owners—to recognize the truth of the proposition that women, children, workers, and slaves, respectively, are moral equals and should be treated as ends in themselves rather than as mere means to ends. We would want an intellectual correction of beliefs such as, say, the following sort of high-toned, serious defense of the inferiority of African Americans:

> Mentally the negro is inferior to the white. The remark of F. Manetta, made after a long study of the negro in America, may be taken as generally true of the whole race: "The negro children were sharp, intelligent and full of vivacity, but on approaching the adult period a gradual change set in. The intellect seemed to become clouded, animation giving place to a sort of lethargy, briskness yielding to indolence. We must necessarily suppose that the development of the negro and white proceeds on different lines. While with the latter the volume of the brain grows with the expansion of the brainpan, in the former the growth of the brain is on the contrary arrested by the premature closing of the cranial sutures and lateral pressure of the frontal bone."

The author goes on to admit that the causal explanation advanced here is not certain, and he attempts to supplement it with the claim that, "[T]he arrest or even deterioration in mental development is no doubt very largely due to the fact that after puberty sexual matters take the first place in the negro's life and thoughts."

The article of which this passage is a part, titled "Negro," did not appear in a trashy pamphlet published by a white hate group or other retrograde members of our species. Rather, it is part of a veritable icon of Western high culture, *The Encyclopedia Britannica* (13th ed. [1926], vol. 19, 344 ff.). Worse yet, this edition was one of the officially designated "scholars' editions," the articles of which were supposed to be definitive resources for future researchers. (In the same edition, the entire entry for "Women" is: "See men.") Today we can snicker at such high-handed attempts to provide scientific credibility for ignorance and crude bias, and we can understand it in terms of the context of the eugenics movement. We can even take comfort in the fact that, no matter what the lunatic fringe are likely to get up to in this country, mainstream America will not return to *that*. But lest we get too cozy, we need to remember that sixty-eight years later, Richard J. Herrnstein's and Charles Murray's *The Bell Curve: Intelligence and Class Structure in American Life* pointed in a very similar direction.

Thus there is still work for education to do here, and in fact Leon J. Kamin (1995, 99-100) has shown how Herrnstein's and Murray's book depends on racist science and logical mistakes so elementary that even first-year logic students would not commit them. Kamin concludes his refutation of the book's core thesis by observing that "*New York Times* columnist Bob Herbert [came] to the conclusion that *The Bell Curve* 'is just a genteel way of calling somebody a nigger.' Herbert is right. The book has nothing to do with science" (ibid., 103). Yet what is of interest in the present context of escaping ideological entrapment is, unless Herrnstein and Murray were outright bigots, one would think that they could not have failed to notice the obvious flaws Kamin pointed out. But perhaps this "not noticing" was itself a product of self-deception and indicative of the fact that racism survives today not so much as an intellectual position, but as a visceral reaction. If this is true, if Hume is correct that reason by itself does not motivate, and if there is a close link between unkindness and disconnection from a world of feelings, then victimizers clearly need affective as well as intellectual transformation. Moreover, an exploiter can also regard an exploitee as an equal on an intellectual plane without any corresponding behavioral change. An exploiter can sincerely give lip service to ideals of freedom and equality, as Herrnstein and Murray do not, and yet behave, even without knowing it, in a consistently contradictory fashion. Because, then, if we want victimizers to change in their "hearts" as well as their "heads," we need to know how to modulate that affectivity in order to stop the victimization.

One tactic is a type of confrontation that attempts to make victimizers see their own acts from the perspectives of their victims. This strategy follows Solon's advice for ridding the world of injustice, noted in Chapter 2, and the Vermont prison therapy for sexual offenders, described in Chapter 3. This was also Hogarth's strategy behind his engravings on cruelty, but with the particular variation of forcing this perception through an "*in terrorem* method to frighten the strong 'into withholding their power to maim'" (Hallie 1982, 33). Whether by fear or more positive means, the general aim is to deter victimizers by getting them to see themselves as the potential victims of their own maiming. This is a method that, if successful, would provide the affective change required but unhappily not the necessary cognitive modification.

It is also the case that an *in terrorem* method of changing hearts is unlikely to be very effective, though in some contexts, it may well be necessary. The main problem in changing dispositions through fear is one of audience. The well disposed will need no lessons, though such instruction might prevent the less firm among them from straying. Such lessons also might deter those merely inclined to victimization, but this will probably not be a very large or powerful group. Also, fear alone will not long discourage those actively disposed to victimization, because the disposition will tend to return when the fear of sanctions is removed.

Nevertheless, Douglass and Hallie are right to exhort us to grasp the meaning of cruelty from the perspective of the victim rather than the victimizer. The epistemological and moral advantage is that it will force victimizers, and us as bystanders, to face the "plain facts" of the victim's suffering. We need to convince victimizers, by some means other than fear, that it is an objective fact rather than a mere subjective opinion that torturing, maiming, killing, and all of the other types of (normative) exploitation and coercion described in this book, are grievously wrong. Locke once pointed out in *An Essay Concerning Human Understanding* (Book II, Chapter XXII) that, "[T]he motive for continuing in the same state of action, is only the present satisfaction in it; the motive to change, is always some uneasiness" (1969, 142). We can then diminish (normative) exploitation and coercion if a brute, empathic connection to victims' suffering, as they themselves live it, makes exploiters uneasy enough to change—either through guilt, remorse, shame, or another causal agency. The empathic bond is crucial. Emotional infection alone, which might well be the most immediate effect of confronting the "plain facts" of victims' suffering, will not suffice because of its ephemerality and our tendencies not to notice disagreeable pain and suffering, as described at several junctures in this book. Creating such empathic bonds is what the previously discussed treatment programs for child molesters did. They diminished harm causing through enforced empathic connections to victims' suffering and therefore made it much more difficult, even if not impossible, for the offenders to deny their victims' pain and suffering.

Because not all of the prisoners reached that perception, it follows that making the perspective of victims visible to their victimizers is not a sufficient condition of stopping victimization. It might or might not be a necessary condition, but it is clearly a strong contributory cause and, even if insufficient, perhaps also the most persuasive corrective possible. Moreover, such real-life experiences can easily be supplemented by imaginative variations in literary narratives, such as those found throughout this book. For Hallie, it was Gothic horror tales. For abolitionists and others before the Civil War, it was *Uncle Tom's Cabin*. Both sorts of fiction were written from the perspective of the victims.

Another famous literary example, also closely related to the subject matter of the previous chapter, consists of the scene in *The Adventures of Huckleberry Finn*, in which Huck faces the terrible dilemma of betraying Jim or helping him escape. Huck must choose between doing what he takes to be the morally correct act of writing a confession to Miss Watson that he has helped her runaway slave escape, or what he believes to be not just a morally wrong act but a *damnably* wrong act of helping his (now) friend Jim. On the one hand, he is miserable because he believes that he has harmed Miss Watson, who had never wronged him. On the other hand, Jim is his one true friend, the friend who helped him night and day during their voyage down the river.

With intentions and consequences of actions thoroughly mixed up in an immoral morality, Huck seeks to extricate himself with the written confession to Miss Watson. He "felt good and all washed clean of sin for the first time," and he knew that he could then pray with a clear conscience (Twain 1959, 209). But he could not do it. He took up the perspective of the victim and allowed his suffering to trump his own conscience. He thought about their long trip down the river, how Jim often stood his watches on top of his own, how they sang and laughed, and how they escaped danger together. He tried to harden his heart against Jim, but to no avail. His attempts miscarried, because he remembered how Jim said he "was the best friend old Jim ever had in the world, and the *only* one he's got now" (ibid., 209–10). Huck then tore up his confession, saying as he did so, "All right, then, I'll *go* to hell" (ibid., 210). He does not change his mind about the immoral morality of his culture, rather, he does what he believes is the morally wrong thing, which is for us the right one. What is essential for the argument here for diminishing cruelty is the way in which adopting the viewpoint of the victim led Huck to assume responsibility for Jim, even, for him, at the cost of his own soul.[10]

The corrective function of taking the victim's perspective is in some respects like that of bringing personal experiences of evil into conjunction with theories that explain it as part of the greater good, that it is illusory, that it is justified as necessary for moral growth, and so forth. Philosophers in their studies or classrooms might be convinced by one or more of these theories, but they will look very different when those thinkers confront the parents whose child has just died. They might not abandon their theories entirely, just as Huck never gave up his own social morality, however, the personal experience of the suffering of the least advantaged and powerful individual or group can do much to tear the veil away from the ideologies behind the convenient rationalizations for not seeing and hearing the victims.

However, even if keeping to the victim's perspective is the best possible remedy to transform exploiters, there are other reasons it is still not a sufficient condition. There are at least three other types of victimizers against whom it will be ineffective. The first are those to whom Hare referred, the "talented torturer or single-minded sadist [who] may understand very well the quality of the suffering he is inflicting, and be spurred on by that very understanding to go on inflicting it" (Hare 1981, 99). These people are only too happy to consider the victim's perspective.

The second group consists of active victimizers or bystanders who are so soaked with concealing ideology that seeing things from the perspective of the victim's suffering would be ineffective, even if they were directly confronted with it, because its value is already discounted and neutralized, as it were, in advance. A clear example of such an anesthetized ideologue is Aunt Sally in *The Adventures of Huckleberry Finn*. After the explosion of a steamboat cylinder head, she has this interchange with Tom Sawyer:

> "'Good gracious! Anybody hurt?'
> "'N'm. Killed a nigger."
> "Well, it's lucky; because sometimes people do get hurt." (Twain 1959, 216)

This remarkable three-line conversation illustrates at a single stroke the immoral morality of a slave-owning culture as well as Aunt Sally's unquestioning acceptance of it. Even if she and her real-life counterparts could be brought to take up their victims' perspectives, her reply here strongly suggests that she would regard their suffering as insignificant as they themselves.

The third class of victimizers and bystanders for whom confrontation with the suffering of their victims is likely to make no appeal often overlaps that of ideologues. Members of this third class are those who have already been the victims of the suffering that they inflict on others, but that fact imposes no detectable restraint on their harming and maiming, because they believe in it. Those who practice genital mutilation are cases in point. They are not necessarily sadists. On the contrary, they may care very much about their victims, but they do not see them as victims or themselves as victimizers because they voluntarily continue a custom, the background social morality of which sanctions their practices. Of what help to them or their terrified victims would it be if they viewed their practice through the eyes of those they mutilate? The "plain facts" of the screams and pain of their victims (as we would see them) are community and historically relative, and the practitioners arguably view themselves as the true guardians of community morality and discipline to which they have already themselves submitted. That they care about the girls at issue may be true, but it is also irrelevant to their cruelty. Thus as we saw in the previous chapter, Nussbaum is correct to argue that local customs should not be immunized from external criticisms. In the case of genital mutilation, the emotions of the practitioner "are only as reliable as the social norms that give rise to them" (Nussbaum 1999, 10), and appeals to care are not likely to stop the mutilation and consequent suffering.

This fact suggests that, even though there are limits to discouraging victimization through somehow getting the victimizer to see the victim's suffering from her point of view, it will probably be most successful when four conditions are met: (1) The relevant social norms must be more compatible with kindness than with cruelty. (2) The victimizer unknowingly engages in exploitation, the remedy for which will be education in the broadest sense possible. (3) The victimizer is otherwise more disposed to kindness than cruelty. (4) The victimizer receives active community support to desist from coercion and/or exploitation. Conditions 2 and 3 are most likely to be met when the victimizer's false consciousness is more or less a passive effect of unseen and unsuspected social conditioning. Of course, that conditioning will also reflect social norms incompatible with the unkindness of the victimization, but as long as the social morality as a whole is humanizing, condition 1 will be met, and there will be hope for reform if the victim can be awakened.[11]

To take a typical example, in 1995, Don Roberts, a building contractor in Muncie, Indiana, discovered in a barn loft a trunk containing a list of Muncie's most prominent men from the early 1920s. The list just also happened to be that of the Ku Klux Klan members in that area from 1923 to 1926, and the trunk also contained assorted Klan paraphernalia, such as hoods and crosses. Mr. Roberts was shocked to discover his father's name on the list. The paper was brittle and crumbling, and he typed the names on a fresh sheet of paper and gave it to the Hamilton County Historical Society. While many local families protested vigorously against publishing the names, others, including Mr. Roberts, were moved "to examine their consciences when it comes to race. 'I look back [at my childhood] and ask myself, 'Why wasn't I upset as a kid when black kids couldn't sit with us in the movie theatre? Why wasn't I upset when they could not swim at the public swimming pool?'"[12]

Mr. Roberts' childhood attitude might well have changed if he had had personal contact with those excluded and had been able to share empathically their suffering. Sharing vicariously their torment from their point of view rather than his own, he could have seen the racist society of which he was comfortably a part from their perspective rather than from that of someone on the right side of the barricade. More precisely, he would have understood for the first time that there was a barricade, and that he was unknowingly complicit in maintaining it. Of course, adults bore the responsibility for the segregated schools, buses, movie theatres, drinking fountains, rest rooms, and the like. Yet social change often begins with the discontented young who are to determined to create a better world.

Growing up at probably the same time as Mr. Roberts, I also remember that I was not bothered by any of these repulsive injustices. However, I also know why. Uncriticized because unrecognized, passive social conditioning, along with a physical insulation from African-American children, conspired to keep my conscience untroubled. I was cut off from the world of their feelings, because I was cut off from them.[13] It was not that Mr. Roberts or I in any way took up an active posture against minority-group children. It was never that conscious or deliberate. Rather, the *status quo ante* was simply there—massively, quietly, successfully. There was no incentive to question these social forces, because we did not suspect that they were there to begin with. Nobody ever told us that African Americans—or, as one said then, "Negroes"—were inferior to whites, because no one had to. It was pervasive and unseen, something in the air, just like the oxygen that we breathed unreflectively. And we were entirely typical of mainstream white society. Certainly exceptional cases existed here and there, but by and large, that society did not recognize its racial injustices until cities starting burning in the 1960s and the Black Power movement frightened people into a belated examination of conscience. These phenomena also functioned on a social plane as an example of Hogarth's *in terrorem* method of deterring future victimizers—with its concomitant weaknesses. Discriminatory behavior returned in the absence of immediate threats.

We were, then, for the most part, good-willed, passive bystanders to racial injustice. We might have been disabused of this insouciance if we had been challenged on an intellectual plane—if, that is, African Americans had defied us to demonstrate some rational relationship between skin color and the ability and right to use public facilities, schools, and so forth. However, for the reasons given above about motivation, this probably would have been ineffective in the absence of fundamental affective change. The power of "the tides of history that bear down on all of us" (Coles 1992, 38) is undoubtedly too great to be deflected by simple rational argument. After all, Martin Luther King himself was very far from enjoying majority support, even in the Black community, and it is arguable that his pleas for justice depended on his death for their ultimate effectiveness.

Additionally, the conditions noted above that make it more likely for active and passive victimizers to recognize the cruelty they perpetuate were not met. (1) The state of American society then was such that the relevant social norms governing race relations were not more compatible with kindness than with cruelty. (2) Many victimizers, both active and passive, unknowingly engaged in exploitation, although (3) they were otherwise more disposed to kindness than cruelty. But the force of (1), coupled with the fact that (4) there was insufficient community support to overcome racism, prevented us from gaining consciousness. Only the violent force of social disruption changed enough minds and perhaps some hearts as well.

There is another case of how satisfying these four conditions can discourage victimizers' cruelty that both returns us to Gilligan's work and to the issue of essentialism and constructivism, nature and culture, and gender and sex, which cropped up at the end of Chapter 4. The example consists of the process of developing from boyhood to manhood. A phenomenology of that process will match Gilligan's reflections on girlhood and womanhood and support her arguments as described above. There is not enough space here to develop such a phenomenology, so I will limit myself to a brief sketch of what it meant to grow up male—by which phase I mean to refer to biology and society, sex and gender—in mid-twentieth-century America. This summary outline will reveal more about the social conditioning forces that Gilligan described. It will also point to how, in relation to gender as opposed to race, the four conditions of reducing victimization might be satisfied. In addition, it will show that there is evidence that the conditioning forces to be described here have not changed appreciably since the experiences occurred to which I shall refer.[14]

The following sketch also has a negative philosophical value, in that it implicitly argues against a universal essence of masculinity. As Judith Butler observes, "[P]henomenologically, there are indeed all sorts of ways of experiencing gender and sexuality" (1995, 24). Therefore, there are other types, formed under different conditions, "marginalized and subordinated" (Connell 1995, 164), which I do not consider here because of their lack of relevance to Gilligan's work.[15] In the formation of gender and sexuality both nature and culture are at work so that the distinction between them "is abstract: everything is cultural in us (our Lebenswelt is 'subjective') (our perception is cultural-historical) and everything is natural in us (even the cultural rests on the polymorphism of the wild Being" (Merleau-Ponty 1968, 253).[16] I shall return to the notion of polymorphism later, but here an immediate consequence is that, as noted in my reply to Bigwood in Chapter 1, "[T]here is not a word, not a form of behaviour which does not owe something to purely biological being—and which at the same time does not elude the simplicity of animal life" (Merleau-Ponty 1962, 189). Therefore, and fortunately, the process of growing up male as I experienced it can be changed, with a consequent diminishment of unkindness to men and women alike.

To begin, then, with boyhood, its first central feature was that its constitutive experiences took their places in a constantly guided process from boyhood to manhood. Although it is true that I had a great deal more leisure time and grew up in a far less dangerous environment than many boys (and girls) today, I never had the sense of gently sideslipping on my own. Rather, it was a question of a youth sculpted by parents, teachers, ministers, and other social influences for a successful transition to adult life. This guidance was far more fundamental than directed responses to the standard adult query, "What do you want to be when you grow up?" The adults in my life were quite prepared for a great variety of answers to that question over the years. What was essential about repeating that question *ad infinitum* was its focus on having to answer it someday.

In terms of maleness, the meaning of boyhood was therefore an uncontroversial, if not always a smooth, problem-free, *preparation* for adult life. There was a rather simple, uncomplicated assumption of power and the enjoyment of life that was designed to fit within a teleological process. As a result, later entry into manhood did not entail anything like the "dissociative split" that Gilligan described for girls who, as women, learn to speak with false voices. Effectively, the male voice remained the same, albeit modulated by all of the usual formative experiences of adolescence. In other words, growing up meant in large part growing into what I had laboriously and carefully trained, and had been trained, to become. And what was that?

The major constituent values of manhood, which we learned very early to start practicing, were autonomy, self-reliance, the ability to assume responsibility, independence, and the toughness of endurance.[17] It is tempting to think that such conditioning must be inconsistent with developing virtues of care, concern, and kindness, but that would be erroneous. In my own case, one part of the moral message behind the former set of qualities consisted of its necessity for instantiating the latter set. Thus on the one hand, a convenient shorthand for reinforcing the first set of masculine characteristics was to say that I had to "be a man." On the other hand, an equally important side of that manliness was to help the weak. God might help those who helped themselves, but we were expected to do for the rest.

The task of being a man, or being a "real man," for which our youth was meant as practice, also distinguished boys from girls in another way. I never heard an adult say to my sister, or any other girl, "Be a woman." Therefore being a man, a real man, presented itself to us as a project at which we could succeed or fail, with predictable social consequences of praise or blame. However, girls were what they were. Their being women apparently was already inscribed in their existence, so that prescription equaled inscription. Simply living would bring them to their biological and cultural destination and destiny. In other words, their essence was seemingly identical to their existence: they were goddesses.

However, this deification was not to last long. In the world of men, rather than boys, as noted in Chapter 4, cosmetics, the weight loss and plastic surgery industries, and other social institutions and forces conspire to reinforce the message that women are not acceptable as they are. Thus the underlying meaning of these social institutions is desacralization, or, as Bartky points out, "The fashion-beauty complex produces in woman an estrangement from her bodily being" (1990, 39). This is because "the 'intimations of inferiority' are clear: Not only must we continue to produce ourselves as beautiful bodies, but the bodies we have to work with are deficient to begin with. . . . [Such] Psychological oppression is dehumanizing and depersonalizing; it attacks the person in her personhood" (ibid., 29).

How could the project of becoming a man have failed? Those who announced and reinforced this task by a plethora of overt and hidden signs did not mean that age alone would ensure success. It was not merely a question of reaching the young years of adulthood. Rather, it was first a question of the boy's successful separation from the mother, the experience that Gilligan noted takes place in the early years for boys but not until adolescence for girls. One measure of successful separation, which thus was not applied to girls, consisted of the repression of feeling and the need for connections. Thus boys at that time strove mightily to avoid sharing feelings—showing any sympathy was a code for weakness—and above all, crying (being a "sissy"). However, there are separations and separations, and Gilligan does not provide anything like a complete picture of those at issue with boys and their mothers. Looking back at my own experiences, I think of them as the emotional equivalent of learning to ride a bicycle without training wheels. The separation presented itself as part of the larger project of launching a self-reliant person into the world, and that type of separation, colored by gratitude, is fully consistent with very strong attachments of love, care, concern, and so forth. I see these experiences now in the way that Gilligan, in another context, describes "the paradoxical truths of human experience—that we know ourselves as separate only insofar as we live in connection with others, and that we experience relationship only insofar as we differentiate other from self" (1982, 1993 printing, 63).

Adolescent years served as a large proving ground and obstacle course for the project of manhood. The boyhood messages did not change, but their implementation became considerably more difficult because of peer pressure, criticism, and wider social influences that held up unattainable but indispensable ideals. The main problem consisted of body image, and it first arose from socially normative pictures (literally) of men. Male body image crises long predated *Baywatch*. For us, the icon of manhood was Charles Atlas. His black and white advertisements in comic books always featured the same beach scene in which a muscle-bound bully kicked sand in the face of a "97-pound weakling." On the blanket beside that deficient specimen of manhood lay curled up a beautiful girl wearing a bikini (which was pretty daring for the times). There was an inset photograph of the spectacularly muscular Mr. Atlas, who promised us all revenge on such bullies after taking his fitness course. Some of the advertisements also featured "before" and "after" scenes. In the latter, the newly empowered former weakling settled the bully's hash—with the girl looking on adoringly.

There are three other significant facts about those advertisements. They would have meant nothing apart from the larger project of our lives, becoming men, which assigned them their meaning. This project entailed having and maintaining a hard, powerful, non-feminine body. In addition, the bully in a certain way stood for all other teenage males. They were our most severe critics and could wield the greatest power over us by merciless criticism and teasing, especially in showers (mandatory) after gym classes.

Finally, the presence of the bikini-clad girl was important, because she represented one main way that girls were "other" for us and than us. In *The Second Sex*, Simone de Beauvoir advances by now well-known arguments about how women define themselves as "other" than men. When we were adolescents, girls were also "other," but in very different ways. Like the girl on the beach blanket, they were witnesses to our successfully becoming men or shamefully failing to do so. They were the attractive softness and temptation to feeling that we so violently repudiated in ourselves. Perhaps, indeed, we rejected it so violently, and did considerable violence to ourselves in the process, to the degree that we recognized our separation from and attraction to it. As Merleau-Ponty phrases it, "The I-other relation [is] to be conceived . . . as complementary roles, one of which cannot be occupied without the other being also: masculinity implies femininity, etc. Fundamental polymorphism by reason of which I do not have to constitute the other *in face of* the Ego" (1968, 220-21). And a few pages later, he says of the "male-female relation," that "each is the *possible of the other*," with a "relation of *Kopulation* where two intentions have *one sole Erfülling*" (ibid., 228; emphasis in original).

Thus Judith Butler observes correctly that "Becoming a 'man' within this logic requires a repudiation of femininity, but also a repudiation that becomes a precondition for the heterosexualization of sexual desire and hence, perhaps also, its fundamental ambivalence. If a man becomes heterosexual through the repudiation of the feminine, then where does that repudiation live except in an identification that his heterosexual career seeks to deny?" (1995, 26). In fact, Butler goes on to say, longing for the feminine is stamped by that disavowal in the sense that the man desires the woman he will never be and does not want to be. Therefore, he covets her. Our detachment from girls' feelings, and from our own, thus carried forward from boyhood the momentum of separation and the fear of shared intimacy. Hence, one of the worst boyhood insults was to accuse a particular boy of playing with dolls. When we were teenagers, we certainly came to share the interests of girls, but on our terms, with as little risk of feeling exposure as possible. As Susan Bordo observes, "[T]he softness and vulnerability shared with the feminine body" is always a "possibility felt to be harbored by the male body and threatening to its masculine stature and status" (1994, 269).

The otherness that girls represented for us also became hierarchical, the perpetuation of patriarchy. In boyhood, it was a question of feeling superior to girls, especially in terms of athletic ability ("throwing like a girl"). During adolescence, we became much more aware of how social structures and practices reinforced this hierarchical relationship, particularly in terms of course tracking in education—literature, art, and home economics for girls, and science, math, and shop classes for boys. Similarly, gender discrimination in employment, of which we could see the results but not the causes, produced nearly all male "commanding" professions of law, medicine, airplane pilots, and so forth, while women generally became secretaries, nurses, and flight attendants (then called "stewardesses").

Bordo is also right to call our attention to "the feminist insight that the personal is the political—that social power and hierarchy are embodied not only in 'external' institutions and forms of organization," such as those just mentioned, "but make their way into the very heart of desire, need, emotion, sexuality" (1994, 278). Thus with the awakening of erotic interests, male life became a volatile, unstable mix of dramatic insecurity about body image, a dramatic increase in self-consciousness, and the flowering of hierarchical relationships with girls as attempted possessions ("my girl"). In response to the turmoil and confusion about self-identity in the wake of bodily and social upheavals, girls became "other" in a more mysterious, tantalizing, and frustrating way. However, the basic contours of the male self remained intact, even if they wavered under the attraction of the feminine. Body image became even more important, because (I think) a hard, tough body functioned as armor for an exceptionally fragile ego. The worst experiences were having that ego crushed by being turned down for a date and being thrown over for another guy. This humiliating experience does not vanish in adulthood, as myriad bar conversations attest.

The sense of sexuality that emerged from this process of development extended the notion of possession and hierarchical dominance to a one-dimensional experience of performance rather than feeling, achievement (scoring) rather than sharing, and penetration rather than communion. As Bordo points out, this conception of male sexuality—as the agent rather than the recipient, "the penetrator not the penetrated"—is not only profoundly engrained in our culture but ultimately goes back to Aristotle. Likewise, "The deep associations of masculinity as active, constitutive (and self-constituting) subjectivity and femininity as a passive, 'natural,' bodily state underlie the equation of penetrability with femininity" (Bordo 1994, 288).[18]

What sort of manhood, finally, emerged to fulfill the process of development? It is a self that is tough and resilient, more nearly active than passive. Its strength, however, no longer derives from efforts to emulate Charles Atlas; body image has taken on a different set of meanings associated with health and survival. (Pain, suffering, and death are the great equalizers.) It is also a self that is autonomous, but at the same time committed to family, colleagues, and other friends. Both halves of that boyhood picture of autonomy—the independent and responsible self—developed according to plan. Nevertheless, these relationships modify the male self rather than bring it into being. As Gilligan puts it, "[T]he sequential ordering of identity and intimacy in the transition from adolescence to adulthood better fits the development of men than it does the development of women" (1982, 1993 printing, 163).

It is also a self that is rather distanced from its feelings and from those of others. It is a distance that does not exist for itself but for the protective space it offers. It is a distance that reflects a fear of trust—not the impersonal variety we repose in our physicians or bankers, but that which conveys a "fear of being really vulnerable, of personally trusting another. . . . The cardinal sin for men is to be weak, vulnerable. . . . It makes genuine, intimate, and fulfilling heterosexual relationships exceedingly difficult—as if they were not difficult enough on their own" (LaFollette 1996, 121).

In terms of those heterosexual relationships, mine was a self in search of reintegration but love on its own nonthreatened terms.[19] Gilligan's own image for such a male self is Virgil's Aeneas (1988, 3-6, 12-13). An equally good example is one of Camille Claudel's sculptures in the Musée Rodin in Paris. This particular bronze consists of an ensemble of three human figures. The central figure is an upright, walking man. An elderly woman stands behind and attempts to embrace him. She has placed her hands very loosely on his arms, and her face is quite close to his. His body is turned away from her. However, his head responds to her touch with an involuntary inclination, although he continues to look away from her. In this ambiguous gesture, he acknowledges her presence without giving into it. Both figures are nude, with the exception of a cape around the shoulders of the woman. The third figure is nude as well. It is that of a young woman kneeling behind the man. Head to one side, arms outstretched, she seems to be imploring him not to leave her. The elderly woman suggests comfort spurned; the younger woman, care, love, and concern. The man intimates the determined energy of self-sufficiency and the refusal of re-lationships. The title of this sculpture is *L'Age mûr* (*Maturity*).

As noted above, these hallmarks of becoming a male self in our type of so-ciety are still very much in evidence. In "The Bully in the Mirror," Stephen S. Hall reports on the troubled life of boys today in much the same terms. He is concerned with the way in which adolescent boys exemplify the "timeless ar-chetypal trajectory to a teenager's battle with body image." Girls' eating dis-orders have long been a focus of study in this area, as we discussed earlier, but it is less well noticed that boys today continue to deal with their anxieties about their bodies by translating "strong and virile"[20] into "bulked up and mus-cular" (1999, 32).

Bordo had discussed this phenomenon five years earlier, but with a concep-tual twist that does not appear in Hall's essay. For Bordo, the contemporary trend toward bulking up has to do with a cultural achievement of difference from women rather than "natural" difference. In her view, "Whereas muscles once signified the brutely 'natural,' the primitive, and thus were usually reserved in cultural representations for the bodies of blacks, slaves, prize-fighters and manual laborers, muscles today have been re-located to the 'civilized' side of the nature/culture duality" (1994, 290–91). The reason is that muscles today are the product of "mind over matter," dedicated workouts in gyms and other venues, to create a masculine body.

Certainly there is a difference here, but it is not one that distinguishes the era in which I grew up from the present one.[21] Her description applies perfectly to my youth. It is also a difference that is not well described in terms of a contrast of nature and culture, even if they constitute a "duality" and if "nature" is en-closed in cautionary quotation marks. It would be more accurate to character-ize the distinction at issue as one between different types of projects in the Lifeworld. In the former, the "natural," muscle formation takes place in the course of other projects. In the latter, muscle formation constitutes the whole or at least main purpose of the project. Today, as when I was young, bulking up was a goal that equally embraced nature and culture. Even for those who went to gyms to work out, it was a question of a natural endowment that distin-guished males from females, and this natural endowment was enhanced under cultural norms for cultural purposes. Moreover, "manual laborers" are not lo-cated on the "nature" side of the duality, and not only because labor is a social concept. During both my high school and college years, the most valued sum-mer jobs were in construction. This was partly because the pay was good, but principally because it served as a functional equivalent of a gym and provided an attractive suntan gratis.

Hall also shows that the same kinds of locker room insults and teasing that we both remember so well are alive and well today in corporate boardrooms, as during a recent high-profile lawsuit with "Michael Eisner dissing Jeffrey

Katzenberg as a 'little midget'." "You would never know," Hall points out, "that for the past quarter-century, feminist thought and conversation has created room for alternatives to traditional masculinity, in which toughness is equated with self-worth and physical stature is equated with moral stature" (1999, 32). Furthermore, with cultural messages about the perfect male body becoming more and more insistent, boys and men both are increasingly at risk for psychopathological problems. One of these, called "body dysmorphic disorder," consists of patients' obsessions with flaws in their appearance that they think they perceive. For men, these usually consist of "receding hairlines, facial imperfections, small penises, [and] inadequate musculature" (ibid., 33). In addition, more and more men are turning to cosmetic surgery these days, with liposuction being the most popular. Advertisers have "commodified boys' bodies" (ibid.) to step up the pressure on men of the unattainable ideal body, while for boys themselves, male action figure toys have become more bulked up and muscular.

In 1988, the U.S. Government Office of Population Affairs, through the Data Archive on Adolescent Pregnancy and Pregnancy Prevention, published a study of teenage boys' sexual attitudes, titled the "National Survey of Adolescent Males." In 1993, one of the lead researchers for the study, Joseph H. Pleck, reported on what he called "masculine ideology," which simply expresses the main points of my own account of growing up male. It "indicates the degree to which boys subscribe to the more traditional standards of male comportment: the need for respect from peers and spouses, a reliance on physical toughness, a reluctance to talk about problems, even a reluctance to do housework" (Hall 1999, 33). A similar problem continues to exist for men who provide adolescents with role models. We speak of men, but never of women, as "helping" with housework. However, Pleck also noted of adolescents, as other researchers have since then, something else that is much more ominous. Just as Gilligan pointed out that care, sympathy, and a concern for relationships place girls at risk, adolescent boys imbued with the "masculine ideology" are equally in danger. There is a high positive correlation between this traditionalist attitude and the risk for dangerous sexual behavior, troubles with alcohol and other drugs, suicide, educational problems and getting into legal trouble.

Sharing feelings is still taboo, lest one be seen as "sensitive," "a code word for 'weak' " (Hall 1999, 34). Moreover, the "culture of cruelty," a phrase taken from Dan Kindlon's and Michael Thompson's *Raising Cain*, is still alive and well in the locker room and beyond: "[A] boy's body image is shaped, if not determined, by the cruelest, most unforgiving and meanest group of judges imaginable: other boys" (Hall 1999, 58), and psychologists have begun to hypothesize a connection between the resultant stress and mental problems. Hall notes that, in his interviews with these youngsters, anxiety about penis size still exists, and many boys these days skip showers after gym class. However, the primary source of angst is chest muscles: "I heard genuine fear in the voices of older boys when they spoke about the impending horror of going to camp or the beach and having to appear in public *without a shirt*" (ibid., 64; emphasis in original).

None of this is necessary, any more than was my traditional socialization as a male in mid-twentieth-century American society. Rather than stating the a priori truths of a bedrock male nature, male ideology is a construction, a story about gender rather than sex. It is only an ideology, and the sole beneficiary of the power it bestows seems to be those capitalist enterprises that trade on commodified bodies. And if it is only an ideology, it can be changed. As Nussbaum puts it, instead of believing in "unchanging male aggression," it is more reasonable to think that men behave in the ways they do "because society gives permission to males to form and to express such attitudes" (1999, 12).

This subject, in the framework of sexism, as well as that of Mr. Roberts in the context of racism, shows how victimizers and other complacent bystanders might be induced to view cruelty from the victim's perspective and thus cease their harm causing. With regard to the first condition of getting the victimizer to take the victim's perspective, that the relevant social norms must be more compatible with kindness than with cruelty, I am inclined to think that we can be a bit more optimistic than was possible when mainstream America was asleep to the evils of segregation. The male ideology itself has lost some of its grip in the presence of publicly discussed alternative masculinities, and men today are much more actively involved with child rearing than they used to be. Further, the prevailing social morality is not as misogynist as it was racist in the 1950s and early 1960s.

The second condition—that victimizers unknowingly engage in exploitation—is satisfied as well for many men, since they do not understand how they have been passively complicit in exploiting women. Most teenage boys meet this condition as well since, as Mr. Kindlon puts it, "They're not even in touch with their emotions, and they're doing things for reasons of which they're not even aware. You're not getting the real story because *they* don't even know the whole story" (Hall 1999, 34). Thus they are in principle educable, and seeing the effects of their acts, social practices, and the like, from the victim's perspective, is the best source of evidence, even if it is not always convincing. The third and fourth conditions may be satisfied as well: adolescent males today are probably more inclined to kindness than cruelty, and they may also be able to obtain community support to combat the effects of the masculine ideology. For example, if adolescent male psychiatric problems continue to increase, the various engines of social persuasion might be mobilized to defeat the power of the ideology, especially the power of advertisers.[22]

The discussion over the last several pages has been devoted to these four conditions that can induce victimizers and complacent bystanders to adopt empathetically the victim's standpoint, and can therefore awaken victimizers to the effects of their actions. The discussion has led us to consider adolescent males who are by turns both victimizers and victims of other boys and, as men, potential victimizers of women. However, if it is correct to say that satisfying these four conditions is not a sufficient condition of diminishing cruelty, to discover what would be sufficient entails transcending attempts to modify the victimizer's cognitive and affective states. It requires attention to the victims, and especially to self-deceived victims of unseen coercion and exploitation.

Freedom and Goodness

How, then, can victims—above all, those who are self-deceived—lead lives of kindness that provide adequate space for suspicion and for diminishing the chances of their own victimization? For those at risk for victimization in situations of unbalanced power, the opposite of suspicion is trust. Thus the previous questions can be rephrased as follows: For those in such situations, and especially for those committed to the vulnerability that opening oneself to the other in kindness requires, what justifies the trust that must underlie such openness?[23]

We saw in Chapter 3 that genuine kindness entails a certain sense of innocence—not that which can be lost, but that which can be gained. To achieve it, we have to become "as wise as a serpent and as guileless as a dove," as the biblical expression has it. As we have also seen, this means that qualities of kindness, sympathy, and care are not blind or indiscriminate but rather are consistent with judgments about the welfare of others, even if the latter do not agree with the content of those judgments. One lesson of a hermeneutics of suspicion is that one must invent ways to be kind that are also consistent with making informed judgments about oneself.

Gilligan has pointed out that, in societies like ours, women are much more likely to exemplify kindness, sympathy, care, and the like than are men, and that men would be morally better off if they developed similar capacities for relationships. Yet the fact that, for now anyway, women especially are inclined to these virtues has an ambiguous normativity. As Wertheimer points out, one might argue that these qualities make women morally superior to men, at least to those who wish to uphold patriarchy. On the other hand, they may equally make women more easily exploitable (1996, 259–60). This ambiguity implies that kindness requires not only trust, but suspicion as well. Even this accommodation to suspicion, though, does not satisfy all feminists. For example, Catharine MacKinnon and Claudia Card argue that women's "instincts" to care for others are not instincts at all. Rather, they "are actually constructs of women's subordination, which frequently serve male interests and work against women" (Nussbaum 1999, 13). Their view is effectively that there is no room for trust, because trust itself is a convenient and deceitful patriarchal tool. Therefore, if genuine kindness is really possible—between men and women, or in any other context—there must be some defensible basis for trust, even while we remain on guard against "emotions formed under conditions of injustice" that may place us at (greater) risk for exploitation (ibid., 13).

Nevertheless, as Nussbaum goes on to say, "[D]uly scrutinized and assessed, emotions of care and sympathy lie at the heart of the ethical life" (ibid., 14). Every society needs them, especially those attempting to overcome a history of substantive injustice. This is what Frederick Douglass recognized when he reached out to sympathetic relatives of his previous owners after the Civil War. He refused to repudiate the value of sympathy, love, and trust, despite those injustices. Nussbaum refuses to accept the similar invitation of some feminists to allow men's long-standing injustices to women to erode the possibility of all trust, even though she points out that—as Douglass' postwar critics also said of him—"sympathy and forgiveness" can appear as "collaboration with oppression" (ibid.).

Therefore, the question becomes, how can feelings of kindness and their supporting feelings of "care and sympathy" be "duly scrutinized and assessed" so that trust is possible on the part of likely victims of exploitation? And in the cases of what I have called "double-blind" exploitation, how can the potential victims be awakened from their indoctrinated slumbers in order to deter their would-be victimizers? For those who are alert to the possibility of exploitation in a particular situation, a necessary and perhaps even sufficient part of the critical scrutiny that they need to direct toward their dispositions to kindness consists of knowledge of all the relevant interests in play. Such knowledge implicates at least four of Nussbaum's "central human functional capabilities" summarized in the last chapter, "senses, imagination, thought"; "emotions," "practical reason," and "affiliation." What is required is a clear awareness of what is at stake for the other party (ies), how a particular act of kindness will serve those interests, and whether serving those interests will be self-destructive. In other words, one has to be "as wise as a serpent" in the care of oneself as well as in the care of the object of one's care.

Annette Baier addresses this connection between knowledge of the other's interests and trust, to which we referred briefly in Chapter 3, when she makes a "tentative" proposal for "a test for the moral decency of a trust relationship." The continuation of such a trust does not have to depend on "successful threats" that the truster holds over the trusted, or on the trustee's "successful cover-up of breaches of trust." In those cases, when the truster found out what the trustee depended on for the trust to continue, that knowledge would be sufficient to undermine the trust (1986, 255). To put it very generally, insofar as what the truster depends on for the trust to continue is something that, once the trusted party realizes what it is, will probably lead to additional abuse and destruction of that trust, then the trust is morally bad. In other words, a relationship of trust will be "morally bad to the extent that either party relies on qualities in the other which would be weakened by the knowledge that the other relies on them" (ibid., 255–56). The essence of the test, then, is to require that both parties expose all their relevant interests in order to see if the bond of trust can survive that exposure.

How would this test fit the instances of trust about which MacKinnon, Card, and Nussbaum are suspicious? Doubtless, the sort of case about which they are most concerned is the type described by Bellah et al. in the previous chapter, that of the traditional sort of wife and mother who devotes herself exclusively to her husband and family, and whose very sense of self-identity and self-worth derives from that relationship and only from that relationship. It is also the sort of case that Nora and Torvald and Edna and Léonce represent. The woman in such a marriage trusts her husband, among other things, to love her exclusively, to help protect her and their children, and to join with her in a mutually fulfilling project of child rearing. For Baier, whether he is trust*worthy* will depend on whether all of his interests in that relationship, fully and candidly revealed, are consistent with those values. He may not be able to articulate all of his interests, or may not want to, but the most decisive factor would surely be whether there are any inconsistencies between his postmarital behavior and his premarital expressions of values and promises. If his actions reveal that he considers her a mere means to his own pleasures, her trust in him would not survive scrutiny. If she continued to overlook patterns of abuse, she would have to retreat to a self-deceived false-consciousness of "blindness, ignorance, and gullibility" (ibid., 256).

However, this is only part of the story. Whether such women could trust their husbands also requires a reference to the social setting in which their marriage commitments were made. Since "preference, emotion, and desire" are shaped in large part by society, "[P]eople's desires and preferences respond to their beliefs about social norms and about their own opportunities" (Nussbaum 1999, 11). When people have been cut off from resources for some capability, for instance, education or simply proper nutrition, it is reasonable to expect them to be slow to desire those things. The chronically weak may not even have a clear idea of what it is like to be strong. Thus "[W]omen's stated satisfactions and preferences . . . may be deformed by intimidation, lack of information, and habit" (ibid., 33). These facts imply two things about the woman described above. Her marital commitment and indeed her very concept of marriage may not be the products of truly informed consent. Instead, they may have been formed under intimidation and fear. Also, she will be able to detect only the abuse that she has been trained to recognize—that which is inconsistent with exclusive love and protection. She will not likely be able to perceive systemic abuse correctly, because she had not been prepared to see it for what it was. She has bought into the game without recognizing that it was a game or what it was. In this state of self-deception, unlike that in which potential victims are already sensitized to the possibility of exploitation, Baier's test of trust would likely be inoperative. That is because it is a *knowledge* test, and when one party to a trust is denied access to relevant knowledge, she cannot place herself in a position required to assess the morality of the trust.

If this is right, it follows that in general for people who are not able to recognize exploitation when they see it, the mere enumeration of interests to check for their trust-weakening coefficients will not suffice as a test of trust. The kindnesses that such people do for their exploiters may therefore forge links in a chain that binds them more closely to those exploiters. Thus, once again, a cognitive solution for deterring victimizers has to be supplemented with one that is affective. For the reasons given in Chapter 5, the best chance that self-deceived victims have of avoiding victimization lies in an institutional, political solution. With an increase in freedom and power to change social structures and practices will come both a changed affectivity more accurately attuned to the presence of exploitation and a reinforced will to resist it.

A clear case in point has occurred recently in Yemen. After thousands of years, women are finally gaining freedom and political rights. With incipient democracy, women are now out of their homes going to university and running businesses, and the government has named its first woman ambassador. In contrast, in Saudi Arabia, women are still not allowed to drive or even carry identity cards, and Kuwait not long ago denied women the right to vote. Perhaps in two or three generations, honor killings and the idea that wives are property, just as goats or camels, will also be historical relics of Yemeni culture recounted to disbelieving children. If so, Yemeni women will appreciate what Edwin Curley calls one of the most basic themes of Spinoza's ethical thinking, "the contrast between the active and the passive emotions, and the importance of diminishing the role that passive emotions play in our lives." Rather than be "controlled by external circumstances," we should act in such a way that our actions reflect our most basic desires: "the striving to persevere in existence and to increase our power of action" (Curley 1991, 38–39).

The armature of the motor of this political solution is again self-attestation and the capable body as the core of human dignity, this time engaged in the process of Dewey's civic liberalism that we considered in Chapter 5. The goal in both cases is open and informed public discussion and resolution of issues, which presupposes that we ought always to maximize freedom of choice and the experience of agency. Or, as Marcel put it, "[S]elf-respect implies precisely that stubborn refusal to let oneself be treated as an instrument" (1963, 150). Moreover, Dewey would agree with Nussbaum's contention that these goals do not express a "mere parochial Western ideology." Rather, they portray the meaning of agency "that has deep roots all over the world; it expresses the joy most people have in using their own bodies and minds" (1999, 11). Politics should attempt to enable the maximum number of people possible to achieve self-attestation.

I mentioned above that Baier's test of trust applies to all classes of exploiters and exploitees, in which the latter are positioned to be able to detect exploitation, both systemic as well as particular situational details. This is, in fact, what happened in some of Laing's and Esterton's families of schizophrenic patients. Some of the children were able, finally, to grasp the sense of the machinations of their well-meaning but harm-causing parents, and so were able to neutralize their influence. Similarly, Douglass recounted how the fully awake slave became immune to the blandishments of the master. To conclude this chapter, let us consider two other simple nongender cases.

The first example concerns corporate exploitation of education. A high school environmental science teacher wrote recently about corporations taking over public school space by advertising their products in the guise of "study aids" and other educational services. What may look to cash-strapped school boards and adminstrators as largesse in the support of education turns out to be rather different in practice. At least 234 companies are now inundating schools with computer software, films, and textbooks of dubious educational value. To take just a few examples, "A lesson in self-esteem sponsored by Revlon includes an investigation of 'good and bad hair days'. . . . Chevron, in a lesson for use in civics or sciences classes, reminds students that they will soon be able to vote and make 'important decisions' about global warming, which the company then rebuts as incomplete science. . . . To teach the 'scientific method,' the Campbell Soup Company once distributed free lesson plans and demonstration kits. The 'Slotted Spoon Test' compared the thickness of Campbell's product, Prego, against a competitor, Ragu. The young scientists were to find Prego thicker; if not, they simply did the lab incorrectly."[24]

Here Baier's test easily applies. What to administrators may look like civic-minded corporate kindness turns out to be blatant commercialism once all of the interests of the companies concerned are clearly identified. The transparent purpose becomes creating future consumers rather than educating children, and once that is obvious, the basis for the trust is shattered. Knowledge of what the corporations are relying on for the continuation of the trust relationship is enough to weaken and destabilize it. And if there could be any possible doubt, it is clearly dispelled by the language of certain marketers who describe children as "born to be consumers," "consumer cadets" whose "consumer embryos" start to "develop in the first year of existence." The latter claim stems from marketers' excitement over "evidence that children as young as 12 months are capable of 'brand associations.'"[25]

The second example is also one of broken trust, or perhaps a case in which no trust could have been operative from the beginning. It concerns the way in which banks, mainly Citigroup, ostensibly help welfare recipients receive their benefits through a network of ATM machines. The District of Columbia and thirty-nine states have hired banks to distribute welfare payments in this way, and the State of New York will pay Citigroup $80 million from 1999 to 2003 for this purpose. The idea of the program was "to reduce fraud, save money, and draw poor people into the financial mainstream." What has actually happened, though, is that the banks, Citigroup especially, are charging welfare recipients fees for withdrawals, and these fees are deducted from their welfare checks. Most regular Citigroup ATM customers do not have to pay these fees. Also, for many months, while Citigroup was struggling to make money off of welfare recipients, the bank blocked access to its two huge networks of ATMs for "hundreds of thousands [of] New York City welfare recipients." The bank did this "by refusing to pay the full fee charged by other banks for each transaction. Payment of the full fee would have allowed poor people to use the same range of ATMs as Citigroup's regular customers."[26]

Here again we have a case in which "knowledge of what the other party is relying on for the continuance of the trust relationship would . . . itself destabilize the relation" (Baier 1986, 255). Once the legislature is apprised of all of Citigroup's and similar financial institutions' interests in providing ATM access to the poor, it will or ought not any longer trust ⅲhem to work for welfare recipients. Legislatures might continue to employ these institutions to distribute welfare payments for some other reason (s)—it might, for example, still be cheaper—but no one could keep up the pretense of believing that the institutions further poor people's interests.

To conclude, the last two chapters have exposed kindness to a hermeneutics of suspicion in a variety of contexts and with different types of criticisms. The previous chapter dealt with the crucial notion of a false consciousness created by self-deception and defended the value of kindness against certain misinterpretations by Hallie and Douglass. It also challenged on their own grounds Nietzsche's likely criticisms of kindness as internally inconsistent. Those criticisms led to a sketch of part of a new moral psychology that revolves around the notion of the capable body—a notion that Nussbaum's list of central human capacities makes socially specific. The present chapter has extended the notion of self-deception that creates a false consciousness to Marx's conception of ideologies in order to show how they mask unkindnesses embedded in capitalism. The hermeneutics of suspicion then extended to Carol Gilligan's research on gender. We examined strategies for diminishing exploitation in terms of judging the exploiter's act from the perspective of the victim and changing the victimizer's cognitive and affective states. In the contexts of both racism and sexism, we identified conditions that had to be satisfied in order to deter the victimizer's harm-causing behavior. Satisfying those conditions turned out to be insufficient for, even if they were a strong contributory cause of, such deterrence. To discover what would be sufficient, we turned our attention to the victims, especially those who are self-deceived. Our discussion led not to a knowledge test of trust, such as Baier proposes, but to an institutional, political solution that, as Douglass knew well, best guarantees freedom and is an indispensable condition of goodness. The aim of this endeavor is to change social structures and practices that contribute to victimization. In the context of advancing that solution, finally, we looked at certain feminist criticisms of Gilligan and, by implication, of women's kindness in general. While admitting the dangers of which they wrote, I have declined their conclusion in favor of a hermeneutically suspicious life of kindness supported and protected by appropriate political and other social institutional changes.

What has to be addressed now is the means to accomplish that objective. How can we continue to live a life of kindness as described in Part One with a properly suspicious attitude? The objects of that suspicion are that through naïveté, one's kindnesses might unwittingly be used by others for exploitative purposes within an unjust social system, regardless of having had the best of motives, and/or harm oneself by permitting oneself to be exploited. How can one best live a non-naïve life of kindness as practical wisdom—maximally seeking the good of others, but not at the inadvertent cost of others or oneself? I shall call this "critical kindness," and it comprises the subject of the final chapter.

Chapter 8

Critical Kindness:
Toward an Aesthetic Humanism

A wide, efficacious love is as difficult as it is rare.
—Philip Hallie, *Tales of Good and Evil, Help and Harm*

Uncritical Praise and the Challenge of Suspicion

Moritz Schlick ends his *Problems of Ethics* (*Fragen der Ethik*) with the following "apostrophe to kindness," that, he asserts, "could be patterned after the Kantian hymn to duty, word for word":

> Kindness, thou dear great name, that containest nothing in thee demanding loveless esteem, but prayest to be followed; thou dost not menace and needst not establish any law, but of thyself findest entrance into feeling, and willingly art revered; whose smile disarms all sister inclinations; thou art so glorious that we need not ask after thy descent, for whatever be thy origin it is ennobled through thee. (1939, 208–209)

Schlick's energetic "apostrophe," completely uninterested in the origins of kindness that evolutionary psychologists are studying, comes at a price. Nowhere in his major work on ethics does he consider, let alone critically discuss, the types of challenges and concerns of a hermeneutics of kindness. His praise of the virtue and his defense of an ethics of kindness float above the suspicions detailed across the last two chapters about the value of kindness and its ability to be corrupted by exploitative power. One task of critical kindness is, therefore, to attempt to justify Schlick's confidence in kindness by bringing his panegyric down to earth. How, against the background of suspicion articulated above, can one lead a life of "ennobled" kindness? How can one critically "revere" kindness?

In the first place, we need a more general understanding of the contours of our vulnerability beyond the contexts of racism, sexism, and capitalism described in the last two chapters. It is not a question of specifying the plethora of possible forms of personal and social exploitation and/or coercion for their own sake,[1] but rather only those to which our acts of kindness expose us. There we can distinguish victimization on both the interpersonal as well as social level. On an interpersonal plane, my act (s) of kindness to the other (s) can expose me to the risk of being used both directly and indirectly as a mere means to an end. I may be exploited directly when my offer to help provides an unexpected target of opportunity for someone bent on an evil purpose. I may also be exploited indirectly in a variety of ways as, for example, when I agree to intercede for someone with a third party without realizing that the person requesting my help intends to exploit or otherwise victimize that third party. Thus I may introduce a male friend to a certain woman without knowing that he will use the date to which she consents on my recommendation in order to take advantage of her.

On a social plane, there are also various forms of direct and indirect exploitation. I can be exploited directly when I make contributions to a clever but fraudulent charity or, say, when my agreement to be an organ donor plays a role in an ER medical team's not doing all that would otherwise be done to revive me. I can be exploited indirectly when I agree to lend my name to a certain organization's advertising campaign, which then uses it to support exploitative purposes of which I knew nothing, and of which I would have disapproved. In addition, competitive business environments provide ample illustrations of acts of kindness that can lead to indirect exploitation. For instance, an act of self-sacrificing kindness might enable that person to secure advantages of power and money over me, or to convince management that the object of my kindness merits those advantages because she is more aggressively competitive.

I must also direct suspicion at myself. For just as I can be an unwitting victim of others, I can unwittingly victimize them both directly and indirectly. Because of self-deception about my motives, and the rationalizations that stem from them, like the "kind" slave owner or the patriarchal husband, I can also misread myself and the facts. At one level, as illustrated in the last two chapters, such misreadings stem from not viewing one's own actions from the point of view of the victim. However, as we have also seen, looking at our acts from the victim's perspective is not sufficient to avoid the danger of a false consciousness, because successfully deceived victims do not know that they are victims. Like many of Laing's and Esterton's schizophrenic children, or like Nora in the beginning of *A Doll's House* and the myriad of real-life women for whom she stood, they do not raise critical questions, because they do not know that anything is wrong. They have not yet "awakened," to use Chopin's term. They are in some ways analogous to the prisoners in the allegory of the cave of

Plato's *Republic*, who cannot distinguish between appearance and reality and can have no consciousness of any other type of reality. As a result, a commitment to avoid victimization entails a willingness to be suspicious of one's own motives even, or especially, if the other party does not.

On an interpersonal level, we have already examined several examples of *apparent* acts of kindness that directly exploit others. For instance, we can greatly harm people through "loving" them inappropriately, and we do not need one of Montaigne's "long interpretations" to understand why. We have also seen that no cases of genuine kindness directly exploit others because, to be authentically kind, such acts must actually pursue the other's good rather than merely intend to do so. Nonetheless, there are instances in which real kindness can indirectly, unknowingly, exploit other people. I might, for instance, lend money to someone to help her escape from poverty, or to get established in the business world, and that money may make the individual concerned an irresistible target for the exploitative/coercive pressures of family or friends. Similarly, in James' *The Portrait of a Lady*, Ralph Touchett talks his father into settling a lot of money on Isabel Archer, and this inheritance, designed to enable her to flourish independently, only sets her up as a prize for the unscrupulous Gilbert Osmond.

On a social plane, we can likewise do acts of kindness for individuals in, say, institutional settings, which have the effect of making them more visible and perhaps advancing their careers, but for which advancements they are not yet ready or possibly even suited. Thus again our acts would have the effect of making the individuals concerned liable to exploitation by those more powerful and capable of manipulating the system. Our actions often have ambiguous results so that kindness can coexist with, and sometimes abet, exploitation and coercion. To take a very different example, Hallie points out that Major Julius Schmähling, who was the German *Kommandant* of the Haute-Loire area of France during the Nazi occupation, turned a blind eye to the Chambonnais' operations of rescuing Jews and treated the civilian population as humanely as possible. Yet he was also a German soldier, charged with keeping the peace in his area. Therefore, Schmähling's kindnesses ambiguously served the causes of good and evil simultaneously: "They saved people's lives in the region of Le Puy, and they advanced the military purposes of a regime dedicated to the mass murder and total domination of millions of human beings" (Hallie 1997, 72).

Schmähling's ambiguity is, however, only an extreme case of a much more ordinary phenomenon. I might buy a garment made in a *maquiladora* factory in order to support as much as possible impoverished workers, but my willingness encourages the exploitation behind the production of the article. My department might hire "adjunct" faculty members so that they can retain some foothold in the job market, but at the price of exploiting them and complicity with an exploitative system. I may make contributions to charities that will provide help to their intended beneficiaries, but also, like international food relief, will prolong wars in impoverished countries by strengthening the combatants. This is only one way in which we can see the truth of Ricoeur's claim that there is an "inevitable place of conflict in the moral life" (1992, 247).

The conclusion toward which this heightened sense of vulnerability leads— at least in what concerns the ways in which I perceive myself at risk—is one of suspicious closure against others. The distinction between the normative and factual senses of solidarity gets sharpened as social cooperation looks to be inevitably risky. Such cooperation takes on a Hobbesian air of the least worst alternative, always underwritten by a profound uneasiness about the other's power and intentions, even to the point of a deep pessimism about the possible value of the other (s). Freud, for example, takes this line when he argues for the unintelligibility of the biblical injunction to love one's neighbor as oneself: "Not merely is this stranger in general unworthy of my love; I must honestly confess that he has more claim to my hostility and even my hatred" (1961, 57). Such an attitude is obviously inconsistent with most acts of kindness and their allied phenomena of hope, sympathy, and compassion. It is a question of a "form of life," as Wittgenstein would say, led by crippled souls for whom happiness, such as it is, is exceptionally insular and conceived as minimal exposure to risk.

However, even if we do not yield to this distorted form of life, as we have seen, non-naïve (critical) kindness requires combining the qualities of being a kind person, as detailed in Part One with the legitimate role of suspicion about others and self. Such a life must be able to hold together, even if in inevitable tension, certain apparently contradictory qualities. Trust must be conjugated with suspicion, openness with closedness, the warmth of generosity with a cautious discipline, the readiness of *disponibilité* with unreadiness, and activity with passivity. There are many ways in which one might describe the result: cautious trust, hesitant openness, a checked readiness, controlled activity, or restrained vitality.

It is true that, at a descriptive level, the practical wisdom that is embedded in genuine acts of kindness provides similar controls. As detailed in Part One, those controls distinguish authentic kindness from naïve and potentially harmful enthusiasm[2] (and from perhaps less naïve but equally harmful neurotic do-gooders). A desire for kindness can provide short-term energy, enthusiasm, and (normative) communion, but practical wisdom furnishes insight, circumspection, directing control, and effectiveness by requiring people to consider whether the announced needs and complaints of those they attempt to help are really in their interests. As we also saw, part of the challenge of kindness considered as an inventive charity consists in helping others in ways that sometimes do and sometimes do not match their expectations.

However, in the context of hermeneutic suspicion, practical wisdom has to go beyond questioning the consistency of the appearances to critically questioning the appearances themselves. It must unveil the framework of interpretation itself in which the phenomena present themselves. The answers one gives to these questions will decide, say, whether the homeless beggar should be pitied as a victim of capitalism or treated as a shiftless ne'er do well who won't apply for a job, because "I don't do mornings."[3] Those answers will also determine what one says to girls and boys (and their parents) to help them avoid growing up in a patriarchal society.

If a life of critical kindness must hold together the opposites listed above, how can they be combined in some form of unity? It will not be a question of a synthesis that could logically or existentially remove all tensions and incompatibilities between them, or use those on one side to absorb those on the other. For Ricoeur is right about inevitable conflict in the moral life. Tragedy can teach us these limits not only on a grand scale of world-historical events but also daily in unwise interventions in other people's lives. Both sets of opposites must be kept, and in tension with each other.

This means that either side of a pair of opposites can prevail in a given situation. Therefore, there are times when one should not be kind—when, say, there are high stakes in terms of possible direct and indirect exploitation and/or coercion, and a substantial risk of playing into evil hands. *Disponibilité* is only a disposition rather than a sufficient condition of performing an act of kindness. Practical wisdom serves as a principle of caution for translating that readiness and its generous warmth into effective ways to help others. By the same token, there are times when one should refuse the genuine and apparent kindnesses of others. For the reasons stated above, authentic acts of kindness can put us in jeopardy, even if they do not intend to harm us. And with apparent acts of kindness, part of the role of practical wisdom, as noted above, consists of conjoining others' offers of help with a calculation of their interests in the outcome.

Thus, for instance, when a bank increases customers' credit card spending limits, it often provides an accompanying explanation that consists of praise for the "excellent manner" in which they have "managed" their accounts (read: paid their bills). However, when the veil of illusion is stripped from this putative reward—when it is reduced to the bank's interest (literally)—it quickly turns out to be a not-so-subtle ploy to get their clients to spend more each month than they can afford and to sink into debt because of the resulting interest payments. In a similar fashion, Douglass' "sober and thoughtful slave" could learn to calculate the interests of the slave owner to tear the veil from his pretense of kindness, just as spouses can attempt to divine a strategy behind their partners' acts in order to determine whether they amount to exploitation or coercion. Of course, in practice, there are limits and difficulties in obtaining the necessary knowledge, and sometimes, as in Schmähling's case, results are ambiguous. However, when there are unavoidable exploitative or coercive effects, the task of practical wisdom is to mitigate the harm caused.

It also follows from the necessity of keeping both trust and suspicion in tension with each other that trust is not cancelled out any more than is suspicion. There are equally times when the grounds for suspicion can be overcome. Ambiguity and the risk of abusing others or being abused still remain, but on these occasions they become acceptable and sometimes become so slight that they virtually disappear. This means that risks, even if unavoidable, are sometimes reasonable.

However, to say that both trust and suspicion must be held together in a dialectical tension does not yet indicate how this might be done. For in choosing to be or not to be kind to others in a given situation, we must give pride of place to one of these opposites. As Patricia Sayre points out (1993, 568), even though we need both, the resulting attitude will be quite different, depending on which one we value up. Therefore, which member of the pair should contextualize the other?

As a matter of a *general* attitude toward others and self, awarding pride of place to suspicion would have very unhappy consequences. Among others, it would greatly reduce Good Samaritanism and other forms of altruism without which society would be substantially impoverished. Indeed, as we saw in Chapter 2, the original Good Samaritan had more reasons than any of the other passersby to be suspicious. Nonetheless, he set aside those reasons, because he was "seized with pity." In addition, the primacy of suspicion would lead to a considerably diminished sense of respect and love for others and oneself. Marcel expresses this well when he correlates a sense of "admiration" for human beings with their readiness to be *disponible* for others. "Admiration" itself, he tells us, "is a form of readiness" (1984, 202).

The upshot here is that kindness is a regulative ideal. In some situations, that may be all that it can be, just as Kant said that no one could prove that morality itself is possible. However, it is still regulative, because it is an ideal. In other situations, we may have various degrees of success in implementing it. Therefore, even if we are not always capable of achieving it, we should not stop trying to bring into existence a world in which it is always realizable. How then can one best go about it?

A Poetics of the Will

The unavoidable presence of conflict in the moral life, along with its inevitable shadow of suspicion, has implications for the concrete means to bring kindness into being. It is a question of a certain type of decision making that is appropriate for this life of critical kindness. This sort of decision making is integrative in nature and guided rather than determined by rules (as with Eliot's "men of maxims"). This integrative quality, and the fact that it is inscribed in an inventive charity, implicates decision making that is much more akin to that of the artist than to that of a Kantian moral subject. It also leads, as we shall see, to a view of kindness that is closely analogous to aesthetic experience[4]—of both artist and spectator—and a new approach to aesthetic humanism in which Schlick's apostrophe can find a home.

Artists resolve a problem by integrating a variety of elements into the most meaningful form possible under conditions imposed by their materials, limited time, and resources. Certain rules serve as guidelines for their creativity. These are embodied in various techniques for preparing the canvas, marble, manipulating the bow of the violin, and the like, as also for the actual creation of the work of art: rules for using the brush or the chisel and mallet for certain effects, for playing the instrument, and so forth. But these technical rules do not account for the creativity of the artwork, and, in any case, artists can and do change techniques to achieve better effects.

Similarly, the decision making involved in performing acts of kindness necessitates the successful integration of trust and suspicion, judgments about how to seek the greatest good possible for the other under the circumstances with the least possible harm. The will that acts of kindness reflect thus has an essentially poetic quality, "the power of unification unfurled by the configuring act constituting *poiesis* itself" (Ricoeur 1992, 142).[5] In acts of kindness this "power of unification" takes the form of binding up wounds and overcoming— or, at least, mitigating, the effects of—alienation and polarized interests. In so doing, kindness becomes analogous to performance art. Moreover, as illustrated above and in Part One, the good of the other that acts of kindness intend includes the requirements of justice as much as possible.[6]

Even though kindness is rule bound to that extent, its poetic activity carries it beyond rules through an inventive charity that seeks the other's flourishing. We considered several examples of this *poiesis* in Part One, such as Dr. Holt's anguish over her terminally ill patients, Aaron Feuerstein's care for, and of, his employees; and Detective Skip Mannain's kindnesses to the family of the slain Mexican worker and to other Mexicans in Poughkeepsie. Also, two clear fictional examples included Dorothea Brooke's simple kindnesses to Rosamond Lydgate in *Middlemarch*, and, in *Shirley*, Hiram Yorke, the factory foreman. When he had to lay off workers, let us recall, he either tried to find them other jobs or relocated them to areas of the country where more jobs were available. The unifying function of such an inventive charity invokes the Old Testament ideal of the embrace of kindness and truth and justice and peace.

Kindness not only helps bring about an external unity among events and human affairs, but it also provides an internal unity as well in the sense of personal integrity discussed in Chapter 2. This is the wholeness that results from resisting degradation into a welter of functions. At first I recoil into myself as self-recovery, but then I balance that centripetal self-withdrawal by a centrifugal affirmation of myself as a totality of relationships through which I am at the disposal of others. That is why Marcel stated that the *disponibilité* that reflects this integrity is the point of departure for the self's "activity and creativeness" (1964b, 43).

Aesthetic experience, whether of the artist or spectator, also provides an internal unity as well as refined perception and discrimination. Monroe Beardsley points out that these are two of the beneficial effects of the experience of aesthetic objects (1958, 574). The internal unity comes about when we contemplate an aesthetic object and "we are taken in hand by it, so to speak, [then] we do often feel a remarkable kind of *clarification*, as though the jumble of our minds were being sorted out" (ibid.). As far as the refined perception and powers of discrimination are concerned, I have already argued that these skills, practiced so well by Eliot and (Henry) James, are necessary for acts of kindness to be effective. It is what Marcel means when he speaks of having an "ear" for experience: "The word 'ear' in its aesthetic sense means something infinitely more subtle, a certain faculty for appreciating relationships" (1973, 6). For without this ability, one could not achieve the situational sensitivity required for practical wisdom to triumph over being one of the "men of maxims," and one would therefore be incapable of appreciating the good of the other. Accordingly, Beardsley argues that if aesthetic experience could make people "more sensitive and perceptive," "then this would have a wide bearing upon all other aspects of our lives—our emotional relations with other people, for example" (1958, 574). To this perception should be compared the discussion in Chapter 2 of the way in which warmth of generosity shows how we are tempered, like a knife or other tool, so that the kind person lives in the state of feeling attunement to the needs and desires of others. This is a particular modality of the more general fact that, as we saw in Chapter 4, our flesh is already adapted for relationships.

Beardsley also observes (1958, 575) that the experience of aesthetic objects develops the imagination so that one can learn to see things from another person's perspective, that of the artist, even when that point of view is quite foreign. This is an attitude, he tells us, that "fosters mutual sympathy and understanding" (ibid.). I can open myself to the work, be taught by it, and learn something new from it—even though, because it requires my active complicity, this experience might be very difficult to attain.[7] The contemplation of aesthetic objects is therefore also, he states, a preventative for mental problems. Conversely, I can always misperceive and distort a work of art by trying to see or listen to it according to the interpretive categories I impose on it. When I impose ideological filters on the work of art, I will find in it only what I put there myself.

Just so, as we have seen at several junctures of this book, kindness rests on the possibility of imaginative self-transposal into the perspective of the other. Indeed, Herbert Spiegelberg seems to have been thinking about the connection of empathy and aesthetic experience when he said of self-transposal that, "An actor impersonating different roles knows best what this implies" (1986, 102). Because this self-transposal allows for an empathetic understanding of others, I can be taught by and learn from them. In addition, the aesthetic experiences of which Beardsley writes can both form a model for, and prepare someone for, heeding Hallie's advice of taking the perspective of the victim instead of the victimizer.

The will that produces acts of kindness is poetic in another way as well, namely, it is expressive. This aspect of *poiesis* is closer to the Heideggerean sense of "bringing forth," of a blossom bursting into bloom, which we examined in Chapter 4. As we saw, for Heidegger, with an artwork the "bursting forth" does occur with the work, but only as it refers to the artist. As a result, both the work produced as well as the activities that are invested in the work are expressive. Value is both brought into being and expressed in the same movement. In kindness, as in artistic creation, "Expression is the revelation of the self, simply because it causes us to actually *be* what is expressed" (Dufrenne 1973, 380).

One might argue that there is a significant disanalogy between the artists' creative activities and results and those inscribed in acts of kindness. The former will express their visions on canvas, in marble, as a way of living the body in the dance, in performing a piece of music, in an actor's playing a role, and so forth. However, when we perform acts of kindness, we do not express our visions in the other in the same way. Because of the necessity to maintain an appropriate absence from the lives of others, it looks as though we cannot invest ourselves in acts of kindness in the way artists do with their materials.

This is true, but it does not follow that acts of kindness are not expressive or that they bear no similarity to those of an artist. For what we express in kind acts is precisely that appropriate absence along with the help offered to the other in need. The content of the expression consists of actions to fulfill a desire to facilitate the successful continuation of the other's projects, and *only* that desire. Our success is measured both by our transcendence of merely having the right intention and our appropriate withdrawal from those projects. For the reasons given above, our integrity is likewise expressed, and that expression can have the effect of aestheticizing the environment. As Wittgenstein pointed out in the *Tractatus* (6.43), "[T]he good or bad exercise of the will does alter the world . . . the effect must be that it becomes an altogether different world. It must, so to speak, wax and wane as a whole. The world of the happy man is a different one from that of the unhappy man" (1961, 147).

Dufrenne insightfully addresses the way in which expression can aestheticize the environment, both in the artist's activities and beyond the art world. In the context of discussing the world expressed in the artwork, he states that it possesses a coherent, unified *Weltanschauung* that "is not a doctrine but rather the vital metaphysical element in all men, a way of being in the world which reveals itself in a personality." It is not surprising, he states, that this *Weltanschauung* can become "the world of the aesthetic object, since each man already radiates a world. There is a nimbus of joy around the joyous man. We say of another that he exudes boredom. The effect is such that ordinary objects can change their appearance through the mere presence of someone" (1973, 177).

Just so, there is a nimbus of kindness around the kind person that equally radiates a world of kindness, and we have already looked at several examples of how kindness can aestheticize the environment. It accounts for the way Maggie Tulliver perceives Dr. Kenn in Eliot's *The Mill on the Floss*. It is what Eliot means in *Middlemarch* when she writes that, as we saw in Chapter 3, the "presence of a noble nature, generous in its wishes, ardent in its charity, changes the lights for us" (1965, 819). It also explains how the "large-minded stranger" in Hardy's *Tess of the D'Urbervilles* was able to shame Angel Clare into returning to his wronged bride.

These examples call our attention to the objective side of aesthetic experiences that, up until this point, has been neglected in favor of their subjective aspects. We must now consider aesthetic objects in order to complete the analogy of aesthetic experiences with acts of kindness and appreciating the kind acts of others. There are two major points about the objects of aesthetic experiences that are pertinent to kindness. First, aesthetic objects present themselves to us as worthy of respect.[8] They impose on us a demand to adapt to them rather than the other way around. Thus, for example, when the orchestra begins to play, the audience (generally) becomes quiet. This is not because, or not only because, the loudness of the music usually drowns out conversation, but rather because the audience acknowledges implicitly the respect owed to the music (and the musicians). The same phenomenon occurs, *mutatis mutandis*, with all other artistic media as well. When the play begins, a hush settles over the audience, because they know that they should be quiet as much as because they do not want to miss any of the lines. Most museum visitors at least make a nominal effort to understand what paintings, sculptures, and so forth express rather than *first* imposing on them their own interpretive grid. As Dufrenne puts it, "I submit myself to the work instead of submitting it to my jurisdiction, and I allow the work to deposit its meaning within me" (1973, 393). This is a necessary condition of fulfilling Beardsley's objective of aesthetic objects teaching us to develop a sympathetic understanding of another person's viewpoint, even if quite foreign to our own.

Similarly, whereas the presence of a tool relates me to its creator only indirectly, the aesthetic object unites us with the artist in an I-Thou relationship "without opposing one to the other" (Dufrenne 1973, 113). Furthermore, despite significant differences in our attitudes toward the lovable and the beautiful, there are similarities relevant to the present discussion. Dufrenne notes that, "A man is as disarmed before his beloved as he is before the aesthetic object. He has as little intention of improving the aesthetic object as of transforming his beloved. He would as little dream of using the one as of abusing the other" (1973, 431). An individual not capable of adopting these attitudes, perhaps because locked in egoistic indifference, will lose the possibility of aesthetic experience just as much as of love. Such a person "degrades the aesthetic to the level of the pleasing and the beloved to an occasion for a series of adventures in which he assumes the role of self-satisfied hero" (ibid.).

It is clear how the presentation of the aesthetic object as worthy of respect has its analogue in a life of kindness. That the other for whom we perform acts of kindness stands in the same relationship to us has been both a stated and an unstated premise of all of the descriptions of kindness in Part One. That the other might be quite alien to us, and that we can in principle overcome this obstacle by opening ourselves to, and learning from, her, was also central to the descriptions of empathy in Chapter 3, and to Scheler's wish to make phenomenology the "guardian of dialogue" (Barber 1993). Indeed, if others could rise no higher in our experience than mere tools, there would be no point to kindness at all, and it is this contrary state that is central to most of the examples of victimization that we have analyzed in Part Two.

However, although treating someone with respect is a necessary condition of kindness, we have already seen in Part One that it is not a sufficient condition. As Kant pointed out, one can adopt a respectful attitude toward others with perfect coldhearted consistency. As a result, the first lesson about kindness that aesthetic objects have to teach us must be supplemented by another. This second point of relevance, perhaps less obvious, is that aesthetic objects offer us the possibility of a depth of experience that stands over against the degradation of the aesthetic described above.[9] That depth is gauged in terms of what we discover about, rather than impose on, the aesthetic object. However, it is equally true that we will not make this discovery or have this depth unless we possess the necessary sensitivity that comes from committing ourselves to the aesthetic object. Thus "The more I lay myself open to the work, the more sensitive will I be to its effects. . . . Aesthetic feeling has depth not only because it unifies us but also because it opens us up" (Dufrenne 1973, 405).

Dufrenne applies to the aesthetic object Merleau-Ponty's phenomenology of the pre-reflective, intelligible body sketched in Chapter 1 in order to argue that, "The supreme proof of feeling's depth is that it is intelligent in a way that intelligence as such can never be. . . . [Aesthetic intelligence can know] a sign which is its own meaning, a smile which is tenderness, a motet which is piety" (1973, 406). The depth of the aesthetic feelings provided by the aesthetic object manifests itself in the same register of bodily intelligibility: "A man knows tenderness in a Mozart andante—that singular nuance of tenderness smiling through tears, that delicate joy which has undergone untold tribulations without becoming lost in them—because his depths have been offered substantial nourishment" (ibid.).

The manner in which aesthetic objects can solicit and nourish depths of feeling has its analogue in kindness as follows. First, what corresponds to the aesthetic object is the act of kindness itself: the project of warmly generous service to the other with which we resonate either as its recipient or as a third party. In addition, the attitude that corresponds to the perception of the aesthetic object is, as noted above, what Marcel terms admiration. Admiration in this sense presupposes respect, but it is distinct from it. That distinction is what Wittgenstein had in mind when he said of G. E. Moore (see Chapter 2) that he liked and respected him, but that the latter did not warm his heart. For that, kindness was necessary along with the second type of innocence distinguished in Chapter 2, which Wittgenstein thought Moore did not possess.

In contrast, Maggie Tulliver does sense the extent of loving kindness in Dr. Kenn, and the depth of that kindness is intimately connected to his ability to aestheticize the environment. Eliot states effectively that these depths are at least partly temporal in that the middle-aged have achieved a stability that serves as a rock of refuge for younger, struggling fellow humans. Indeed, she says, the middle-aged constitute a sort of "natural priesthood" (1985, 553). This suggests that there is yet another intimate connection between possessing depths of kindness and maturity. To some degree there is a correlation with chronology, but the latter is neither sufficient nor necessary for maturity. There are some middle-age and older people who will always be immature, and there are occasional youngsters who are precociously mature.

At whatever age, though, the correlation between maturity and depths of kindness appears to rest on the fact that such people are self-assured, non-manipulative, have no need of hidden agendas, and the like. Hence, we return once more to the theme of the capable body at the core of self-esteem, and to the theme of strength advanced in Chapter 6 as part of a new moral psychology. Moreover, although we are rarely able to perceive directly the struggles that it entails, our admiration also extends to the *Aufhebung* behind that strength. This is so, because we suppose that most people are like us, and that, as noted in Chapter 2, Hume pointed out correctly that there is "some particle of the dove kneaded into our frame, along with the elements of the wolf and serpent" (1957, 92). Thus we implicitly conclude that most other people also struggle to rechannel energies into acts of kindness that would have been invested in gaining power over others.

As with aesthetic feelings, the admiration of these depths of kindness opens us up and "broadens us" (Marcel 1984, 202). But just as aesthetic objects differ in their capacities to generate depths of feelings, so also acts of kindness have varying abilities to stimulate corresponding degrees of admiration. We saw in Chapter 1 that acts of kindness fall along a scale of seriousness from the trivial to what Judith Jarvis Thomson called "splendid Samaritanism." Thus other things being equal, a minor act such as picking up a dropped umbrella will not usually produce any deep resonance of feeling,[10] whereas staying up all night consoling the grief-stricken relative of a suicide will normally provoke great admiration. Similarly, Wittgenstein was filled with admiration—a revealing phrase—for his physician who offered him his own house, rather than a hospital, as a place to die. This is why, as noted in Chapter 3, Wittgenstein correlated kindness with being human, not in terms of species membership but rather in a normative sense of fulfillment of our best possibilities.

It is this sense of being human that is at issue in one of the significations of kindness specified by the Dictionary of the French language, *Le Robert*.[11] Under the "second meaning" of *Gentil*, from the Latin *gentilis*, "from family or race," the authors specify "noble by birth" and "noble of heart" in the ethical sense of nobility. The former yields the sort of ideological self-deceptions illustrated in Chapter 6. The nobility of heart, which is of interest here, reflects a kindness that, as a virtue, gives human action dignity by distinguishing and elevating it. It is a quality that indicates the development of virtue: human beings can elevate themselves by kindness to an ethical excellence. As such, kindness honors both the agent and the recipient of the act (s).

Kindness thus actualizes what is most proper to human beings as such, and this quality is contingent, since we can also act with indifference. This is to say that human beings are capable of nobility by elevating themselves, by making their initial condition one of value, and this is an essentially human capacity, because lower life-forms do not perform these valorizing activities. But precisely because kindness is not necessary for actions, but a contingent quality of them, it has an ethical value.

Marcel's own description of the connection between kindness and being human is a "*gaudium essendi*, the joy of existing," without which "we will have only a mutilated and deformed idea of our situation" (1973, 42). The joy of existing provides us with a "primordial existential assurance" (ibid., 43) that not only furnishes the correlation between maturity and the depths of kindness, noted above, but also hope, as described in Chapter 2.

Marcel was also quite worried, correctly, that depth of feeling in contemporary society tends to degenerate into superficiality, joy into "satisfactions" (1984, 202), being into having. By this he means material satisfactions in the ownership of property, which we discussed in Part One in terms of the cycle of insatiable acquisition, boredom, desire, greater acquisition, and so on. At bottom, satisfactions do not satisfy. "Having" does not provide security, and the Rolling Stones provided the leitmotif for this self-defeating way of life when they famously sang, "I can't get no satisfaction."[12] The unhappiness of the acquisitive consciousness forms a stark contrast to the "joy of existence"—as is immediately apparent in any shopping mall before Christmas. It is a question of both a spiritual and an aesthetic degradation, and we shall return to this theme below in terms of the possibilities of aesthetic humanism.

Before doing so, there is one final aspect of the way in which a life of kindness is analogous to aesthetic experience, and that has to do with self-judgment. That is, because acts of kindness honor both agent and recipient, and because kindness is a contingent quality of action for which the agent alone is responsible, kindness also serves as a criterion of self-assessment. But kindness has a wider moral significance, because it can also serve as a vehicle of self-judgment for those who observe others perform such acts. Dufrenne notes that, in the experience of aesthetic objects, "I must make myself conform to what feeling reveals to me and thus match its depth with my own. . . . through feeling, I myself am put in question" (1973, 377). Acts of kindness perform the same function.

Suppose that I see, hear, or read about someone's performing a great act of kindness—especially one of "splendid Samaritanism." For example, some years ago a splendid Samaritan in Miami intervened to save a girl from being gang-raped. Her car had broken down in the wrong place at the wrong time, and she was desperately pleading with the gathering mob to call her father. A total stranger went to her aid, was assured that she was all right but did not believe it, and defended her at the risk of his life. In the event, although she escaped harm (I think), he was severely beaten and subsequently hospitalized.

Now I might read about this case with cold indifference, but if I have any feelings of admiration for the depths of that man's kindness, with its attendant risks and dangers, those feelings *necessarily* put me in question. My admiration is not one thing to which my self-evaluation is adventitiously conjoined. Rather, if there is any depth of feeling with which I resonate that kindness, I cannot admire and not question myself. This is only a particular modality of the facts that, as discussed in Chapter 5, the possibility of community is already schematized in our flesh, and the self is solidary, not solitary. I am necessarily implicated, because through this bodily resonance I am *moved*—perhaps quite against my will—to ask myself what I would have done under the circumstances, whether I would have had the necessary courage to perform the act (s) in question, and so forth. Thus Gilligan notes correctly, "As the knowledge that others are capable of care renders them lovable rather than merely reliable, so the willingness and the ability to care becomes a standard of self-evaluation" (1988, 16).

Aesthetic Humanism

There is at least one more way in which kindness is analogous to aesthetic experience, and that concerns the way in which our experiences of aesthetic objects can underpin a sense of humanism. Dufrenne argues explicitly for such a humanism, and, as we shall see, much of what he says is directly applicable to kindness. The last two paragraphs of the previous section have opened the way to understanding the role of kindness in an aesthetic humanism, because they describe the way in which third parties—and, by extension, larger groups and even whole communities—can use the experience of kindness in their own moral evaluations and therefore make ethical advances.

For Dufrenne, aesthetic humanism is the ability of experiences of works of art to solicit and nourish our specifically and universally human capacities as social acts. When we contemplate an aesthetic object, we "transcend [our] singularity" and open ourselves "to the universally human." Hence, "[A]esthetic contemplation is in essence a social act, much as are, according to Scheler, loving, obeying, and respecting" (1973, 68). The "humanist significance of aesthetic experience" is that it provokes the spectator "to realize the human within him at the same time that he recognizes the human as surrounding him in public" (ibid., 69).

Art therefore "creates a communion which did not exist prior to it" (ibid., 70). Within that communion I know the other through feelings of participation in our mutual contemplation of the work. Who makes up this communion, and what are our relationships with them? Dufrenne makes a distinction between the masses and the subset of them who comprise the public of a particular artwork. From the spectator's point of view, the communion consists of the public that "tends toward humanity," a movement made possible by the work (ibid.), and that public transcends I-Thou relationships. This is because the work creates in its public "a participation, not a cooperation. In this sense, the cohesion of the group is precarious" (ibid., 66). Dufrenne writes here solely from the spectator's perspective, but if we install ourselves in that of the performer, other, more intimate relationships are possible in the public devoted to a particular work. Thus Schutz notes that the "mutual tuning-in relationship" in music is that by which "the 'I' and the 'Thou' are experienced by both participants as a 'We' in vivid presence" (Schut 1964, 161).

For Dufrenne, this movement of the public "toward humanity" would not take place if the work did not give evidence of its creator and, "through him, of the civilization which has inspired him" (Dufrenne 1973, 158). The work is, therefore, a concrete universal in the sense explicated in the Introduction. Thus an obscure artist, "buried in the anonymity of remote ages . . . really has something to say; a humanity in search of itself stammers through him" (ibid., 104). That emergent humanity constitutes "something general [that] resides at the heart of the singular [work of art]"; hence, "it is in the great works of man, as embodied in philosophy and art, that we come across the active creation of humanity" (ibid., 480–481). We identify with this creation through feelings of participation, as when, for example, we recognize joy in Mozart's *Jupiter* symphony. The essence of the symphony is therefore "a means of realizing a human essence by assuming the human condition precisely in its singularity" (ibid., 482).

What is true of works of art in their role of advancing an aesthetic humanism applies equally well to kindness in the ethical realm. Contemplating acts of kindness likewise leads us out of our singularity and opens us to what is universally human. Here also we recognize the universally human within us and with and in others. For example, when we consider the stranger's act of saving the Miami girl from vicious sexual assault, we become aware of a possibility not particular to that splendid Samaritan. We are cognizant of the fact that all of us may have to face the dreadful choice between life and limb and saving a victim. We are also aware through media distribution of the story that wider circles of anonymous readers also recognize these facts and perhaps reflect on the same questions we do. Thus our contemplation of this admirable act of kindness becomes a social act.

Dufrenne points out that, in the creation of a public for an artwork, a communion is created that did not exist before it. Our participation with others in this public is based on our feelings for the work and on those feelings we share with others who make up that public. We also saw that that public had a "precarious" unity, even though it made progress toward humanity in its mutual participation that would have been impossible without the work.

These descriptions apply as well to social contemplation of acts of kindness. Acts of kindness bring about a communion that would not otherwise have emerged because, as noted above, my feelings of admiration for the other's kindnesses necessarily put me in question, and what is true of me is true of all other observers who respond admiringly to the act of kindness in question. They make up the public of that act. The unity of the group, also one of participation rather than cooperation, is likewise precarious because of its anonymous membership and because its boundaries will fluctuate substantially depending on who continues to contemplate the act and how they conclude their self-examinations. Even so, members of the group can make some progress toward humanity in contemplating the act, examining their own lives, and through whatever social action is appropriate to improve society—in the Miami case, eliminating the conditions that made the act of sacrifice necessary.

Art and communion are also intimately linked in one other way that directly conjoins kindness and aesthetic experience. Marcel notes in his essay on "Authentic Humanism" that the "fundamental existential assurance" that makes hope possible "relates to the structural conditions that allow an individual to open himself to others" (1973, 39)—or that prevent that openness. As detailed in Part One, these structural conditions include the political process, racism, sexism, poverty, class prejudice, and the like, as well as architecture and urban design that mold people's lives. Here it is a question of the aesthetic quality of these latter two factors and their implications for the connection between aesthetic humanism and kindness.

This is effectively the theme of postmodernist rejections of modernist architecture, particularly the Bauhaus school and its grand rational planners such as Le Corbusier and Mies van der Rohe.[13] That is, one important aspect of postmodern architecture is the way in which it criticizes the unkindness of architectural modernism. The latter "originated with an enlightened ideal: rational design was to be consistent with a rational society based on the myth of modernization and the rejection of the past; machinism is seen as the source of happiness and blossoming as, for example, in Le Corbusier's house-machine" (Compagnon 1994, 117). Thus, for example, the Bauhaus school insisted that "Form follows function," and insisted on a universal "geometrical purism" (ibid., 116).

However, as Compagnon goes on to point out, in the wake of the Bauhaus' exile to the United States, technology "had given birth to totalitarianism," and the "fiasco of modernism" was soon clear (ibid., 117). Thus architectural postmodernism based itself on the facts that not only had modernism not led to genuine liberation, but that, quite to the contrary, it had contributed directly to increasing social alienation. Peter Blake, as Compagnon points out, dates "the end of modernism as July 15, 1972, at 3:32 P.M. (more or less), when several St. Louis apartment buildings built in the 1950s were dynamited because they had become uninhabitable" (ibid., 118).[14] Some of Le Corbusier's *cités radieuses* almost came to the same end, a fate that, for Compagnon, "perfectly illustrates the deterioration of the myth of modernism with its metaphors of the machine and the factory" (ibid.).

Architectural postmodernism, in contrast, rejects functional universalism. It is eclectic, local, and based on "a tolerant syncretism." It counters modernist geometrical purity with "ambiguity, plurality, and coexistence of styles" (Compagnon 1994, 116, 119). It is also playful, self-parodying, and even anarchic, but more livable and humane. It is kinder, because it does not consist of massive projects fueled by an optimistic vision imposed on people's lives but rather celebrates their diversity, self-determination, creativity, and spontaneity.[15]

In a similar way, kindness celebrates the freedom of the spirit rather than a vision of rules imposed on it. As noted in Part One, the life of kindness is subject to rules without being rule determined. The people of whom we have the fondest memories are not hide-bound rule followers, such as Eliot's "men of maxims," but those who adapted rules to an ardent, inventive charity. In so doing, they showed that kindness bespeaks one of the best possibilities of human existence, not as naïve enthusiasm but as the critical enterprise of realistically seeking the good of the other as explained throughout this book. Filtered by legitimate suspicion, it still remains against all obstacles, risks, and disappointments, attached through feelings of admiration for others to whom it wishes to be of service. It is a courageous struggle to persevere in the type of innocence that can be gained rather than that which can be lost, and to bring goodness into being within what well-founded suspicion reveals as the limits of one's situations.

Kindness is a difficult commitment because, although continually praised, it is paradoxically and deeply counter-cultural. There are at least three reasons for this. Our culture continues to stress hardness and toughness, it fosters a distrust of anything that looks "soft," and it mistakenly consigns kindness to that denigrated category. By the same token, it overlooks the real strength required to be kind. In addition, also ingrained in our culture is a radical individualism that, as noted in Chapter 5, does not logically imply, but is much more congenial to, egoistic indifference.

It also follows that a life of kindness is much more likely to flourish in a society whose young develop morally along the lines that Gilligan describes as typical for girls than according to those that have traditionally obtained for boys in this country. Bordo is surely right when she complains of the "depressing . . . fact that when masculinity gets symbolically 'undone' in this culture, the deconstruction nearly always lands us in the territory of the degraded, while when femininity gets symbolically undone, the result is an immense elevation in status. . . . The macho-woman pays homage to the heroic myths of masculinity" (1994, 290).[16] Part of the challenge to the role that kindness will play in human flourishing in the twenty-first century and beyond will be to develop other and more honorable ways of becoming men and women.

The third reason that a life of kindness is counter-cultural is because it has become increasingly difficult to reach the depths of feelings that nourish kindness and that are necessary for an aesthetic humanism. There is much in our culture that distorts and compresses those depths into shallow, ephemeral gratification. This is what Marcel meant when he wrote that the joy of existence has been degraded to satisfactions that leave us without existential assurance and hope. However, it was not Marcel, but another French philosopher, Gilles Lipovetsky, who most compellingly illustrated this transition of mass culture to the ephemeral, and his own view of that culture is much more nuanced than Marcel's. Rather than consigning these contemporary trends to a "sociology of shadows," he would locate them somewhat ambiguously closer to the light.

In *The Empire of Fashion* (1994), Lipovetsky argues in relevant part that the hallmarks of mass culture are its ephemerality and superficiality, and fashion is both its general form as well as driving force. In turn, Lipovetsky takes clothing as the most representative area of fashion and focuses most of his attention on it. He wants to underscore the increasing power of fashion in society, as well as fashion's ability to cast its aura of evanescence and attractiveness over much of the rest of society—for example, the extension of the consumer mentality to voting. As he sees it, fashion is no longer merely decorative, but rather has firmly established its hegemony by being woven into the very warp and woof of the structure of society.

The current era of fashion is that of open, more democratized fashion, as opposed to hierarchical, aristocratic, sumptuary fashion of haute couture that concentrated on luxury, privilege, and conspicuous consumption. It is to that phase, which lasted until the 1950s, that the class-based explanations of mass culture in the writings of Jean Baudrillard and especially Pierre Bourdieu are most relevant. The revolution that brought it down "corresponds to the emergence of what Americans were the first to call 'ready-to-wear,' " (Lipovetsky 1994, 90), which in turn was made possible because of improved manufacturing technology that produced great quantities of good-quality clothing at a reasonable cost.

The democratic ideal of egalitarianism is only one factor responsible for the era of open fashion. It is also a question of a synergy of values that include sports and "the new individualist ideal of the youthful look" (ibid., 99). For sports as for clothing, the combination of mass-produced objects and the leisure to enjoy them has motivated the emergence of a "hedonistic, juvenile mass culture" (ibid.). This is to say that a youth aesthetics has replaced a class aesthetics. As Yves Saint-Laurent observed, elegance is no longer the goal; rather, it is now seduction. Role models are reversed: "Before," Saint-Laurent states, "a girl wanted to look like her mother. Today, it's the other way around" (ibid., 100). The old haute couture that served as a mark of distinction for the successful woman has given way to "the new requirement of individualism: a youthful appearance" (ibid.).

Diverse styles of clothing reflect this pursuit of youthfulness. Fashions have replaced fashion, and informal, casual clothes have supplanted formal wear. Previous taboos have been abolished in favor of democratically pluralistic approaches to youthful appearances. Elegance has yielded to clothes that can be torn, frayed, and sloppy but also frivolous and irreverent. Indeed, it is very difficult to be absolutely *out* of fashion. This tolerant, youthful aesthetics, as Lipovetsky sees it, also leads to greater kindness. People no longer ridicule the handicaps of others and/or make fun of outdated clothing. Similarly, "Flexibility in fashion, deep aversion to violence and cruelty, a new sensitivity toward animals, an awareness of the importance of listening to others . . . efforts to find peaceful solutions to social conflicts—these are all aspects of the same general process of modern democratic civilization" (ibid., 119–20).

A cult of the body also functions in tandem with the cult of youthful appearance.[17] It demands "the same narcissistic self-surveillance, the same need for information, and the same adaptation to novelty" (ibid., 102). Anyone who has seen skin cream commercials on television has observed this dynamic. Body works are youth works for men as much as for women. In fact, in France, if not also in the United States, older men now spend more time at it than do women.

For Lipovetsky, the era of open fashion is also that of "consummate fashion," the hegemony of fashion. Fashion is not confined to one sector of the social world; rather, it is the "general form at work in society as a whole." Everyone is to some extent involved with fashion, "and the triple operation that specifically drives fashion is increasingly implemented: the operation of *ephemerality*, *seduction*, and *marginal differentiation*." Advertising "has replaced ideological solemnity, while the seductiveness of consumption and pop psychology" has displaced traditional disciplines of democracy (ibid., 131; emphasis in original). It is not that this fashion form of "ephemerality, seduction, and marginal differentiation" affects everything in society or that it affects equally everything it does influence. There are, after all, as he points out, economic catastrophes, murders, nuclear disasters, wars, racism, labor strikes, and so forth to which fashion is irrelevant. Rather, the fashion form is a matter of a "dominant historical tendency" that significantly colors our social atmosphere (ibid., 132). Accordingly, we now have designer pasta, computers, eyeglasses, sunglasses, and a plethora of accessory items that are much more cheerful and playful manifestations of personalized lifestyles. Contrary to the "form follows function" design spirit of the Bauhaus, and in which design has been opposed to fashion, Lipovetsky points out that the aesthetic appearance of the product is now seen as integral to the design, to the function of the product.

The fashion form is also deeply embedded in advertising. Advertising is "communication structured like fashion, more and more under the sway of the spectacular, personalized appearance, pure seduction. . . . Everywhere we turn we encounter reality cosmeticized, value added in the fashion mode" (ibid., 158–59). Both in form and content, advertising seduces through the power of frivolous, ephemeral images. It entices and incites rather than controls. Its power has nothing to do with a "panoptic totalitarian logic" (ibid., 163) à la Foucault. Rather than threatening freedom, advertising actually appeals to a low level of it "where a state of indifference reigns, where there is an excess of choice among scarcely differentiated options" (ibid., 165). And what works for things works for people as well: they are marketed according to the same fashion dynamic of ephemerality, seduction, and marginal differentiation. In other words, how they are dressed (literally) is not a decorative addition but is integral to the design of the "product." Marginal differentiation here entails that there are few substantial differences between, say, television news anchors or packaged political candidates for whom ephemeral sound bites and photo opportunities take the place of reasoned public discourse.

The same principles apply to the media generally, "a powerful machine controlled by the laws of accelerated renewal, ephemeral success, seduction, and marginal differences" (ibid., 174). Mass media culture is a "culture of consumption, wholly constructed in view of immediate pleasure and mental recreation. Its seductiveness stems in part from its simplicity" (ibid., 178). Previous generations were connected much more intimately to their pasts. But today, all mass cultural products are perishable; speed conquers all. Frenetic activities on television screens portray American society as an exhausting search for instant gratification. As Lipovetsky sees it, "A culture of narrative is being replaced, as it were, by a culture of movement; a lyric or melodic culture is being superceded by a cinematic culture constructed around shock and the deluge of images. . . . Only pure stimulation remains, without memory: reception in the fashion mode" (ibid., 179–180). Moreover, the kind of electronic stimulation with which Lipovetsky was familiar consisted of television, radio, and movies. Since he wrote, the Internet has come to be a much more important source of such stimulation and, what he would predict, its hottest sector, the World Wide Web, has grown by leaps and bounds because of the discovery that it could become a tool of frivolous consumption. Indeed, it is not too much to say that a new phase of consummate fashion has arisen in mass-media culture with the Internet and the Information Age generally.

For Lipovetsky, the fashionable world of the mass media gives us "the best and the worst, inseparably: news around the clock, and zero-degree thinking" (ibid., 11). They show us everything almost completely devoid of judgment. Thus they reinforce the tolerant, non-coercive, pluralistic *Zeitgeist* of fashion. The media "help orchestrate the new profile of anxious but tolerant narcissistic individualism with open morality and a weak or inconsistent superego. In various realms the media have succeeded in replacing churches, schools, families, political parties, and labor unions as agencies of socialization and transmission of knowledge" (ibid., 193). (You can even go to church on the Web.)

Mass media give us more information than ever before, but the knowledge that results is fragile and superficial. The great ideologies of the past presented themselves as valid beyond the immediacy of the present. In contrast, mass-media information offers "fewer speculative syntheses, but more facts; less meaning, but more technical details" (ibid.). We hear fewer reasoned arguments, but we get more news flashes about events.

These reflections on the ephemerality of mass culture are doubly interesting for kindness. One of these interests points toward the fact that, as explained in Chapter 3, there are certain senses in which a less judgmental culture does increase in kindness. Nevertheless, as we also saw, individuals or whole cultures deficient in the capacity for judgment, as Lipovetsky takes them to be, face severe obstacles to kindness and the moral point of view generally. Hence, there are important implications for democracy in the hegemony of fashion, of which he is well aware, and for education, which he does not mention in *The Empire of Fashion*.

The second and closely related interest concerns the consequences for aesthetic humanism posed by ephemeral mass culture. Even if one does not accept that the fashion form dominates in contemporary society, an unbiased observer would have to admit its prevalence. Even vice these days lives in the fashion mode.[18] Further, despite the fact that the ascendancy and democratization of fashion have led to greater tolerance and more autonomy, it remains true that the increase in the fashion form does rest in large part on a narcissistic individualism inscribed in the intertwining cults of the body and youthful appearance. This fact suggests that the prevalent conception of self-identity, or individuality, is that which has no depth of character development or other aesthetic depths of the type described by Dufrenne. Rather, this fashionable self lives at the level of the aesthetic in Søren Kierkegaard's sense. This is the life of the butterfly that flits from one ephemeral seductive pleasure to another, but this time in an image culture. The downside of this style of life, as Kierkegaard knew well, is that "The euphoria of fashion has its counterparts in dereliction, depression, and existential anguish. . . . We have more personal autonomy, but also more personal crises" (Lipovetsky 1994, 241). However, although Kierkegaard thought of the aesthetic as merely a "stage on life's way," contemporary mass culture appears to have enshrined it.

The ephemerality of experience, the absence of judgment, and the intertwined cults of narcissistic youth and the body hardly conduce to experiences of kindness that both draw from, and contribute to, the depths of experience that will anchor an aesthetic humanism. Yet perhaps the conflict can be mitigated by Dufrenne's distinction between the masses and the public of the artwork. By analogy, admiration for acts of kindness as well as encouragement for developing lives of kindness can flourish in groups or individually, because the acts at issue can also have their publics that are distinct from the masses. Of course, those "publics" will be influenced by mass culture. However, the very fact that contemporary mass culture has widened the boundaries of tolerance and autonomy may provide individuals and groups the freedom they need to remain counter-cultural until society changes enough to rediscover the depths of experience beneath the images and ephemeral appearances. Concomitantly, they will come to appreciate the truth of Auden's observation that, "We must love one another or die" (1979, 88), and that love does not live on appearances alone.

Notes

Notes to Introduction

1. The progenitor of this reexamination was Alisdair MacIntyre (1981). Other recent works in this area are George Fletcher (1993), J. R. Lucas (1993), Terrance Mc-Connell (1993), and Martha C. Nussbaum (1990, 1994, 1995a, 1999).
2. For further details on these developments and on the resurgence of virtue ethics generally, see Midgley (1993).
3. See Schlick (1939), see especially the last chapter, "What Paths Lead to Value Fulfillment [*Wertwollen*]?" There is no word for "kindness" in ordinary German. Schlick uses *Das Güte*, as distinct from the more shallow, ephemeral phenomenon of *Freundlichkeit*. In ordinary German, *freundlich* could sometimes be synonymous with "kind," but more serious discussions distinguish them. Thus Otto Friedrich Bollnow states, "Goodness [*Güte*] in many respects is related to friendliness [*Freundlichkeit*]. . . . Friendliness lives more on the surface, but goodness is rooted really in the depth of the heart" (1962, 12–13). Elsewhere, on p. 9, he notes that in the history of the German language, the "present-day meaning" of *Güte* developed from *Herzengüte*.
4. For a more detailed consideration of this theme, along with related comments on Spencer's *Faerie Queen*, see "Kindness" in Hamrick (1985a, 203–204).
5. "A White Supremacist Group Seeks a New Kind of Recruit," by Pam Belluck, *The New York Times*, July 7, 1999, p. 1.
6. By "decency" I do not mean merely a negative or minimal morality, only beyond which is something morally worth praising. Thus Philip Hallie writes, "To follow the negative ethic you need only clean hands, not active ones. The negative laws make up the ethic of decency. . . . But to follow the positive ethic, to be one's brother's keeper, is to be more than decent; it is be active, even aggressive. It involves going out of one's way for another. . . . If the negative ethic is minimal, the positive ethic is maximal" (1982, 168–69; see also 1997, 26–27, 175–76). Throughout this book, my use of "decency" will embrace both the active and the passive, the doing of good as well as the avoidance of evil, caring for others in addition to avoiding harming them. This use of the term corresponds more closely to the ordinary English of "doing the decent thing," though Hallie is right that it does not reach superogatory acts.
7. One regrets the absence of a contemporary Erasmus to capture properly the pathetic aspects of the 1980s. More than 400 years ago, the gentle humanist from Rotterdam had Folly opine, "Most foolish of all, and the meanest, is the whole tribe

259

of merchants, for they handle the meanest sort of business by the meanest methods, and although their lies, perjury, thefts, frauds and deceptions are everywhere to
be found, they still reckon themselves a cut above everyone else simply because their
fingers sport gold rings" (Erasmus 1971, 142). How might Erasmus have updated
his description of merchants if Leona Helmsley, Charles Keating, Carl Ichan, and
Martin Milken had been in the audience? Perhaps just the trappings changed:
Rolexes and BMWs for gold rings. *Plus ça change.*

8. The mid-1990s rash of layoffs—ironically balanced these days by acute labor shortages—was graphically illustrated in a series of seven front-page stores in *The New
York Times* during the first week of March 1996. The title of the first article, "On
the Battlefields of Business, Millions of Casualties," could well have stood as the
title for the whole series, but just as revealing were the other titles: "The Company
as Family, No More," "Big Holes Where the Dignity Used to Be," "A Hometown
Feels Less Like Home," "In the Class of 70, Wounded Winners," "The Politics of
Layoffs: In Search of a Message," and "A Search for Answers to Avoid the Layoffs."

9. "At the richest time in the nation's history, housing that the poor can afford is at an all-
time low, fueling an increase in homelessness, according to the United States Conference of Mayors." "Homeless Defy Cities' Drives to Move Them," by Evelyn Nieves,
New York Times, December 7, 1999, p. 1. The same article details the popularity of
laws passed in many cities to prosecute the homeless who sleep in public spaces.

10. See "Gap Between Rich and Poor Found Substantially Wider," by David Cay Johnston, *The New York Times*, September 5, 1999, p. A14. See also "In a Time of
Plenty, the Poor Are Still Poor," by Richard W. Stevenson, *The New York Times*,
January 23, 2000, section 4, p. 3. The latter article reports that, according to the U.S.
Census Bureau, the poverty rate in 1998 was 12.7 percent, which was less than 15.1
percent in 1993 but almost identical to the rate at the height of the last economic
expansion in 1989. "And it is worse than in 1969, the year the previous record-
setting expansion ended, when 12.1 percent of Americans lives in poverty." As far
as income is concerned, the average for those of the poorest 20 percent of Americans dropped 5 percent "between the late 1970s and the late 1990s, after adjusting
for inflation." In contrast, the Economic Policy Institute and the Center on Budget
and Policy Priorities report that the average income in the top 20 percent of families rose 33 percent.

11. "Clinton's Cosmetic Poverty Tour," *The New York Times*, July 8, 1999, p. A.25.
When Rudolph Giuliani, the mayor of New York City, infamously decided to have
the homeless arrested, "The *New York Post* quoted one man swept up in the crack-
down as follows: 'I'm not on crack, I'm not mentally ill. I just could not afford to pay
rent.' " See Molly Ivins, "When the Boom Ends, Many People Will Be Flat
Busted," *St. Louis Post-Dispatch*, December 5, 1999, p. B3.

12. "More Working Families Turn to Food Pantries," *St. Louis Post-Dispatch*, March
11, 1998, p. A4. The article also reports, "Hunger experts said one reason [for food
pantries serving more and more of the working poor] is corporate downsizing and
a technology-driven economy that leave people without key skills in dead-end,
low-wage jobs." As one reporter noted on its 150th anniversary, the *Communist
Manifesto* "recognized the unstoppable wealth-creating power of capitalism, pre-
dicted it would conquer the world, and warned that this inevitable globalization of

national economies and cultures would have divisive and painful consequences." Paul Lewis, "Marx's Stock Resurges on a 150-Year Tip," *The New York Times,* June 27, 1998, p. A17.

13. "The Poor Still Pay More," by Molly Ivins, *St. Louis Post-Dispatch,* April 12, 2000, p. B15. Furthermore, the IRS even subjects the poor to audits more than it does the rich. See "I.R.S. More Likely to Audit the Poor and not the Rich," by David Cay Johnston, *The New York Times,* April 16, 2000.

This demonization of the poor has returned *con brio* as a critique of "compassionate conservatism." Dinesh D'Souza, for instance, a scholar at the American Enterprise Institute and who also worked in the Reagan White House, decries "the propensity of the poor to indulge in social pathologies, be it drugs, alcohol, wife beating, divorce, illegitmacy or abortion." Walter Goodman, "Let Them Eat Microchips, *The New York Times,* March 4, 2001, p. 4–3. Clearly D'Souza never watched *Dallas* or, in an earlier age, *Peyton Place,* but in any case, his view is that "[T]he guy who is worth little has probably produced little of value. By the same token, the guy who's earning twice as much as you is most likely—perish the thought—twice as good as you are" (*Ibid.*). Goodman is right to conclude that "[I]n a philosophy where the losers have only themselves to blame, you can't go wrong by picking on the undeserving poor" (*Ibid.*)

14. "In Television's New Reality, Temptation Puts Vows to Test," by Bill Carter, *The New York Times,* January 8, 2001, front page.

15. Elián is "the latest pawn in our culture's increasingly pornographic exploitation of children." As one network executive put it, "For TV, it's plain old voyeurism." Janet Reno's appeal to "turn off the TV lights" on Elián went unnoticed. Why were we so willing to blame either his Miami relatives or Fidel Castro, "but not our own voyeuristic enabling of the worst excesses of our media culture?" "America Finds Another Jon Benet," by Frank Rich, *The New York Times,* April 22, 2000, p. A27. See also "Television's New Voyeurism Pictures Real-Life Intimacy," by Bill Carter, *The New York Times,* January 30, 2000, p. 1.

16. "IPO Outlook: 'Adult' Web Sites Profit, Though Few Are Likely to Offer Shares," by Dunstan Prial, *Wall Street Journal,* March 8, 1999, p. B10: "'What's really successful is hardcore pornography,'" said Mark Hardie, a senior research analyst at Forrester Research in Cambridge, Mass. But the raunchier the content, the less chance there is that an investment bank would touch an IPO proposal by the operator of such a site,' he said." In addition, a number of American corporations— including General Motors (GM), AT&T, Time Warner, Marriott International, and Hilton—make millions of dollars every year on sex films. GM alone makes more money on pornography each year through its subsidiary DirecTV than does Larry Flynt's *Hustler* enterprises. See "Technology Sent Wall Street into Market for Pornography," by Timothy Egan, *The New York Times,* October 23, 2000, p. 1.

17. Effectively, what President Clinton was arguing for consists of what Daniel Goleman has described as "managing your emotions." Goleman (1995, 43) points out the obvious necessity of such a skill for maintaining civility and even democracy itself. In Chapter 5 we shall examine certain institutional examples of these skills.

18. "Have a #%!&$! Day: Looking for Civility in America," *The New York Times,* October 18, 1993, p. B4.

19. Heidegger's example, cited by Merleau-Ponty (1968, 115, n. 2), concerns the former's high school that, "For us who look at it or ride by, it is different than for the pupils who sit in it. . . . You can, as it were, smell the being of this building in your nostrils. The smell communicates the being of this essent far more immediately and truly than any description or inspection could ever do" Heidegger (1959, 33).

20. As far as Husserl is concerned, it is worth considering here Ludwig Landgrebe's arguments in his analysis of Husserl's lectures published as "First Philosophy," vol. 2, originally given in 1922–1923. There Husserl tried to "reduce" down to a givenness of pure apodicticity, but according to Landgrebe, he discovered that the project fails, since horizons are ever-present and essential. The desired foundation is not workable (Landgrebe 1970, 259–306). I am indebted to Claude Evans for this reference.

21. The address was given at Victoria University, Wellington, New Zealand, on March 31, 1995. It was reprinted and cited, in *The New York Review of Books*, vol. XLII, no. 11, June 22, 1995, p. 36. Havel also appropriately commended those intellectuals "who are mindful of the ties that link everything in this world together, who approach the world with humility, but also with an increased sense of responsibility, who wage a struggle for every good thing" (1995, 37).

22. Schneider himself now appears to have been a fraud, but the value of Merleau-Ponty's strategy, I believe, can survive this inconvenient intrusion of fact! For more on Schneider's case, see Howard Gardner (1975, 143–47).

23. Ms. Maclaren used this expression in a paper titled "Emotion, Blind Recognition, and the Habit Body: a Merleau-Pontian Rethinking of James and Sartre on Emotions," read to the Merleau-Ponty Circle meeting in Wrexam, Wales, July 1999.

24. As we shall see below, this is only one of many similarities in Ricoeur's and Nussbaum's views of the relationships of philosophy and literature. These resemblances are striking, because *Love's Knowledge* is devoid of references to *Time and Narrative*, just as, later, *Poetic Justice* was of *Oneself as Another*. Ricoeur, for his part (1992, 191, 243), was aware of and admired Nussbaum's *The Fragility of Goodness*. Carol Gilligan is a good example of a thinker who employs Ricoeur's and Nussbaum's insights about literature "depragmatizing" the Lifeworld. See, for instance, her instructive uses of Checkhov (1982, 1993 printing, 5), Virgil (1988, 3–6, 13–14), and Jane Austen (1988, 18).

25. Compare Merleau-Ponty's argument, within the context of Gestalt psychology, that every elementary perception has a figure-ground structure and "is therefore already charged with *meaning*" (1962, 4; emphasis in original).

26. Nussbaum cites approvingly Paul Gewirtz's claim that "Literature makes its special claims upon us precisely because it nourishes the kinds of human understanding not achievable through reason alone but involving intuition and emotion as well" (1988, cited at Nussbaum 1990, 43n). I agree with his view of literary understanding, but his suggestion that philosophy is based solely on reason devoid of "intuition and emotion" is mistaken. Phenomenologists have long shown why such a split between the cognitive and the emotive is insupportable. There are differences between philosophy and literature, but this is not one of them.

27. Cf. Merleau-Ponty's self-direction to "Make an analysis of literature in this sense: as *inscription* of Being" (1968, 197).

28. "We could never have loved the earth so well if we had had no childhood in it. . . . Our delight in the sunshine on the deep bladed grass today, might be no more than the faint

perception of wearied souls, if it were not for the sunshine and the grass in the far-off years, which still live in us and transform our perceptions into love" (Eliot 1985, 74). As Mikel Dufrenne notes (1973, 402–403), "[P]sychology tends to accentuate child-hood experiences, not merely because they come from childhood but because they are decisive, because the man repeats the child. . . . We are authorized to seek depth in the past because we can afterward verify that it was pregnant with a future."

29. At a certain juncture in the story, James writes about a crucial encounter between the Prince and Charlotte Stant. They stood silently, "facing and faced," "grasping and grasped," "meeting and met." Then "everything broke up, broke down, gave way, melted and mingled. Their lips sought their lips, their pressure their response and their response their pressure; with a violence that had sighed itself the next moment to the longest and deepest stillnesses they passionately sealed their pledge (James 1985, 259).

30. As far as I know, it has never been pointed out how this claim is necessarily true. A thought, or anything else, cannot simultaneously be the contained as well as the container. Thus phrased, Merleau-Ponty's point runs parallel to Bertrand Russell's well-known argument that sets cannot be members of themselves (1964, 262ff.).

Notes to Chapter I

1. Updike (1983, 34), cited at Leder (1990, 74).
2. Suffering differs from pain, both logically and phenomenologically. Erich Loewy argues that "pain can become suffering when it is seen to serve no purpose and, in that sense, to have no meaning" (1991, 4). This cannot be right. Literally painstak-ing care (of children, aged parents, patients, and the like) can be both painful and meaningful (purposeful) suffering. More generally, Loewy claims, "Pain is neither a necessary nor a sufficient condition of suffering" (ibid., 8). He is correct about the latter because, for instance, those whose exercise regimens are driven by the maxim, "No pain, no gain," will not only not suffer in the presence of pain but will posi-tively rejoice in its presence. But it is wrong to say that pain is not a necessary con-dition of suffering, a claim that he supports with examples that are implausible on their faces. One of them is that a mother could undergo the "extreme suffering" of "watching her child being beaten to death while she stands helplessly by" with no physical pain (ibid.). Surely such a claim constitutes a *reductio ad absurdum* of the mind-body dualism on which it implicitly rests, regardless of the author's intent, for we are being asked to envisage the possibility of a most intense mental anguish with no physical pain, and such a claim has no support in anything that we know about human experience.
3. I have learned over the years from my many disabled students why this consequence is only probable. In general, the disabled have been among the most determined, well-motivated students in my classes. They have learned how to revalorize their re-maining capacities to preserve as much of a sense of an "I can" as possible and to use them as a foundation for self-esteem.
4. See also here Tom Attig (Hamrick 1985a, 161–76).

5. The current euphemism for "handicapped" is "physically challenged." These are *not* synonyms, for my response to a challenge—in my own eyes and in those of others as well—ought to be to try to meet it. Whether successful or not, my self-esteem would rise, and possibly my value (valor) in the eyes of the Other as well. If someone intervened merely in an effort to meet such a challenge, we would call it an interference rather than an intervention, meddling rather than helping. On the contrary, in the present situation, we can see clearly that there are more layers of meaning than someone simply being challenged. See also Chapter 3 for a further discussion of aberrations in similar euphemisms.

6. These contentions mirror settled points of criminal law in which the absence of agency, as in posthypnotic suggestions and sleepwalking cases, negates the necessary *mens rea* required for a crime. Two other pertinent defenses are coercion, as in acting with a gun at one's head, and duress. See Leo Katz (1987, 62–72, 113–22) and Sanford H. Kadish and Monrad G. Paulsen (1975, 76–80, 561–76). The relevance of these legal distinctions to a discussion of kindness is that, while it is very difficult to conceive of an act of kindness being done under coercion, the matter of duress is much more obscure. Suppose a neurotic student did me (what I took to be) a kindness, but whose motive (I subsequently discover) was fear of failing my course. Would it be an act of kindness? If we are tempted to answer negatively, what should we say about Scrooge helping Tiny Tim? About acts of charity by religious believers driven by fear of eternal punishment?

7. See especially Ricoeur's arguments (1992, 77–87) against G.E.M. Anscombe and Donald Davidson for a phenomenology of intentional projects ("similar to the one I once sketched out at the beginning of *The Voluntary and the Involuntary*" [Ricoeur 1992, 86]) that are teleological and not reducible to an ontology of causally determined, agent-less events. We shall return to the subject of motivated freedom in Chapter 3.

8. For a full account of the Trocmés and their fellow villagers, see Hallie (1982, 1997, and especially 1979).

9. See here Sandra Bartky's invaluable studies of psychological oppression (1979, 1990) resulting from "psychic alienation," a concept borrowed from Frantz Fanon, which stems from "stereotyping, cultural domination, and sexual objectification" (1990, 23). In the following chapter, we shall discuss René Magritte's illustration (literally) of this phenomenon, and of much else, in his drawings titled *Le Viol* (*Rape*).

10. For two of the most recent treatments of this disheartening subject, see Brumberg (1997) and Hesse-Biber (1996).

11. The French translation is more graphic and, I believe, revealing, than the pallid English verb "moved." It says that the Good Samaritan saw the victim and was "seized" with pity: "[il] fut saisi de pitié." See also here Wuthnow (1991, 169).

12. Even though omissions to act are thus really actions after all, it is still true that someone has omitted to do something in lieu of something else. Therefore, in what follows, I shall continue to refer to them as omissions to act.

13. One of the oldest senses of "tact" is touch (Lat. *tactus*) from which we also derive "tactile." See *The Shorter Oxford English Dictionary, On Historical Principles*, 2232.

14. This argument simply adapts to the case of persons and kindness, Merleau-Ponty's more general claim that, in perception, "The senses intercommunicate by opening

on to the structure of the thing. One sees the hardness and brittleness of glass. . . . One sees the springiness of steel, the ductility of red-hot steel, the hardness of the plane blade, the softness of shavings" (1962, 229). Compare Wittgenstein's remark, " 'We *see* emotion.'—As opposed to what?—We do not see facial contortions and *make the inference* that he is feeling joy, grief, boredom. We describe a face immediately as sad, radiant, bored, even when we are unable to give any other description of the features. – Grief, one would like to say, is personified in the face. This is essential to what we call 'emotion' " (1990, §570).

15. For more on this point, see Hamrick (1994, 78ff.).

16. For a valuable commentary on the relationship between Merleau-Ponty's phenomenology and *Beloved*, see Diane Enns (1995, 263–79).

17. Compare George Eliot's *The Mill on the Floss* when Philip praises Maggie's eyes: "They're not like any other eyes. They seem trying to speak—trying to speak kindly" (1985, 260).

18. The reason for the qualifier, "human," in this sentence is that, as the work of Frans B. M. de Waal and others shows, the behavior of some other animals evidences kindness, care, and compassion as well. See, for example, De Waal (1996), especially in chapter 2 on "Sympathy" the section titled "Simian Sympathy" (78–82). Elsewhere, Schlick (1939, 164) rejects classical modernist divisions between nature and culture for human beings and argues, against Hobbes, that it is impossible to think adequately about human existence with no reference to culture. But he does not hold on to this insight when he describes the smile and its natural significance. Even more naively, Lawrence J. McGarry has argued that kindness is a "positiveness resonating with our nature," and that, "Nothing is more immediately obvious to us than that we *feel* comfortable in atmospheres of pleasantness, kindness, and uncomfortable in unpleasant, negative ones. And this is so *no matter what our cultures have conditioned us to like or dislike, to feel good or bad about*" (1986, 98, 100; emphasis added). These are the last words of McGarry's book. Unfortunately, he does not go on to answer the obvious question of how kindness could make us feel comfortable and how unkindness could produce discontent, while at the same time we have been conditioned in a contradictory manner. Moreover, to say that "we feel comfortable in atmospheres of pleasantness" and "uncomfortable in unpleasant" ones seems to mean no more than the unilluminating tautology that we feel pleasant in pleasant atmospheres and uncomfortable in uncomfortable ones.

19. It is worth noting here Carol Bigwood's attempt to use Merleau-Ponty's phenomenology of the body as an antidote to certain "poststructuralist feminist theorists [who] hold that the body is merely the product of cultural determinants and that gender is a free-floating device" (1991, 54). She is correct, in my view, not to dismiss the "nature" half of the nature-culture unity of human existence. But in pursuit of a "new model of the body that leads neither to biological determinism nor to gender skepticism and cultural relativism" (ibid., 56), she perhaps goes too far in relying on what she claims is Merleau-Ponty's "attempt to recover a non-cultural, non-linguistic body that accompanies and is intertwined with our cultural existence" (ibid.). The very point of Merleau-Ponty's argument is to deny the possibility of distinguishing nature from culture, so that the natural body could stand by itself and accompany a cultural body, and vice versa. In other words, for Merleau-

Ponty, culture is not a veneer covering a natural base from which it could be detached. It is not clear whether her use of "accompanies" implies this latter view that Merleau-Ponty rejects.

20. An illuminating example, and of Merleau-Ponty's more general argument about culture and nature, concerns certain Asian–Afro-American conflicts. Florence King notes that, "Explaining what it is about Asians that Blacks don't like, the embattled Korean grocer whose Brooklyn store has been the target of a year-long boycott told the *Washington Post:* 'Because we don't laugh so much and don't smile so much, it doesn't seem like we're very kind people.' Blacks are now demanding smiling good cheer of Asians just as white Southerners once demanded it of them" (1992, 54–55).

21. For a more complete discussion of such indirect problem solving relevant to the notion of motivated freedom, see Alfred Schutz (1973, 31–38, 172–75) and James L. Marsh (1989, 134). Also important here, as Marsh adds, following Schutz, is the fact that there are two kinds of motives: " 'because' motives deriving from the person's past and 'in order to' motives present in a project directed toward the future" (ibid.).

22. It is also true that deception and fraud are never completely off the agenda with people we know well, or think we know well. As Geoffrey Moore points out in his Introduction to James' *The Portrait of a Lady*, "It is a constant theme of James's: being taken in by someone you have learned to trust" (James 1986, 18). Likewise, deception about kindness is possible, not only about our perception of other people's actions but also about oneself as well. We will study problems of self-deception in Part Two below.

23. John Locke appears to hold implicitly the contrary view. In his *A Letter Concerning Toleration*, he considers a magistrate who "is afraid of other churches, but not of his own, because he is kind and favorable to the one, but severe and cruel to the other. These he treats like children and *indulges them even to wantonness.* Those he uses as slaves, and how blamelessly soever they demean themselves, recompenses them no otherwise than by galleys, prisons, confiscations, and death" (1950, 53; emphasis added).

24. Brown and Gilligan (1992). See especially "Jesse: Tyranny of Nice and Kind" (53-62). In reviewing this work, Carolyn G. Heilbrun noted that Brown and Gilligan "discovered the startling veracity of young female thought and expression, and the even more amazing submergence of that veracity as adolescence proceeded. The girls were now seen to have moved from 'authentic into idealized' relationships,' sacrificing truth on the altar of niceness" (Heilbrun 1992, 13–14). It is not clear whether Ms. Heilbrun would equate kindness and niceness as Brown and Gilligan apparently do, but they are clearly different here. For girls to be nice to boys, and women to men, in these ways is certainly most unkind to themselves and arguably to boys and men also insofar as it contributes to unjustified male illusions of superiority, consequent discriminatory behavior patterns, and long-term psychological damage. For more on this subject, see Chapter 7.

25. "Réponse à Bordes," in *Oeuvres complètes*, I:136, 137, n. 1. Oddly, Rousseau adds that this gentleness of indifference is the "gentleness which inspires people with the taste for literature."

26. For additional reasons to distinguish gentleness from kindness, see part 2, chapter 2, of Foucault's (1977) *Discipline and Punish,* "The Gentle Way in Punishment."

27. "Treblinka's Other Monster," *The New York Times*, August 21, 1993, p. 13. Franz remained unrepentant after the war and was sentenced to life imprisonment by a German court in 1965. When he was arrested in 1959, he had in his apartment a photograph album of his years at Treblinka that bore the inscription, "The Best Years of My Life." He was quietly released from prison in 1993.

28. The phrase "intend to" is necessary here because, first, kindness can be the instrument of unintended, unsuspected harm. Second, there are certain ambiguous cases in which we can intend to do kindnesses, but which cause unintended, but foreseen, harm or the risk of harm. These types of cases find a fictional embodiment in an event that takes place at the end of Robert Louis Stevenson's *Treasure Island*. The crew refused to take back to England three pirates who were kneeling in supplication on a sand spit past which the *Hispaniola* sailed. Jim recorded the crew's deep regret, but that they "could not risk another mutiny; and to take them home for the gibbet would have been a cruel sort of kindness" (Stevenson 1911, 270). The general form of this type of cruel kindness appears, then, to amount to providing short-term aid necessary for the welfare of the other, but at the price of causing, or taking the risk of causing, more serious long-term harm. We will look at certain non-fictional examples in Chapter 3.

Notes to Chapter 2

1. One finds the same theme in Dufrenne (1973, 381) and in Emerson: "In strict science all persons underlie the same condition of an infinite remoteness" (1937, 108). However, it is equally important to stress that, as we saw in the last chapter, Wild, Emerson, and Levinas provide us with only half of the picture of how the Other appears to us. Given our common lexicon of corporeity, as described earlier, I and the Other are so closely bound together in common situations that communication and community are what is primary. This primacy is shown in our initial conviction that we have something in common with the stranger.

2. This fictional example apparently has a real historical importance. I remember reading years ago in a now unfindable volume of *American Heritage* that Aaron Burr was shown this passage some time after his famous duel with Alexander Hamilton. He is said to have replied that, had he read the text earlier, he would have been swayed more by kindness than justice, and Hamilton would still be living.

3. There are sometimes cases of seeming inconsistencies in kindness that turn out not to be such. Hitler, for example, was apparently kind to (Aryan) children and to all lobsters, which he could never bear to eat or see killed. But he befriended these defenseless beings only because doing so fed his colossal egoism and meglomania.

4. Merleau-Ponty's pertinent comments about Schneider also apply, *mutatis mutandis*, to the egoistic (in Schlick's sense) inability to perceive the appeal of the other. In both cases there are "deficiencies affecting the junction of sensitivity and significance, deficiencies which disclose the existential conditioning of both. . . . In the normal subject the object 'speaks' and is significant . . . whereas in the patient the meaning has to be brought in from elsewhere by a veritable act of interpretation" (1962, 131).

5. Martha Nussbaum argues for the same position for the same reasons (1995a, 60–63). It is striking to read her descriptions of the intelligibility and intentionality of the emotional life in apparent unawareness of its long phenomenological explication from Heidegger and Scheler through Sartre, Merleau-Ponty, and Ricoeur, among others.

6. Marx's view of the relationship between compassion and sympathy is not entirely clear, for he uses the same word, *Mitleid*, for both. But, as noted below, he also writes of sympathy consolidating itself in the virtue of compassion. In the absence of any attempt to distinguish them, I shall construe them as synonyms.

7. It is revealing about the appalling harm that affectlessness caused in the twentieth century that *L'Etranger* became "Gallimard's all-time best-selling novel. . . . [This affectlessness], too, can be called a plague, and it comes out very strongly in Camus's play 'Caligula' (1945)" (*The Economist*, April 27, 1996, p. 93, in a review (unsigned) of Olivier Todd, *Camus: Une Vie* (Paris: Gallimard, 1996).

8. Even Kant, curiously enough, seems to admit this, at least once, when he argues, "It is a duty not to shun sick-rooms or prisons and so on in order to avoid the pain of compassion, which one may not be able to resist. For this feeling, though painful, nevertheless is one of the impulses placed in us by nature for effecting *what the representation of duty might not accomplish by itself* (1964b, §35, 122; emphasis added).

9. This is how Hobbes defended the consistency of his egoistic ethics, even though he gave alms to a beggar. He did it, he explained, not for the sake of the beggar but to relieve his own pain in seeing the beggar. At the other end of the social spectrum, Lord Henry, the aloof aristocrat in Oscar Wilde's *The Picture of Dorian Gray*, remarks, "I can sympathize with everything, except suffering. . . . I cannot sympathize with that. It is too ugly, too horrible, too distressing" (Wilde 1985, 46).

10. On the indifference to pain and suffering generally, see W. H. Auden's instructive poem *Musée de Beaux Arts*. The painting referred to is very probably Pieter Bruegel the Elder's *Fall of Icarus* in the Musées royaux des Beaux-Arts in Brussels.

11. This type of aversion can also be attributable to family as much as to racial identification. At a certain point in *Jane Eyre*, for instance, the young Jane came to live with her Aunt, Mrs. Reed. Jane was related to Mr. Reed, who had died, and who had made his wife promise that she would "rear and maintain" Jane. But, Charlotte Brontë, tells us, it was against her nature. In the absence of any connection of blood, it was "irksome" to have "to stand in the stead of a parent to a strange child she could not love, and to see an uncongenial alien permanently intruded on her own family group" (1966, 48).

12. I am indebted to Michael Barber for pointing out this fact.

13. Ovid, *Metamorphoses Book VIII.* (1970, 106–112).

14. Once in a small village in the French Alps, the very kind owner of our hotel came to our table after dinner with a nervous question. "Monsieur, I have heard it said that in America the value of a man is judged by the amount of money he makes. Could that possibly be true?" (*Horreur!*)

15. Mr. Eliot's moral failure is also the same as that of Blanche Ingram in *Jane Eyre* (Brontë 1966, 215) and of the protagonist and narrator of Josephine Hart's *Damage*. Musing on the causes of the tragedy that dissipate him, he speculates on "Some

deep failure of the soul perhaps. An inherited emptiness. . . . A flaw in the psyche, discovered only by those who suffer from it" (Hart 1991, 165).

16. Compare the treatment of employees in our contemporary age of downsizings to Charlotte Brontë's description of Hiram Yorke, the foreman of a wealthy mill owner, in *Shirley*. Yorke was a kind and fatherly person both to employees and to the poor of the neighborhood. Whenever he had to fire people "he would try to set them on to something else; or, if that was impossible, help them to remove with their families to a district where work might possibly be had" (Brontë 1974, 79). See also "Downsizing: How It Feels to Be Fired," *The New York Times*, March 17, 1996, E5.

17. "At the Bar," by David Margolick, *The New York Times*, April 17, 1992, B9.

18. "Parody Puts Harvard Law Faculty in Sexism Battle," *The New York Times*, April 27, 1992, p. A8.

19. Blake (1906, I, 75). Blake's view goes back to at least ancient Greece: " 'It was an excellent saying of Solon's,' wrote Richard Bentley, 'who when he was asked what would rid the world of injuries,' replied: 'If the bystanders would have the same resentment with those that suffer wrong'" (Hay 1960, 4). R. M. Hare describes certain other cases in which the answer would also be "yes," but very far removed from what Blake or Solon had in mind: "A talented torturer or single-minded sadist may understand very well the quality of the suffering he is inflicting, and be spurred on by that very understanding to go on inflicting it" (1981, 99).

20. Originally published in 1933, "On the Ontological Mystery" followed a play entitled *Le Monde cassé* (*The Broken World*). Marcel's denunciation of the reduction of Being to having converges on Conrad's *The Heart of Darkness* which, its editor points out, "can be seen as the first twentieth-century novel, with its climate of doubt and vagueness, its loss of moral confidence, its need for 'belief' in the midst of moral wilderness, its exploration of the subconscious, and its affirmation of individual freedom" (Conrad 1983, Introduction, 23–24).

21. See also here Willard Gaylin (1992) for the picture he paints of men denied the intimacy of love and who get caught up, and caught, in an adolescent time warp of insecurity marked by a mania of acquisition of symbols of professional accomplishment and status. And it is, of course, women who are the ultimate emblem of such narcissistic achievement ("trophy wives").

22. For an identical conception of hope on a political plane, see Havel's "The Politics of Hope" in *Disturbing the Peace* (1990, 181).

23. Marcel also claims that real presence, as distinguished from that which is merely physical, "is something which reveals itself immediately and incontrovertibly in a look, a smile, an accent, a shaking of hands" (1964b, 40). For reasons already noted above, this claim cannot be true, at least without serious qualification. Clever acting, deception, fraud, and seduction can never be excised completely from the social agenda, even if in certain cases it would take a lot of intellectual work just to raise the hypothesis. The ambiguity of behavior never completely disappears. Werner Marx makes the same mistake when he says of the person of "responsible readiness," "He knows immediately who and what accord with his compassion in each case" (1992, 64).

24. It is interesting that Marcel does not anticipate Levinas and Marx by attacking Heidegger for privileging the ontological over the personal. Marcel's last writings

are heavily indebted to the later Heidegger, and passages such as that referenced by this note show that the former considered the latter's language adequate for expressing important truths about human being.

25. In a similar vein, Richard Williams, executive director of the American Indian College Fund, writes à propos of President Clinton's televised announcement that he is part Cherokee—because his grandmother was one-quarter Indian—that tribal membership "is about much more than a fraction of blood. (The government actually forced this standard upon tribes.) It is about keeping traditions alive and being responsible for our people. . . . My tribe, the Oglala Lakota Sioux, describes our shared responsibility with the words 'mitakuye oyasin.' It means 'we are all related.' " See "The Part-Cherokee President," *The New York Times*, July 16, 1998, p. A25.

26. For more on this subject, see Hamrick 1985b, 46-48.

27. It should be pointed out that the Lakota were hardly the only Native Americans to defend such values. For example, the Cheyenne view of wealth was that it was "not to be hoarded or to be self-consumed. . . . Its value derives from its being given away. Chiefs, who are the greatest exemplars of Cheyenne virtues, are the greatest givers" (Hoebel 1960, 94).

28. This is not to say that Marcel would have nothing to learn from Marx. He could certainly have endorsed Marx's famous descriptions of "Alienated Labor" in the *Economic and Philosophic Manuscripts of 1844*, or similar accounts in Thoreau's *Walden* and Tocqueville's second volume of *Democracy in America*. But for Marcel, the "solution" would always have transcended Marx's solution to a problem, because labor, or performing functions, could never have belonged to the essential being of the worker. For more on this subject, see Hamrick (1985b 142, 153 n. 16).

29. For more on this topic, see Hamrick (1985b, 51–52).

30. For Levinas, as we shall see below, these claims are unconditional. Sidgwick gives us a more traditional conception of such claims in his view that generosity is a type of benevolence or "Chivalry toward adversaries or competitors [which] seems to consist in showing as much kindness and regard for their well-being as is compatible with the ends and conditions of conflict" (1913, 326).

31. Dorothea echoes Blake's belief when she asks, "How can we live and think that anyone has trouble—piercing trouble—and we could help them, and never try?" (Eliot 1965, 853). Such simplicity in kindness is also consistent with regret and/or repentance at being too much at the disposition of the other—as Dorothea learns from her disastrous marriage to Mr. Casaubon. Timon of Athens learns the same lesson, as does old Mrs. Linton in Emily Brontë's *Wuthering Heights*, when she takes the ill Catherine to Thrushcross Grange to convalesce: "But the poor dame had reason to repent of her kindness; she and her husband both took the fever, and died within a few days of each other" (1959, 89–90).

32. Michael Shea, housing director for ACORN (the Association of Community Organizations for Reform Now), observes, "Few bankers do this out of the goodness of their hearts. . . . If there was no community pressure and the law, few banks would do something. But now a lot of bankers see it's in their self-interest." See "New Hope in Inner Cities: Banks Offering Mortgages," *The New York Times*, March 14, 1992, p. 1. There was no significant improvement by the end of the

decade. According to both ACORN and the Department of Housing and Urban Development, the principal cause of denying home mortgages to minority group members was discrimination. See "Bias Worsens for Minorities Buying Homes," by Peter T. Kilborn, *The New York Times*, September 16, 1999, p. A15.

33. See John Boswell's masterful treatment of this theme (1990). The hard-edged charity dispensed to abandoned children was usually fatal. "In Renaissance cities," for example, "the infants disappeared quietly and efficiently through the revolving doors of state-run foundling homes, out of sight and mind, into social oblivion, or, more likely, death by disease" (433). They "either died among strangers or entered society as strangers. Mostly they died" (434).

34. Hence, Sir James Fitzjames Stephen's high-pitched vexation: "A very large proportion of the matters upon which people wish to interfere with their neighbours are trumpery little things which are of no real importance at all. The busybody and world-betterer who will never let things alone, or trust people to take care of themselves, is a common and contemptible character" (1967, 159).

35. There is at least one text in which Marcel does come close to stating this implication (1984, 201–202).

36. Compare Albert Camus' description in *The Plague* of attempts by Dr. Rieux, Rambert, and Tarrou to converse through plague masks: "Whenever any of them spoke through the mask . . . it was like a colloquy of statues" (1972, 193). Likewise, Isabel Archer Osmond, in James' *The Portrait of a Lady*, confronts her cousin Ralph in the aftermath of her bad marriage. Her face became a mask: "There was something fixed and mechanical in the serenity painted on it; this was not an expression, Ralph said—it was a representation, it was even an advertisement" (1986, 443).

37. The emphasis on both visual and linguistic expression in the living face owes a lot to Merleau-Ponty. But there are also very old echoes in Levinas' thought here. In terms of "the language of the eyes," compare Emerson's view, "We have a great deal more kindness than is ever spoken. . . . Read the language of these wandering eye-beams. The heart knoweth" (1937, 105). On the importance of vocal expression, compare Erasmus' claim, "[S]peech is the least deceptive mirror of the mind" (1971, 67). Similarly, the actor, David Suchet, has a "great theory" of acting that "you find the person, or '*per-son*,' through sound. . . . So '*per-son*' becomes personality." See "David Suchet Is Poirot to TV Viewers," *St. Louis Post-Dispatch*, May 20, 1992, 4F. Also, Carol Gilligan's (1982, 1993 printing) *In a Different Voice* shows us how the self can develop through talking and listening. It gains strength in and through these relationships rather than in the (typically masculine) accumulation of power.

38. Levinas contends that politics and war are closely bound up with each other and that both are opposed to morality because they are acts of totalizers. An interesting example of his point may be found in the writings of William Penn. "Princes," he tells us, . . . [should choose wives] such as they Love, and not by *Proxy* merely to gratify [political] Interest; and ignoble Motive; and that rarely begets, or contines that *Kindness* which ought to be between men and their Wives. . . . Besides, it is certain, Parents Loving Well before they are Married, which very rarely happens to princes, *has Kind and Generous Influences upon their Offspring: Which, with their Example, makes them better Husbands, and Wives, in their Turn*" (n.d., 16–17; emphasis in original).

39. The rejection of egocentricity for heterocentricy has seen a parallel decentering of individual rights and duties, identified with masculinity, in favor of an ethics of care and responsibility, identified with the feminine. See Larrabee (1993) for a valuable collection of essays on this topic.

40. In this respect, his closest real-life variant is Kenneth Starr, that hyper-repressed voyeur and stalker who embodies exactly Santayana's definition of a fanatic as someone who redoubles his effort after having forgotten his aim. Both are idolaters in Marcel's sense of the word.

41. Actually, in his religious fanaticism, Werle is a Norwegian Angel Clare. He is so psychologically rigid and devoted to absolutes to the exclusion of people who must live under such rules and principles that he would have made the Pharisees blush. His unkindness even extends to convincing the daughter, Hedwig, to sacrifice the wild duck in the attic as her most precious possession. It would be a "free-will offering" (Ibsen 1984, 288) so that her father would love her. But instead of killing her pet, she commits suicide. As Erasmus' Folly knew well, sometimes "turning a blind eye" and "building up illusions" are much better at keeping friendships together than is the truth (1971, 91).

42. Compare here the following comments by the editor of *Sense and Sensibility*: "[W]hile she [Jane Austen] saw with unsparing clarity just how much cruelty, repression, and malice the social forms made possible, how much misery they generated, she knew that a world in which everyone was totally sincere, telling always the truth for the sake of their feelings and never any lies for the feelings of others, would be simply an anarchy, everybody's personal 'form' cancelling out everybody else's" (Austen 1982, 16).

43. Peter Johnson points out correctly that innocents in this first sense of the term are essentially ignorant because "they are incapable of envisaging moral conduct in any other way" (1988, 10; cited in Wolgast 1993, 304, n. 15). Johnson (1998) and Stuart Hampshire (1989) are concerned exclusively with the connection between innocence in this first sense and politics. As such, their arguments lie outside of our concerns here. Kant also had this sense of innocence in mind when he wrote, "Innocence is a splendid thing, only it has the misfortune not to keep very well and to be easily misled" (1964a, 72).

44. Wittgenstein ascribes this sense of innocence to G. E. Moore—what was "no credit" to him—and uses his example to distinguish between being "kind" and "kindly": "I *like* and greatly respect Moore; but that's all. He doesn't warm my heart (or very little), because what warms my heart most is human kindness, and Moore—*just like a child*—is not kind. He is kindly and he can be charming and nice to those he likes and he has great *depth*.—That's how it seems to me. If I'm wrong, I'm wrong" (Malcolm 1972, 80). This is the source that Wolgast sought when she said, "Wittgenstein is reported to have distinguished between the innocence of a child . . . and 'the innocence a man has fought for,' of which only the latter is commendable" (1993, 299, n. 7).

45. Compare Louis Althusser's descriptions of two real-life clergy. The first, a veteran of World War I, had "seen it all before, was exceedingly indulgent. . . . [He] was always chewing on the same pipe he had had in the trenches. He too was the good 'father' figure" (1993, 72). In the middle of a raging quarrel between the local count

and the school master, "The priest was a decent chap and politically shrewd, [but he] behaved in such a way that he did not have an enemy in the place" (ibid., 73). The second priest was Pope John XXIII: "It was springtime, and this pure-hearted man was enchanted by the flowers and the children. He had the appearance of a Burgundian who enjoyed red wine, but beneath that exterior he was a totally artless and profoundly generous man with a slightly Utopian vision" (ibid., 346). It is clear from the context that Althusser uses "artless" to denote innocence in the second rather than the first sense.

Notes to Chapter 3

1. For further details about self-transposal, see Hamrick 1990.
2. This was the question that Dale Singer, an editor of the *St. Louis Post-Dispatch*, faced with his father, Phil. "Yet the main question in Phil's case became a simple one: Was there any sense, or any kindness, in bringing him back from the brink of death, to return him to the nursing home where only a feeding tube would keep him away from another ambulance ride to the hospital?" See "Deciding on Death," *St. Louis Post-Dispatch*, January 6, 1991, p. D1. Note the similarity of these types of agonizing decisions to the "cruel kindness" that Jim contemplates in *Treasure Island* (see Chapter 1), of rescuing the pirates only to take them home to face possible hanging.
3. Care for the dying can be unkind in other ways as well. One such example is health care professionals who construe their jobs as pain relief with or without the informed consent of the patient. Another is attempts to keep the patient alive at all costs, so that "the operation was a success, but the patient died." I am indebted to my colleague, Clyde M. Nabe, for several examples of such unkindnesses. See also here Nuland 1994, especially pp. 61–62, 250–60.
4. I am indebted to Kwame Anthony Appiah for directing me to this text, as well as to *Nervous Conditions*, referred to below.
5. "Minister to Go on Trial for Homeless Campsite," The Associated Press, *The New York Times*, July 7, 1997, p. A13.
6. There is another similarity with Aristotle as well. In his view, generosity and self-control are both moral virtues (1962, 32). We have already discussed generosity as one essential condition of being a kind person; self-restraint is its complement.
7. Foot also holds, as does A.D.M. Walker (1989), that there is a necessary incompatibility between virtues such as justice and charity, in that the development of the one would entail the diminishment of the other. As we shall see below, the relationship between them is not that simple, and there is a strong sense of mutual dependence. As Daniel Putnam puts it, "The just person needs to weigh the demands of kindness and empathy" in order to humanize the administration of justice, just as "the kind person must weigh the demands of justice if kindness is not to become exploitation. . . . Without such weighing, we either have excess . . . mimicry, or luck" (1990, 517).
8. I am indebted to Ms. Rose Bateman for retrieving this reference. Darley and Batson argue that some of the seminarians who did not stop might well have been

more conflicted than callous. That is, they were hurrying because "the experimenter, *whom the subject was helping*, was depending on him to get to a particular place quickly" (1973, 203; emphasis in original). However, the conflict and self-absorption hypotheses are not rivals. Some seminarians may have been genuinely torn between the two desires, but others could well have been self-absorbed, precisely because they focused intently on pleasing the experimenter and thus had to hurry.

9. Writers such as D. H. Lawrence provide us with stirring examples of the powers of the involuntary, particularly when no effort can manipulate it to produce acts of kindness. See, for instance, in *Sons and Lovers*, Mrs. Morel's inability to love her husband, even after his serious work accident (1982, 86), and the impossibility of kindness in the relationship between Paul and Miriam (ibid., 418). These lovers *manqué* are trapped in the mire of deeply conflicted feelings of possession, belonging, and a triangle of antagonism with Paul's mother.

10. But not by Ricoeur. Writing of "feelings that are revealed in the self by the other's suffering" (1992, 191), he adds: "In this regard, feelings of pity, compassion, and sympathy, formerly exalted by English-language philosophy, deserve to be rehabilitated. In this perspective, Max Scheler's analyses devoted to sympathy, hate, and love remain unequaled" (ibid., 192, n. 29).

11. In Scheler's view, Darwin, to some extent, Herbert Spencer, and Nietzsche were all guilty of confusing emotional infection with genuine fellow-feeling. The former two tried "to derive fellow-feeling from the herd-consciousness and herd-behaviour of the higher animals," while Nietzsche, "arrived at a completely *misguided evaluation* of fellow-feeling, and especially of pity. . . . Suffering itself does *not* become infectious through pity. Indeed, it is just where suffering is infectious that pity is completely excluded" (Scheler 1954, 17).

12. Brian Carr has pointed out that Aristotle's *Rhetoric* depicts pity as a "quite self-centered emotion," and that Martha Nussbaum's defense of compassion as "the basic social emotion," which is based directly on Aristotle's account of pity, "manifests the same peculiar tendency" (Carr 1999, 425). He then develops a position on compassion that strongly resembles Scheler's view of fellow-feeling, Stein's view of empathy, and Spiegelberg's concept of self-transposal. "[C]ompassion," he argues, "is a social virtue precisely because it involves an act of transcending the self-centred standards of judgment which Aristotle and Nussbaum rest their analyses on" (Carr 1999, 425).

13. One of the staples of the multiple *Star Trek* television series is not merely toleration of difference but respect and even reverence for it. It is appropriate that this lesson has its most visible television presentation in a work of science *fiction* away from Earth.

14. E. B. Titchener coined the word "empathy": "This is, I suppose, a simple case of empathy, if we may coin that term as a rendering of *Einfühlung*." (1909, 21).

15. Compare Michel Henry's complaint about Husserl: "Desire directed towards a possible response, emotion in the face of reciprocity of this desire, a feeling of presence or absence, solitude, love, hate, resentment, boredom, pardon, exaltation, sadness, joy, amazement—such are the concrete modalities of our life such as it is lived with the other, such as it is a feeling-with, sym-pathy in all its forms. Of all that, what does Husserl's Fifth Cartesian Meditation tell us? Not a word" (1990, 140).

16. Hence, Marianne Sawicki is wrong to accept, as it appears that she does, Theodor Lipps' view that *Einfühlung* is "the way one overtakes and saturates someone else" (1997, 123). Compare also Stein's and Spiegelberg's point about empathy, a study that showed that student nurses suffering from "empathic overarousal" became so obsessed by their terminally ill patients' plight that it became "difficult to remain in the same room as the patients" (Hoffman 1984, 295). Stein and Spiegelberg would argue that, as the boundaries between the nurses and patients broke down, their connection was no longer empathic. The same lesson applies in other contexts as well. One therapist appeals to Maimonides in arguing for "the importance of seeing the person who is suffering, not just the suffering. 'To care about the individual is one thing; to overidentify with their pain doesn't help them a bit' " (Wuthnow 1991, 206).

17. On a sociopolitical level, this equation gets expressed in the jejune notion of patriotism as inconsistent with criticism of the government. This was a common conservative response during the Vietnam War.

18. Nussbaum argues accordingly, "The ability to imagine vividly, and to assess judicially, another person's pain, to participate in it, and then to ask about its significance, is a powerful way of learning what the human facts are and of acquiring a motivation to alter them" (1995a, 91). The rest of *Poetic Justice* illustrates this conviction in terms of sexual harassment, racism, and homophobia.

19. The way Marcel might well play off judgment and duty against kindness is presented vividly in Allende's *House of the Spirits* when Esteban explains to Father Antonio his proposal of giving monthly allotments of cash to his estranged sister, Férula: "I must explain that I'm not doing this out of kindness but because of a promise" (1986, 133). The explanation comes some pages later: Esteban "recalled his childhood, when she [Férula] surrounded him with dark solicitude, wrapping him in debts of gratitude so huge that as long as he lived he would never be able to pay them back" (ibid., 152). Marcel might also point out that kindness is often presented as something above and beyond duty in other kinds of contexts as well—beyond, say, the wooden, rule-bound performance of a job description. From this angle, the bored, insolent clerk, just as does Esteban, embodies an unavailability rooted in some type of alienation.

20. Such laws also exist in a few American legal jurisdictions and in every jurisdiction in the case of child abuse. The biblical tale of the Good Samaritan also provides the same lesson, but with a curious twist. The Good Samaritan, perceived as a member of a despised, impure minority, had every right to judge his intervention inappropriate. If the victim recovered, he might well express great anger at his rescuer for having used impure oil and wine to treat his wounds (see *Leviticus* 11:44), and if the victim died, the Good Samaritan would face the blood wrath of his family. The Good Samaritan ends by ignoring all of these legitimate judgments and reasons for nonintervention because, as noted in the previous chapter, he was "seized with pity." I am indebted to the Reverend Donald Molitor for these biblical facts and reference.

21. Compare with Eliot's diagnosis Ibsen's character, Gregers Werle, and his real-life counterpart, Kenneth Starr, as well as Sartre's wonderful portrait of M. Achille and his friends in *Nausea*: "[T]hey baptized their little obstinacies and some proverbs in

the name of experience, and they turned themselves into automatic vending machines: two sous in the slot to the left and *voilà* anecdotes wrapped in silver paper; two sous in the slot to the right and one gets invaluable pieces of advice that stick to your teeth like soft caramels" (1965, 100).

22. There is also a curious example of this view of judgment in Mr. Glegg who, Eliot tells us, would have grown misty eyed "with true feeling" at the sale of a widow's belongings—which he could have prevented with an easy five-pound donation—but who never would have dreamed of helping someone out of poverty. The reason is that charity "always appeared to him as a contribution of small aids, not a neutralising of misfortune" (Eliot 1985, 187). This is another example of the phenomenon studied earlier of the way that kindness is nested in a context of other values and presents itself as conditioned by that value structure.

23. Dirk Johnson, "When Money Is Everything, Except Hers," *The New York Times*, October 14, 1998, p. A1.

24. Thus Anna Quindlen writes of a physician who, as a third-year medical student making rounds in the wards, joined other students who "stood around the sickbed of one of their own professors and discussed his case without even acknowledging the man beneath the sheets." See "The Human Touch," *The New York Times*, May 14, 1994, p. B15. There are, however, signs of some change in American medical schools, where teaching compassion has suddenly become politicaly and medically correct. "Medical Schools Discover Value in Dispensing Compassion," by John Langone, *The New York Times*, August 22, 2000, p. D7.

25. It is a pleasure to note that the best student in my last logic class was a young woman with spina bifida, confined to a wheelchair. Indeed, I have had many disabled students in my classes over the years, and I have never heard one of them use their disabilities as excuses for not turning in assignments, earning poor grades, and so on. In contrast, too many fully able students are experts at such excuses and proficient whiners.

26. Compare Denver's experience of having Beloved look at her in Toni Morrison's (1988) epic: "It was lovely. Not to be stared at, not seen, but being pulled into view by the interested, uncritical eyes of the other (118)."

27. R. D. Laing once observed that the psychiatric vocabulary has many words for disturbed persons, but none for *disturbing* ones (Laing & Esterton 1964, 149n.).

28. "Les limites de la tolérance," by Henri Behar, *Le Monde*, June 4, 1992, p. 24.

29. "The Word Police Are Listening for 'Incorrect' Language," by Michiko Kakutani, *The New York Times*, February 1, 1993, p. B4.

30. One more similarity between Nussbaum's *Poetic Justice* and Ricoeur's *Oneself as Another* is that both take pains to point out that they do not wish to abolish a morality (and legality) of rules but only to show their insufficiency for practical wisdom.

31. In contrast, the Do Something Kindness and Justice Challenge offers program materials for schoolchildren to encourage them to perform acts of kindness as a way of life. More than 14,000 schools in fifty states use the program materials.

32. Isabel Archer Osmond knew this in her discussion with Lord Warburton in the theatre. James tells us that her conversation with him "pointed to presence of mind: it expressed a kindness so ingenious and deliberate as to indicate that she was in undisturbed possession of her faculties" (1986, 350). George Eliot paints a similar

picture of such mindfulness in the character of Lucy Deane in *The Mill on the Floss*. She was "a woman who was loving and thoughtful for other women, not giving them Judas-kisses with eyes askance on their welcome defects, but with real care and vision for their half-hidden pains and mortifications, with long ruminating enjoyment of little pleasures prepared for them" (1985, 477).

33. Another example is Nurse Rooke in Jane Austen's *Persuasion*. She is a model of practical wisdom. She "thoroughly understands when to speak. She is a shrewd, intelligent, sensible woman. Hers is a line for seeing human nature; and she has a fund of good sense and observation which, as a companion, make her infinitely superior to thousands of those who having only received 'the best education in the world,' know nothing worth attending to" (1982, 168).

34. At one level, a certain factual ignorance is unavoidable. We rarely, if ever, know fully all that our faces express or what our voices convey, let alone find ourselves in control of their multiple meanings. The case is no different for other types of expression—say, for painters or novelists—and the reason is the same: "Like the weaver, the writer [and everyone else expressing anything] works on the wrong side of his material" (Merleau-Ponty 1964b, 45). But just as this lack of certitude does not stand in the way of expression, it likewise does not bar us from performing acts of kindness or excuse us from the obligation of becoming as context sensitive as possible. This lesson stands out clearly in the passage cited from Wright's *Native Son*.

35. There is an incident in *Tess of the D'Urbervilles* that ties together all of these senses of kindness transcending justice, but not being inconsistent with practical wisdom. Tess is writing a letter to her estranged husband in Brazil: "The punishment you have measured out to me is deserved—I do know that—well deserved—and you are right and just to be angry with me. But, Angel, please, not to be just—only a little kind to me, even if I do not deserve it, and come to me!" (Hardy 1978, 417).

36. "Japan Confronting Gruesome War Atrocity," by Nicholas D. Kristof, *The New York Times*, March 17, 1995, pp. 1, A10.

37. Goleman also notes that, in language that reflects closely Merleau-Ponty's notion of the reversibility of flesh, "[S]everal theories of psychoanalysis see the therapeutic relationship as providing just such an emotional corrective, a reparative experience of attunement. *Mirroring* is the term used by some psychoanalytic thinkers for the therapist's reflecting back to the client an understanding of his inner state, just as an attuned mother does with her infant" (1995, 101–102).

Notes to Chapter 4

1. Consider, for example, parents who pay $70 per hour for Little League baseball instruction for their children. Bernard Beck, a sociologist at Northwestern University, advances an insightful explanation for this behavior. Well-educated and highly successful parents take a "management-style approach" to child rearing, he writes, and they tend to look on their progeny as "growth stocks." These parents have had successful careers, "and use the same goal-oriented principles when it comes to raising their kids. They study what's needed for success. They look at the competition. It's

all a very rational, very market-oriented approach." See "The Latest Sandlot Twist: Paid Tutors for Little Leaguers," by Dirk Johnson, *The New York Times*, June 24, 1999, p. A 20. Similarly, Marian Salzman, president of The Intelligence Factory, speaking about the increasing popularity of male nannies, asserts that, "Parents always have to be managing their assets, including their children." See *The American Way*, (American Airlines flight magazine), October 2000, p. 54. I am indebted to Kenneth Stikkers for this latter example.

2. The effectiveness of these techniques cannot be doubted. In World War II, the U.S. Army discovered that only 15 to 20 percent of soldiers shot to kill the enemy. "By the Korean War, around 55 percent of the soldiers were willing to fire to kill. And by Vietnam, the rate rose to over 90 percent" (Grossman 1998, 3).

3. "Poor Children with Bad Teeth Have Trouble Finding Dentists," by Carey Goldberg, *The New York Times*, June 26, 1999, p. A8.

4. "How Fathers Can Help Daughters in the Body-Image Battle," by Abby Ellin, *The New York Times*, September 18, 2000, p. B7.

5. "In Quest for the Perfect Look, More Girls Choose the Scalpel," by Jane Gross, *The New York Times*, November 29, 1998, p. 1.

6. "So Much Work, So Little Time," by Steven Greenhouse, *The New York Times*, September 5, 1999, Section 4, p. 1. Shor also said in an interview that, if she were to rewrite her book, she would title it *The Even More Overworked American*.

Since Schor's book appeared, other have argued that Americans had more leisure time than in previous decades, less leisure time, and about the same. The latest studies have tried to resolve the confusion by distinguishing between *groups* that claimed to have more or less leisure time. That is an empirical question that cannot be answered here. But what does seem incontestable is that, for many, even if not all, workers, the several factors that she describes as key to understanding diminished leisure time only grew worse throughout the decade.

7. "Deny Rape or Be Hated: Kosovo Victims' Choice," by Elisabeth Bumiller, *The New York Times*, June 22, 1999, p. 1. One Kosovar husband interviewed for this article stated that, if she admitted to him that she had been raped, "I would ask for a divorce—even if I had 20 children."

8. "Arab Honor's Price: A Woman's Blood," by Douglas Jehl, *The New York Times*, June 20, 1999, p. 1. The reporter notes that, "female chastity is seen in the Arab world as an indelible line, the boundary between respect and shame. . . . It is an unforgiving logic, and its product, for centuries and now, has been murder—the killings of girls and women by their relatives, to cleanse honor that has been soiled." The article goes on to state that, although a few modernizers across the Arab world are trying to tighten the laws against honor killings, they are fighting against the overwhelming weight of history and tradition.

9. Even more oppressively, values prevailing in some cultures make mere *being* female a possible death sentence. The UN Population Fund's "State of World Population Report 2000" states that at least 60 million girls, mostly in Asia, are "missing." Either they have been killed outright or have not been given the same health protection in childhood as boys. See "Violence against Women Is Culturally Rooted, Report Says," *St. Louis Post-Dispatch*, September 21, 2000, p. A9. See also Nussbaum 1999 (32) and "Modern Asia's Anomaly: The Girls Who Don't Get Born," by Celia W. Dugger, *The*

New York Times, May 6, 2001, p. 4–4, for an account of the use of ultrasound machines to determine sex *in utero* in order to abort unwanted female fetuses.

10. There are now Internet sites based on the premise that, "Students are not merely consumers of knowledge" but are *only* consumers. These sites offer courses along with ads for on-line shopping in order to "make money from people who might shop while they study." "Why not," they argue, "use education as a marketing tool to attract potential shoppers the way other sites use free e-mail or home pages?" See "Education: Web's New Come-On," by Lisa Guernsey, *The New York Times*, March 16, 2000, p. D1.

11. Even worse, schools sometimes lie to these students by encouraging them with "A's" to think that they are very good in a particular subject, so that university courses bring both a rude awakening and an understandable resentment. See also "At Least They Have High Self-Esteem," by Ben Wildavsky, *U.S. News and World Report*, February 7, 2000, p. 50.

12. "The New Measure of Man," *The New York Times*, July 8, 1994, p. A15. This article consists of excerpts from his speech accepting the Philadelphia Liberty Medal at Independence Hall on July 4, 1994.

13. See "Is the Sun Setting on Farmers? Many Can't Survive the 'New Agriculture.'" by David Barboza, *The New York Times*, November 28, 1999, Section 3, pp. 1, 14.

14. Ellen Goodman, "Silicone Story's Sad Lessons," the *Boston Globe*, reprinted and cited in the *St. Louis Post-Dispatch*, July 13, 1998, p. D7.

15. Ellen Goodman, "As Technology Brings the Office Home—and on Vacation—Where's Life?" the *Boston Globe*, reprinted and cited in the *St. Louis Post-Dispatch*, September 1, 1999, p. B7.

16. Leonore Tiefer, a psychologist at the New York University School of Medicine, argues this way. Perhaps thinking of Foucault, she states that labeling sexual changes of diminished desire and/or arousal as "bad," and therefore a "problem," leads us to "invent a universal model, a normative view of sex" (Hitt 2000, 41).

17. As Merleau-Ponty saw in sketching out an ontology of the flesh, such theoretical disputes between "nature" and "social construction" cannot be solved within the opposition of phenomenology and scientific realism. Sexual dysfunction, analyzed precisely within this dichotomy in *Phenomenology of Perception*, is another example of how starting with the "'consciousness'-'object' distinction" can never explain how it is that an "objective" event such as a "cerebral lesion" "could entail a massive disturbance" in our relationships with our Lifeworld (1968, 200).

18. Such thinking also illustrates a very old doctrine in Western philosophy, that there is no such thing as unused power. This view extends back at least as far as Parmenides and Plato and descends to us through St. Anselm's ontological argument for the existence of God and the tradition of medieval realism that that argument represents, as well as through Spinoza's metaphysics.

19. Certain claims to the contrary have been made on the Internet, and perhaps we are now on the cusp of "trophy babies" in addition to "trophy wives." As Kant pointed out, we can either have a price—even a "fancy" market price—or dignity (1964a, 102). What goes for babies goes for children as well. In a stunningly frank dissolution of human dignity in the icy waters of cash value, the March 4, 2001 issue of *The New York Times Magazine* published a photographic spread (pp. 50–58) titled

"Me and My Hero." The sub-title was "A reminder that everybody needs somebody to look up to." The photographs display children with the adults they idolize. For example, one of the photographs shows a little boy with the cardiothoracic surgeon who repaired his heart, while another photo shows an eleven-year-old boy who had had one of several necessary operations posed beside Christopher Reeve in his wheelchair. The copy for each photograph sketches the attraction that the chosen adult had for the child, and then ends up revealing the true nature of the "story," namely, advertising the clothing the child is wearing along with its price. Thus in the first example we read: "'Dr. Laks is my hero because he opened my chest and fixed my heart.' Haskell's top, $19, and shorts, $25, from Ralph Lauren Childrenswear. At Bloomington's, Dillards's." (p. 52).

20. "As Abortion Rate Decreases, Clinics Compete for Patients," by Gina Kolata, *The New York Times*, December 30, 2000, front page.

21. Heidegger's word for "revealing" is *das Entbergen*, "which connotes an opening out from protective concealing, a harboring forth. . . . Heidegger's central tenet [is] that it is only as protected and preserved—and that means as enclosed and secure—that anything is set free to endure, to continue as that which it is, i.e., to be." (1977, 11, n. 10). We shall return to this theme in the following chapter's discussion of community.

22. Some instructive examples are Dolores Keane's *Solid Ground* and Clannad's *Coinleach Ghlas an Fhómhair* and *The Green Fields of Gaothdobhair*.

23. The "non-human" is meant here in a collective sense. I do not mean that humanness depends on convivial contact with *all* of nature. That would be naively romantic. Nature provides many encounters of the fanged kind, for example, none of which is desirable. Furthermore, one searches in vain through Thoreau's rhapsodies on nature for references to those infuriating New England pests, blackflies and mosquitoes.

24. In his last "Conversation" with Ricoeur, Marcel admitted that his earlier view of technology was "perhaps . . . overly hostile." He rejected this view as "absurd. I would no longer condemn a single instance of technology. I believe that technology is good in itself." This softer criticism does not fit very well with his uniformly negative remarks in *Tragic Wisdom* about the American space program, but in any event, his considered judgment seems to be that the value of technology rests on its ability to respect "a certain core of the sacred in man" and "the integrity of man as sacred" (Marcel 1973, 247, Ricoeur's words).

25. An analogous picture of centered harmony of nature and home occurs in *The Mill on the Floss*. Eliot writes of "what an old-fashioned man like Tulliver felt for this spot [the mill] where all his memories centred and where life seemed like a familiar smooth-handled tool that the fingers clutch with living ease" (Eliot 1985, 352). A few pages later, the author contrasts this picture of harmony of nature and home with the way in which "good society" has "its claret and its velvet carpets, its dinner-engagements six weeks deep," and rests on exploiting the working class that, in their hovels, experiences no such "harmony of nature and home" (ibid., 385).

Professor Ernie Sherman has noted that, for Merleau-Ponty, we all live in a world habitat that is in one sense familiar and familial. In the sense of kindness as belonging to the same kind, we are all kindred expressions of the flesh of the world. Unkindness, in the moral sense, manifests itself in social actions, processes, and mechanisms, such as those Eliot describes that cut out other people from participation. "Absolute Habitation," a paper read to the 1998 annual general meeting of the Merleau-Ponty Circle at Salisbury State University.

26. Scheler's linguistic descriptions of this worldview and his recommended perceptual reconnections are both practically identical to Abram's, from whose discussions and references his voice is unfortunately absent.

27. Compare Merleau-Ponty's "working note" for the continuation of *The Visible and the Invisible:* "Do a psychoanalysis of Nature: it is the flesh, the mother. A philosophy of the flesh is the condition without which psychoanalysis remains anthropology" (1968, 267). Ecofeminists have also been concerned to point out the connection between the male oppression of both women and nature. See, for example, Merchant 1980, 1995.

28. "Be It Ever Less Humble: American Homes Get Bigger," *The New York Times,* October 22, 2000, Section 4, p. 5.

29. "U.S. Goes on Energy Splurge after Falling Off Its Diet," *The New York Times,* October 22, 1998, pp. C5–6. While this book was in press, President Bush declared his unwillingness to follow the Kyoto Accords.

30. "The New Measure of Man," *The New York Times,* July 8, 1994, p. A15.

31. In addition, studies have shown that playing with animals helps diminish patients' depression, and that "patients who can see trees and other greenery from their hospital rooms recover faster and do better than those who look out to brick walls or ventilation machinery." As a result, the Joint Commission for the Accreditation of Healthcare Organizations is now "circulating for review new guidelines that would ascertain whether patients' rooms have views of nature and how much of the view can be seen while lying flat in bed" (Wiley 1999, 22). Studies have also shown that patients in the ICU do better when they have views of nature or can even view a painting of nature on a barren wall. Views of nature and audio tapes of babbling brooks and birds singing have also helped patients waiting for biopsies and heart procedures, because they reduce stress (ibid., 24).

32. See Hopkins (1996, 114), "God's Grandeur."

33. In this task, Hopkins would find an ally in Jean-Marie Schaeffer, who defends the "sacralization of poetry," because it is a "restorer," not simply of "Art," but more generally—and *through* this sacralization—in a resacralization of being, of life, and of the universe" (Schaeffer 1992, 116; emphasis in original).

34. Today evolutionary psychologists want to explain how other animals, and impliedly human beings, are capable of qualities such as kindness, compassion, and altruism generally. One hypothesis is that of mutual back-scratching: self-interested behavior for mutual convenience. One selfish chimp, say, in a cooperative community could take food it did not hunt and, by taking fewer risks, could get more genes into the next generation. Another hypothesis holds that kindness is an expression of self-interest, because it creates a reputation of trustworthiness that would have long-term genetic payoffs to outweigh the short-term losses of cooperation. In other words, altruism is an illusion, a rationalization of self-interest. As against such reductive thinking, we have known at least since Bishop Butler's criticisms of Hobbes that altruism and self-interest are not necessarily inconsistent with each other, that both are real, and that neither can be reduced to the other. In this regard, the present book uses phenomenology as a way of "saving the phenomena" rather than having them explained away.

35. It is not clear that earthworms experience pain the way we do—sensuous, affective suffering—but, like ants, their nervous systems do equip them with nociceptors that are sensitive to discomfort and from which they want to flee. It would be interesting to know what percentage of those who fish would continue to use earthworms as bait if they were aware of their victims' adverse reactions to having hooks threaded through them.

Notes to Chapter 5

1. For a lengthier discussion of the internal and external aspects of rules and the applicability of the distinction beyond the realm of law, see Hamrick (1987, 130 ff.) and (1983, 187 ff.).
2. One possible example of stupidity consists of school policies that used to force all left-handed schoolchildren to sit in right-handed desks, because being right-handed was considered the "proper" way to write. How should we account for this wrongheaded normativity if not due to stupidity? Ignorance? Neglect? All three? But of course, this particular example of normativity has a history at least as old as the Romans for whom *sinister* meant "left," and *dexter* meant "right."
3. "Hospital Turns Poor Couple Away," Ann Landers' column in the *Boston Globe*, August 10, 1989, p. 82.
4. "Louisiana Settles Suit, Abandoning Private Youth Prisons," by Fox Butterfield, *The New York Times*, September 8, 2000, p. A12.
5. "Profits at Juvenile Prisons Earned at a Chilling Cost," by Fox Butterfield, *The New York Times*, July 15, 1998, p. 1. In March 2000, a Louisiana state judge had six teenage boys removed from another privately run juvenile prison because "they had been brutalized by guards, kept in solitary confinement for months with no reason, and deprived of shoes, blankets, education, and medical care." See "Privately Run Juvenile Prison in Louisiana Is Attacked for Abuse of 6 Inmates," by Fox Butterfield, *The New York Times*, March 16, 2000, p. A14.
6. The Texas Defender Service has released a chilling report on capital punishment in Texas. Having an incompetent, drunk, drugged, or sleeping defense attorney has routinely been dismissed as grounds for appeal. The report, titled "A State of Denial: Texas Justice and the Death Penalty," also details the official use of obviously false evidence, the withholding of beneficial evidence, and threats made against witnesses. See "The Death Capital," by Bob Herbert, *The New York Times*, October 16, 2000, p. A27. Such officials can count on support at the federal appellate level as well: one enthusiastic death penalty devotee is Edith Hollan Jones, who sits on the U.S. Fifth Circuit Court of Appeals. "Once, during a last-ditch oral argument on the eve of an execution, she famously complained that the proceedings were keeping her from a birthday party for one of her children." See "Death Takes a Holiday," by Bob Herbert, *The New York Times*, August 19, 1999, p. A21.
7. Kozol later (1995) narrowed his analysis to the South Bronx. He shows us a ghetto of poor children whose entrapment is hardly adventitious. Rather, it is the effect of avarice, disregard, racism, and convenience.

8. Kozol himself argues strongly for equalized funding, and his own position has been attacked as too simplistic (Schrag 1991, 20), which it is. But even Schrag does not quarrel with Kozol's descriptions of inner-city schools, and Schrag's assertion that equalization "tends to destroy local accountability and erode the supports and sense of mission that make strong schools possible" (ibid., 20) ignores the dialectical relationships between schools and society. Society will have to deal, one way or another, with the consequences of systemic discrimination.

9. Sometimes such pathological detachment is attributable to just plain ignorance. Hallie recounts a stunning example of a recovered drug addict from Harlem who had just barely escaped death. At the end of his speech to a group of people in Middletown, Conn., "a Middletown woman stood up and said, in all earnestness: 'I just can't understand drug addiction. All *I* need in order to get high is to see a beautiful sunset.' And she sat down." The young man simply looked away in silence. He saw, as she did not, "the dark space that separates intimate knowledge from smug gentility" (1997, 199).

10. As against Foucault, Gauchet and Swain do not take the State to be a tyrant so much as a failed master, less evil than a bureaucratic organization that made mistakes. In the asylums, doctors failed to achieve the 90 percent cure rate they had promised. It was closer to 40 percent which is amazing enough, but not enough to defeat government skeptics.

11. Texas' rate of executions is the usual focal point of skepticism about "compassionate conservatism." However, one can also wonder about the meaning of that concept when it was the premise behind Governor Bush's veto of Senator Rodney Ellis' bill that would have guaranteed indigent defendants access to legal counsel within twenty days. The bill had been passed unanimously by the (Republican-controlled) Texas Senate and House of Representatives.

12. See here Derrida (1997, 276-78). Also, it is interesting to note that, for Ricoeur, "in the case of sympathy that comes from the self and extends to the other, equality is reestablished *only* through the shared admission of fragility and, finally, of mortality" (Ricoeur 1992, 192, emphasis added). "Only" seems wrong: I may sympathize with another non-native speaker trying to pronounce the letter "g" in Dutch or with someone trying to master her temper, but these experiences only vaguely implicate fragility and mortality, if at all. Ironically, what these experiences do reference are two of Ricoeur's aspects of the involuntary, life situation and character.

13. Damon (1999, 76) records that 10 percent of American children had "enough problems to warrant psychiatry" in 1976, and that by 1989, the figure had almost doubled to 18.2 percent. However, he does not address the question of true need for psychiatric help as opposed to (educational) system-created needs.

14. According to a recently released report by the Peter D. Hart Research Associates for the AFL-CIO, "Only two in five young workers expressed confidence that employers would treat their employees fairly." See "Young Workers Start Out Optimistic, Become Disillusioned, Labor Study Says," by Philip Dine, *St. Louis Post-Dispatch*, September 1, 1999, p. 1. Ellen Goodman adds another dimension to this perception in the context of technology in the high-speed office discussed in the previous chapter. She writes, "Even in good times, the luckiest of workers remain[s] insecure

about a future that seems as planned for obsolescence as this year's software. In the fast-forward workplace, you stay up-to-speed or fall behind." See "As Technology Brings the Office Home—and on Vacation—Where's Life?" in the *Boston Globe*, reprinted and cited in the *St. Louis-Post Dispatch*, September 1, 1999, p. B7.

15. "The Decline of the Nice-Guy Quotient," by Daniel Goleman, *The New York Times*, September 10, 1995, p. See also Goleman 1995 for an extended discussion of "emotional" rather than "cognitive" intelligence.

16. "Holistic Law Tries to Make Every Case a Civil One," by Pamela Ferdinand, the *Washington Post*, May 17, 1998, p. A13.

17. "A Push from the Top Shatters a Glass Ceiling," by Reed Abelson, *New York Times*, August 22, 1999, p. A23. How this sensitivity to inclusiveness came into being is an instructive story in terms of empathy, kindness, and connections to the world of feelings. In 1981, the company's future chief executive, Lewis E. Platt, was a typical white, male, workaholic manager. Then his world collapsed. His wife, Susan, died of cancer, and suddenly he had to step into the unaccustomed role of taking care of his two daughters, ages nine and eleven. He quickly learned the exhausting daily fate of single parents, usually mothers. His subsequent memos as chief executive "remind[ed] male colleagues of some of the built-in disadvantages women operate under . . . [while] two-thirds of male managers have stay-at-home wives." As a result of this sensitivity to inclusiveness, there have been dramatic employee retention benefits for the company, especially among women.

18. In her "Afterword," Doris Hallie noted that her husband "yearned for a oneness with humankind and with nature. He loved his moments of joy—*jouissance*—as he called it, but he was forever aware of the dark side, that hurricane" of human evil (1997, 209).

19. See the note in Chapter 1 regarding Florence King's report on cultural misunderstandings in Brooklyn between African Americans and Korean grocers.

20. "Whale Hunt Affirms Makah Values and Roles," by the Rev. Donald W. Johnson, the *St. Louis Post-Dispatch*, June 1, 1999, p. B15.

21. "Testing the Limits of Tolerance As Cultures Mix," by Barbara Crossette, *The New York Times*, March 6, 1999, p. A15.

22. "Detective's Kindness Helps Awaken a City," by Joseph Berger, *The New York Times*, January 7, 1999, p. A29.

23. Testimony elicited in congressional hearings from some of the *maquiladora* workers have revealed the frightening human toll of U.S. companies' financial bonanzas. These children are not allowed to talk, they do not earn enough money for proper nutrition, they can go to the bathroom only twice a day, and they are discouraged from asking for medical attention. Their bosses will not let them go to school in the evening (how could they stay awake?), because they would have to leave their sweatshops too soon. In short, "All that is joyful in life is being wrung from the youngsters who are fed into the wretched, soulless system of the maquiladora assembly plants. Is a Gap shirt worth it?" See Bob Herbert, "Children of the Dark Ages," *The New York Times*, July 21, 1995, p. A11. Six years later, things are no better. In Acuña, Mexico, "as in other border settlements, Mexican workers earn such miserable wages and American companies pay such minimal taxes that its schools are a shambles, its hospital crumbling, its trash collection slapdash, and its sewage lines

collapsed. Half of Acuña's 150,000 residents now use backyard latrines." Sam Dillion, "Profits Raise Pressure on Border Factories," *The New York Times*, February 15, 2001, p. A1.

24. The Philosophy for Children program mentioned earlier seeks to instantiate Dewey's call for renewed civic debate in a respectful, reasoned manner. Its goal is not acceptance of all competing perspectives but rather respectful appreciation. It aims for what Sandel called a "deliberative" sort of mutual respect and toleration while pressing forward as far as the evidence and reason will carry the group toward a consensus about the best answer. Children learn invaluable lessons about rights and responsibilities of public speech. Since the program effectively attempts to fulfill Santayana's virtue of "intellectual kindness or courtesy to all possible wills," Philosophy for Children functions as a model for democratic decision making.

25. "Downside of Doing Good: Disaster Relief Can Harm," by Paul Lewis, *The New York Times*, February 27, 1999, p. A19.

26. "In Japan, Nice Guys (and Girls) Finish Together," by Nicholas D. Kristof, *The New York Times*, April 12, 1998, Section 4, p. 7.

27. "The New Measure of Man," *The New York Times*, July 8, 1994, p. A15.

28. The degree of isolation in suburbia, as well as the quality of its residents' lives, depends largely on the type of suburb at issue. Over the last thirty years or so, some suburbs have become low-density cities that have their own cultural facilities, hospitals, university campuses, and multiple types of housing, in addition to the standard shopping malls. Moreover, they have been the source of many new jobs, particularly for married and middle-class women who wanted to return to the workforce. See "After Decades of Dismissal, the Suburbs Win Converts," by Iver Peterson, *The New York Times*, December 5, 1999, p. 1.

29. Sandel calls this the "constitutive view," because it "describe[s] not just a *feeling* but a mode of self-understanding partly constitutive of the agent's identity. . . . For them [the participants], community describes not just what they *have* as fellow citizens but also what they *are*" (1998, 150; emphasis in original).

30. "[N]ative Americans have sought to focus on their group or society, within which the self achieves meaning; non-natives have concentrated on the self, especially in its struggles against a larger group. For many Indians, the telling of a merely individual story would be not just impertinent, but also downright misleading." See "Tales of the Dispossessed," by Mark Abley, *The Times Literary Supplement*, February 16, 1996, p. 7.

Notes to Chapter 6

1. In my first venture into a phenomenology of kindness many years ago, I argued that kindness involves respect for others in a Kantian sense, as ends in themselves, and I also attempted an answer to Douglass and Philip Hallie on that basis (Hamrick 1985a, 215–16). I now regard that answer, which I shall discuss below, as not entirely incorrect, but rather as hermeneutically naïve. It did not sufficiently come to grips with problems of immoral moralities and multiple interpretations.

2. A sample of this advice runs as follows:
"'You are too lenient, too lenient by far, Léonce,' asserted the Colonel. 'Authority, coercion are what is needed. Put your foot down good and hard; the only way to manage a wife. Take my word for it.' The colonel was perhaps unaware that he had coerced his own wife into her grave" (Chopin 1982, 290).

3. Compare with these characters another who consciously manipulates women and views them as "toys" (Ibsen's dolls). Rev. Helstone in Charlotte Brontë's *Shirley*, whom we already encountered in Chapter 2, is the polar opposite of Henry Higgins: "At heart he could not abide sense in women: he liked to see them as silly, as light-headed, as vain, as open to ridicule as possible; because they were then in reality what he held them to be, and wished them to be—inferior: toys to play with, to amuse a vacant hour, and to be thrown away" (1974, 138).

4. I have added the qualification of sincerity for two reasons. First, it is necessary for the argument in this section that attempts to make the strongest case possible against kindness. Second, I have included it for the sake of a logically complete typology of slave owners. Historical accounts and slave narratives describe at least three types of slave owners. There were those who sincerely believed that African and Creole slaves were not (fully) human and therefore had no rights. This is the attitude of antebellum Southern (and much of Northern) society, which Twain captures so graphically in *Huckleberry Finn*. At the opposite extreme, there were slave owners who knew that their livelihood depended on unspeakably cruel immorality. Either they knew and did not care, or they knew and repressed this inconvenient knowledge. And there were probably others who had doubts and likewise ignored or repressed them, though here the literature is much less clear.

5. It is important to note that Laing rejected the view that, to put it crudely, the children's parents made them sick. He also declined to follow those who held that mental illness was a myth (personal interview). His view can best be described as claiming that the parents at issue were necessary, but not sufficient, causes of their children's mental problems. Since Laing's work and death, considerable progress has been made in tracking a genetic basis for schizophrenia. Therefore, perhaps we should say that the behavior of rigidly controlling parents such as those he studied consists of a strong contributory, rather than a necessary, cause.

6. This is just one example of how "The modern self's expressive freedom goes hand in hand with the modern world's instrumental control" and can sometimes conflict with it (Bellah, et al. 1985, 124). Similarly, after a friend's house was burglarized, the police showed a singular lack of enthusiasm about the chances of catching the thieves and recovering his lost property, but they did provide cards from psychologists working for victims' services who would provide him with counseling. Rather than receiving the help he needed, my friend was caught in "the tension between conceptions of people as ends in themselves and as a [mere] means to organizational ends" (ibid., 125).

7. It is highly regrettable that Douglass could not have read Nietzsche, especially his penetrating analyses of retribution in *On the Genealogy of Morals*. Michael Moore (1987) points out neatly how Nietzsche would explain Mrs. Auld's heightened opposition. It consists of the sublimation of an impulse that she could not recognize consciously because of conflict with her husband. Therefore, she dishonestly

"ignored" it by transmuting her guilty conscience into more vocal opposition. Moore points out how this classic Shakespearean response of "protesting too much" underwrites people's intense opposition to the types of crimes to which they are most attracted. Hence, their strongly retributive impulses to punish offenders take the place of this sublimated self-recognition. Freud's notion of trauma as repression (*Verneinung*) leads to the same conclusion, because it reveals vulnerabilities in (here) victimizers who then repress the cause (s) of these threats (Freud 1953–74, I, 352–57).

8. As we have seen in the discussion of Werner Marx's ethics, the German word for "pity" or "compassion" is *Mitleid*, literally, "suffering-with." Marx founds his ethics of compassion on a capacity for this feeling, which he terms *Mitleidenkönnen*. Of course, Nietzsche would have no higher regard for his approach to ethics than he would of any of the others described here.

9. There are other dimensions of the moral value of forgetting, as in gift giving. Nietzsche's naturalistic view of moral values accounts for gratitude as the expression of a desire to rectify a power imbalance when someone does me a favor or gives me a gift. I cannot recoup my power in the situation directly, so I try to make it up by thanking the individual. On this reading, gratitude is, therefore, a gentle form of revenge. However, Boltanski argues against sociological critiques of gift giving based on self-interest that, "inspired by the Nietzschean critique, denounce the illusion of the freely given and unveil the interests hidden under the illusion of disinterestedness" (Boltanski 1990, 201). Instead, someone "in a state of agapè gives, without preoccupying himself with a gift in return, and then forgets" (ibid., 241). The person in a state of agape has no calculus for valuing gifts and judging the proper return gift in order to keep the scales of power even. To this state of love should be compared the consciousnesses of all of the *fearful* holiday shoppers who buy according to what has been bought for them.

10. For a detailed discussion of the capable body, nature, and law, see Hamrick (1987), especially chapters 6 and 7.

11. Nussbaum records that, "The 'capabilities approach' was pioneered within economics by Amartya Sen and has been developed by both Sen and me in complementary but not identical ways" (1999, 379, n. 26). Sen's latest reflections on the subject are included in his *Development as Freedom* (New York: Alfred A. Knopf, 1999).

12. Against the suspicion that basic human rights are merely the product of Western cultural history, Ricoeur states that, "It is as though universalism and contextualism overlapped imperfectly on a small number of fundamental values, such as those we read in the universal declaration of the rights of man and of the citizen." At the intersection of the universal and the historical, these values can be defended as universally binding. However, we also need to allow for this claim to be questioned "on the level of the convictions incorporated in concrete forms of life." This discussion will be fruitless, however, unless each of the discussants acknowledges that "potential universals are contained in so-called exotic cultures." Thus, for Ricoeur, the "notion of universals in context or of potential or inchoate universals is . . . the notion that best accounts for the reflective equilibrium that we are seeking between universality and historicity" (1992, 289).

Notes to Chapter 7

1. This same text, at p. 177 ff., offers a spirited defense of the continuing relevance of Marx's solutions as well as his criticisms.

2. "Guatemala passed a law recommended by the World Health Organization forbidding makers of baby formula to claim that expensive formula (rather than free mother's milk) is necessary for fat, healthy babies. Gerber Products convinced the United States to challenge that law in the WTO. The mere threat of a trade challenge caused Guatemala to drop its law." See "WTO's Record Explains Protests in Seattle," by Donnella H. Meadows, the *St. Louis Post-Dispatch*, November 29, 1999, p. B7.

3. "U.S. Effort to Add Labor Standards to Agenda Fails," by Steven Greenhouse and Joseph Kahn, *The New York Times*, December 3, 1999, p. 1.

4. "Shipwreck in Seattle," by David E. Sanger, *The New York Times*, December 5, 1999, Section 1, p. 14.

5. "The notion that human beings are born with inalienable rights had to be reconciled with the fact that women could not vote and did not have equal property rights. So the ideal of the 'passionless' woman, who was 'the angel of the house,' was born as a rationalization for preserving the traditional hierarchy." See "The Opposites of Sex: The 'Normal' and the Not," by Dinita Smith, *The New York Times*, May 13, 2000, p. A17. The point under discussion comes from Carol Groneman (2000).

6. Goldman (1993, 148–49) cites a number of studies that failed to find any statistically meaningful gender differences as measured by Kohlberg's cognitive stage theory, as well as other studies that did conclude that "females were more likely to choose personal over impersonal dilemmas as problems to talk about and to identify personal problems as the sort they confronted. Moreover, personal dilemmas were more likely to elicit a 'care' response than a 'justice' or 'rights' response. Controlling for dilemma *content*, however, sex differences were still not found to be significant."

7. See, for example, Freud's *"Civilized" Sexual Morality and Modern Nervous Illness* (1908) (1953–1974, IX: 199) which anticipates the same argument in *The Future of an Illusion* (1927) (1953–1974, XXI: 48).

8. It should be noted that Nietzsche writes here without the slightest trace of irony or sarcasm, as could well be expected from one who wrote so much else about women that is prejudicial, inaccurate, and morally outrageous. His attitude here is purely compassionate.

9. "[her]" is included in the cited text. The author cites here Jean Hampton (1991, 54).

10. The editor comments on this passage: "Surely not all of *Uncle Tom's Cabin* embodies a greater indictment of the slave-based code than this scene, in which the *right* course is shown to be perfectly evil and the *wrong* perfectly good—shown not by expostulation but by a literarily complex irony and by a good person's dreadful dilemma, both of them under perfect control" (288). Perhaps, however, there is another contender for this accolade. Toni Morrison shows us in *Beloved* the terrible dilemma of a mother who kills her baby to prevent her from growing up in slavery.

11. Diminishing cruelty by getting the victimizer to adopt the perspective of the victim has many social applications—for example, in law. The fourth chapter of Nuss-

baum's *Poetic Justice* provides a quick review of certain legal cases in which empathic links to victims might well have changed judges' minds. But there are many more cases too lengthy to summarize here. Three relevant and important U.S. Supreme Court decisions are *Bradwell v. Illinois*, 16 Wall. 130 (1873) (upholding an Illinois law barring women from practicing law); *San Antonio Independent School District et al. v. Rodriguez*, 411 U.S. 1 (1973) (overturning a lower court ruling that upheld a challenge to the Texas system of financing public schools with local property taxes); and *General Electric Co. v. Gilbert*, 429 U.S. 125 (1976) (upholding a private disability insurance plan that covered all risks except pregnancy). *Gilbert* proved to be too strong for the legislative stomach and was remedied legislatively by the Pregnancy Disability Act of 1978.

12. "Old List of Klan Members Revives Racist Past in an Indiana City," by Dirk Johnson, *The New York Times*, August 2, 1995, p. A8.

13. The best dramatic picture that I have ever seen of what America was like during my youth was the short-lived, excruciatingly accurate television series *I'll Fly Away*. I will always be curious to know whether its low viewer ratings were due in whole or in part to its uncomfortable truth.

14. An earlier version of the following section—titled "Growing Up Male"—read to the Merleau-Ponty Circle's annual general meeting at George Washington University, September 2000, generated many helpful criticisms, especially from Gail Weiss.

15. Interested readers may wish to consult, besides Connell's book, May, Strikwerda, and Hopkins (1996); Berger, Wallis, and Watson (1995); and Silverman (1992).

16. Nussbaum states that, "The philosophical tradition suggests that even something as apparently deepseated as the character of a person's erotic desire may contain a socially learned component" (1999, 12). Merleau-Ponty's phenomenology of the body showed a long time ago why a person's erotic desire *must* always contain "a socially learned component."

17. If this sounds rather like an advertisement for Dodge trucks—"RAM tough"—the association is no accident. Advertisers use the same qualities traditionally associated with masculinity to sell products to men, and a ram is a male animal. The announcer's "macho" voice reinforces the impression. Indeed, it sounds as though either he is bench-pressing 200 pounds and/or is about to have a hernia. Given this cluster of values, it is most improbable that any such ad will mention the fact that a ram is a male *sheep*.

18. Other images are equally possible, as Bordo notes: "[T]he vagina could just as easily be imagined as actively holding, containing, or enclosing the penis as being 'penetrated' by it" (1994, 288–89). She goes on to point out, following Richard Mohr, that homosexuality is "deeply subversive of sexism," because it eliminates the "dominance of the penetrator" in favor of a type of sexual "democracy" in which "active/passive roles appear as easily reversible and none is privileged" (ibid., 289).

19. The same desire for reintegration shows itself in male friendships. Some years ago, there was a beer commercial that caught this insight exactly. A group of men sat around a campfire by a lake. As they toasted each other with beer bottles, one of them spoke to and for the whole group when he said, "It doesn't get any better than this." However, as the advertisers knew very well, that commercial was no more

about beer than, say, the story of Jonah was about the anatomy of whales. It was really about the elusive end of friendship to which the beer company hoped their product would be seen as a means.

20. The importance of virility for male self-esteem and esteem in the eyes of others could not be clearer than in Tony Blair's 5 percent increase in approval ratings upon the announcement of his wife's unexpected pregnancy. In addition, how many people know anything about Senator Strom Thurmond apart from his age and legendary virility? Even the appearance of virility is effective for self-esteem, as the wildly enthusiastic and largely male response to Viagra shows.

21. Body images in these two eras do differ dramatically in one respect, however. Today, "Gay and straight, male and female, blue-collar and white-collar, everyone in our culture today (who can afford to) is getting hard and ripped." Challenges to gender divisions in the workforce have "consisted largely in permission for women to do men's work and embody a masculinist ethos and aesthetics." However, this change is asymmetrical in that it still violates cultural norms for men to do women's jobs. When they do undertake them, they usually "masculinize" them in order to avoid the appearance of softness (Bordo 1994, 290, 292–93).

22. For example, Eric Harris, one of the Littleton killers, apparently complained repeatedly about his height and particularly that his brother was taller than he (Hall 1999, 32). Perhaps that report, if true, will lead some people somewhere to be more reflective about their complicity with the male ideology. In terms of the "female ideology," that "thin" = "beautiful," editors of women's fashion magazines have sometimes decried young girls' eating disorders just as firmly as they have declined responsibility for them. They argue that their magazines merely reflect prevailing codes of beauty rather than create them. The disingenuousness of that reply is risible, however, because young girls form their ideals of beauty in part—perhaps in large part—on the basis of pictures of emaciated supermodels in those very fashion magazines. Perhaps that would begin to change as well if the tide of public opinion turned in the direction of perceiving those pictures as threats to public health. As long as male and female ideologies remain highly profitable and publicly uncriticized, young people will continue to be harmed.

23. Not all cases of exploitation involve betrayals of trust. For example, Douglass stated many times that slaves had no reason to trust the slave owner, because their welfare turned exclusively on the latter's character, state of mind, whims, and so forth.

24. "Schools with a Slant," by John F. Borowski, *The New York Times*, August 21, 1999, p. A23. The author also notes that, "A few years ago, Consumers Union . . . analyzed 111 'sponsored educational materials' for a study of commercialism in schools. It found that roughly 80 percent included blatant bias, commercial pitches, inaccuracies, or all three."

25. George Will, "Peddling an Ethic of Selfishness to 'Consumer Cadets,'" *St. Louis Post-Dispatch*, May 7, 2001, p. E9.

26. "A.T.M. Cards Fail to Live Up to Promise to Poor," by David Barstow, *The New York Times*, August 16, 1999, p. 1. Barstow also writes that, "When informed about the imminent publication of the article," Citigroup made some cosmetic changes in the interest of welfare recipients, but the latter still have less access than regular customers do, and they still have to pay special fees to use the machines.

Notes to Chapter 8

1. Readers interested in the wider concepts of coercion and exploitation should consult, *inter alia*, Wertheimer (1987, 1996) for a variety of important examples, spurious examples, and analyses of the concepts of coercion and exploitation.

2. Compare Sartre's statement that Merleau-Ponty "told me that the communists were right to distrust intellectuals. They were always seduced by the particular action proposed, badly equipped to undertake it, and above all to make it come to an end. They were quickly enamoured of it and even more quickly disenchanted, thus in the same breath abandoning the common enterprise and returning implacably to their precious studies" (1984, 140).

3. "For Caseworker, Helping Is a Frustrating Struggle," by Jason DeParle, *The New York Times*, December 10, 1999, p. 1.

4. This assertion will surprise those who are used to thinking of ethics in terms of rule-based deontologies or utilitarianisms (or consequentialisms). Rule-based duties, it will be held, are radically different than ephemeral aesthetic pleasures. But that is not the sense of the aesthetic employed here, and kindness that is closely analogous to aesthetic experience is much closer to what, say, Ricoeur designated as ethics as opposed to morality.

5. Ricoeur often announced, but never wrote, the third volume of *The Philosophy of the Will*, a "Poetics of Will." Of course, I do not claim that this section represents even part of what he necessarily would have written. However, I do believe that his thought could have gone in this direction. The *poiesis* that he explores attaches to the creation of meaning generally, and that sense is equally well intended here. However, there is nevertheless a will behind acts of kindness, and it is the decision making of that will that is of primary interest here.

6. As William Frankena pointed out some years ago, neither Kant nor anyone else has ever given us a completely conflict-free system of rules of justice (1973, 32–33), and that is not yet to say anything about the practical difficulties in seeking justice.

7. Beardsley takes no notice of the difficulty of developing this sympathetic imagination before controversial artworks that violate the received morality of a particular culture—for instance, Andres Serrano's *Christ Pissed*, in which he placed a cruxifix in a jar of his own urine, or Robert Mapplethorpe's homoerotic photographs. However, he might reply that he refers only to possible effects of contemplating aesthetic objects, not that every such experience will have the effects for which he hopes.

8. One might object that this is precisely what is not true of controversial artworks that violate mainstream cultural morality, and not even true of the avant-garde generally. But even criticisms of such works, be they ever so strident, tacitly acknowledge the normative demand that those works make on us to be evaluated in and of themselves apart from official party lines and other ideologies.

9. It is of course true that not all aesthetic objects have the capacity to provide depth in our experiences of them. This is, in fact, one of the main ways that most people evaluate works of art. Those works that cannot do this we say cannot "speak to us," and they diminish in our view into triviality. The word "art" is often used in a normative sense to mean only "good art," but that is a mistake. "Art" also has a more basic descriptive sense that allows us to distinguish good art from bad art.

10. One can imagine, of course, many circumstances in which other things are not equal. If, say, the person who picked up the umbrella had to make a great effort to do so—he or she might have long been in physical therapy following a severe automobile accident—then our admiration would be considerably different than for an able-bodied individual. Also, sometimes people working in service industries have such consistently bad experiences with customers that any ordinary kindness tends to get magnified into heroic virtue.

11. I owe this reference and commentary on it to Professor Didier Dupont of Lille. In our many café conversations and visits to art museums and artists' workshops in Paris, he perfectly illustrated the aesthetic and moral qualities that he himself explicated.

12. The next line, "I can't get no girlie action," extends the degradation of being to having, the depths of meaningful experience to superficial, ephemeral satisfactions, beyond the ownership of property. This degraded sense of sexuality is caught exactly in the popular idiom of "having sex." It is deeply symbolic that a certain entertainment network voted this song the best in rock and roll in the last millennium.

13. In France, in fact, the term *postmodernisme* was originally limited to architecture and probably had a more exact meaning in that field than anywhere else, certainly in philosophy.

14. Compagnon does not mention it, but the name of those apartment buildings was the Pruitt-Igoe Complex.

15. Wittgenstein is an example of a thinker who makes the same criticisms of modernism as do the postmodernists, but he remains within modernism. As opposed to Carnap, whose thought "is part of the same cultural spirit as the Bauhaus and Le Corbusier's Cité radieuse," Wittgenstein's modernism, as Hilary Putnam pointed out, "is anguished and suffering." He wanted "to reestablish the legitimacy of the natural, of the traditional, of organic development, of formations that spontaneously arise in the absence of any ambitious total plan" (Descombes 1993, 162).

16. A recent Ford truck television commercial illustrates exactly Bordo's point. A hardened, suntanned range worker fixes fence posts—which he throws into and from his truck—while the male voice-over favorably contrasts his tough solitude with those who have seen the film *You've Got Mail*, which, the unseen male observes, is about falling in love, boy kissing girl, and so on.

17. See "Après-Face-Lift Spas Are Thriving in California," by Carey Goldberg, *The New York Times*, October 28, 1996, p. B2.

18. "[I]n our pampered, narcissistic culture, vices are affectations. . . . [T]here is no more appalling sight than a table of complaisant and self-important young men and women blowing smoke from their Robustos and Belicosos. . . . But then, maybe our stylized and commercialized vices are perfect for our times. Annoying, prosperous, mildly guilty, but of no real consequence." See "Vice Takes a Holiday," by Maureen Dowd, *The New York Times*, December 31, 1997, p. A15. As Lipovetsky would say, "Vice in the fashion mode."

Bibliography

Abram, David. 1988. "Merleau-Ponty and the Voice of the Earth." *Environmental Ethics* 10, 101–20.

———. 1996. *The Spell of the Sensuous: Perception and Language in a More-than-Human World.* New York: Pantheon Books.

Achebe, Chinua. 1992. *Things Fall Apart.* Introduction by Kwame Anthony Appiah. New York: Alfred A. Knopf, Everyman's Library. First published in 1958. London: William Heinemann Ltd.

Albaret, Céleste. 1973. *Monsieur Proust.* Paris: Laffont.

Alejandro, Roberto. 1993. *Hermeneutics, Citizenship, and the Public Sphere.* Albany: State University of New York Press.

Allende, Isabel. 1986. *House of the Spirits.* Translated by Magda Bogin. New York: Bantam Books. Originally published in 1982 as *La Casa de los Espiritus.* Barcelona: Plaza y Janés, Editores. S. A.

———. *Eva Luna.* 1989. Translated by Margaret Sayers Peden. New York: Bantam Books. Originally published in 1987 as *Eva Luna.* Barcelona: Plaza y Janés Editores, S.A.

Althusser, Louis. 1993. *The Future Lasts Forever.* Edited by Olivier Corpet and Yann Moulier Boutang. Translated by Richard Veasey. New York: The New Press. Originally published in 1992 as *L'avenir dure longtemps.* Paris: Éditions STOCK/IMEC.

Aristotle. 1941. *The Poetics.* Translated by Ingram Bywater. Pp. 1455–87 in Richard McKeon, ed., *The Basic Works of Aristotle.* New York: Random House.

———. 1962. *Nicomachean Ethics.* Translated with Introduction and Notes by Martin Oswald. Indianapolis: Library of Liberal Arts Press.

Attig, Tom. 1985. "Existential Phenomenology and Applied Philosophy." Pp. 161–76 in William S. Hamrick, ed., *Phenomenology in Practice and Theory.* Dordrecht: Martinus Nijhoff.

Auden, W. H. 1979. *W.H. AUDEN, Selected Poems.* New York: Vintage Books, new ed.

Austen, Jane. 1966 [1816]. *Emma.* Edited with an Introduction by Ronald Blythe. Harmondsworth: Penguin Books.

———. 1982 [1818]. *Persuasion.* Edited with an Introduction by D.W. Harding. Harmondsworth: Penguin Books.

———. 1982 [1811]. *Sense and Sensibility.* Edited with an Introduction and Notes by Tony Tanner. Harmondsworth: Penguin Books.

Austin, J. L. 1962. *Sense and Sensibilia.* Oxford: The Clarendon Press.

Baier, Annette. 1986. "Trust and Antitrust." *Ethics* 96: 2. (January): 231–60.

Balzac, Honoré de. 1987 [1833]. *Le médecin de compagne.* Edited by Maurice Bouet. Paris: Librairie Larousse.

Barber, S.J., Michael D. 1993. *Guardian of Dialogue: Max Scheler's Phenomenology, Sociology of Knowledge, and Philosophy of Love.* Lewisburg: Bucknell University Press.

Barnett, Mark A. 1987. "Empathy and Related Responses in Children." Pp. 146–62 in Eisenberg and Strayer, eds. *Empathy and Its Development.* Cambridge: Cambridge University Press.

Baron, Robert A. and Donn Byrne. 1987. *Social Psychology: Understanding Human Interaction.* Boston: Allyn and Bacon, Inc., Fifth Edition.

Barthes, Roland. 1985. *The Responsibility of Forms.* Translated by Richard Howard. Berkeley: University of California Press. Originally published as in 1982 *L'Obvie et l'obtus.* Paris: Éditions de Seuil.

Bartky, Sandra Lee. 1979. "On Psychological Oppression." Pp. 252–58 in Sharon Bishop and Marjorie Weinzweig, eds. *Philosophy and Women.* Belmont, Calif.: Wadsworth Publishing.

———. 1990. *Femininity and Domination: Studies in the Phenomenology of Oppression.* New York and London: Routledge.

———. 1998. "Body Politics." Pp. 321–29 in Alison M. Jaggar and Iris Marion Young, eds. *A Companion to Feminist Philosophy.* Oxford: Blackwell Publishers.

Beardsley, Monroe C. 1958. *Aesthetics: Problems in the Philosophy of Criticism.* New York: Harcourt, Brace and Company.

Beauvoir, Simone de. 1953. *The Second Sex.* Translated and Edited by H.M. Parshley. New York: Knopf. Originally published in 1939 as *Le deuxième sexe.* Paris: Gallimard.

Bellah, Robert N., Richard Masden, William M. Sullivan et al. 1985. *Habits of the Heart.* New York: Harper & Row. 2d ed., 1996. Berkeley: University of California Press.

———. 1992. *The Good Society.* New York: Alfred A. Knopf.

Berger, Maurice, Brian Wallis, and Simon Watson, eds. 1995. *Constructing Masculinity.* New York and London: Routledge.

Bernasconi, Robert, and Simon Critchley, eds. 1991. *Re-Reading Levinas.* Bloomington: Indiana University Press.

Berne, Eric, M. D. 1964. *Games People Play.* London: Penguin Books.

Bigwood, Carol. 1991. "Renaturalizing the Body (with the Help of Merleau-Ponty)." *Hypatia* 6: 3: 54–73.

Blake, William. 1906 [1789]. "On Another's Sorrow," Book I of *Songs of Innocence.* in Edwin J. Ellis, ed., *The Poetical Works of William Blake.* London: Chatto & Windus.

Bloom, Amy. 2000. "Generation Rx." *New York Times Magazine,* (March 12): 23–24.

Blum, Lawrence. 1987. "Particularity and Responsiveness." Pp. 306–37 in J. Kagan and S. Lamb, eds., *The Emergence of Morality in Young Children.* Chicago: University of Chicago Press.

Bollnow, Otto Friedrich. 1962. *Einfache Sittlichkeit.* Göttingen: Vandenhoeck & Rupprecht.

Boltanski, Luc. 1990. *L'Amour et la Justice comme compétences.* Paris: Éditions Métailié.

Bordo, Susan. 1994. "Reading the Male Body." Pp. 265–306 in Laurence Goldstein, ed., *The Male Body: Features, Destinies, Exposures.* Ann Arbor: University of Michigan Press.

Boswell, John. 1990. *The Kindness of Strangers: The Abandonment of Children in Western Europe from Late Antiquity to the Renaissance.* New York: Vintage Books.

Bridges, Thomas. 1994. *The Culture of Citizenship.* Albany: State University of New York Press.

Brontë, Charlotte. 1966 [1847]. *Jane Eyre.* Edited by Q. D. Leavis. Harmondsworth: Penguin Books.

————. 1974 [1849]. *Shirley.* Edited by Andrew Hook and Judith Hook. London: Penguin Books.

Brontë, Emily. 1959 [1847]. *Wuthering Heights.* New York: Signet Books.

Brown, Lyn Mikel, and Carol Gilligan. 1992. *Meeting at the Crossroads: Women's Psychology and Girls' Development.* Cambridge, Mass.: Harvard University Press.

Brumberg, Joan Jacobs. 1997. *The Body Project.* New York: Random House.

Bury, Emmanuel. 1996. *Littérature et politesse, L'invention de l'honnête homme (1580–1750).* Paris: Presses Universitaires de France.

Butler, Judith. 1995. "Melancholy Gender/Refused Identification." Pp. 21–36 in Berger, Wallis, and Watson, eds. *Constructing Masculinity.* New York and London: Routledge.

Camus, Albert. 1972. *The Plague.* Translated by Stuart Gilbert. New York: Alfred A. Knopf. Originally published in 1947 as *La Peste.* Paris: Gallimard.

Carr, Brian. 1999. "Pity and Compassion as Social Virtues." *Philosophy* 74: 411–29.

Cash, Wilbur J. 1941. *The Mind of the South.* New York: Alfred A. Knopf.

Cataldi, Suzanne L. 1993. *Emotion, Depth, and Flesh, A Study of Sensitive Space.* Albany: State University of New York Press.

Chakravarty, Amiya, ed. 1961. *A Tagore Reader.* Boston: Beacon Press.

Chekhov, Anton. 1988 [1886]. "Heartache." Pp. 120–25 in *A Doctor's Visit: Short Stories.* Edited with an Introduction by Tobias Wolff. New York: Bantam Books.

Chopin, Kate. 1982 [1899]. *The Awakening.* Pp 39–122 in Jerome Beaty, ed., *The Norton Introduction to the Short Novel.* New York: W. W. Norton & Company.

Coetzee, J. M. 1995. "The Artist at High Tide." *The New York Review of Books* XLII: 4 (March 2): 13–16. This is a review of Joseph Frank, 1995. *Dostoevsky: The Miraculous Years, 1865–71.* Princeton: Princeton University Press.

Cohen, Richard A., ed. 1986. *Face to Face with Levinas.* Albany: State University of New York Press.

Coles, Robert. 1992. Review of W. W. Meissner's *Ignatius of Loyola, The Psychology of a Saint. New York Times Book Review,* September 20th, p. 38.

Collins, Randall. 1994. *Four Sociological Traditions.* New York and Oxford: Oxford University Press.

Compagnon, Antoine. 1994. *The Five Paradoxes of Modernity.* New York: Columbia University Press. Originally published in 1990 as *Les Cinq Paradoxes de la Modernité.* Paris: Éditions de Seuil.

Connell, R.W. 1995. *Masculinities.* Cambridge: Polity Press.

Conrad, Joseph. 1985 [1902]. *The Heart of Darkness.* Edited with an Introduction by Paul O'Prey. London: Penguin Books.

Cox, Harvey. 1966. *The Secular City.* Rev. ed. New York: Macmillan.

Cullity, Garrett. 1994. "International Aid and the Scope of Kindness." *Ethics* 105: 1 99–127.

Curley, Edwin. 1991. "A Good Man Is Hard to Find." Presidential address delivered before the Eighty-Ninth Annual Central Division Meeting of the American Philosophical Association, April 26. Pp. 29–45 in the *Proceedings and Addresses of the American Philosophical Association*, vol. 65, no. 3 (November).

Dalai Lama. 1990. *The Dalai Lama: A Policy of Kindness*. Edited by Sidney Piburn. Ithaca, N.Y.: Snow Lion Publications.

Damon, William. 1999. "The Moral Development of Children." *Scientific American* (August): 72–78.

Dangarembga, Tsitsi. 1988. *Nervous Conditions*. Seattle: Seal Press.

Darley, John M., and Daniel C. Batson. 1973. "From Jerusalem to Jericho: A Study of Situational and Dispositional Variables in Helping Behavior." *Journal of Personality and Social Psychology* 27: 191–204.

Davis, O.S.B., Cyprian, Reverend. 1990. *The History of Black Catholics in the United States*. New York: Crossroad Publishing.

Darwin, Charles. 1898 [1871]. *The Descent of Man and Selection in Relation to Sex*. Second Edition, Revised and Augmented. New York: D. Appleton and Company.

Descombes, Vincent. 1992. *Proust: Philosophy of the Novel*. Translated by Catherine Chance Macksey. Stanford, Calif.: Stanford University Press. Originally published in 1987 as *Proust: Philosophie du roman*. Paris: Les Éditions de Minuit.

———. 1993. *The Barometer of Modern Reason*. Translated by Stephen Adam Schwartz. New York and Oxford: Oxford University Press. Originally published in 1988 as *Le Baromètre de la raison moderne*. Paris: Odéon.

Derrida, Jacques. 1988. "The Politics of Friendship." *Journal of Philosophy*. LXXXV: 11: 632–44.

———. 1994. *Specters of Marx*. Translated by Peggy Kamuf, with an Introduction by Bernd Magnus and Stephen Cullenberg. New York and London: Routledge. Originally published as *Spectres de Marx*. 1993. Paris: Editions Galilée.

———. 1997. *Politics of Friendship*. Translated by George Collins. London and New York: Verso. Originally published in 1994 as *Politiques de l'amitié*. Paris: Editions Galilée.

De Waal, Frans B. M. 1996. *Good Natured: The Origins of Right and Wrong in Humans and Other Animals*. Cambridge, Mass.: Harvard University Press.

Dickens, Charles. 1995 [1854]. *Hard Times, For These Times*. Edited with an Introduction and Notes by Kate Flint. London: Penguin Books.

Douglass, Frederick. 1962 [1862]. *Life and Times of Frederick Douglass*. Introduction by Rayford W. Logan. New York: Collier Books.

———. 1988 [1845] *Narrative of the Life of Frederick Douglass, An American Slave*. Harmondsworth: Penguin Books.

Dufrenne, Mikel. 1973. *The Phenomenology of Aesthetic Experience*. Translated by Edward Casey, Albert A. Anderson, Willis Domingo, and Leon Jacobson. Evanston, Ill.: Northwestern University Press. Originally published in 1967 as *Phénoménologie de l'expérience esthétique*. Paris: Presses Universitaires de France.

Edmundson, Mark. 1997. "On the Uses of a Liberal Education." *Harper's Magazine* (September): 39–49.

Eisenberg, Nancy, and Randy Lennon. 1983. "Sex Differences in Empathy and Related Capacities." *Psychological Bulletin* 94:100–31.

Eisenberg, Nancy, and Janet Strayer. 1987. *Empathy and Its Development.* Cambridge: Cambridge University Press.

Eliot, George. 1965 [1871]. *Middlemarch.* Edited with an Introduction by W. J. Harvey. London: Penguin Books.

———. 1985 [1880]. *The Mill on the Floss.* Edited with an Introduction and Notes by A. S. Byatt. London: Penguin Books.

Emerson, Ralph Waldo. 1937 [1841]. "Friendship." Pp. 105–20 in Charles W. Eliot, LL.D., ed., *Essays and English Traits.* The Harvard Classics. New York: P. F. Collier & Son.

Enns, Diane. 1995. " 'We-Flesh,' Remembering the Body *Beloved.*" *Philosophy Today* 39:3/4 (fall), 263–79.

Erasmus of Rotterdam. 1971 [1511]. *Praise of Folly* and *Letter to Martin Dorp 1515.* Translated by Betty Radice with an Introduction and Notes by A.H.T. Levi. London: Penguin Books.

Erdoes, Richard. 1972. *The Sun Dance People: The Plains Indians, Their Past and Present.* New York: Alfred A. Knopf.

Erikson, Erik H. 1969. *Gandhi's Truth.* New York: W. W. Norton & Company.

———. 1976. "Reflections on Dr. Borg's Life Cycle." *Daedalus* 105:1–29.

Feinberg, Joel. 1973. *Social Philosophy.* Englewood Cliffs, N.J.: Prentice Hall.

———. 1988. *Harmless Wrongdoing.* New York and Oxford: Oxford University Press.

Fink, Eugen. 1933. "Die phänomenologische Philosophie Husserls in der gegenwärtigen Kritik." *Kantstudien* 38: 321–83.

Flaubert, Gustave. 1964 [1856]. *Madame Bovary.* Translated by Mildred Marmur, with a Foreword by Mary McCarthy. New York: Signet Books.

Fletcher, George P. 1993. *Loyalty.* Oxford: Oxford University Press.

Finnis, John. 1980. *Natural Law and Natural Rights.* Oxford: Clarendon Press.

Foot, Philippa. 1978. *Virtues and Vices and Other Essays in Moral Philosophy.* Oxford: Basil Blackwell.

Forster, E. M. 1985 [1910]. *Howards End.* Introduction by Samuel Hynes. New York: Bantam Books.

———. 1986 [1923]. *A Room with a View.* New York: Vintage Books.

Foucault, Michel. 1977. *Discipline and Punish, The Birth of the Prison.* Translated by Alan Sheridan. New York: Vintage Books. Originally published in 1975 as *Surveiller et Punir: Naissance de la prison.* Paris: Gallimard.

———. 1986. *The Care of the Self.* Translated by Robert Hurley. New York: Random House. Originally published in 1984 as *Le Souci de soi.* Paris: Gallimard.

Frankena, William. 1973. *Ethics.* 2nd ed. Englewood Cliffs, N.J.: Prentice Hall.

Freud, Sigmund. 1953–1974. *The Standard Edition of the Complete Psychological Works of Sigmund Freud.* Edited by James Strachey et al. London: Hogarth Press.

Friedmann, Wolfgang. 1973. "Phenomenology and Legal Science." Pp. 343–65 in Maurice Natanson, ed., *Phenomenology and the Social Sciences*, vol 2. Evanston, Ill.: Northwestern University Press.

Gadamer, Hans Georg. 1975. *Truth and Method.* Translated by G. Barden and J. Cumming. New York: Seabury Press. Originally published in 1960 as *Wahrheit und Methode.* Tübingen: J.C.B. Mohr (Paul Siebeck).

Gardner, Howard. 1975. *The Shattered Mind.* New York: Alfred A. Knopf.

Gare, Arran E. 1995. *Postmodernism and the Environmental Crisis.* London and New York: Routledge.

Gauchet, Marcel, and Gladys Swain. 1980. *La pratique de l'esprit humain.* Paris: Gallimard.

Gaylin, Willard. 1992. *The Male Ego.* New York: Viking Press.

Gewirth, Alan. 1978. *Reason and Morality.* Chicago: University of Chicago Press.

Gewirtz, Paul. 1988. "Aeschylus' Law." *Harvard Law Review* 101: 1043–55.

Gilligan, Carol. 1982, 1993 printing. *In a Different Voice.* Cambridge, Mass.: Harvard University Press.

———. 1988. "Remapping the Moral Domain: New Images of Self in Relationship." Pp. 3–20 in Carol Gilligan, Janie Victoria Ward, Jill McLean Taylor, with Betty Bardige, eds., *Mapping the Moral Domain.* Cambridge, Mass.: Harvard University Press.

Gilligan, Carol, and Grant Wiggins. 1988. "The Origins of Morality in Early Childhood Relationships." Pp. 111–38 in Carol Gilligan, Janie Victoria Ward et al., *Mapping the Moral Domain.*

Goldman, Alvin I. 1992. "Empathy, Mind, and Morals." Presidential address delivered before the Sixty–Sixth Annual Pacific Division Meeting of the American Philosophical Association in Portland, Oregon, March 27. Pp. 17–41 in *Proceedings and Addresses of the American Philosophical Association,* vol. 66, no. 3.

———. 1993. *Philosophical Applications of Cognitive Science.* Boulder: Westview Press.

Goleman, Daniel. 1995. *Emotional Intelligence.* New York: Bantam Books.

Gordon, Robert M. 1986. "Folk Psychology As Simulation." *Mind and Language* 1:158–71.

———. 1992. "The Simulation Theory: Objections and Misconceptions." *Mind and Language* 7:11–34.

Gray, Thomas. 1963 [1742]. *Elegy Written in a Country Churchyard.* P. 341 in J. B. Priestley and Josephine Spear, eds., *Adventures in English Literature.* New York: Harcourt, Brace & World.

Groneman, Carol. 2000. *Nymphomania: A History.* New York: W. W. Norton & Company.

Grossman, David. 1998. "Trained to Kill." *Christianity Today.* August 10, pp. 1–8.

Gunther, Gerald. 1975. *Cases and Materials on Constitutional Law,* 9th ed. Mineola, N.Y.: Foundation Press, Inc.

Habermas, Jürgen. 1987. *The Philosophical Discourse of Modernity.* Translated by Frederick G. Lawrence. Cambridge, Mass.: MIT Press. Originally published in 1985 as *Der philosophische Diskurs der Moderne: Zwölf Vorlesungen.* Frankfurt-am-Main: Suhrkamp Verlag.

———. 1995. *Justification and Application: Remarks on Discourse Ethics.* Translated by Ciaran Cronin. Cambridge, Mass.: MIT Press. Three of the five essays originally appeared in *Erläuterungen zur Diskursethik.* 1991. Frankfurt am Main: Suhrkamp Verlag.

Hahn, Lewis Edwin, ed. 1995. *The Philosophy of Paul Ricoeur.* Chicago and LaSalle: Open Court Press, Library of Living Philosophers, Vol. XXII.

Halfon, Mark S. 1989. *Integrity: A Philosophical Inquiry.* Columbus: Ohio State University Press.

Hall, Stephen S. 1999. "The Bully in the Mirror, the Troubled Life of Boys." *The New York Times Magazine* (August 22): 31–64.

Hallie, Philip. 1979. *Lest Innocent Blood Be Shed: The Story of the Village of Le Chambon and How Goodness Happened There.* New York: Harper & Row.

———. 1981. "From Cruelty to Goodness." *The Hastings Center Report* 11: 3 (June): 23–38.

———. 1982. *Cruelty.* Middletown, Conn.: Wesleyan University Press.

———. 1995. "Camus's Hug." *American Scholar* 64: 3 (summer): 428–35.

———. 1997. *Tales of Good and Evil, Help and Harm.* Foreward by John J. Compton, Afterword by Doris A. Hallie. New York: HarperCollins.

Hammer, Dean C. 1995. "Václav Havel's Construction of a Democratic Discourse: Politics in a Postmodern Age." *Philosophy Today* 39: 2/4 (summer): 119–30.

Hampshire, Stuart. 1989. *Innocence and Experience.* Cambridge, Mass.: Harvard University Press.

Hampton, Jean. 1991. "Two Faces of Contractarian Thought." Pp. 31–55 in Peter Vallentyne, ed., *Contractarianism and Rational Choice.* New York and Cambridge: Cambridge University Press.

Hamrick, William S. 1978. "Persons and Other Students." *Man and World* 11: 1/2: 78–95.

———. 1983. "Language and Abnormal Behavior: Merleau-Ponty, Hart, and Laing." *Review of Existential Psychology and Psychiatry 18:1–3, 181–203.*

———. ed. 1985a. *Phenomenology in Practice and Theory.* Dordrecht: Martinus Nijhoff.

———. 1985b. "Redeeming the Earth: Tragic Wisdom and the Plains Indians." *Journal of the British Society for Phenomenology* 16: 1 (January): 36–54.

———. 1987. *An Existential Phenomenology of Law: Maurice Merleau-Ponty.* Dordrecht: Martinus Nijhoff.

———. 1990. "Coercion and Exploitation: Self-Transposal and the Moral Life." *Journal of the British Society for Phenomenology* 21: 1 (January): 67–79.

———. 1994. "Perception, Corporeity and Kindness." *Journal of the British Society for Phenomenology* 25:1 (January): 74–84.

Hardy, Thomas. 1978 [1891]. *Tess of the D'Urbervilles.* Introduction by A. Alvarez and edited by David Skilton. Harmondsworth: Penguin Books.

———. 1981 [1878]. *The Return of the Native.* Edited with an Introduction by George Woodcock. Harmondsworth: Penguin Books.

———. 1982 [1874]. *Far From the Madding Crowd.* Edited with an Introduction by Ronald Blythe. Harmondsworth: Penguin Books.

Hare, R. M. 1963. *Freedom and Reason.* Oxford: The Clarendon Press.

———. 1981. *Moral Thinking.* Oxford: The Clarendon Press.

Hart, H.L.A. 1961. *The Concept of Law.* Oxford: The Clarendon Press.

Hart, Josephine. 1991. *Damage.* New York: Alfred A. Knopf.

Havel, Václav. 1990. *Disturbing the Peace: A Conversation with Karel Hvizdala.* New York: Alfred A. Knopf. Originally published in 1986 as *Dálkový výslech.* Prague: Rozmluvy.

———. 1991. *Open Letters, Selected Writings 1965–1990.* Selected and Edited by Paul Wilson. New York: Alfred A. Knopf.

———. 1993. *Summer Meditations.* Translated by Paul Wilson. New York: Vintage Books.

Hay, Malcolm. 1960. *Europe and the Jews: The Pressure of Christendom on the People of Israel for 1900 Years.* Boston: Beacon Press. First ed., 1950, *The Foot of Pride.* Boston: Beacon Press.

Hegel, G.W.F. 1967. *Hegel's Philosophy of Right.* Translated by T. M. Knox. New York and Oxford: Oxford University Press.

Heidegger, Martin. 1959. *Introduction to Metaphysics.* Translated by Ralph Mannheim. New Haven and London: Yale University Press. Originally published in 1953 as *Einführung in die Metaphysik.* Tübingen: Max Niemeyer Verlag.

———. 1962. *Being and Time.* Translated by John Macquarrie and Edward Robinson. London: SCM Press. Originally published in 1927 as *Sein und Zeit.* Tübingen: Max Niemeyer Verlag.

———. 1977. *The Question Concerning Technology and Other Essays.* Translated and with an Introduction by William Lovitt. New York: Harper Torchbooks.

Heilbrun, Carolyn G. 1992. "How Girls Become Wimps." *The New York Times Book Review* (October 4): 13–14.

Henry, Michel. 1990. *Phénoménologie Matérielle.* Paris: Presses Universitaires de France.

Herrnstein, Richard J., and Charles Murray. 1994. *The Bell Curve: Intelligence and Class Structure in American Life.* New York: The 0Free Press.

Hesse-Biber, Sharlene. 1996. *Am I Thin Enough Yet?* New York: Oxford University Press.

Hitt, Jack. 2000. "The Second Sexual Revolution." *The New York Times Magazine* (February 20): 34–69.

Hoebel, E. Adamson. 1960. *The Cheyennes: Indians of the Great Plains.* New York: Holt, Rinehart, and Winston.

Hoffman, Martin L. 1984. "Empathy, Its Limitations, and Its Role in a Comprehensive Moral Theory." Pp. 283–302 in William M. Kurtines and Jacob L. Gewirtz, eds., *Morality, Moral Behavior, and Moral Development.* New York and Chicester: John Wiley & Sons.

———. 1987. "The Contribution of Empathy to Justice and Moral Judgment." Pp. 47–80 in Eisenberg and Strayer, eds., *Empathy and Its Development.* Cambridge: Cambridge University Press.

Holler, Clyde, ed. 2000. *The Black Elk Reader.* Syracuse, N.Y.: Syracuse University Press.

Holmes, Stephen. 1993. *The Anatomy of Antiliberalism.* Cambridge, Mass.: Harvard University Press.

Holt, Kay G., M. D. 1994. Letter to the Editor. *Journal of the American Medical Association,* 271:1 (January 5) 23.

Hopkins, S. J., Gerard Manley. 1996. *Selected Poetry.* Edited with an Introduction and Notes by Catherine Phillips. Oxford: Oxford University Press.

Hugo, Victor. 1987 [1862]. *Les Misérables.* Translated by Lee Fahnestock and Norman MacAfee, based on the classic C. E. Wilbour translation. New York: Penguin Books.

Hume, David. 1957 [1751]. *An Inquiry Concerning the Principles of Morals.* Edited and with an Introduction by Charles W. Hendel. Indianapolis: Library of Liberal Arts.

———. 1967 [1739]. *A Treatise of Human Nature.* Edited by L. A. Selby-Bigge. Oxford: Clarendon Press.

Husserl, Edmund. 1970. *The Crisis of European Sciences and Transcendental Phenomenology.* Translated by David Carr. Evanston: Northwestern University Press. Originally published in 1954 as *Die Krisis der europäischen Wissenschaften und die transzendentale Phänomenologie: Eine Einleitung in die phänomenologische Philoso-phie*, ed. Walter Biemel. The Hague: Martinus Nijhoff.

Ibsen, Henrik. 1981. *Four Major Plays*. Translated by James McFarlane and Jens Arup, with an Introduction by James McFarlane. New York: Oxford University Press.

———. 1984. *Four Great Plays*. Translated by R. Farquharson Sharp, with an Introduction and Prefaces to each play by John Gassner. New York: Bantam Books.

James, Henry. 1985 [1904]. *The Golden Bowl*. Edited with an Introduction by Gore Vidal and Notes by Patricia Clark. London: Penguin Books.

———. 1986 [1881]. *The Portrait of a Lady*. Edited with an Introduction by Geoffrey Moore and Notes by Patricia Clark. London: Penguin Books.

James, William. 1910. *Pragmatism: A New Name for Some Old Ways of Thinking*. New York: Longmans, Green, and Co.

———. 1911 [1897]. *The Will to Believe and Other Essays in Popular Philosophy*. London: Longmans, Green, and Co.

Johnson, Peter. 1988. *Politics, Innocence, and the Limits of Goodness*. New York and London: Routledge.

Kadish, Sanford H., and Monrad G. Paulsen. 1975. *Criminal Law and Its Processes, Cases, and Materials*. 3d. ed. Boston: Little, Brown and Company.

Kamin, Leon J. 1995. "Behind the Curve." *Scientific American* (February): 99–103.

Kant, Immanuel. 1964a [1785]. *Groundwork of the Metaphysics of Morals*. Translated by H. J. Paton. New York: Harper Torchbooks.

———. 1964b. [1797]. *The Metaphysical Principles of Virtue, Part II of The Metaphysics of Morals*. Translated by James Ellington, with an Introduction by Warner Wick. Indianapolis: Library of Liberal Arts.

Katz, Leo. 1987. *Bad Acts and Guilty Minds*. Chicago: University of Chicago Press.

Kindlon, Daniel J. 1999. *Raising Cain: Protecting the Emotional Life of Boys*. New York: Ballantine Books.

King, Florence. 1992. *With Charity toward None: A Fond Look at Misanthropy*. New York: St. Martin's Press.

Kleinman, Arthur. 1988. *The Illness Narratives: Suffering, Healing, and the Human Condition*. New York: Basic Books.

Kozol, Jonathan. 1991. *Savage Inequalities: Children in America's Schools*. New York: Crown Publishers.

———. 1995. *Amazing Grace: The Lives of Children and the Conscience of a Nation*. New York: Crown Publishers.

Kriegel, Blandine. 1995. *The State and the Rule of Law*. Translated by Marc A. LePain and Jeffrey C. Cohen, with a Foreword by Donald R. Kelley. Princeton, N.J.: Princeton University Press. Originally published in 1989 as *L'État et les esclaves: Réflexions pour l'histoire des états*. Paris: Éditions Payot.

Lachs, John. 1994. *The Journal of Clinical Ethics* (spring): 10–15.

LaFollette, Hugh. 1996. "Real Men." Pp. 119–34 in May, Strikwerda, and Hopkins, eds., *Rethinking Masculinity*. Lanham, Md.: Rowman & Littlefield, 2d ed.

Laing, R. D. 1971. *Knots*. London: Penguin Books.

Laing, R. D., and A. Esterton. 1964. *Sanity, Madness, and the Family*. Harmondsworth: Penguin Books.

Landgrebe, Ludwig. 1970. "Husserl's Departure from Cartesianism." Pp. 259–306 in R. O. Elvton, ed. *The Phenomenology of Husserl*. Chicago: Quadrangle Books.

Laqueur, Thomas. 1994. "Closing Time." *London Review of Books* (August 18): 7–8.

La Rochefoucauld, François, duc de la. 1959 [1665]. *Maxims*. Translated with an Introduction by Leonard Tancock. London: Penguin Books.

Larrabee, Mary Jeanne, ed. 1993. *An Ethic of Care: Feminist and Interdisciplinary Perspectives*. New York and London: Routledge.

Lawrence, D. H. 1982 [1913]. *Sons and Lovers*. Harmondsworth: Penguin Books.

———. 1983 [1915]. *The Rainbow*. Edited with an Introduction and Notes by John Worthen. Harmondsworth: Penguin Books.

———. 1985 [1921]. *Women in Love*. Harmondsworth: Penguin Books.

Leder, Drew. 1987. "Towards a Phenomenology of Pain." *Review of Existential Psychology Psychiatry* 19:2/3: 255–66.

———. 1990. *The Absent Body*. Chicago and London: University of Chicago Press.

Lee, Dorothy. 1959. *Freedom and Culture*. Englewood Cliffs, N.J.: Prentice Hall.

Lennon, Randy, and Nancy Eisenberg. 1987. "Gender and Age Differences in Empathy and Sympathy." Pp 195–217 in Eisenberg and Strayer eds., *Empathy and Its Development*. Cambridge: Cambridge University Press.

Levin, David M. 1985. *The Body's Recollection of Being, Phenomenological Psychology, and the Deconstruction of Nihilism*. London: Routledge & Kegan Paul.

———. 1991. "Visions of Narcissism: Intersubjectivity and the Reversals of Reflection." Pp. 47–90 in M. C. Dillon, ed., *Merleau-Ponty Vivant*. Albany: State University of New York Press.

———. 1998. "Tracework: Myself and Others in the Moral Phenomenology of Merleau-Ponty and Levinas." *International Journal of Philosophical Studies* 6:3 (October): 345–92.

Levinas, Emmanuel. 1972. *Humanisme de l'autre homme*. Montpellier: Fata Morgana.

———. 1979. *Totality and Infinity*. Translated by Alphonso Lingis. The Hague: Martinus Nijhoff. Originally published in 1961 as *Totalité et infini, essai sur l'extériorité*. The Hague: Martinus Nijhoff.

———. 1981. *Otherwise than Being or Beyond Essence*. Translated by Alphonso Lingis. The Hague: Martinus Nijhoff. Originally published in 1974 as *Autrement qu'être ou au-delà de l'essence*. The Hague: Martinus Nijhoff.

———. 1987. *Collected Philosophical Papers*. Translated by Alphonso Lingis. Dordrecht: Martinus Nijhoff.

———. 1990. *Ontology and Alterity in Merleau-Ponty*. Translated by M. B. Smith. Evanston, Ill.: Northwestern University Press. Originally published in 1983 as "Notes on Merleau-Ponty," pp. 181–186 in O. Hoeffe and R. Imbach, eds., *Paradigmes de théologie philosophique. En hommage à Marie-Dominique Philippe, O.P.* Fribourg: Éditions Universitaires.

Linden, George W. 1977. "Dakota Philosophy." *American Studies* 18: 2 (fall): 17–43. Reprinted with slight alterations in Clyde Holler, *The Black Elk Reader*. Syracuse, N.Y.: Syracuse University Press, 209–40.

Lipovetsky, Gilles. 1994. *The Empire of Fashion: Dressing Modern Democracy*. Translated by Catherine Porter. Princeton, N.J.: Princeton University Press. Originally published in 1987 as *L'Empire de l'éphémère: La mode et son destin dans les sociétés modernes*. Paris: Editions Gallimard.

Llewelyn, John. 1995. *Emmanuel Levinas: The Genealogy of Ethics*. London and New York: Routledge.

Locke, John. 1950 [1689]. *A Letter Concerning Toleration*. New York: Liberal Arts Press.

———. 1969 [1690]. *An Essay Concerning Human Understanding*. Oxford: The Clarendon Press.

Loewy, Erich H. 1991. *Suffering and the Beneficent Community: Beyond Libertarianism*. Albany: State University of New York Press.

———. 1997. *Moral Strangers, Moral Acquaintance, and Moral Friends: Connectedness and Its Conditions*. Albany: State University of New York Press.

Lucas, J. R. 1993. *Responsibility*. Oxford: Clarendon Press.

Lyotard, Jean-François. 1988. *The Differend: Phrases in Dispute*. Translated by Georges Van Den Abbeele. Minneapolis: University of Minnesota Press. Originally published in 1983 as *Le Différend*. Paris: Les Éditions de Minuit.

MacIntyre, Alisdair. 1981. *After Virtue*. Notre Dame, Ind.: Notre Dame Press.

———. 1988. *Whose Justice? Which Rationality?* Notre Dame, Ind.: Notre Dame University Press.

Malcolm, Norman. 1972. *Ludwig Wittgenstein: A Memoir*. London, Oxford, and New York: Oxford University Press.

Manent, Pierre. 1994. *An Intellectual History of Liberalism*. Translated by Rebecca Balinski, with a Foreword by Jerrold Seigel. Originally published in 1987 as *Histoire intellectuelle du libéralisme: Dix leçons*. Paris: Calmann-Lévy.

Manvell, Roger, and Heinrich Fraenkel. 1965. *Himmler*. New York: G. P. Putnam's Sons.

Marcel, Gabriel. 1963. *The Existential Background of Human Dignity*. Cambridge, Mass.: Harvard University Press.

———. 1964a. *Creative Fidelity*. Translated by Robert Rosthal. New York: Noonday Press. Originally published in 1940 as *Du Refus à l'invocation*. Paris: Gallimard.

———. 1964b. "On the Ontological Mystery." Translated by Manya Harari. Pp. 9–46 in Manya Harari, *The Philosophy of Existentialism*. New York: Citadel Press. Originally published in 1932 as *Position et approches concrètes du mystère ontologique*. Paris: Desclée de Brouwer.

———. 1967. *Searchings*. Westminster, Md.: Newman Press. Originally published in 1964 as *Auf der Suche nach Wahrheit und Gerechtigkeit*. 1964. Frankfurt: Verlag Knecht.

———. 1973. *Tragic Wisdom and Beyond*. Translated by Stephen Jolin and Peter McCormick. Evanston, Ill.: Northwestern University Press. Originally published in 1968 as *Pour une sagesse tragique*. Paris: Librairie Plon.

———. 1984. "Reply to Otto Friedrich Bollnow." Translated by Susan Gruenheck. Pp. 200–203 in Schilpp and Hahn, eds., *The Philosophy of Gabriel Marcel*. La Salle, Ill.: Open Court Press.

Marsh, James L. 1989. *Post-Cartesian Meditations*. New York: Fordham University Press.

———. 1995. *Critique, Action, and Liberation*. Albany: State University of New York Press.

———. 1999. *Process, Praxis, and Transcendence*. Albany: State University of New York Press.

Martin, Richard P., ed., 1991. *Bullfinch's Mythology*. New York: HarperCollins.

Marx, Werner. 1987. *Is There a Measure on Earth?* Translated by Thomas Nenon and Reginald Lily. Chicago: University of Chicago Press. Originally published in 1983 as *Gibt es auf Erden ein Maß? Grundbestimmungen einer nichtmetaphysischen Ethik.* Hamburg: Felix Meiner Verlag.

————. 1992. *Towards a Phenomenological Ethics.* Translated by Stefaan Heyvaert, with a Foreword by Thomas Nenon. Albany: State University of New York Press. Originally published in 1986 as *Mitleidenkönnen als Maß.* Hamburg: Felix Meiner Verlag.

May, Larry, Robert Strikwerda, and Patrick D. Hopkins, eds., 1996. *Rethinking Masculinity: Philosophical Explorations in Light of Feminism.* Lanham, Md.: Rowman & Littlefield, 2d ed.

McConnell, Terrance. 1993. *Gratitude.* Philadelphia: Temple University Press.

McGarry, Lawrence J. 1986. *Kindness and Human Nature.* Philadelphia: Villanova Press.

McTaggart, John McTaggart Ellis. 1906. *Some Dogmas of Religion.* London: Edward Arnold.

Mead, George Herbert. 1934. *Mind, Self, and Society.* Chicago: University of Chicago Press.

Mead, Rebecca. 1999. "Eggs for Sale." *New Yorker Magazine* (August 9): 56–65.

Merchant, Carolyn, ed. 1980. *The Death of Nature: Women, Ecology, and the Scientific Revolution.* New York: Harper & Row.

————. 1995. *Earthcare: Women and the Environment.* New York : Routledge.

Merleau-Ponty, Maurice. 1962. *Phenomenology of Perception.* Translated by Colin Smith. London: Routledge. Originally published in 1945 as *Phénoménologie de la perception.* Paris: Gallimard.

————. 1964a. "The Primacy of Perception and Its Philosophical Consequences." Pp. 12–42 in James Edie, ed., *The Primacy of Perception and Other Essays.* Evanston, Ill.: Northwestern University Press. Originally published in 1947 as "Le Primat de la perception et ses conséquences." *Bulletin de la Société Française de Philosophie* LXI.

————. 1964b. *Signs.* Translated by Richard McCleary. Evanston, Ill.: Northwestern University Press. Originally published in 1960 as *Signes.* Paris: Gallimard.

————. 1964c. *Sense and Non-sense.* Translated by Hubert L. and Patricia Allen Dreyfus. Evanston: Northwestern University Press. Originally published in 1948 as *Sens et non-sens.* Paris: Nagel.

————. 1964d. *Eye and Mind.* Translated by Carleton Dallery. Evanston, Ill.: Northwestern University Press. Originally published in 1964 as *L'Œil et l'esprit.* Paris: Gallimard.

————. 1968. *The Visible and the Invisible.* Text established by Claude Lefort and translated by Alphonso Lingis. Evanston, Ill.: Northwestern University Press. Originally published in 1964 as *Le Visible et l'invisible.* Paris: Gallimard.

————. 1970. *Themes from the Lectures at the Collège de France 1952–1960.* Translated by John O'Neill. Evanston, Ill.: Northwestern University Press. Originally published in 1968 as *Résumés de Cours, Collège de France 1952–1960.* Paris: Gallimard.

————. 1973. *The Prose of the World.* Translated by John O'Neill. Evanston, Ill.: Northwestern University Press. Originally published in 1969 as *La Prose du Monde.* Text established by Claude Lefort. Paris: Gallimard.

Midgley, Mary. 1993. "Virtuous Circles." *Times Literary Supplement* (June 18): 3–4.

Mill, John Stuart. 1956 [1859]. *On Liberty.* Edited and with an Introduction by Currin V. Shields. Indianapolis: Liberal Arts Press.

Miller, Arthur. 1976 [1953]. *The Crucible.* Harmondsworth: Penguin Books.

Monroe, Kristen Renwick. 1996. *The Heart of Altruism: Perceptions of a Common Humanity.* Princeton, N.J.: Princeton University Press.

Montaigne, Michel de. 1958 [1588]. *The Complete Essays of Montaigne.* Translated by Donald M. Frame. Stanford, Calif.: Stanford University Press.

Moore, Michael S. 1987. "The Moral Worth of Retribution." Pp. 79–219 in Ferdinand Schoeman, ed., *Responsibility, Character, and the Emotions.* Cambridge: Cambridge University Press.

Morrison, Toni. 1988. *Beloved.* New York: Penguin Books.

Muldoon, Mark S. 1997. "Ricoeur and Merleau-Ponty on Narrative Identity." *American Catholic Philosophical Quarterly* LXXI: 1: 35–52.

Neihardt, John G. 1961 [1932]. *Black Elk Speaks: Being the Life Story of a Holy Man of the Oglala Sioux.* Lincoln: University of Nebraska Press. Originally published in 1932. New York: William Morrow & Company.

Newman, Judith. 1999. "Passion Pills." *Discover Magazine* (September): 66–73.

Nietzsche, Friedrich. 1966. *Beyond Good and Evil.* New York: Vintage Books.

———. 1968a. *The Will to Power.* Translated by Walter Kaufmann and R. J. Hollingdale and edited by Walter Kaufmann. New York: Vintage Books.

———. 1969. *On the Genealogy of Morals.* Pp. 15–200 in *On the Genealogy of Morals* and *Ecce Homo,* translated by Walter Kaufmann. New York: Vintage Books.

———. 1974. *The Gay Science.* Translated and with a commentary by Walter Kaufmann. New York: Vintage Books.

Nuland, Sherwin B. 1994. *How We Die: Reflections on Life's Final Chapter.* New York: Alfred A. Knopf.

Nussbaum, Martha. 1990. *Love's Knowledge.* New York and Oxford: Oxford University Press.

———. 1994. *The Therapy of Desire.* Princeton, N.J.: Princeton University Press.

———. 1995a. *Poetic Justice.* Boston: Beacon Press.

———. 1995b. "Objectification." *Philosophy and Public Affairs* 24: 4: 249–91.

———. 1996. "Compassion: The Basic Social Emotion." *Social Philosophy and Policy* 13:1: 27–58.

———. 1999. *Sex and Social Justice.* New York and Oxford: Oxford University Press.

O'Brien, Niall Rev. 1988. *Revolution from the Heart.* New York and Oxford: Oxford University Press.

O'Hara, Charles B. 1956. *Fundamentals of Criminal Investigation.* Springfield, Ill.: Thomas.

Oliner, Samuel P., and M. Pearl. 1988. *The Altruistic Personality: Rescuers of Jews in Nazi Europe.* New York: Free Press.

Ovid. 1970. *Metamorphoses, Book VIII.* Edited with an Introduction and Commentary by A.S. Hollis. Oxford: The Clarendon Press.

Pascal, Blaise. 1965 [1662]. *Pensées.* Edited by Michel Autrand. Paris: Bordas.

Paton, H. J. 1965. *The Categorical Imperative.* New York: Harper Torchbooks.

Penn, William. n. d. *William Penn's Plan for the Peace of Europe.* Boston: Directors of the Old South Work, Old South Meeting House.

Peperzak, Adriaan T., ed. 1995. *Ethics As First Philosophy: The Significance of Emmanuel Levinas for Philosophy, Literature, and Religion.* New York and London: Routledge.

Pope, Alexander. 1903 [1734]. *Moral Essays.* Pp. 156–75 in Henry W. Boynton, ed., *The Complete Poetical Works of Alexander Pope.* Boston and New York: Houghton, Miflin, and Company.

Putnam, Daniel. 1990. "The Compatibility of Justice and Kindness." *Philosophy* 65: 516–17.

Rawls, John. 1996. *Political Liberalism.* New York: Columbia University Press.

Regan, Tom. 1985. *The Case for Animal Rights.* Berkeley: University of California Press.

Reiman, Jeffrey. 1987. "Exploitation, Force, and the Moral Assessment of Capitalism: Thoughts on Roemer and Cohen." *Philosophy and Public Affairs* 16: 1 (winter): 3–41.

Richards, Norvin. 1992. *Humility.* PhiladelphiaPA: Temple University Press.

Ricoeur, Paul. 1965. *Fallible Man.* Translated by Charles A. Kelbley. Chicago: Henry Regnery. Originally published in 1960 as *L'Homme faillible.* Paris: Aubier, Editions Montaigne.

———. 1966. *The Voluntary and the Involuntary.* Translated by Erazim V. Kohák. Evanston, Ill.: Northwestern University Press. Originally published in 1950 as *Le Volontaire et l'involontaire.* Paris: Aubier Éditions Montaigne.

———. 1970. *Freud and Philosophy.* Translated by Denis Savage. New Haven, Conn.: Yale University Press.

———. 1973. *Interviews: Paul Ricoeur, Gabriel Marcel.* Pp. 217–56 in Gabriel Marcel, *Tragic Wisdom and Beyond.* Evanston, Ill.: Northwestern University Press.

———. 1984. *Time and Narrative,* vol 1. Translated by Kathleen McLaughlin and David Pellauer. Chicago: University of Chicago Press. Originally published 1985 as *Temps et récit I.* Editions de Seuil.

———. 1988. *Time and Narrative,* vol. 3. Translated by Kathleen Blamey and David Pellauer. Chicago: University of Chicago Press. Originally published in as *Temps et récit III.* Paris: Éditions de Seuil.

———. 1992. *Oneself as Another.* Translated by Kathleen Blamey. Chicago and London: University of Chicago Press. Originally published in 1990 as *Soi-même comme un autre.* Paris: Éditions du Seuil.

———. 1995. "Intellectual Biography." Pp. 3–53 in Lewis E. Hahn, ed. *The Philosophy of Paul Ricoeur.* Chicago and LaSalle: Open Court Press.

Rochlitz, Rainer. 1994. *Subversion et subvention: Art contemporain et argumentation esthétique.* Paris: Gallimard.

Rosenthal, Sandra B. 1996. "Self, Community, and Time: A Shared Sociality." *Review of Metaphysics* 50 (September): 101–19.

Ross, W. D. 1930. *The Right and the Good.* Oxford: Clarendon Press.

Rousseau, Jean-Jacques. 1825. *Oeuvres complètes de J.J. Rousseau.* Edited by P.R. Anguis. Paris: Librarie Dalibon.

Russell, Bertrand. 1964. "The Philosophy of Logical Atomism." Pp. 323–43 in *Logic and Knowledge,* edited by Robert C. Marsh. London: Macmillan.

Sacks, Peter. 1996. *Generation X Goes to College*. Chicago and LaSalle: Open Court Press.

Salinger, J. D. 1991. *Franny and Zooey*. Boston: Little, Brown, and Company.

Sandel, Michael J. 1996. "Dewey Rides Again." A review of *John Dewey and the High Tide of American Liberalism* by Alan Ryan, *New York Review of Books* (May 9): 35–38.

———. 1998. *Liberalism and the Limits of Justice*. 2d ed. Cambridge: Cambridge University Press.

Santayana, George. 1964. *The Wisdom of George Santayana*. Edited by Ira D. Cardiff. New York: Philosophical Library.

Sartre, Jean-Paul. 1956. *Being and Nothingness*. Translated by Hazel Barnes. New York: Philosophical Library. Originally published in 1943 as *L'Etre et le néant*. Paris: Gallimard.

———. 1963. *The Psychology of Imagination*. Translated by Forrest Williams. New York: Citadel Press. Originally published in 1948 as *L'Imaginaire*. Paris: Gallimard.

———. 1965. *Nausea*. Translated by Robert Baldick. New York: Penguin Books. Originally published in 1938 as *La Nausée*. Paris: Gallimard.

———. 1984. "Merleau-Ponty [I]." Translated by William S. Hamrick. *Journal of the British Society for Phenomenology* 15:2 (May): 123–54.

Sawicki, Marianne. 1997. "Empathy before and after Husserl." *Philosophy Today* 41:1 (spring): 123–27.

Sayre, Patricia A. 1993. "The Dialectics of Trust and Suspicion." *Faith and Philosophy*, 10:4 (October): 567–84.

Scarry, Elaine. 1985. *The Body in Pain*. New York: Oxford University Press.

Schaeffer, Jean-Marie. 1992. *L'art de l'âge moderne, L'esthétique et la philosophie de l'art du XVIIIe siècle à nos jours*. Paris: Gallimard.

Scheler, Max. 1954. *The Nature of Sympathy*. Translated by Peter Heath. New Haven, Conn.: Yale University Press. Originally published in 1913 as *Zur Phänomenologie der Sympathiegefühle und von Liebe und Hass*. Halle: Niemeyer.

———. 1973. *Formalism in Ethics and Non-Formal Ethics of Values*. Translated by Manfred S. Frings and Roger L. Funk. Evanston, Ill.: Northwestern University Press. Originally published in 1913 as *Der Formalismus in der Ethik und die materiale Wertethik*. Fifth rev. ed. 1966. Bern: A. Francke AG Verlag.

Schmitt, Richard. 1959. "Husserl's Transcendental-Phenomenological Reduction." *Philosophy and Phenomenological Research* 20: 238–45.

Schilpp, Paul A., and Lewis Edwin Hahn, eds., 1984. *The Philosophy of Gabriel Marcel*. LaSalle, Ill.: Open Court Press. Library of Living Philosophers, vol. 17.

Schlick, Moritz. 1939. *Problems of Ethics*. Translated by David Rynin. New York: Prentice Hall. Originally published in 1930 as *Fragen der Ethik*. 1930. Wien: Verlag von Julius Springer.

Schnapper, Dominique. 1994. *La communauté des citoyens, Sur l'idée moderne de nation*. Paris: Gallimard.

Schoeman, Ferdinand, ed. 1988. *Responsibility, Character, and the Emotions*. Cambridge: Cambridge University Press.

Schopenhauer, Arthur. 1965 [1841]. *On the Basis of Morality*. Translated by A.F.J. Payne. Indianapolis: Bobbs-Merrill.

Schrag, Peter. 1991. "Savage Equalities." *New Republic* (December 16): 18–20.

Schutz, Alfred. 1962. *Collected Papers, Vol. I, The Problem of Social Reality.* Edited and introduced by Maurice Natanson, with a Preface by H. L. Van Breda. The Hague: Martinus Nijhoff.

————. 1964. *Collected Papers, Vol. II, Studies in Social Theory.* Edited and introduced by Arvid Brodersen. The Hague: Martinus Nijhoff.

————. 1967. *The Phenomenology of the Social World.* Translated by George Walsh and Frederick Lehnert. Evanston, Ill.: Northwestern University Press. Originally published in as *Der sinnhafte Aufbau der sozialen Welt.* Vienna: Julius Springer Verlag.

Sensat, Julius. 1984. "Exploitation." *Noûs* 18: 1 (March): 21–38.

————. 1973. *The Structures of the Life-World.* Translated by Richard Zaner and H. Tristam Englehardt, Jr. Evanston, IL: Northwestern University Press.

Shakespeare, William. 1939 [1600–01]. *The Tragedy of Hamlet, Prince of Denmark.* Edited by George Lyman Kittredge. Boston: Blaisdell Publishing Company.

————. 1975 [1596–97]. *The Merchant of Venice.* Pp. 175–202 in *The Complete Works of William Shakespeare.* New York: Crown Publisher.

Shelley, Mary. 1985 [1818]. *Frankenstein, or the Modern Prometheus.* Edited and with an Introduction and Notes by Maurice Hindle. London: Penguin Books.

Sidgwick, Henry. 1913. *The Methods of Ethics.* London: Macmillan.

Silverman, Kaja. 1992. *Male Subjectivity at the Margins.* New York and London: Routledge, Chapman and Hall.

Singer, Peter. 1990. *Animal Liberation.* 2d ed. New York: New York Review of Books/Random House.

Skaggs, Peggy. 1985. *Kate Chopin.* Boston: Twayne Publishers.

Smith, Adam. 1976 [1759]. *The Theory of Moral Sentiments.* Edited by D. D. Raphael and A. L. Macfie. Oxford: Clarendon Press.

Smith, John. 1984. "The Individual, the Collective, and the Community." Pp. 337–51 in Paul A. Schilpp and Lewis E. Hahn, eds., *The Philosophy of Gabriel Marcel.* LaSalle, Ill.: Open Court Press.

Society of Friends. 1960. "Christian faith and practice in the experience of the Society of Friends." Pp. 470–80 in *London Yearly Meeting of the Religious Society of Friends.* London: Headley Brothers, Ltd.

Sokolowski, Robert. 1985. *Moral Action: A Phenomenological Study.* Bloomington: Indiana University Press.

Solomon, Robert C. 1985. "A More Severe Morality: Nietzsche's Affirmative Ethics." *Journal of the British Society for Phenomenology* 16:3 Number (October): 250–67.

Spiegelberg, Herbert. 1984. "Three Types of the Given: The Encountered, the Search-Found, and the Striking." *Husserl Studies* 1:69–78.

————. 1986. *Steppingstones toward an Ethics for Fellow Existers.* Dordrecht: Martinus Nijhoff.

Stein, Edith. 1964. *On the Problem of Empathy.* Translated by Waltraut Stein, with a Foreword by Erwin W. Straus. The Hague: Martinus Nijhoff. Originally published in 1917 as *Zum Problem der Einfühlung.* Halle.

Steinbeck, John. 1976 [1939]. *The Grapes of Wrath.* New York: Penguin Books.

Stephen, Sir James Fitzjames. 1967 [1873]. *Liberty, Equality, Fraternity.* Edited and with an Introduction and Notes by R. J. White. Cambridge: Cambridge University Press.

Sterne, Laurence. 1987 [1760]. *The Life and Opinions of Tristram Shandy, Gentleman.* Edited and with an Introduction and Notes by Ian Campbell-Ross. Oxford: Oxford University Press.

Stevenson, Robert Louis. 1911. *Treasure Island.* New York: Charles Scribner's Sons.

Tanner, Christine A., Patricia Benner, Catherine Chesla, and Deborah R Gordon. 1993. "The Phenomenology of Knowing the Patient." *IMAGE: Journal of Nursing Scholarship,* 25: 4 (winter): 273–80.

Taylor, Charles. 1992. *The Ethics of Authenticity.* Cambridge, Mass.: Harvard University Press.

Thomas, R. S. 1985. *Poems of R. S. Thomas.* Fayetteville: University of Arkansas Press.

Thomson, Judith Jarvis. 1971. "A Defense of Abortion." *Philosophy and Public Affairs* 1:1 (fall): 47–66.

Thucydides. 1951. *The Complete Writings of Thucydides, The Peloponnesian War.* The unabridged Crawley translation, with an Introduction by John H. Finley Jr. New York: Modern Library.

Titchener, E. B. 1909. *Lectures on the Experimental Psychology of the Thought-Processes.* New York: Macmillan.

Tolstoy, Leo. 1985. *The Kreuzer Sonata and Other Stories.* Translated and with an Introduction by David McDuff. Harmondsworth: Penguin Books.

Toombs, S. Kay. 1987. "The Meaning of Illness: A Phenomenological Approach to the Patient-Physician Relationship." *Journal of Medical Philosophy* 12: 219–40.

———. 1988. "Illness and the Paradigm of Lived Body." *Theoretical Medicine* 9: 201–26.

Tucker, Robert C. 1978. *The Marx-Engels Reader.* 2d ed. New York: W.W. Norton & Company.

Twain, Mark. 1959 [1859]. *The Adventures of Huckleberry Finn.* Afterword by George P. Elliott. New York: New American Library, Signet Books.

Updike, John. 1983. "Pain." *The New Republic* (December 26): 34.

Valéry, Paul. 1957. *Oeuvres I.* Paris: Gallimard.

Walker, A.D.M. 1989. "Virtue and Character." *Philosophy* 64: 349–62.

Wertheimer, Alan. 1987. *Coercion.* Princeton, N.J.: Princeton University Press.

———. 1996. *Exploitation.* Princeton, N.J.: Princeton University Press.

Wharton, Edith. 1986 [1920]. *The Age of Innocence.* Introduction by R.W.B. Lewis. New York: Collier Books.

Whitehead, Alfred North. 1933. *Adventures of Ideas.* New York: Macmillan.

Wilde, Oscar. 1985 [1891]. *The Picture of Dorian Gray.* Edited by Peter Ackroyd. London: Penguin Books.

Wiley, John P., Jr. 1999. "Help Is on the Way." *Smithsonian Magazine* (July): 22–24.

Williams, Tennessee. 1972. *A Streetcar Named Desire.* New York: Signet Books.

Willimon, William H. 1982. "The Limits of Kindness." *Christian Century* 99: 13 (April 14): 447–49.

Wittgenstein, Ludwig. 1961. *Tractatus Logico-Philosophicus.* Translated by D. F. Pears and B. F. McGuinness, with an Introduction by Bertrand Russell. London: Routledge & Kegan Paul.

———. 1968. *Philosophical Investigations.* Translated by G.E.M. Anscombe. Oxford: Basil Blackwell.

———. 1990. *Remarks on the Philosophy of Psychology (II).* Edited by G. H. von Wright and H. Nyman and translated by C. G. Luckhardt and M.A.E. Aue. Oxford: Basil Blackwell.

Wolgast, Elizabeth. 1993. "Innocence." *Philosophy* 68: 297–307.

Woolf, Virginia. 1992 [1927]. *To the Lighthouse.* Introduction by Quentin Bell. London: Vintage Books.

Wordsworth, William. 1975 [1798]. *Lines Written a Few Miles Above TINTERN ABBEY.* London: Thomas Jenkins (Printers) Ltd.

Wright, Richard. 1993 [1940]. *Native Son.* New York: HarperCollins.

Wuthnow, Robert. 1991. *Acts of Compassion: Caring for Others and Helping Ourselves.* Princeton, N.J.: Princeton University Press.

Yeats, W. B. 1976. *The Collected Poems of W. B. Yeats.* New York: Macmillan.

Zaehner, R. C. 1962. *Hinduism.* London: Oxford University Press.

Index